A DICTIONARY OF ECONOMICS

About the Authors

HAROLD STEPHENSON SLOAN was educated at Columbia University, from which he received both his baccalaureate and graduate degrees. In 1946, the University of Denver conferred upon him its honorary doctorate of laws, in recognition of his work in economic education, and in 1960 he received an honorary degree of doctor of science from Fairleigh Dickinson University. Following a relatively extensive business career, he taught economics at various institutions and from 1929 to 1936 served on the economics faculty of the New Jersey State Teachers College, rising to the rank of Associate Professor. From 1936 to 1945 he served as vice-president and first executive director of the Alfred P. Sloan Foundation, Inc., and held the position of Visiting Professor of Economics at New York University. The following year he was appointed Adjunct Professor of Economics in the Graduate School of Arts and Science, New York University, which post he held until 1958. In 1959 he was appointed Professor of the Inter-American Course in Education and Economic Development held in Bogotá, Colombia, S.A., and in 1963 served as consultant to the U. S. Agency for International Development Educational Project in Peru, S.A. Currently he is Director of Research at Fairleigh Dickinson University and Visiting Lecturer at Teachers College, Columbia University. He is author of *Today's Economics*, *Farming in America*, and coauthor of *Classrooms in the Factories*, *Classrooms in the Stores*, and *Classrooms in the Military*.

ARNOLD JOHN ZURCHER received his baccalaureate degree from Oberlin College, his A. M. from Cornell University, and his Ph. D. from Princeton. Although he has filled teaching assignments at various institutions, his teaching career has been largely confined to New York University, where he began as Instructor in Political Science in 1928 and rose to the rank of Professor in 1940. In addition he is also Coordinator of the Area of Studies Program in the Department of Government in the University's Graduate School. In 1945 he joined the staff of the Alfred P. Sloan Foundation, and became a vice-president and the executive director of that organization. Among various volumes of which he is author or part author are *The Experiment With Democracy in Central Europe*, *Propaganda and Dictatorship*, *The Governments of Continental Europe*, *Constitutions and Constitutional Trends Since the Second World War*, and *The Struggle To Unite Europe, 1940–1958*. He has also shared with Professor E. C. Smith the editorship of the *New Dictionary of American Politics* (published by Barnes & Noble, Inc.) and is a major contributor to that volume.

EVERYDAY HANDBOOKS

A DICTIONARY OF ECONOMICS

FOURTH EDITION REVISED

BY

Harold S. Sloan
Columbia University

Arnold J. Zurcher
New York University

BARNES & NOBLE, INC., • N. Y.
Publishers • Booksellers • Since 1873

L. C. Catalogue Card Number: 64-18785

This is an original Handbook (Number 266) in the Everyday Handbook Series. It was written by distinguished educators, carefully edited, and produced in the United States of America in accordance with the highest standards of the publishing industry.

PREFACE TO THE THIRD EDITION

The new edition of this dictionary has expanded considerably the material which appeared in the previous editions. All together some 300 new terms have been added, bringing the total number of entries to more than 2,800. Some of these new terms are words or phrases that have only recently come into significant use in economics; a few others are terms inadvertently overlooked in the first edition. By far the largest block of new entries are of a statistical nature. Their inclusion reflects the extraordinary growth of quantitative methods and statistical and mathematical analyses in economic practice and theory. An effort has also been made to give adequate space to the concepts of the more recent economic theorists, especially to the Keynesians. In the appendix appears still another new feature: excerpts from various public and private financial reports analyzed in terms of words and phrases defined elsewhere in the dictionary, and a list of the monetary units of the nations of the world. The former should prove helpful both as detailed explanations of important economic tabulations and as specific applications, in appropriate context, of a multitude of economic expressions.

Incorporation of this material in the new edition will, it is hoped, contribute substantially to the achievement of the purpose originally set for the dictionary, viz., to provide a reference volume of maximum utility to the broadest possible constituency. To create such a volume, the authors have culled significant terminology from the literature of the various areas into which the study of formal economics is usually, albeit somewhat arbitrarily, classified. In addition to statistical methods and concepts, these areas include economic history and theory, international trade, finance and exchange, international commercial policy, public finance, fiscal policy, taxation, money, and credit. An examination has also been made of certain of the more specialized areas of economic study such as business cycles, price policies and price mechanisms, agricultural and labor economics, industrial organization, and the problem of social welfare. Words and phrases in common use in these more specialized areas have also been included. Moreover, in view of the scope of public regulation of economic life, so characteristic of the present day, an effort has been made to incorporate brief digests or descriptions of the more important relevant American statutes and judicial decisions and American and international regulatory agencies.

Interspersed among the more formal economic terms the reader will also find not a few words or phrases derived from the nomenclature of what may be termed "practical" or "business" economics. The terms thus defined may relate to accounting, marketing, corporate financing and organization, insurance, securities and investment, industrial and public relations, production costs and techniques, and other activities directly involving business, commercial, or banking practice. Inclusion of entries from subjects such as these is necessary if the book is to achieve the authors' objective of serving the maximum readership. Incorporation of such entries may also serve, in some small measure, to overcome what is often little more than an arbitrary and misleading distinction in the study of economics between subject matter primarily concerned with economic theory and subject matter concerned with the practical application of economic principles.

No effort has been spared by authors and publishers to make this dictionary an efficient and authoritative reference tool. No term has been included unless formal investigation indicated that it was commonly used in economic discussion. Where authorities differ as to the term's precise meaning, or where more than one common meaning exists for a term, the reader has been advised of such difference or variation in meaning. The authors have also tried to indicate whatever variations may exist between the technical and popular meanings of particular terms and between the meaning of a word or phrase in formal economics and in commercial and financial practice. In every instance American usage has been the guide.

Throughout the book formal definitions have often been supplemented by detailed explanations where such a procedure seemed necessary; and the explanations occasionally embrace specific illustrations of the application of a concept where illustrations are possible and seem desirable. Definitions of the more generic terms are usually followed by an extensive list of cross-references to other terms in the book which extend or illustrate the definition or are otherwise relevant. Moreover, when the content of a particular definition or explanation contains terms defined elsewhere in the book, such terms are usually printed in small capitals. Wherever, in the interest of greater clarity, the authors deem it advisable that the reader investigate elsewhere in the book the meaning of a term which may be used in the context of a particular definition, such a term is followed by the Latin abbreviation (*q.v.*). Descriptions of public regulatory agencies and digests of statutes and judicial decisions are necessarily brief. In each case only essential data are given. Where these are insufficient for the reader's purposes, the entry will at least assist him in his effort to find further and more authoritative information in such official publications as the *United States Government Manual*, the *Statutes at Large*, or the official reports of the courts.

Despite the existence of numerous encyclopedias and other reference works of lesser stature in the economic area, a dictionary of the scope and character described above apparently fulfills a real need. At any rate such a conclusion is implied by the favorable reception accorded the earlier editions. The book found immediate favor with students and teachers in our schools and colleges, in graduate schools of arts and science, and in professional schools of business administration. A brisk demand also developed among professional persons interested in public affairs and among those concerned with the more "functional" aspects of economic life, particularly those engaged in industry, commerce, and banking. In the preface to the first edition the authors expressed the hope that their effort at achieving precision in economic terminology might persuade some of the general public, who consult economic literature infrequently, that the subject of economics is perhaps not quite so dismal as it is sometimes declared to be. Apparently more than one layman has found a use for this volume. Whether such use has in turn contributed towards overcoming in some degree the poor reputation hitherto accorded the subject of economics remains to be seen.

It is notorious that leading economists often differ sharply on the precise significance to be attached to many of the words and phrases that are part of their professional vocabulary. Such differences sometimes provoke serious controversy; and even the most impartial lexicographer may fail to find common ground. Hence, when the authors undertook preparation of the first edition of the dictionary they were well aware that any effort to standardize the meaning of economic terminology, however sincerely made, might evoke as much censure as praise. There has been some of both but, rather surprisingly, more of praise than of censure. For both praise and censure the authors are extremely grateful. Only through the informed comment of colleagues and professional experts and the criticism of the users of this book can the problem of economic nomenclature be brought under constant attack. Only if the authors' professional colleagues and the users of this book make known their comments, criticisms, and suggestions can any effective advance be made in standardizing economic terminology. The authors remain persuaded, moreover, that such an effort is worth while. Lack of understanding by student and layman of the meaning of terms in economics has frequently led to grave misconceptions and has aggravated the misunderstanding which too often afflicts the public's effort to deal with economic questions. The vast changes which have occurred in economic life in recent years, including the increase of regulatory agencies, both national and international, and the growing importance of economic factors in national and international politics have added many new words and phrases in the economic area. Without some guide such as this book professes to offer, terminological confusion is intensified and prevailing uncertainty and misunderstanding are aggravated.

Many have contributed ideas, criticisms, and suggestions in the course of the development of this book, and the authors acknowledge all such help with genuine appreciation. Dozens of reviews and scores of letters of comment have been received concerning the first edition. They have been of immense help to authors and publisher. The authors wish particularly to express their thanks to the officers of the Irving Trust Company, the Chase National Bank, Moody's Investors Service, and the Bank of North Dakota for their assistance in verifying certain definitions. Their thanks go also to John C. Pelegrine, at one time general counsel of the Curtiss-Wright Corporation, and to Arthur G. H. Power of Conboy, Hewitt, O'Brien and Boardman, who have offered valuable suggestions on definitions of a legal nature; to James F. Kenney for assistance on entries relating to accountancy; to Professor Paul Clifford of the New Jersey State Teachers College at Montclair for assisting in some of the mathematical computations; to Miss Cecile Stierli and Mrs. Muriel P. Gaines for various contributions they have made to the physical preparation of the manuscript; to Anne and Wallace Clark of Buttzville, New Jersey, who have contributed liberally to the finished product by their painstaking editing and proofreading; to Mrs. Carol Ann Luten for her careful reading of the manuscript of the first edition and her numerous suggestions for its improvement; and to Dr. Gladys Walterhouse for similar services in connection with the preparation of the manuscript of the third edition. Finally, they wish to express their gratitude to Mrs. Harold S. Sloan for her invaluable editorial assistance.

While the aid thus extended has been of inestimable value, no responsibility rests with those who have so generously given it. The authors alone are responsible for the sins of omission and commission.

New York City

H. S. S.
A. J. Z.

PREFACE TO THE FOURTH EDITION

In preparing this new edition of the Dictionary, the authors have sought to bring up to date all entries which deal with relatively current or fluid situations or which describe the purpose and operation of various private and public agencies. Occasionally, moreover, certain existing definitions or descriptions have been expanded because developments since the publication of the previous edition have enhanced the significance of the subjects they define or describe.

Substantial additions have also been made to the list of entries described or defined in the earlier editions, thereby bringing the total to some 3,000 words, phrases or titles. Among these newer entries are to be found certain recent judicial decisions of broad social significance, descriptions of new public bodies, and interpretations of words or phrases that have recently come into general use in the literature of economics and in allied or sub-disciplines. An effort has been made, especially, to bring together some of the newer words or phrases that have gained currency in such fields as business management, public administration, accounting, business practices, and statistics, and as a result of the growing use of automatic computer devices in business and economic research.

H.S.S.
A.J.Z.

FUNDAMENTAL RELATIONSHIPS IN ECONOMIC LIFE

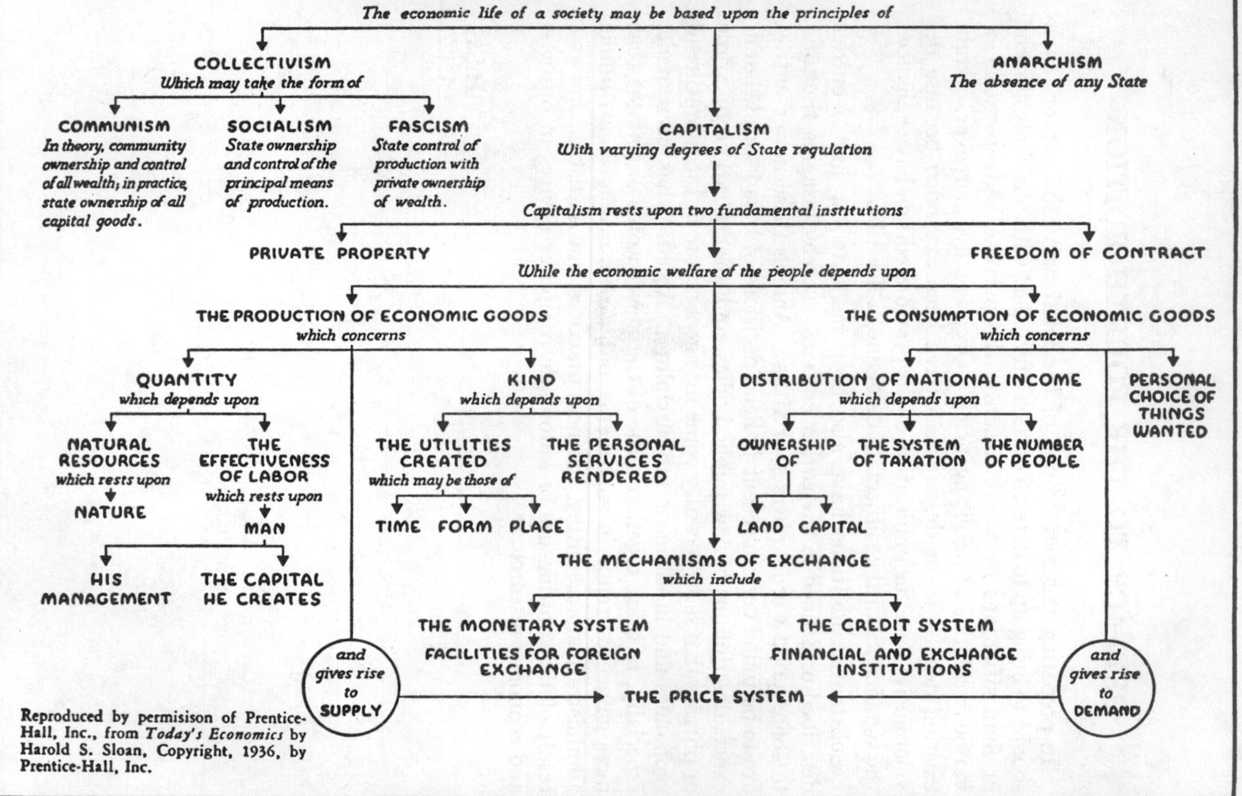

The economic life of a society may be based upon the principles of
COLLECTIVISM
Which may take the form of
COMMUNISM
In theory, community ownership and control of all wealth; in practice, state ownership of all capital goods.
SOCIALISM
State ownership and control of the principal means of production.
FASCISM
State control of production with private ownership of wealth.
CAPITALISM
With varying degrees of State regulation
ANARCHISM
The absence of any State
Capitalism rests upon two fundamental institutions
PRIVATE PROPERTY
FREEDOM OF CONTRACT
While the economic welfare of the people depends upon
THE PRODUCTION OF ECONOMIC GOODS
which concerns
QUANTITY
which depends upon
NATURAL RESOURCES
which rests upon
NATURE
THE EFFECTIVENESS OF LABOR
which rests upon
MAN
HIS MANAGEMENT
THE CAPITAL HE CREATES
KIND
which depends upon
THE UTILITIES CREATED
which may be those of
TIME
FORM
PLACE
THE PERSONAL SERVICES RENDERED
THE CONSUMPTION OF ECONOMIC GOODS
which concerns
DISTRIBUTION OF NATIONAL INCOME
which depends upon
OWNERSHIP OF
LAND
CAPITAL
THE SYSTEM OF TAXATION
THE NUMBER OF PEOPLE
PERSONAL CHOICE OF THINGS WANTED
THE MECHANISMS OF EXCHANGE
which include
THE MONETARY SYSTEM
FACILITIES FOR FOREIGN EXCHANGE
THE CREDIT SYSTEM
FINANCIAL AND EXCHANGE INSTITUTIONS
and gives rise to SUPPLY
THE PRICE SYSTEM
and gives rise to DEMAND

Reproduced by permisison of Prentice-Hall, Inc., from *Today's Economics* by Harold S. Sloan, Copyright, 1936, by Prentice-Hall, Inc.

KEY TO ABBREVIATIONS

Commonly used for certain public agencies and other organizations described in this book

Agency or Organization	*Abbreviation*
Agricultural Research Administration	ARA
American Federation of Labor and Congress of Industrial Organizations	AFL-CIO
Atomic Energy Commission	AEC
Bureau of Employees' Compensation	BEC
Civil Aeronautics Board	CAB
Committee for Economic Development	CED
Commodity Credit Corporation	CCC
Commodity Exchange Authority, Council of Economic Advisers	CEA
European Payments Union	EPU
European Recovery Program	ERP
Export-Import Bank	EIB
Farm Credit Administration	FCA
Farmers Home Administration	FHA
Federal Aviation Agency	FAA
Federal Crop Insurance Corporation	FCIC
Federal Deposit Insurance Corporation	FDIC
Federal Housing Administration	FHA
Federal Mediation and Conciliation Service	FMCS
Federal National Mortgage Association	FNMA
Federal Power Commission	FPC
Federal Public Housing Authority	FPHA
Federal Reserve System	FRS
Federal Trade Commission	FTC
Food and Agriculture Organization of the United Nations	FAO
General Accounting Office	GAO
General Agreement on Tariffs and Trade	GATT
General Services Administration	GSA
Health, Education, and Welfare, Department of	HEW
Housing and Home Finance Agency	HHFA
Industrial Workers of the World	IWW
Internal Revenue Service	IRS
International Bank for Reconstruction and Development	IBRD
International Civil Aviation Organization	ICAO
International Confederation of Free Trade Unions	ICFTU
International Cooperation Administration	ICA

KEY TO ABBREVIATIONS

Agency or Organization	*Abbreviation*
International Labor Organization	ILO
International Monetary Fund	IMF
International Refugee Organization	IRO
International Telecommunications Union	ITU
International Trade Organization	ITO
Interstate Commerce Commission	ICC
Labor Statistics, Bureau of	BLS
Maritime Administration	MA
National Aeronautics and Space Administration	NASA
National Association of Manufacturers	NAM
National Bureau of Standards	NBS
National Industrial Recovery Act	NIRA
National Labor Relations Board	NLRB
National Mediation Board	NMB
National Security Council	NSC
Organization of American States	OAS
Organization for Economic Cooperation and Development	OECD
Organization for European Economic Cooperation	OEEC
Production Credit Corporation	PCC
Public Housing Administration	PHA
Railroad Retirement Board	RRB
Reconstruction Finance Corporation	RFC
Rural Electrification Administration	REA
Securities and Exchange Commission	SEC
Social Security Administration	SSA
Soil Conservation Service	SCS
Temporary National Economic Committee	TNEC
Tennessee Valley Authority	TVA
United Nations	UN
United Nations Educational, Scientific and Cultural Organization	UNESCO
United Nations Relief and Rehabilitation Administration	UNRRA
United States Employment Service	USES
United States Tariff Commission	USTC
Universal Postal Union	UPU
Veterans Administration	VA
World Federation of Trade Unions	WFTU
World Health Organization	WHO

A

ability-to-pay principle of taxation. The principle that a tax should be levied upon individual taxpayers in accordance with their ability to pay the tax rather than in proportion to the direct benefits received from the state, or the cost to the state of the services rendered individual taxpayers. This principle is generally applied today as, for example, in the case of PROGRESSIVE TAXATION on income. Also called *faculty principle of taxation.*

abrasion. As applied to coins, the loss in weight due to wear while in circulation.

absolute advantage. See explanation under COMPARATIVE ADVANTAGE.

abstinence theory of interest. See AGIO THEORY OF INTEREST.

accelerated depreciation. Unusually rapid depreciation due to special conditions. Such depreciation may be caused by overloading of machinery, lack of skilled employees, or inability to provide proper maintenance or to obtain repair parts. See also DEPRECIATION.

accelerating premium. Under certain incentive wage systems, a bonus which becomes progressively larger as production increases.

acceleration principle. An explanation used by Keynesian economists showing how an increase or decrease in consumer expenditures may cause changes in new CAPITAL FORMATION. For example, a sufficient increase in consumer demand for a commodity may result in added facilities for producing it, and, conversely, a sufficient decrease in consumer expenditures may result in failure on the part of producers to replace worn-out equipment, or DISINVESTMENT. The acceleration factor, or *coefficient of acceleration* as it is sometimes called, is the ratio of change in investments to change in consumer expenditures. Thus, if increased consumer expenditures of $4,000,000 cause increased capital investments of $2,000,000, the acceleration factor, or coefficient of acceleration, is $\frac{1}{2}$. The equation is:

$$\frac{\Delta I}{\Delta C} = \frac{2{,}000{,}000}{4{,}000{,}000} = \frac{1}{2}.$$

See also INDUCED INVESTMENT, KEYNESIAN ECONOMICS.

acceptance. A draft or bill of exchange on the face of which the debtor against whom the draft or bill is drawn has affixed his signature indicating his intention to pay. See also BANK ACCEPTANCE, TRADE ACCEPTANCE.

acceptance bill. See explanation under BILL.

acceptance supra protest. An agreement to pay a protested note, draft, or similar credit instrument by a person other than the debtor named on the document. See also PROTEST.

accommodation paper. A promissory note that has been indorsed by one or more persons in order that the one who originally made that note may obtain credit at a bank. If the credit is advanced by an individual, the accommodation paper might contain only the signature of the debtor without indorsements.

account. As applied to bookkeeping, a ledger record displaying charges or debits on the left-hand side of the page and credits on the right-hand side. Each account bears either a proper name or a title descriptive of the item to which the debits and credits are applied; for example, capital account, cash account, bank account, sales account. For terms applied to some of the common groups of accounts see ACCOUNTS PAYABLE, ACCOUNTS RECEIVABLE, BILLS PAYABLE, BILLS RECEIVABLE, CONTROLLING ACCOUNT, IMPERSONAL ACCOUNT, NOMINAL ACCOUNT, OPEN ACCOUNT, PERSONAL ACCOUNT, REAL ACCOUNT, SUSPENSE ACCOUNT.

accountant. A person versed in bookkeeping methods and in the preparation of statements displaying the assets and liabilities and the operating results of business and other enterprises. See also CERTIFIED PUBLIC ACCOUNTANT.

accounts payable. A term used in double-entry bookkeeping to indicate the records of the amounts credited to others for goods and services purchased, and the amounts paid for those purchases. See also ACCOUNT.

accounts receivable. A term used in double-entry bookkeeping to indicate the records of the amounts charged to others for goods and services sold, and the amounts received. See also ACCOUNT.

accrual basis. The entry of financial transactions on accounting records prior to the actual receipt or expenditure of the funds involved in such transactions; for example, charging purchases before bills covering those purchases are paid and crediting sales before the money income represented by those sales is received.

accrued interest. Interest that has accumulated but which has not been paid or collected. In the case of bond purchases, it is customary for the buyer to pay the seller accrued interest up to but not including the date of delivery, in addition to the purchase price. See also INTEREST.

accumulated dividend. A dividend which has not been paid when due and which has become a liability of the corporation, to be paid, presumably, at some future time. See also DIVIDEND.

accumulation. In calculating the yield on a bond, the difference between the face value and the cost if the bond is purchased at a discount. See also DISCOUNT.

accumulative dividend. See CUMULATIVE DIVIDEND.

acid-test ratio. In a BALANCE SHEET, the proportion of the sum of cash, ACCOUNTS RECEIVABLE, and the market value of SECURITIES, if any, to CURRENT LIABILITIES. If, for example, the balance sheet shows $5,000 cash, $1,000 in accounts receivable, and securities valued at $3,000, and the current liabilities amount to $3,000, the acid-test ratio is 3 to 1. The acid-test ratio is frequently used as one test to determine CREDIT RATING. Sometimes called *quick ratio*.

acknowledgment. A personal declaration before an officer designated by the state, or before a court of law, that a certain act is one's own. The act of signing certain documents is often required to be so acknowledged in order to make certain the identity of the person signing the document.

across-the-board. A popular term frequently applied to a wage policy which provides for a uniform increase of wages for all employees of an establishment.

active stock. See explanation under CAPITAL STOCK.

active trade balance. See FAVORABLE BALANCE OF TRADE.

actuary. As used in the United States, a person who calculates insurance risks and premiums. In Europe the term is sometimes applied to a clerk, especially one employed by a corporation.

***Adair* v. *United States*.** An early case, 208 U. S. 161 (1908), in which the United States Supreme Court declared unconstitutional an act of Congress outlawing yellow-dog employment contracts in interstate commerce. Such contracts called for a promise by a prospective employee not to join a labor union. The court based its decision on the theory that legislative interdiction of such contracts violated contractual liberty protected by the due process clause of the 5th Amendment. The case is similar to *COPPAGE* v. *KANSAS* (*q.v.*).

Adamson Act. An act of Congress, 1916, establishing the 8-hour day as the basis of pay for railroad employees in interstate commerce.

Addyston Pipe and Steel Co. case. A case, *United States* v. *Addyston Pipe and Steel Co.*, 175 U.S. 211 (1899), in which the Supreme Court of the United States liberalized somewhat its earlier ruling in the KNIGHT CASE (*q.v.*) involving the application of the Sherman Antitrust Act. In the instant case, the court applied the act to a combination among certain steel companies to fix prices of their product in the United States, declaring that the commerce power of Congress extended to the regulation of contracts among individuals or companies if such contracts directly and substantially affected interstate and foreign commerce. See also SHERMAN ANTITRUST ACT.

adjuster. A person who examines the damage and estimates the loss created by a fire, or other disasters covered by insurance, and attempts to arrive at an agreement with the insured in settlement of the claim against the insurance company.

adjustment bond. See explanation under BOND.

Adkins* v. *Children's Hospital. See MINIMUM-WAGE CASES.

Adler* v. *Board of Education. A case, 342 U. S. 485 (1952), in which the Supreme Court of the United States upheld New York's so-called Feinberg Law (1949). This provided for the removal of teachers and other employees in the state's public schools who advocate overthrow of the government by unlawful means. Power of removal was extended to public-school employees who belong to organizations which the state's educational authorities, after appropriate hearings, had listed as subversive in their aims. Individuals identified as members of such organizations were presumed to be disqualified from holding a position in the educational system, such presumption being subject to later review by a court or similar body.

administered price. A predetermined price arrived at from a calculation of costs and desired profits, from a fairly accurate knowledge of the total quantity of goods likely to be offered on the market, and from an estimate of the probable sales volume at the predetermined price. The process of establishing an administered price cannot be described either as COMPETITION or MONOPOLY, but is one which combines elements derived from both of these concepts. It suggests the existence of an OLIGOPOLY or a DUOPOLY. See also MONOPOLISTIC COMPETITION, PRICE.

administrator. A person authorized to settle an estate when the deceased has left no will or has named no executor. In common speech the term may refer to a person who manages business affairs of any kind or the activities of some public agency.

admission temporaire. The free admission of dutiable goods which are destined for export after undergoing some sort of processing.

ad valorem duty. A customs duty based on the value of the goods. Such a duty is a fixed percentage of the foreign or domestic valuation of imported goods. It is used in contradistinction to SPECIFIC DUTY. See also CUSTOMS DUTY.

advance. A loan.

advance bill. See explanation under BILL.

advertising. The art of making known to the public, in one way or another, goods and services offered for sale, and various methods of persuasion to induce the public to buy those goods and services.

advertising agency. An individual or organization that prepares and places advertising for others.

advice. As used in commercial affairs, information concerning a shipment of goods or some other matter pertaining to a business transaction.

affidavit. A written statement to which the maker takes oath or makes affirmation before a notary public or other officer authorized by law to administer an oath or affirmation. See also NOTARY PUBLIC.

afforestation. The creation of a forest where none existed before; for example, planting trees on submarginal soil or on abandoned farm or grazing land. There is said to be as much as 80,000,000 acres of idle land in the United States suitable for afforestation. The term should not be confused with REFORESTATION.

agent. Generally any person who acts for another with the latter's consent. The term is sometimes used also to indicate a broker, as in the case of an insurance agent.

agents of production. See FACTORS OF PRODUCTION.

aggregate corporation. A corporation consisting of more than one person. See also CORPORATION.

aggregative index number. An INDEX NUMBER (*q.v.*) computed by finding the sum of the figures applicable to each period of time under consideration, assigning the index number 100 to the period designated as the base period, and finding for each of the other periods a figure which bears the same relation to 100 that the sum of the figures for that period bears to the sum of the figures of the base period.

Example:

Item	Period	
	1940	1941
A	9.00	10.00
B	5.00	4.00
C	7.00	9.00
Totals	21.00	23.00
Index No.	100	x

$x : 100 :: 23.00 : 21.00.$

$x = 109.52$, index number for 1941.

This method provides no logical means for assigning relative importance to the various items constituting the lists of figures. The resulting index numbers, therefore, even though mathematically valid, may fail to disclose the full significance of changes that may have occurred from one period to another. For example, in calculating variations in the cost of living, changes in consumer buying habits will alter the relative quantities of various commodities purchased, and may affect the cost of living quite as much as do price changes. For this reason, a WEIGHTED AVERAGE is often incorporated in this method of constructing an index number. In the case of a cost of living index, the weights might logically be the quantities purchased. For tests to determine the mathematical validity of an index number, see FACTOR REVERSAL TEST, TIME REVERSAL TEST.

agio. A premium paid for the exchange of one kind of money for another. The premium may be for the exchange of the money of one nation for the money of another, or it may be in the form of an allowance for coins, short in weight due to wear, exchanged for coins of full weight. Occasionally the term is used to indicate a premium paid for a foreign BILL OF EXCHANGE.

agio theory of interest. The theory that explains interest as a premium paid for the immediate possession of goods which otherwise could be had only at some future time. This premium is paid, according to the theory, because most people expect to be more bountifully supplied with goods in the future than they are at the moment, because present satisfactions are more vivid than future possibilities, or because present goods may offer the possibility of immediately increasing the profits of production. Also called *abstinence theory of interest*. See also INTEREST.

Agricultural Adjustment Act (first). An act of Congress, 1933, designed to control the prices of farm products by regulating the production of those products. Farmers were asked to co-operate by reducing acreage planted in certain products, and received cash payments from the government to compensate them for such reduction in acreage. The funds for these payments were to be raised by a PROCESSING TAX (*q.v.*). This tax was declared unconstitutional by the Supreme Court in 1936. See also HOOSAC MILLS CASE.

Agricultural Adjustment Act (second). An act of Congress, 1938, which redefines and extends the agricultural policies of the first act of that name, held unconstitutional by the courts in 1936. As supplemented by more recent statutes and a variety of executive orders, this new act continues the provision of earlier legislation for MARKETING AGREEMENTS and AGRICULTURAL PARITY payments for certain agricultural staples. It also continues the policy of SOIL CONSERVATION, inaugurated by the Soil Conservation and Domestic Allotment Act of 1936, authorizing payments out of the federal treasury to farmers and others who carry out approved soil-conservation policies. In addition, the new act provides producers of certain staples with a system of insurance against growing hazards, and, through loans to farmers on surpluses, has developed the nucleus of the idea of the *ever-normal granary*.

Agricultural Adjustment Act case (second). A case, *Mulford* v. *Smith*, 307 U. S. 38 (1939), in which the Supreme Court of the United States sustained the constitutionality of the second AGRICULTURAL ADJUSTMENT ACT (1938). The precise issue in the case was the act's provision for tobacco-marketing quotas and the imposition of penalties on those who exceeded such quotas. The court argued that Congress' real motive in passing this act, which was the general stabilization of agriculture, was irrelevant to the act's validity, it being clear that the attempt to regulate the flow of an agricultural commodity to the market affected interstate commerce, that such regulation was an attempt to "foster, protect and conserve that commerce" or to "prevent the flow of commerce from working harm to the people of the nation," and hence was within the competence of Congress.

Agricultural Credit Act. An act of Congress, 1923. It provided for the establishment of 12 FEDERAL INTERMEDIATE CREDIT BANKS (*q.v.*).

agricultural economics. That part of the study of economics which treats particularly of the production and distribution of agricultural products together with the economic agencies serving agriculture such as credit institutions, marketing associations, and the like. See also ECONOMICS.

agricultural ladder. A figurative expression of the idea that farmers start as farm laborers, then successively become share croppers, tenant farmers, and owner-operators.

agricultural parity. A price for certain farm products which is assumed to give those products an exchange value, for things that the farmer needs to buy, equivalent to that which existed at a specified period of time called the "base period." For most farm products to which the legal requirement for parity applies, parity for a particular product at a specified time is now computed (1961) by first dividing the average price for the ten-year period just preceding by the average INDEX NUMBER for all prices received by farmers during the same period. The resulting quotient, called the adjusted base-period price, is then multiplied by the current index number (1910–1914 =100) of prices paid by farmers, which now includes farm wage rates. Thus, the average price received by farmers for rough rice from 1947 to 1958 was $5.04 a bag, and the average index number of prices received by farmers was 262, resulting in an adjusted base-period price of $1.92. When multiplied by the 1958 index number of prices paid by farmers (308), the result is $5.91. See also PARITY.

Agricultural Research Administration. A major division of the United States Department of Agriculture responsible for co-ordinating most of the department's bureaus and offices engaged in experimental, demonstration, or research activities. The name was changed in 1953 and the division was known thereafter as the AGRICULTURAL RESEARCH SERVICE.

Agricultural Research Service. A major division of the United States Department of Agriculture engaged in experimental, demonstration, and research activities relating to the production and utilization of farm products. It is also responsible for the control and regulatory programs involving the enforcement of plant and animal quarantines, the eradication of animal and plant diseases, meat inspection, and related work. Projects are carried on at the Agricultural Research Center, Beltsville, Md., as well as in other localities in the United States and in foreign countries. Much of the research is in co-operation with state agricultural experiment stations.

agricultural revolution. 1. In England, the transition from medieval to modern conditions in rural areas during the 18th century. Lands formerly held in common were enclosed for the benefit of great landowners. As a result of these *enclosures* yeoman farmers were thrown out of work, causing great distress and unrest. 2. The application of modern science and technology to the cultivation and exploitation of land, a development especially apparent after 1870, although its beginnings may be noted earlier in the 19th century.

Agriculture, Department of. One of the more important administrative units of the federal government with a secretary of cabinet rank, created February 9, 1889. Traditionally, its prime objective has been the conduct of educational and research activities of immediate benefit to the farm community. In recent decades, however, the department has acquired additional responsibilities of a regulatory and enforcement nature. It now has direct or indirect responsibility for the administration of many federal agricultural-aid programs, among them programs for the stabilization and extension of agricultural markets, the extension of various forms of credit to the agricultural community, the administration of agricultural price-support policies, the promotion of land-resource conservation, and of other programs to assist farmer and rancher. Some of its principal subsidiary units are the SOIL CONSERVATION SERVICE, the Forest Service, the Agricultural Marketing Service, the FARMERS HOME ADMINISTRATION, and the COMMODITY CREDIT CORPORATION.

Aldrich-Vreeland Act. An act of Congress, 1908, which authorized associations of national banks to issue bank notes secured by commercial paper and state and municipal bonds. The act was regarded as a temporary one pending a reorganization of the banking system. Hence, the act provided for appointment of a *National Monetary Commission* to make a thorough investigation of the then existing banking facilities of the country. The establishment of the FEDERAL RESERVE SYSTEM was the ultimate outcome of this investigation.

allonge. An extra piece of paper attached to a document to provide space for indorsements when no space is left for this purpose on the document itself.

allowed time. The time allowed employees for machine upkeep, fatigue, and personal needs in calculating the base pay in piecework or other incentive pay systems.

amalgamation. The condition resulting when a new corporation is formed to absorb two or more existing corporations. The term is also often used interchangeably with MERGER. See also COMBINATION.

American Column and Lumber Co. v. United States. See LUMBER INDUSTRY CASE.

American Communications Association* v. *Douds. A case, 339 U. S. 382 (1950), in which the Supreme Court of the United States upheld the validity of the provisions of the Taft-Hartley Act of 1947 which withdraw collective bargaining and other privileges guaranteed to labor unions by the National Labor Relations Act (1935) when officers of such labor unions refuse to swear or affirm that they are not members of the Communist party or of any organization which advocates the overthrow of the government by force and violence. See also LABOR-MANAGEMENT RELATIONS (TAFT-HARTLEY) ACT, NATIONAL LABOR RELATIONS (WAGNER-CONNERY) ACT.

American Economic Association. A professional organization of economists founded in 1885 to stimulate thought and discussion relating to economic problems and to encourage research in that field. The association is composed of approximately 7,700 members and publishes the *American Economic Review* and occasional monographs.

American Farm Bureau Federation. An organization of farmers, with a nation-wide constituency, founded in the United States in 1920. Originating at the beginning of a long postwar agricultural depression, its purpose was to attempt to meet the pressing economic problems of agriculture. To that end it proceeded to emulate industry by advocating control over production. It organized the FARM BLOC in 1921 for political action, and later carried on a campaign to induce farmers to withhold wheat from a glutted market. The Farm Bureau claims at least 1,628,295 members (1964), with 49 state farm bureaus. The American Farm Bureau Women's Committee also claims a large membership.

American Federation of Labor and Congress of Industrial Organizations. A national organization of labor unions, formed in 1955 by the merger of the previously separate AFL and CIO. The organization comprises 134 national and international unions with a total membership of 13½ million, and some 500 directly affiliated local unions with about 100,000 members, whose occupations do not fall within the jurisdiction of established national unions. There are 6 autonomous trade and industrial departments within the AFL–CIO, 51 state bodies, and 838 local central bodies. The AFL–CIO is financed by per capita dues paid by its affiliates. The federation exercises no authority over member unions except to require them to abide by its constitution and ethical-practices codes, under penalty of suspension or expulsion.

American Stock Exchange. One of the two principal stock exchanges in New York City. It was organized before the Civil War, and for many years conducted its trading in the open street. For that reason it was known as the CURB EXCHANGE. Since 1921 it has been located at 86 Trinity Place.

American system. The policy of encouraging American industry through protective tariffs, and of promoting extensive internal improvements. The term thus used was common during the early part of the 19th century and was usually attributed to Henry Clay.

***American Tobacco Co.* v. *United States*.** A case, 328 U. S. 781 (1946), in which the United States Supreme Court appears to have taken the position that PRICE LEADERSHIP (*q.v.*) and the resulting phenomenon of parallel pricing in an oligopolistic market were illegal, whether or not such pricing was predicated upon an agreement between the individual firms.

amortization. **1.** A provision made in advance for the gradual liquidation of a future obligation by periodic charges against the capital account or by the creation of a money fund sufficient to meet the obligation when due. **2.** As applied to the process of calculating net yield on a bond bought at a premium, the periodic subtraction from the current yield of a proportionate share of the premium between the date of the purchase of the bond and the date of its maturity. See also CURRENT YIELD, PREMIUM.

analog computer. A calculating machine which solves problems by using electrical circuits for simulating physical phenomena. It expresses results in approximate figures proportional to the magnitude of the phenomenon under study. An analog computer is thus a continuous-reading device in which numbers are represented by physical magnitudes such as flow, temperature, or pressure. Although commonly mechanical rather than electrical, a simple clock mechanism or automobile speedometer functions in a manner similar to that of an analog computer. A clock computes divisions of the day by means of a minute hand which revolves 24 times as fast as the earth. A speedometer computes speed by means of a dial or a pointer, the movement of which is in proportion to the revolutions per unit of time of the automobile wheels.

anarchism. A theory of society which advocates the abolition of all forms of coercive government. Such a theory anticipates that harmony among the members of society as well as the production of necessary and desired goods can be attained by voluntary co-operation. Private property would be abolished and collective ownership by co-operating groups substituted. See also ECONOMIC SYSTEM.

annual wage. A provision in law or labor-management contracts which guarantees a wage earner stable employment at established rates of pay for a period of at least 1 year.

annuity. The payment to or receipt by a beneficiary of a fixed amount of money at uniform intervals of time. Usually an annuity is paid out of a fund created at one time or accumulated over a period of years, and payments may liquidate such a fund on the basis of generally accepted statistics indicating the life expectancy of the annuitant. Provisions for an annuity are sometimes incorporated in life-insurance policies and may be paid either to the insured or to beneficiaries. See also DEFERRED ANNUITY, LIFE ANNUITY, SURVIVORSHIP ANNUITY.

annuity bond. See explanation under BOND.

antagonistic co-operation. A term used to describe the thesis that it is not mutual good will that engenders human co-operation but practical necessity. Antagonisms are suppressed because it is mutually advantageous to do so.

antibank movement. Legislative enactments and constitutional provisions promulgated during the 1840's and early 1850's that discouraged normal banking operations and even prohibited banking in the states of Arkansas, California, Florida, Illinois, Iowa, Minnesota, Oregon, and Texas, and in the District of Columbia. The movement was an extreme reaction against the WILDCAT BANKING

ERA and the result of a disposition to hold the banks responsible for the DEPRESSION of 1837–42.

anticipation rate. An extra discount sometimes permitted on an invoice in addition to the cash discount stated in the terms for payment. If the stated terms are, for example, 2 per cent for cash in 10 days or 90 days extra, the customer may pay the bill within 10 days, deducting not only the 2 per cent but an additional anticipation rate calculated on the basis of, say, 6 per cent per annum for 90 days or $1\frac{1}{2}$ per cent. On an invoice of $1,000 the calculation would be as follows:

Invoice	$1,000.00
2 per cent cash discount	20.00
	980.00
Anticipation rate, $1\frac{1}{2}$ per cent	14.70
	$965.30

Anti-Corn-Law League. An organization founded in Manchester, England, in 1839 under the leadership of Richard Cobden to seek repeal of the CORN LAWS.

antidumping duty. A tariff duty which attempts to discourage or prevent dumping; that is, the importation of goods to be sold at a price less than that for which they are sold in the country of origin. Such a duty may achieve its purpose if it equals the difference between the selling price of the goods in the country of origin and the selling price in the country where the goods have been dumped. See also CUSTOMS DUTY.

Anti-injunction (Norris-LaGuardia) Act. An act of Congress, 1932, which protects labor by regulating the issuance of injunctions, outlawing yellow-dog contracts, protecting union officials from the consequences of certain unauthorized acts committed by union members, and requiring trial by jury in certain contempt-of-court cases. See INJUNCTION, YELLOW-DOG CONTRACT.

Antiracketeering Act. An act of Congress, 1934, which, with subsequent amendments, makes it a federal offense directly or indirectly to delay, by robbery or extortion, the movement of any article in interstate commerce.

Antistrikebreaking (Byrnes) Act. An act of Congress, 1936, which, as amended in 1938, prohibits the willful transportation between the states of any person employed for the purpose of interfering by force or threats with peaceful picketing during any labor dispute or with the self-organization or collective bargaining of employees. The act does not apply to common carriers.

antitrust. A term descriptive of any policy or action which has for its object the curtailment of monopolistic power.

antitrust acts. See CLAYTON ACT, SHERMAN ANTITRUST ACT.

Antitrust Division. A division of the United States Department of Justice charged with the enforcement of antitrust and related legislation. It receives complaints and conducts investigations in co-operation with the Federal Bureau of Investigation and the Federal Trade Commission. Criminal prosecutions and suits in equity are instituted when necessary to curb monopolies and restraints of interstate and foreign trade.

Apex Hosiery case. A case, *Apex Hosiery Co.* v. *Leader*, 310 U. S. 469 (1940), in which the Supreme Court of the United States ruled that the loss of production and trade entailed by a sit-down strike to coerce an employer into signing a closed-shop agreement was not substantial enough to constitute the kind of restraint of interstate commerce which the Sherman Antitrust Act was intended to curb and that, therefore, the provisions of the Sherman Act were not applicable to the strike.

applied economics. The application of economic theory to the solution of economic problems. See also ECONOMICS.

apportioned tax. A tax, the proceeds of which are distributed among other political units after having been collected by one of them. Thus, in some of the states of the United States, property taxes may be collected by the county and subsequently shared by the state government, the counties, and other subdivisions. See also TAX.

appraisal. A formal valuation of property, made by a competent authority.

appreciation. A more or less permanent increase in value because of an upward change in the MARKET PRICE or because of inherent qualities that enhance the desirability of, and hence the DEMAND for, a product over a period of time.

apprentice. A person who learns an art, trade, or calling by association with, and under the supervision of, skilled workers. Apprenticeship is of ancient origin. It is identified particularly with a medieval GUILD where apprentices served under master craftsmen in return for the opportunity to learn a trade. During recent years, in the United States, employers and labor unions in certain industries, notably the printing and building trades, have developed systematic plans for apprenticeship training. The Bureau of Apprenticeship and Training of the United States Department of Labor formulates standards for the welfare of apprentices and for their instruction.

appropriation. The action of setting money aside and formally authorizing its expenditure, especially such action when taken by a legislature or similar public body. See also LUMP-SUM APPROPRIATION, ITEMIZED APPROPRIATION.

appropriation, law of. See MARXIAN LAW OF CAPITALIST ACCUMULATION.

arbitrage. The process of buying a thing in one market and selling it at the same time in another market in order to take advantage of price differences.

arbitration. An arrangement whereby two parties to a dispute agree to the appointment of an impartial chairman or group of competent persons to decide the issue, the disputants agreeing to abide by the decision rendered. Arbitration is often used in labor and industrial disputes.

arbitration of exchange. The payment by a person in one country of a debt payable in another country by means of a bill of exchange purchased in a third country. The price of BILLS OF EXCHANGE payable in the currencies of foreign countries differs in the various financial centers of the world. It may be more profitable, therefore, at any particular moment for a person in the United States, for example, wishing to settle a debt in London, to purchase a bill of exchange in France payable in English currency rather than to purchase a bill in New York payable in English currency. Such an operation may be more profitable even if it is necessary first to purchase a bill in New York payable in French currency.

area agreement. As applied to labor relations, an agreement signed by a labor union or unions and individual employers engaged in a particular industry within a geographic area. The latter is usually more extensive than that enclosed by the boundaries of a municipality.

area sample. A limited number of observations selected from an entire aggregate of phenomena on the basis of geographical subdivisions. For example, suppose that a sample of SPENDING UNITS within a state is desired, and there exists no comprehensive list from which such a sample might be obtained. The state, in such a case, might be divided into geographical units, say counties, and a certain number of counties selected for the sample. Each county included in the sample might then be divided into municipalities and a certain number of municipalities selected for the sample. Each municipality included in the sample might then be divided into streets and a certain number of streets selected for the sample. Finally, from each street included in the sample, a certain number of spending units might be identified. See also SAMPLING.

arithmetic chart. See explanation under RATIO CHART.

arithmetic mean. A calculated average computed by finding the sum of the numbers to be averaged and dividing the result by the total quantity of numbers. The mathematical formula is:

$$M = \frac{\Sigma m}{N}$$

when

M = arithmetic mean,
m = numbers to be averaged,
N = total quantity of numbers.

The arithmetic mean is the average most commonly used. It emphasizes extremes, however, and is hence unsuitable for certain types of economic computation. For example, out of 25 contributions, one $10 contribution, when all the rest are less than $1, makes the average contribution seem unduly large if computed according to the arithmetic mean. See also MEAN.

articles of incorporation. A document setting forth the purpose, duration, principal place of business, and other details of a proposed corporation. It is submitted to an appropriate government official for approval, and, if approved, copies of the document must usually be filed in one or more government offices in order that the existence of the corporation be made a matter of public record. Also called *certificate of incorporation.*

artificial capital. See explanation under CAPITAL GOOD.

artisan. A person skilled in some trade or craft; for example, a carpenter, mechanic, or mason.

Aski trading system. A form of exchange control prevailing in Germany during the 1930's according to which payment for certain imports was made in special German marks, these, in turn, being acceptable in payment for exported German goods. The term is an abbreviation of German words meaning "foreigners' special accounts for domestic payments." See also EXCHANGE CONTROL.

assaying. The testing of an ore or other commodity by chemical means or otherwise to determine its degree of purity. The United States government maintains *assay offices* for the testing of bullion used in coins and a customs laboratory to test imported ores for the determination of a DUTY.

assay office. See explanation under ASSAYING.

assembly-line technique. A system of production in which, by a rather extreme application of the principle of division of labor, a number of individual, interchangeable parts, or subassemblies, are brought together into a completely assembled or finished unit. A conveyor belt is frequently used to carry the work under construction between lines of employees, each of whom performs a given operation on the partially constructed unit as it reaches a designated point in the line, the last employee in the line performing his operation to complete the unit. See also INTERCHANGEABLE PARTS, DIVISION OF LABOR.

assented stock or bond. A stock or bond, the owner of which has agreed to some voluntary organizational change in the corporation issuing the stock or bond and has deposited it pending the issue of a definitive stock certificate or bond. A stock or bond, the owner of which has not consented to the change, is called a *nonassented stock or bond.*

assessable stock. See explanation under CAPITAL STOCK.

assessment. 1. A valuation placed upon property for the purpose of taxation; usually called a *tax assessment.* See also EQUALIZATION OF ASSESSMENTS, SPECIAL ASSESSMENT. 2. A demand for payment, the liability for which has already been incurred. Thus, the owners of certain classes of CAPITAL STOCK may be assessed for additional payments; or the holders of shares of stock, not fully paid for, may be assessed the unpaid balance, or a part of it.

assessor. 1. A person with specialized knowledge who assists a judge in cases requiring such knowledge. 2. A government official, usually appointed or elected locally, who appraises property for purposes of taxation.

asset. As used in accounting, something of value that is owned. It may be something tangible or something intangible such as a claim on another person. For some of the more important kinds of assets see ASSET ENTER MAINS, CAPITAL ASSET, CURRENT ASSET, EARNING ASSET, EQUITABLE ASSET, FIXED ASSET, INTANGIBLE ASSET, LEGAL ASSET, ORDINARY ASSET, QUICK ASSET, SLOW ASSET, WASTING ASSET. See also FROZEN, LIQUID.

asset and liability statement. Usually a balance sheet. The term is sometimes used by accountants, however, to indicate a statement of what is owned and what is owed, prepared from single-entry books or sources other than double-entry books. See also BALANCE SHEET.

asset enter mains. A term used in the transactions of executors or trustees, indicating an asset available to meet immediate obligations. See also ASSET.

assignat. A form of paper currency issued by the Revolutionary government in France between 1790 and 1795. It was secured by expropriated lands of the church and the *émigré* nobility. The assignats were redeemed in 1796 by another form of paper currency, and both were subsequently repudiated.

assignee. One to whom a title, interest, or right of some kind has been transferred. The person from whom the transfer is received is the assignor.

assignment. The formal transfer of any property or right from one person to another.

assimilation. As applied to finance, the purchase by the general public of a new issue of securities, and the establishment of their price in the stock markets.

association agreement. As applied to labor relations, an agreement signed by an association of employers and a labor union or a board representing several unions.

assumed bond. See explanation under BOND.

assumption of risk. A common-law doctrine that an employee assumes the risk of personal injury when engaged in an unusually dangerous or hazardous occupation. Such a doctrine has now been largely replaced in most of the states of the United States by WORKMEN'S COMPENSATION LAWS.

assurance. A term used by some insurance companies instead of the term "insurance."

astronomical theory of the business cycle. A theory that attempts to correlate the constantly recurring economic crises with the periodic appearance of sunspots. The varying intensity of the sun's rays is said to cause good and bad harvests, and these, in turn, to influence economic life. The theory was suggested to Stanley Jevons, an English economist, by the apparent regularity of the 10-year intervals between economic crises during the 19th century. See also BUSINESS CYCLE.

Atomic Energy Act. An act of Congress, 1946. The act stated that "subject at all times to the paramount objective of assuring the common defense and security, the development and utilization of atomic energy shall, so far as practicable, be directed towards improving the public welfare, increasing the standard of living, strengthening free competition in private enterprise and promoting world peace." The act provided for public assistance to private research, the dissemination of technical knowledge (consistent with national security), federal research and development, and control over the production, ownership, and use of fissionable materials. The administration of the act was committed to an Atomic Energy Commission of five members, assisted by a board of civilian advisers and a military liaison committee.

Atomic Energy Commission. See UNITED STATES ATOMIC ENERGY COMMISSION.

atomistic society. An economy in which there is a distinct preponderance of small, independent, producing units. The term is used to indicate the condition that existed previous to the establishment of huge aggregates of capital in industry and trade, originally organized as such or created through an AMALGAMATION, HOLDING COMPANY, MERGER, or TRUST.

at the market. An order to a stockbroker to buy or sell immediately regardless of the market price.

auction sale. A sale in which goods are offered to the highest bidder. Such a sale usually involves a series of oral bids which begin at a low price and proceed to the highest one offered, at which point the sale is consummated. See also DUTCH AUCTION.

audit. A verification of an accounting record.

austerity program. A national economic policy which deliberately reduces the level of living of the people in order to accomplish desired ends such as a balanced budget, increased capital equipment, the payment of the external national debt, or the balancing of international payments.

Austrian school. See MARGINAL UTILITY SCHOOL.

autarchy. Economic self-sufficiency. In a more general sense the term is used to indicate complete sovereignty.

automatic balance. As applied to economic life, the idea that automatic forces always restore equilibrium when excesses occur. Thus, when interest rates are too low, savings are curtailed, and the demand for capital will force an advance. In international trade an excess of exports will be checked by the importation of gold and the resulting advance in the general price level. Prices, when too high, will meet resistance through lack of purchasing power, and when too low will be advanced through increased consumer demand.

automatic checkoff. See explanation under CHECKOFF.

automatic wage adjustment. A system of wage payments which provides for advancing or lowering employees' wages according to some factor other than the purely economic demand for labor. This factor may be an advance or decline in the cost-of-living index, or of prices or profits. The term may also refer to wage adjustments made in accordance with some established formula relating to years of employment or to a record of service.

automation. The performance of tasks, formerly requiring human labor and some thought, by self-acting and self-regulating machines. The term was first applied to the mere automatic transfer of materials from one machine tool to another, each machine tool performing some operation contributing to the completion of the final product. Only human labor was thus replaced. With the advance of technology, communication was added, and a variety of precision controls were perfected. Communication occurs when the machine tools, or other fabricating or processing devices, follow a sequence of "instructions" such as might be programed in an ELECTRONIC DATA PROCESSING machine. Control is effected when any deviation from a predetermined program actuates a mechanism that causes the necessary correction to be made. These two latter functions replace human thought, at least on a low level.

autonomous investment. New CAPITAL FORMATION motivated by reasons independent of the rate of interest or the level of NATIONAL INCOME. Public INVESTMENTS are usually of this nature. Investments deemed necessary for the national defense, those designed for PUMP PRIMING purposes, or for the general peacetime welfare of the community, such as public parks, baths, playgrounds, etc., are cases in point. Even PUBLIC WORKS of a SELF-LIQUIDATING nature may be undertaken with little regard for the rate of interest or the level of national income. Private investments are not generally autonomous. Only when made on the basis of long-term plans divorced from considerations of immediate profits and losses can they be so regarded. The term is used in contradistinction to INDUCED INVESTMENT. See also INVESTMENT.

autonomous tariff system. A system of tariff duties in which the rates are established by legislative action exclusively, and not wholly or partly by commercial treaties. The term is used in contradistinction to CONVENTIONAL TARIFF SYSTEM. See also TARIFF.

autonomous variable. In statistics, a variable that depends, in part, upon factors other than those which are strictly economic; for example, changes due to political, social, or psychological influences.

avail. In general, an amount remaining after the deduction of expenses or a discount; for example, the PROCEEDS of a promissory note, the amount of an estate after the debts have been paid, or the income from an auction sale after the deduction of selling expenses.

average. A medial numerical figure calculated from other unequal numerical figures, or placed in a medial position with reference to them. For calculated averages, see ARITHMETIC MEAN, GEOMETRIC MEAN, HARMONIC MEAN, MOVING AVERAGE, WEIGHTED AVERAGE. For positional averages, see MEDIAN, MODE. For quadratic mean, see STANDARD DEVIATION.

B

backlog. An accumulation. For example, a backlog of orders indicates orders as yet unfilled.

back spread. The condition which exists when the difference in price of the same commodity or security in two markets is less than normal. The term is used in contradistinction to SPREAD which indicates a price differential greater than normal. The terms are used in ARBITRAGE transactions.

backtracking. As applied to labor relations, the policy of retaining employees with the longest record of service in preference to those with shorter records when the labor force of an establishment is being reduced. Sometimes called ***bumping***.

Bailey* v. *Drexel Furniture Co. See CHILD-LABOR CASES.

bailment. Generally, the transfer under a contract by one person to another of goods, money, or other valuable personal property for safekeeping or for some specified purpose.

balance of payments. In the case of any particular country, the difference between the total payments made to foreign nations and the total receipts from foreign nations during a given period of time. The payments and receipts include gold, all merchandise and services such as freight and insurance charges, the expenditures of travelers, capital movements as occasioned by loans and their repayment, and the interest charges for servicing the loans. Computation of a particular country's balance of payments may be limited to its economic relations with another country or group of countries, or it may include its economic relations with the whole world. In calculating the balance of payments reference is sometimes made to INVISIBLE ITEMS OF TRADE and to VISIBLE ITEMS OF TRADE (*qq.v.*).

balance of trade. In the case of any particular country, the difference between the money value of that country's merchandise imports and exports. The balance of trade constitutes an important item in calculating a nation's BALANCE OF PAYMENTS. Traditionally, reference is sometimes made to a FAVORABLE BALANCE OF TRADE and to an UNFAVORABLE BALANCE OF TRADE (*qq.v.*).

balance sheet. A condensed list of assets and liabilities displaying net worth or a deficit as of a given date. Also called ***financial statement***. See also ASSET, LIABILITY.

bank. A general and somewhat vague term applying to a large number of different kinds of financial institutions carrying on one or more of the functions of deposit, discount, investment, and issue, and offering other financial services of various kinds. There are also many financial institutions not designated as banks which carry on one or more of the functions above mentioned. For terms referring to different kinds of banks and banking see BANK OF ISSUE, CENTRAL BANK, COMMERCIAL BANK, CO-OPERATIVE BANK, INDUSTRIAL BANK, INVESTMENT BANKING, LAND BANK, MEMBER BANK, MORRIS PLAN BANK, NATIONAL BANK, PRIVATE BANK, SAVINGS BANK, STATE BANK, TRUST COMPANY.

For some of the more important institutions and groups of institutions commonly referred to as banks see BANK FOR CO-OPERATIVES, BANK FOR INTERNATIONAL SETTLEMENTS, BANK OF NORTH DAKOTA, BANK OF THE UNITED STATES, EXPORT-IMPORT BANK OF WASHINGTON, FEDERAL INTERMEDIATE CREDIT BANK, FEDERAL LAND BANK, FEDERAL RESERVE BANK, INTERNATIONAL BANK FOR RECONSTRUCTION AND DEVELOPMENT, JOINT-STOCK LAND BANK. See also BANKING SYSTEM.

bankable bill. See explanation under BILL.

bank acceptance. A draft or bill of exchange accepted for payment by a bank. See also ACCEPTANCE, BILL OF EXCHANGE, DRAFT.

bank call. A demand by an appropriate government official made upon banks for balance sheets showing their financial condition as of a specified date. In the United States such demands may be made by a state superintendent of banks or by the federal bureau of the COMPTROLLER OF THE CURRENCY.

bank clearings. See CLEARINGS.

bank credit. Credit created by a bank by adding the proceeds of a loan to a depositor's account. Such credit may be created by discounting a depositor's promissory note, in which case the face value of the note becomes an ASSET of the bank, and the amount of the discount, DEFERRED INCOME, in the form of unearned interest. Such credit may also be created by the purchase, by the bank, of United States government bonds, in which case the purchase price of the bonds may be placed to the government's credit to be drawn when needed, and the bonds become an asset of the bank. See also CREDIT.

bank debits. The value of checks and commercial paper charged to depositors' accounts by banks within a certain territory during a designated length of time. The statistics are based on reports from member banks and are compiled by the FEDERAL RESERVE BANKS. They serve as a general index of the volume of business being transacted.

bank deposit. The right to receive a stated sum of money from a bank, this right having been created by previously paying an equivalent amount of money or other currency to the bank, or by a credit to the depositor's account of the proceeds of a loan made by the bank. Evidence of a bank deposit is the bank's books of account and the depositor's passbook, duplicate deposit slip, or other form of receipt. A bank deposit may be classified as a DEMAND DEPOSIT, DERIVATIVE DEPOSIT, PRIMARY DEPOSIT, or TIME DEPOSIT.

banker's bill. See explanation under BILL.

bank examiner. A public official who periodically audits the accounts of banks under his jurisdiction to determine whether their practice conforms with the law and whether they are in sound financial condition. The examination of national banks is under the jurisdiction of the United States Comptroller of the Currency, who appoints the examiners. Each bank is examined at least twice a year and more often if deemed necessary. State banks are examined by bank examiners appointed under the laws of the individual states of the United States.

bank for co-operatives. One of a system of 13 credit institutions, one operating nationally and 12 regionally, which were created by act of Congress in 1933 to provide both short- and long-term credit to farm co-operatives. These banks are a part of the FARM CREDIT ADMINISTRATION, an independent agency of the executive branch of the Government. See also BANK.

Bank for International Settlements. A bank organized in 1930, under a Swiss charter, by representatives of the central banks of certain western European states and by representatives of banking interests of the United States, to administer reparations payments under the YOUNG PLAN and engage in a limited general banking business. Thirty years after its founding, the Bank had become a respected and influential fiscal institution largely because of its distinguished leadership. Among its many specialized activities is that of acting as the fiscal agent for the 5-man High Authority of the Coal and Steel Community. The High Authority is the directing agency of the Community. See also BANK.

Bankhead-Jones Farm Tenant Act. An act of Congress, 1937, which authorizes the Farm Security Administration (later the Farmers Home Administration) to finance 40-year mortgage loans to enable tenant farmers, and others in a like position, to purchase small farms.

bank holiday. Any holiday or other period during which banks are legally permitted to remain closed. The term is applied particularly to the period from March 4 to 14, 1933, when a presidential proclamation closed all banks in the United States pending examination into their operations and the restoration of public confidence.

Banking (Glass-Steagall) Act. An act of Congress, 1933. It denied commercial banks and trust companies the right to engage in INVESTMENT BANKING, established the FEDERAL DEPOSIT INSURANCE CORPORATION, and canceled the DOUBLE LIABILITY feature of national-bank stock.

banking system. A term indicating the general characteristics of the structure and operation of a nation's banks. See BANK, BRANCH BANKING, CHAIN BANKING, UNIT BANKING.

bank note. A form of paper currency carrying a bank's promise to pay a specific amount of money to the bearer on demand. Bank notes were issued by NATIONAL BANKS in the United States from 1863 to 1935. They were secured by certain United States bonds bearing the circulation privilege. On August 1, 1935, all of these bonds were retired. No national-bank notes have been issued, therefore, since that date.

bank of issue. A bank that issues bank notes. See also BANK, BANK NOTE.

Bank of North Dakota. A bank owned and operated by the state of North Dakota, officially designated as the "State of North Dakota doing business as the Bank of North Dakota." The bank opened for business in 1919. Its capital was obtained through the sale of bonds — since retired. It conducts a commercial banking business, accepting time and checking accounts from individuals and corporations. Loans are made only to state departments, political subdivisions of the state, and to individuals only under the Federal Housing Administration, G.I. Bill, or Farmers Home Administration. It is the only bank of its kind in the United States (1964).

Bank of the United States. A quasi-public bank, operating under a congressional charter, which through a central office and various branches did a general banking business throughout the United States, issued bank notes, and served as a depositary for federal funds and as a fiduciary agent for the United States government. Technically there were two such banks. The first, created at the instance of Hamilton and the Federalists in 1791, ceased operations with the expiration of its 20-year charter in 1811. The second bank was chartered in 1816, also for 20 years. President Jackson became its unrelenting foe. In 1833 he ordered the federal government's deposits removed and, by his use of the veto and other tactics, succeeded in defeating legislation to recharter the bank. It accordingly ceased operating as the Bank of the United States in 1836. See also BANK.

bank post remittance. A foreign bill of exchange converted into a money order or cash by the bank to which it is directed, the money order or cash then being forwarded by mail to the payee.

bank reserves. The amount of money kept available by a bank to meet the demands of depositors. Since the demands of depositors for money normally represent only a small proportion of a bank's deposits, it is never necessary for a bank to have on hand an amount of money equal to the total deposits entrusted to it. In the United States the amount of money that a bank must keep available for such a purpose is specified by law in the form of a percentage of its deposits. The *legal reserve* requirement of a bank which is a member of the FEDERAL RESERVE SYSTEM depends upon the location of the bank and is determined by the Board of Governors of the Federal Reserve System for all member banks similarly located. The reserves must be kept on deposit with the district federal reserve bank. The legal reserves of state banks in the United States are specified in the laws of the several states. In addition to its legal reserves, a bank also has *primary reserves* consisting of cash on hand and deposits with other banks. A bank's callable loans, its commercial paper eligible for REDISCOUNT, and the government bonds that it owns are sometimes said to make up its *secondary reserves*. See also RESERVES.

bankruptcy. The condition of a debtor who has been adjudged insolvent by a court of competent jurisdiction and whose existing property is administered under the court's order for the benefit of his creditors. This condition may be brought about by a petition filed with the court by the insolvent debtor himself, in which case it is known as *voluntary bankruptcy;* or it may be brought about by a petition filed with the court by the requisite number of creditors, in which case it is known as *involuntary bankruptcy*.

bankruptcy acts. Various acts passed by Congress under its constitutional power to make uniform laws on the subject of bankruptcy. Such national laws supersede existing state legislation on the same subject. Among the more recent federal acts are those of 1898 and 1933. The latter act, amended somewhat in 1934, was passed during the depths of an economic depression and was designed to ease the lot of certain creditors. Railroads and other corporations, unable to meet maturing fixed obligations, were permitted to reorganize under their existing management or under the control of a trustee, and to scale down or otherwise modify their liabilities. Certain classes of individual debtors were also given the opportunity by law to make compositions with their creditors or to secure an extension of time for the payment of indebtedness. In 1938 Congress passed the Chandler Act to consolidate existing bankruptcy legislation. See also BANKRUPTCY.

bankruptcy case. See *STURGES* v. *CROWNINSHIELD.*

barometer stock. See explanation under CAPITAL STOCK.

barter. The direct exchange of one commodity or service for another without the use of money.

base pay. Wages exclusive of overtime, bonuses, or premiums of any kind.

base period. See explanation under INDEX NUMBER.

base rate. As applied to the payment of wages for labor, the pay for a specified amount of production. When bonuses are paid for production beyond a certain minimum, the base rate determines the point from which any increased production and pay are calculated.

basic crops. A term used to designate certain staple commodities subject to price supports. In the long-range farm-price support program enacted by Congress in 1949 the basic crops named were: wheat, corn, cotton, rice, peanuts, and tobacco.

basic yield. The annual return, expressed as a percentage, on a hypothetical investment presenting no risk. In the United States, the nearest approach to a basic yield is the return on long-term federal bonds.

basing-point system. The selection by a seller of a certain place called the "basing point," from which freight charges, paid by the buyer, are calculated, regardless of the actual place from which the goods are shipped. If, for example, the seller has a plant in San Francisco and another in Chicago, and the basing point is San Francisco, a buyer nearer to Chicago than to San Francisco will have to pay the equivalent of freight charges on his order from San Francisco even though his goods are produced and shipped from the Chicago plant. Recent court decisions in the United States will have the effect of outlawing this practice.

bazaar. A market place, particularly one where fancy goods are sold.

bear. As applied to trading on the security exchanges, a slang expression indicating a person who believes that the value of corporate stocks will decline. Used in contradistinction to BULL.

bearer. As used in banking practice, the person who possesses a check, note, or other such instrument, particularly a person who possesses such an instrument made "payable to the bearer," or who can collect on it by virtue of the indorsements which it carries.

Bedford Cut Stone Co.* v. *Journeymen Stone Cutters' Assn. A case, 274 U. S. 37 (1927), in which the Supreme Court of the United

States, following its decision in the DANBURY HATTERS' CASE (*q.v.*), held that the federal antitrust laws prohibited a national labor organization from instructing its members not to work on an unprocessed commodity, in this instance quarried stone, which their employer had purchased from a nonunion enterprise.

Beech-Nut Packing case. A case, *Beech-Nut Packing Co.* v. *Federal Trade Commission*, 257 U. S. 441 (1922), in which the Supreme Court of the United States upheld an order of the Federal Trade Commission requiring a company to desist from certain practices involving maintenance of resale prices by local dealers. The case is one of the earlier judicial precedents establishing that the Sherman Act is violated when producers or distributors of products exact promises from dealers or solicit their co-operation to maintain fixed resale prices. The decision has been modified as a result of legislation permitting resale price agreements, which the courts have sustained. See *OLD DEARBORN DISTRIBUTING CO.* v. *SEAGRAM DISTILLERS CORP.*

beneficiary. One who receives something as a gift. The term is commonly applied to the person named in a life-insurance policy who receives the proceeds upon the death of the insured.

benefit society. See BUILDING AND LOAN ASSOCIATION.

benefits-received principle of taxation. The principle that taxes should be levied upon individual taxpayers in proportion to the benefits they receive from the state. To a certain extent this principle is used in the case of special assessments for improvements, but its general application is subject to the same difficulties as is the COST-OF-SERVICE PRINCIPLE OF TAXATION (*q.v.*). Sometimes called *compensatory principle of taxation.*

Benelux. A term used to identify the CUSTOMS UNION and certain limited aspects of an economic union which have come into being among the Low Countries.

bequest. Usually a gift of personal property provided for in a will. Also called *legacy*.

Beveridge plan. A plan elaborated by Sir William Beveridge in 1942 for revising the British social-insurance system. The plan provided for eight primary causes of need: (1) unemployment; (2) disability; (3) loss of means of support when not regularly employed; (4) retirement; (5) marriage needs of women; (6) expenses of childhood; (7) funeral expenses; and (8) sickness or incapacity.

bid. An offer to buy at a stipulated price.

bidding. 1. Making an offer of a price. 2. As applied to labor relations, the procedure of notifying employees of other jobs in a plant or industry in order that any who wish to do so may apply.

big board. The New York Stock Exchange.

Big Five. A term applied to the five permanent members of the Security Council of the United Nations: the United States, the Union of Socialist Soviet Republics, the United Kingdom, France, and Free China. See also SECURITY COUNCIL, UNITED NATIONS.

bilateral agreement. An agreement between two parties.

bilateral monopoly. The condition which would exist if there were only one buyer for a commodity or service, the entire supply of which was controlled by one seller.

bill. As used in commerce and finance, a generic term identifying a variety of documents having to do with currency, the shipment of goods, and the collection of debts. The term is used as an abbreviation of BILL OF EXCHANGE or as synonymous with DRAFT, often in association with any one of a number of qualifying or descriptive adjectives. Thus, *acceptance bill* is a bill of exchange accepted for eventual payment; *advance bill*, one drawn in advance of a shipment; *bankable bill*, one easily discounted; *banker's bill*, one drawn on a bank; *blank bill*, one with the name of the creditor omitted; *clean bill*, one with no documents attached; *continental bill*, one payable on the continent of Europe; *credit bill*, one drawn against credit already established by the debtor; *demand bill*, one payable at sight; *documentary bill*, one having documents attached; *domestic bill*, one drawn and payable in the same country (in the United States one drawn and payable in the same state); *finance bill*, one drawn by a bank in one country on a bank in another country usually against securities held by the latter bank, and good for a relatively long period of time; *foreign bill*, one drawn in one country and payable in another (in the United States a bill drawn in one state and payable in another); *inland bill*, one drawn in one country and payable in the same country; *investment bill*, one purchased at a discount for the interest it will yield at maturity; *payment bill*, one presented for payment rather than for acceptance; *prime bill*, one which is an excellent credit risk; *sight bill*, same as demand bill; *time bill*, one payable at a future date. See also BILL OF CREDIT, BILL OF EXCHANGE, BILL OF LADING, BILL OF SALE, ORDINARY BILL.

bill of credit. In the United States, an unsecured promissory note issued by a government and intended to circulate as money. Article I, Sec. 10, of the Constitution enjoins the states against emitting bills of credit, but no such injunction applies to the federal government, since it issued such notes as GREENBACKS, and its authority to do so was upheld by the courts. See LEGAL TENDER CASES.

bill of exchange. A sight or time draft arising from payments to or from a foreign country. Occasionally the term is applied to domestic drafts. See also BILL, DRAFT.

bill of lading. A contract between a shipper and a transportation company in which the latter agrees to transport goods under specified conditions which limit its liability. A bill of lading may be a STRAIGHT BILL OF LADING or an ORDER BILL OF LADING. See also THROUGH BILL OF LADING.

bill of sale. A document which formally transfers ownership of property specified in the document from one person to another.

bills payable. A term used in double-entry bookkeeping to indicate the records of the value of promissory notes and commercial paper credited to others, and the amounts paid on such obligations. Also called *notes payable.* See also ACCOUNT.

bills receivable. A term used in double-entry bookkeeping to indicate the records of the value of promissory notes and commercial paper charged to others, and the amounts paid on such obligations. Also called *notes receivable.* See also ACCOUNT.

bimetallism. A monetary system in which the monetary unit is defined by law in terms of two metals, presumably gold and silver, in a specific ratio of weight one to the other, each metal being accepted in unlimited quantities for coinage, and each kind of coin being made legal tender. Also called *double standard.* See also COMPENSATORY PRINCIPLE OF MONEY, LEGAL TENDER, MONETARY SYSTEM.

binary notation. A system of numbering which employs 2 as the number base instead of 10 as in the decimal system. The two digits, or bits as they are called in the binary system, are 0 and 1. These bits are the same as the digits 0 and 1 in the decimal system. Thereafter, binary numbering annexes 0 to double a number and adds one to form the intervening odd numbers. Thus 2 is 10 in the binary system, 3 is 11, 4 is 100, 5 is 101, 6 is 110, 7 is 111, etc. Various adaptations of binary notation are widely used in DIGITAL COMPUTERS.

binder. As applied to insurance, a temporary document informing the person insured that the risk is covered. An insurance policy usually replaces the binder within a period of 15 days.

birth rate. The number of births per 1,000 persons in any given area during the period of a year. This is called the *crude birth rate.* If corrections are made to allow for differences in the composition of the population, the crude birth rate becomes a *refined birth rate.* Thus, the birth rate established for 1,000 women of childbearing age would be a refined birth rate.

bituminous coal cases. Two cases which came before the Supreme Court of the United States to test the validity of two separate acts of Congress purporting to establish fair-practice codes for the soft-coal industry. In 1935 Congress passed the first of these acts, popularly known as the first Guffey Coal Act. In the case of *Carter* v. *Carter Coal Co.*, 298 U. S. 238 (1936), the Supreme Court held the act invalid because of its attempt to fix wages and control working conditions in the mines. The majority of the court considered this to be an attempted regulation of production and not of commerce and hence an effort to exercise a power which belonged to the states and not to Congress. The second Guffey Coal Act, passed in 1937, re-enacted price-fixing provisions of the first act, and this regulation was sustained in *Sunshine Anthracite Coal Co.* v. *Adkins*, 310 U. S. 381 (1940).

black Friday. A term designating any one of a number of historic dates occurring on Fridays when disastrous financial events took place. Two of the most important instances are: (1) Friday, May 11, 1866, when Overend and Gurney, an important banking concern in London, failed, with resultant widespread financial distress; (2) Friday, September 24, 1869, when the United States government purchased with gold 4 million dollars' worth of its bonds in the open market, thus breaking the corner in gold then being manipulated by Jay Gould and James Fiske.

black list. As applied to industrial disputes, a list of the names of certain workers believed to have incited discontent in some plant, circulated among other employers as a warning against employing the workers whose names appear on the list.

black market. A general term indicating all transactions in violation of price and rationing laws.

Bland-Allison Act. An act of Congress, 1878, which authorized the Secretary of the Treasury to purchase not less than $2,000,000 and not more than $4,000,000 worth of silver monthly and coin it into silver dollars of 412½ grains. Provision was also made for silver certificates to be issued against an equivalent deposit of silver dollars in the Treasury.

blank bill. See explanation under Bill.

blanket bond. See explanation under Bond.

blank indorsement. An indorsement that specifies no particular person to whose order a check, note, or similar paper is made payable or to whom it is assigned, and which is therefore payable to bearer. The term is used in contradistinction to special indorsement. See also Indorsement.

blighted area. A neighborhood which has deteriorated in appearance because of land use inharmonious with the surroundings, and often as a result of the inability or unwillingness of property owners to rebuild, renovate, or even maintain their properties in good repair. As a community grows, business establishments frequently encroach upon adjacent residential areas, causing families to move to outlying districts. The neighborhoods thus vacated are left in a transition stage, with consequent neglect characteristic of blighted areas.

blocked exchange. The condition which exists when importers and others, desiring to make payments abroad, are prohibited from doing so by their government; that is, they are blocked from purchasing bills of exchange payable in foreign currencies. Under such conditions deposits in local currency are sometimes made to cover the prospective remittances, but foreign creditors must wait until the block is removed or they find some way of using the local currency credited to them. See also EXCHANGE CONTROL.

***Block* v. *Hirsh*.** See RENT-CONTROL CASE.

blue eagle. An emblem used by the National Recovery Administration of the United States government in 1933. It appeared on citations issued to employers who agreed to a general code of fair competition formulated by the administration.

blue-sky laws. Laws which protect the inexperienced investor against fraud and misrepresentation in the purchase of corporate securities.

board of directors. See explanation under DIRECTOR.

board of trade. 1. In the United States, usually a voluntary community organization of business and professional men having as its object the promotion of civic, industrial, and general social welfare. Frequently called *chamber of commerce*. 2. In the case of the CHICAGO BOARD OF TRADE the term refers to a COMMODITY EXCHANGE.

***Boling* v. *Sharpe*.** See *BROWN* v. *BOARD OF EDUCATION OF TOPEKA*.

bond. 1. A written obligation under seal. See also FIDELITY BOND, SURETY BOND. 2. A certificate of indebtedness. In the latter sense, and as generally regarded in the security markets, a bond is evidence of a debt issued by a government, an agency of a government, or by a private corporation.

A *public bond* is one issued by a foreign government or its subdivisions, or by the federal government of the United States, an agency of the federal government, a territory, a colonial possession, one of the various states of the United States, or any one of many local subdivisions of a state such as a county, township, borough, parish, or school district, as well as any one of a great variety of special assessment districts such as a district engaged in levee construction, drainage of farm lands, building of irrigation works, construction of roads, and other similar projects. A bond which is a direct obligation of the United States government is designated by the words "United States of America" as a part of the title.

Savings Bonds are special United States bonds, issued (1964) in two series, E and H. Series E bonds are sold at a discount and mature in 7 to 10 years, depending upon the date of purchase, but may be retained 10 years beyond the date of maturity or exchanged for H bonds. The approximate investment yield for the entire period from issuance to maturity is 4.06 per cent. The interest of H bonds is paid semiannually. They mature in 9 to 10 years, depending upon date of purchase. The approximate investment yield on the face value from each interest date to maturity is 4.00 per cent.

Some federal agencies have authority to issue obligations guaranteed by, or on the credit of, the United States government. The principal agencies having such authority are COMMODITY CREDIT CORPORATION, FEDERAL DEPOSIT INSURANCE CORPORATION, FEDERAL HOUSING ADMINISTRATION, POSTAL SAVINGS SYSTEM, PUBLIC HOUSING ADMINISTRATION, and TENNESSEE VALLEY AUTHORITY.

The principal federal agencies issuing obligations not guaranteed by the United States government are the BANKS FOR COOPERATIVES, FEDERAL HOME LOAN BANK SYSTEM, FEDERAL INTERMEDIATE CREDIT BANKS, FEDERAL LAND BANKS, FEDERAL NATIONAL MORTGAGE ASSOCIATION, and THE FEDERAL SAVINGS AND LOAN INSURANCE CORPORATION.

A bond issued by a colonial possession is called a *colonial bond* or *insular bond;* one issued by a city, town, or village, a *municipal bond.* A bond issued by a state is called a *state bond,* and one issued by a territory, a *territorial bond.* In a few cities of the United States certain *municipal bonds* are called CORPORATE STOCK. A business corporation bond is customarily spoken of as an *industrial*, *public-utility*, or *railroad bond*, according to the nature of the business carried on by the issuing corporation.

Bonds carry an almost infinite variety of titles which, in addition to the name of the issuing agency, the interest rate, and date of maturity, may indicate in a general way the purpose of the issue, the form of the issue, the nature of the security, if any, pledged in support of the bond, and the terms of payment of interest and principal.

The purpose for which a bond is issued is frequently indicated by such terms as : "bridge," "construction," "development," "dock and wharf," "equipment," "ferry," "highway improvement," "public works," "purchase money," "reclamation," "school," or some other such descriptive term appearing as a part of the name of a bond. An *adjustment bond* is issued to aid in the recapitalization of a business. *Consol* or *consolidated bonds* are issued to retire two or more outstanding issues and thus bring the indebtedness together under one issue. An *interest bond* is a bond issued to pay the interest on other bonds when the necessary cash is not available. A *refunding bond* is issued to retire other indebtedness. A *reorganization bond* is the same as an adjustment bond, defined above. A *tax-anticipation bond* is issued by a governmental unit in order to raise immediate cash and is frequently accepted in payment of taxes when the taxes are due. A *terminal bond* is usually one sold to finance the construction of a railroad terminal. The term may also refer to a bond covering terminal-leave pay, given by the United States government to privates and noncommissioned officers who served in the armed forces during World War II. In 1947 such bonds were made redeemable in cash, before maturity. The term *unified bond* is the same as a consolidated bond, defined above.

The name of a bond may give some indication of the form in which it is issued. A *coupon bond* has coupons attached — one for each interest date — which can be torn off and deposited as checks. Transfer is effected by delivery. An *interchangeable bond* can be exchanged for one issued in another form — a coupon bond for a registered bond, for example. An *interim bond* is a temporary certificate to be exchanged for a definitive bond in due course of time. A *registered bond* is recorded in the name of the owner. Interest is paid by check, and transfer of ownership requires formal notice. A *registered coupon bond* is registered in the name of the owner, but it has coupons attached, payable to the bearer.

Bonds may be unsecured or secured. The term *debenture bond* usually indicates an unsecured bond backed only by the general credit standing of the issuing agency. Direct obligations of governments are generally unsecured, being backed only by the taxing power of the government. However, a *revenue bond* is backed by revenue received from a specific project such as the Golden Gate Bridge of San Francisco and the Triboro Bridge of New York, and a *special-assessment bond* is backed by the power of the government to assess particular individuals for benefits presumably received in the form of public improvements financed by the bond issue.

Other bonds are secured in varying degrees often indicated in a general way by the name of the bond. An *assumed bond* is guaranteed in the matter of principal, interest, or both by a corporation other than the one issuing the bond. The term *blanket bond* indicates, as a rule, a general mortgage pledged as security, but it may be subject to an indefinite number of prior claims on the mortgaged property. A *bottomry bond* is secured by a mortgage on a ship. A *collateral trust bond* is secured by deposits of other securities with a trustee. A *divisional bond* has the backing of a mortgage on some part or division of a railroad. An *equipment trust bond* is usually secured by tangible property, the title of which rests with a trustee while the property is leased to the user, usually a railroad or an air-line company. An *extension bond* is one secured by a mortgage on property coming into possession of a railroad or other agency by virtue of an extension of its services. The term *first-lien bond* indicates a first claim on whatever property, tangible or intangible, is pledged to secure the loan. A *guaranteed bond* is the same as an assumed bond, defined above. An *indorsed bond* is also the same as an assumed bond. A *junior-lien bond* is one that ranks inferior to some other issue in the matter of its claim on the property pledged as security. A *joint and several bond* is one for which the payment of the entire principal and interest is guaranteed by two or more parties. A *land-grant bond* is usually issued by a railroad and secured by a lien on land granted to the railroad by the government. The term *mortgage bond* indicates a pledge of real estate or other property. Mortgage bonds are usually classified as first, second, or third, indicating priority of claims against the security. An *overlying bond* is subject to the prior claims of some other bonds. A *plain bond* is the same as a debenture bond, defined above. The term is also used to indicate a bond on which certain terms and conditions pertaining to the bond have not been stamped thereon. A *prior-lien bond* enjoys a prior lien over some other issue on the property pledged for security, but itself may be subject to prior claims of other issues. A *sinking-fund bond* is one paid from a SINKING FUND (*q.v.*). The sinking fund may be invested until the bonds are due, or, if the bonds are subject to "call from sinking fund," numbers identifying the bonds may be drawn by lot and the corresponding bonds redeemed, or the sinking fund may be used to buy the bonds in the open market. A *stamped bond* is one on which special terms and conditions have been stamped. The term *underlying bond* means that such a bond has a priority claim against the property securing its payment.

The name of the bond may indicate the terms of payment of the interest, principal, or both. An *annuity bond* bears no maturity date, the interest continuing indefinitely. A *callable bond* is redeemable upon due notice to the bondholder. A *continued bond* need not be presented for payment at maturity, but may be held for an indefinite period at the same rate of interest or possibly some different rate. A *convertible bond* grants the holder the right to exchange it for some other type of security, usually common or preferred stock. A *currency bond* may be paid in any kind of legal tender. The term *deferred bond* indicates that the payment of interest is postponed for a specified length of time. An *extended bond* is one the maturity date of which has been postponed with the sanction of the bondholders. A *gold bond* specifies that payment shall be made in gold coins of a certain weight and fineness. Such a clause has no real significance in the United States since the possession of gold coins is illegal. An *income bond* is one the payment of interest on which is contingent upon current earnings. *Installment bonds* are paid off in installments over a period of years. An *irredeemable bond* is the same as an annuity bond, defined above. A *legal-tender bond* is the same as a currency bond. A *noninterest-bearing discount bond* provides that the interest shall be paid, together with the principal, upon maturity. An *optional bond* may be redeemed previous to the maturity date if the issuing agency so elects. A *participating* or *profit-sharing bond* is one that shares in the profits of the issuing agency in addition to a guaranteed interest rate. A *passive bond* bears no interest. Presumably it holds some other advantage for the owner. The term is rarely used. A *perpetual bond* is the same as an annuity bond, defined above. A *redeemable bond* is the same as a callable bond, defined above. *Serial bonds* represent an issue of bonds the maturity dates of which are arranged through a series of years. The terms of serial bonds are usually the same, regardless of maturity date, although sometimes the terms may differ according to the dates on which the bonds are due. *Series bonds* are bonds which are issued at regular intervals over a period of years. All the bonds have the same backing, but the terms may differ according to the year a series is issued. For bonds of historic interest see FIVE-TWENTY BOND, TEN-FORTY BOND, LIBERTY BOND.

bonded goods. Imported goods stored in a bonded warehouse; so called because the owners of the goods have deposited a bond guaranteeing that the duty will be paid when and if the goods are withdrawn for domestic sale. See also BONDED WAREHOUSE.

bonded warehouse. A warehouse in which goods, subject to excise taxes or customs duties, are temporarily stored without the taxes or duties being paid. Security is given for the payment of all taxes and duties that may eventually become due, and the establishment is supervised by public revenue officers.

Bonneville Power Administration. A division of the United States Department of the Interior which administers the distribution of power generated at the Bonneville Dam on the Columbia River in the states of Oregon and Washington, and which acts as the marketing agency for power generated at the Grand Coulee Dam on the Columbia River in Washington. It is anticipated that the administration will act in the same capacity for other proposed projects of a similar nature in the Pacific Northwest.

bonus. A payment, usually in money, in addition to payments normally due for services rendered.

bonus stock. See explanation under CAPITAL STOCK.

book credit. See STORE CREDIT.

bookkeeping. The systematic recording of business transactions so as to show the state of the business at any time. See also DOUBLE ENTRY, SINGLE ENTRY.

book value. As applied to stocks, the proportionate amount of money that would accrue to each share of outstanding capital stock of a corporation if all the corporation's assets were converted into cash at the values appearing on the books, and all of its creditors and other prior claimants, if any, were paid in full. See also VALUE.

boom. Rapid growth in market values and expansion of business facilities and activity.

boondoggling. Wasteful or UNECONOMIC labor. The term was commonly used in America during the depression years following 1929 when government efforts to create employment sometimes resulted in useless or frivolous activity.

boot. As applied to trading, something given in addition to the thing exchanged to equalize the exchange.

bottomry bond. See explanation under BOND.

bounty. An additional payment or subsidy sometimes supplied by a government to encourage a particular industry or the export of specified commodities. See also EXPORT BOUNTY.

bourgeoisie. The middle class. In feudal society this term identified merchants, independent artisans, and similar groups, and distinguished them from the nobility and gentry on the one hand and the manual workers and peasantry on the other.

bourse. A French word meaning a stock or some similar exchange. It is commonly used on the continent of Europe.

boycott. Concerted action by a group involving refusal to have business or other relations with another person or group with a view to punishing the latter or securing redress of some grievance. A boycott is often used in labor disputes, a union resorting to it in order to compel an employer to meet its terms. When those instituting a boycott bring pressure directly upon the person or group against whom they have a grievance, the boycott is called a *primary boycott* and it remains such even if those instituting the boycott use noncoercive tactics such as publicity or peaceful picketing to influence others to join with them. A boycott becomes a *secondary boycott* if those instituting action attempt to increase pressure against the object of their grievance by coercing third parties into assisting them. Thus, efforts of a union to force an employer against whom its members have no grievance, by strike or other coercive tactics, to cease doing business with an employer against whom its members do have a grievance would be a secondary boycott. The same would be true in a case where employees of a factory not on strike were ordered by a union not to process the goods of an employer whose employees were on strike, the purpose of such an order being to aid the striking employees.

branch banking. A banking system in which there are relatively few parent institutions each of which has branches operating over a wide area, thus enabling a single banking organization to operate over a considerable territory. Branch banking has shown considerable development in the United States in recent years, although a NATIONAL BANK may not establish new branches except in cities where the principal office of the bank is located, and only some nine states permit a STATE BANK to operate a state-wide system of branches. See also BANKING SYSTEM.

Brannan plan. A plan for a direct federal subsidy to farmers proposed by Charles F. Brannan, United States Secretary of Agriculture, early in 1949. It would eliminate the existing system of parity payments, allow agricultural commodities to seek their own price level on a free market, and compensate farmers, by means of the subsidy, for the difference between the market price thus obtained and the higher price level established for farm produce during the ten-year period, 1939–49. See also AGRICULTURAL PARITY.

brassage. A charge made by the government for converting bullion into coins. This charge is just sufficient to cover the costs of the coinage.

brazen law of wages. See IRON LAW OF WAGES.

break-even chart. A graphic device in which one curve shows the total FIXED COSTS and VARIABLE COSTS of an enterprise and another curve shows the total INCOME, both at various production levels. The intersection of the two curves represents the break-even point. The appended diagram shows a break-even chart when the following conditions prevail:

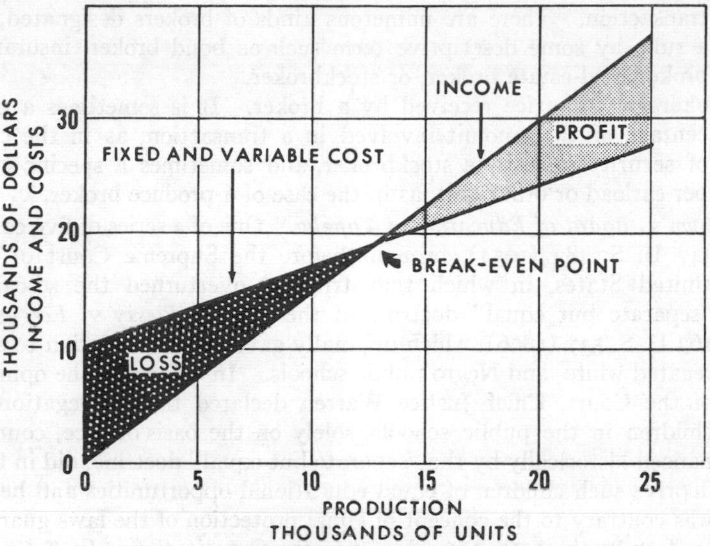

$10,000.00 = fixed costs.
0.70 = LABOR and material COST per unit of product.
1.50 = selling PRICE per unit of product.
x = quantity sales necessary to break even.
$10,000.00 + 0.70$x$ = total fixed and variable costs.
$10,000.00 + 0.70$x$ = 1.50x$.
x = 12,500 = break-even point shown on chart.

breakthrough. A vague popular term indicating some basic new discovery. Progress in some given area of knowledge may seem to remain static for a relatively long period of time. When an important advance is made in such an area, there is said to be a breakthrough. Although, as currently used, this word is especially applicable to technological advances and scientific discoveries, it is occasionally used to signal some advance in the field of applied economics or some field peripheral to economics. The more effective use of automated devices in economic statistics provides an illustration.

broad market. As applied to security exchanges, a period during which a large variety of stocks and bonds are bought and sold. See MARKET.

broker. A person who acts as an intermediary between two or more persons engaged in a business transaction of some kind. His services may consist of effecting a sale or of facilitating the arrangements preparatory or subsequent to a sale or to some other similar transaction. There are numerous kinds of brokers designated, as a rule, by some descriptive term such as bond broker, insurance broker, real-estate broker, or stockbroker.

brokerage. The fee received by a broker. It is sometimes a percentage of the amount involved in a transaction, as in the case of security sales by a stockbroker, and sometimes a specific sum per carload or other unit, as in the case of a produce broker.

Brown* v. *Board of Education of Topeka. One of a series of five cases, 347 U. S. 483 (1954), brought before the Supreme Court of the United States, in which that tribunal overturned the so-called "separate but equal" doctrine of the case of *Plessy* v. *Ferguson*, 163 U. S. 537 (1896), which originally gave judicial sanction to segregated white and Negro public schools. In delivering the opinion of the Court, Chief Justice Warren declared that segregation of children in the public schools, solely on the basis of race, countenanced historically by the "separate but equal" doctrine, did in fact deprive such children of equal educational opportunities and hence was contrary to the concept of equal protection of the laws guaranteed under the 14th Amendment to the Constitution. In *Boling* v. *Sharpe*, 347 U. S. 497 (1954), the Court took the same position with respect to public-school segregation in the District of Columbia, declaring such segregation forbidden by the guarantee of due process in the 5th Amendment to the Constitution.

Brown* v. *Maryland. See ORIGINAL-PACKAGE CASES.

bubble. As applied to SPECULATION, any unsound business venture where the price of participation advances to a point having no relation to the value of the assets or to the possibilities for profit from the operation of the venture. In this sense, the term was first used during the early part of the 18th century when joint-stock undertakings came into popular favor but when the uses of CREDIT were little understood. The most famous bubbles of the time were the MISSISSIPPI BUBBLE in France and the SOUTH SEA BUBBLE in England, both of which reached their climax in 1720.

bucket shop. A place where bets are made on the prices of securities or commodities bought and sold on the stock and commodity exchanges. The bettors do not themselves trade in the securities or commodities. Such operations are considered to be wagers, and the maintenance of a bucket shop is generally held to be illegal.

budget. A formal estimate of future income and expenses, covering a definite period of time. Budgets are commonly used wherever necessary and desirable expenses must be carefully weighed against anticipated income. Thus, they are applicable as much to personal affairs and private enterprise as they are to public finance. The

United States government provided for an annual budget in the *Budget and Accounting Act* of 1921 and vested its preparation and administration in the director of the federal Bureau of the Budget. Practically all of the states of the United States have also established an executive or legislative budget agency, and equivalent agencies are common in most American municipalities. See also CAPITAL BUDGET; BUDGET, BUREAU OF THE.

Budget and Accounting Act. See explanation under BUDGET.

Budget, Bureau of the. A division of the executive office of the President of the United States which prepares and administers the annual federal budget and assists in the formulation of governmental fiscal programs.

buffer stock plan. A term used by a few economists to describe a plan to overcome possible disastrous effects of cyclical fluctuations upon certain industries, particularly raw-material industries. Because of the technical nature of their operations some industries, notably those engaged in certain mining operations, cannot reduce their output rapidly when demand lessens and prices fall. If resulting losses compel the closing of plants, productive capacity is often lost when the products are again in active demand. The buffer stock plan proposes an intergovernmental agency which, under proper safeguards, would offer to buy at a minimum price any quantity of a given commodity and to sell any quantity of that commodity at a maximum price. Thus, it is argued, in times of depression the price could not fall below the minimum, and in times of prosperity, as long as the agency possessed stocks, the price could not rise above the maximum. The price would thus be stabilized within limits presumably narrower than those occasioned by cyclical fluctuations.

building and loan association. A general term indicating an organization, usually incorporated under the law of one of the states of the United States, that provides a presumably safe investment for the savings of its members and serves as a source of loans to its members for home-building purposes. Organizations of this nature are known as CO-OPERATIVE BANKS in Massachusetts, *homestead-aid benefit associations* in Louisiana, and *benefit societies, building societies,* or *mutual loan associations* in various other places. Many of these state-chartered building and loan and similar associations have been converted into FEDERAL SAVINGS AND LOAN ASSOCIATIONS.

building society. See BUILDING AND LOAN ASSOCIATION.

bulk-line costs. Costs at which 80 to 90 per cent of the total supply of a product is said to be produced. The term was used during

World War I when the United States government investigated the costs of various products in the course of determining and fixing fair prices for such products. See also COST.

bull. As applied to trading on the security exchanges, a slang expression indicating a person who believes that the value of corporate stocks will advance. Used in contradistinction to BEAR.

bullion. Gold or silver considered as a metal without regard to its form or any value that may be stamped upon it. Bullion usually is in the form of bars or ingots but may be in the form of old coins or foreign coins.

bumping. See BACKTRACKING.

***Bunting* v. *Oregon*.** A case, 243 U. S. 426 (1917), in which the Supreme Court of the United States upheld an Oregon statute limiting the working day in certain industries to 10 hours and prescribing pay at the rate of time and one-half for employment beyond 10 hours. In effect, the court's decision in this case removed the judicial obstacle to state regulation of the maximum working day, which had been interposed by earlier decisions such as that of *LOCHNER* v. *NEW YORK* (*q.v.*), and gave judicial blessing to such legislation as a proper exertion of the state's police power and a necessary limitation on the contractual freedom of employer and employee.

bureau. For official and other agencies in which "bureau" is the first word of the title, see under descriptive title of agency, e.g., BUDGET, BUREAU OF THE.

business affected with a public interest. Any business, especially a public utility, which, because of the virtual absence of any competitive conditions in the area in which it operates, and because of the important contribution it makes to the public welfare and convenience, may be subject to governmental regulation in respect to rates and services.

business agent. As applied to labor unions, a full-time employee of such organizations who negotiates labor agreements with employers, observes the manner in which such agreements are carried out, and attempts to secure faithful performance of the terms of the agreements.

business barometer. A statistical device that estimates the extent of business activity by means of composite index numbers. See also INDEX NUMBER.

business cycle. A recurring sequence of changes in business activity. Beginning with a period of PROSPERITY, business activity declines until a low point, called a DEPRESSION, is reached. A period of recovery then follows when business conditions become more and more active until prosperity is again restored and a cycle is thus completed. There are many explanations of the business cycle. For some of the more important see ASTRONOMICAL THEORY OF THE BUSINESS CYCLE, CREDIT THEORY OF THE BUSINESS CYCLE, PSYCHOLOGICAL THEORY OF THE BUSINESS CYCLE, OVERSAVING THEORY OF THE BUSINESS CYCLE.

Business Economics, Office of. A unit of the United States Department of Commerce. It develops statistics for gauging national economic activity, analyzes current business conditions and future prospects, and conducts economic research in co-operation with other government agencies, business organizations, and educational institutions. It publishes the official monthly journal, *Survey of Current Business*.

business interruption insurance. See USE AND OCCUPANCY INSURANCE.

buyers' market. The condition which exists when, under competitive conditions, the schedules of supply and demand are such that market prices are at a relatively low level, giving the buyers an advantage. In other words, the sellers are disposed to accept a low price rather than fail to dispose of their goods and services, and the buyers are disposed to retain their money rather than to acquire the goods and services at anything but a low price. The term is used in contradistinction to SELLERS' MARKET. See also DEMAND, SUPPLY.

buyer's monopoly. The condition which exists when there are numerous sellers but only one buyer. For example, during World War II the British government controlled the refrigeration space on ships serving South America. The South American meat packers, therefore, had virtually but one customer — the British government. Also called *monopsony*. See also MONOPOLY.

buyers' strike. A concerted movement by consumers to refrain from buying until prices are reduced.

buyer's surplus. The hypothetical difference between what a buyer actually pays for a product and what he would have been willing to pay if necessary.

buying on margin. The practice of purchasing securities paid for in part out of funds borrowed by using the purchased securities as collateral. Buying on margin is done in anticipation of an advance in price. If an advance occurs, it may enable the trader to pay the loan and make a profit. If the market price declines, however, the value of the collateral deposited to secure the loan may depreciate to such an extent that it has to be sold to liquidate the loan.

In that event the trader loses all that he has advanced. It is to prevent such a loss that a STOP-LOSS ORDER is given. Also referred to as *marginal trading*.

by-product. A product resulting as an incident of the manufacture of some other product. In the production of lignite coal, for example, coal-tar dyes, ammonium salts, and other valuable derivative products are produced.

Byrnes Act. See ANTISTRIKEBREAKING ACT.

C

cable transfer. Usually a foreign bill of exchange by cable, resorted to in order that a transfer of funds may be effected without delay.

cadastre. An official inventory of the real property in any district and the appraised values of such property. The inventory is used for apportioning taxes.

caisse de compensation. A voluntary FUND established in various localities in France during the early part of the 20th century, to which employers contributed and from which allowances were paid to married employees to enable them to maintain their accustomed LEVEL OF LIVING while rearing children. The plan was eventually merged with a national population policy aimed at raising the BIRTH RATE, and in 1932 a compulsory system of contributions for family allowances was established.

call. 1. A privilege accorded a trader, for a fee, to buy a specified quantity of a given stock or commodity within an agreed length of time at a stipulated price. 2. A demand for a payment on part-paid stock of a corporation. See also CAPITAL STOCK.

callable bond. See explanation under BOND.

callable preferred stock. See explanation under CAPITAL STOCK.

call-back pay. The extra amount paid to employees when they are recalled to their places of work because of an emergency, after having left for the day.

call loan. A loan payable on demand. See also LOAN.

call pay. Pay guaranteed an employee who reports for work in an establishment and has no work assigned him.

cambist. 1. A person who buys and sells bills of exchange or who is a specialist in matters pertaining to foreign exchange. 2. A volume supplying data about the currencies of various countries, the rates of exchange, and related matters.

Cambridge school. A school of economic thought based chiefly on the writings of the English economist, Alfred Marshall (1842–1924), and those who followed his ideas and elaborated upon his doctrines. The Cambridge school represents a synthesis of the ideas of various schools of thought, with modifications and additions of its own Thus it follows closely the findings of the CLASSICAL SCHOOL but emphasizes the limitations of some of the classical doctrines, notably that of *LAISSEZ FAIRE*. It adopts the methods of the German HISTORICAL SCHOOL in considering the origin and development of economic forces but subjects these to critical analysis. It makes use of the conception of MARGINAL UTILITY developed by the MARGINAL UTILITY SCHOOL and accepts MATHEMATICAL ECONOMICS as one method of presentation. Many modern ideas have been developed by writers of the Cambridge school, including the NEOCLASSICAL THEORY OF VALUE, and various contemporary theories of money and foreign trade. Also called *neoclassical school*. See also SCHOOLS OF ECONOMIC THOUGHT.

Cameralism. A variety of mercantilism that appeared in Germany and Austria during the middle part of the 18th century. Its economic theory was closely interwoven with considerations of financial policy, governmental administration, and technology. Hence, Cameralism was concerned not only with the best ways in which a state might acquire wealth but also with the best uses to which that wealth, once acquired, might be put. The term is sometimes used today to indicate an economic theory which places particular and perhaps undue emphasis upon public revenue as a factor in national prosperity. Sometimes spelled *Kameralism*. See also MERCANTILISM, SCHOOLS OF ECONOMIC THOUGHT.

canons of taxation. Stipulations as to a sound tax policy. Those set forth in Adam Smith's *Wealth of Nations* are as follows: (1) A tax should be apportioned among the taxpayers in proportion to the revenue they receive under the protection of the state; (2) a tax should be certain and not arbitrary; (3) a tax should be levied at the time when it is most convenient for the taxpayers to pay it; and (4) a tax should cost as little as possible to collect.

capillarity, law of. As applied to population growth, the generalization that as civilization advances, individuals avoid parenthood in order that they may devote their time and means to advancing their social status. The ambition to rise in the social scale is thus likened to the phenomenon of liquids rising by capillary attraction. The term is attributed to Arsène Dumont (1849–1902), a French sociologist, who, together with others, rejected the MALTHUSIAN THEORY OF POPULATION in favor of the idea that BIRTH RATES decline as STANDARDS OF LIVING increase. Although the theory seems applicable in some cases, the science of demography has not as yet offered a thoroughly satisfactory, comprehensive explanation of changes in the rate of population growth.

capital. One of the major factors of production consisting of property from which an income is derived, expressed in terms of money. Popularly, the term is frequently used interchangeably with CAPITAL GOOD. A distinction is sometimes made between *money capital*, or that part of the capital held in the form of money and bank deposits, and *property capital*, or that part of the capital held in the form of evidences of ownership such as stocks, bonds, and mortgages. Then again, such instruments, together with money, are sometimes referred to as *lucrative capital* in contradistinction to capital goods. A few economists include acquired knowledge within the meaning of capital on the ground that it, too, is a source of income. In business practice the term may refer merely to the net worth of an enterprise, or it may refer to all of the more permanent investments made by the owners or borrowed by them on a long-term basis. In a still more general sense, the term may refer to the total assets of an enterprise. Capital is classified in various ways. The terms VENTURE CAPITAL and SECURITY CAPITAL indicate the degree of risk involved in its use. See also FACTORS OF PRODUCTION, FROZEN, LIQUID, WORKING CAPITAL.

capital asset. As applied to income-tax computations in the United States, the term refers only to items not bought and sold in the ordinary course of the taxpayer's business. Thus, a washing machine would be a capital asset when used in a commercial laundry, but it would be an ORDINARY ASSET to the dealer in such machines. Generally, in commercial speech the term is synonymous with FIXED ASSET. See also ASSET.

capital budget. That part of a budget which considers capital sales and purchases as distinct from other income and expenditures. See also BUDGET.

capital consumption allowance. A deduction made in the amount of the GROSS NATIONAL PRODUCT when reconciling the total gross national product with the total NATIONAL INCOME. Capital consumption allowance consists of: (1) DEPRECIATION charges; (2) accidental damage to fixed capital such as that caused by transportation wrecks, fire, hurricanes, etc.; and (3) capital outlays charged to current expense, such as the purchase of new CAPITAL GOODS which are used up during the current period.

capital expenditure. An amount paid for the acquisition of an asset. See also ASSET.

capital formation. The creation of capital goods. Capital formation is made possible through savings. Savings may be spent directly for labor, materials, and other expenses involved in the creation of capital goods, or, through the purchase of a security, they may be loaned to others for such a purpose. If deposited in a bank, they may become the basis of a bank loan used to create capital goods. See also CAPITAL GOOD.

capital-gains tax. In the United States a federal tax levied upon the profits from the purchase and sale of capital assets. Such profits are reported as income. Losses sustained in a like manner are deductible from income under specified conditions. See also TAX.

capital good. A material economic good other than land which is used for the production of wealth. Most authorities exclude land from the meaning of this term on the ground that capital goods are created by man and are, for all practical purposes, unlimited in quantity whereas land is an original gift of nature and is limited in quantity. Other authorities regard land as a particular kind of capital good, terming it *natural capital*, thereby distinguishing it from other capital goods which they designate as *artificial capital*. Still other authorities make the term "capital goods" synonymous with WEALTH. They prefer to use such terms as *instrumental capital* or *producers' capital* to indicate wealth used to produce additional wealth, and the term *consumers' capital* to indicate what others would call CONSUMER GOODS. However defined, the term "capital goods" normally excludes such items as stocks, bonds, mortgages, and money which are sometimes called REPRESENTATIVE GOODS. Capital goods are occasionally classified according to their durability as FIXED CAPITAL GOODS and CIRCULATING CAPITAL GOODS, and again, according to their degree of specialization as FREE CAPITAL GOODS and SPECIALIZED CAPITAL GOODS. The distinction between capital goods and CAPITAL should be noted. Capital goods are sometimes called *intermediate goods* because of their function of serving consumers only indirectly in the satisfaction of their WANTS. When so designated, however, CONSUMER GOODS, while still in the possession of producers or MIDDLEMEN, must be considered capital goods serving consumers indirectly.

capitalism. An economic system based upon the private ownership of all kinds of property and the freedom of the individual to contract with others and to engage in economic activities of his choice and for his own profit and well-being. Such governmental restrictions as are placed on private property and freedom of contract are designed for the protection of the public. Zoning restrictions regulating building operations or land use and the exclusion of agreements involving an illegal act are cases in point. In a capitalistic economy the government plays a relatively minor role in economic life, its functions being mainly those of maintaining order, preventing abuses, and carrying on such activities as private enterprise cannot pursue with reasonable assurance of profit. Also called *free enterprise.* See also ECONOMIC SYSTEM, STATE CAPITALISM.

capitalistic production. See INDIRECT PRODUCTION.

capitalization of land taxes. Capitalization at a prevailing rate of interest of the sum paid as taxes on a piece of land, the result of such calculation being the amount by which the capital value of the land in question might be reduced in case it were offered for sale. For example, if the annual taxes on a piece of land are, let us say, $100 and the prevailing rate of interest is 4 per cent, a capital sum of $2,500 will be needed to yield an amount equal to the taxes. This sum of $2,500 may be taken into consideration by a prospective purchaser and deducted from the price that he would otherwise be willing to pay.

capitalized value. The value arrived at by dividing annual earnings by a stipulated rate of interest, usually the prevailing rate. Thus, if the net earnings of a productive enterprise are, let us say, $2,550 per year, and the prevailing rate of interest is 3 per cent, then the capitalized value is $85,000. See also VALUE.

capitalized-value standard. As applied to the valuation of a corporation's capital assets, the value as determined by dividing the annual earnings by a stipulated interest rate. Virtually identical with EARNING-CAPACITY STANDARD. See also CAPITALIZED VALUE.

capital levy. A nonrecurring tax on capital. The term may refer to a special nonrecurring tax placed only on new capital values acquired during some particular period such as during a war. Thus conceived, a capital levy is similar to a CAPITAL-GAINS TAX except that it is levied on an appraised instead of a realized gain. Or the term may refer to a levy on the entire existing capital in a nation. As such, a capital levy is similar to a general PROPERTY TAX levied only at one particular time.

capital liability. A fixed liability which is incurred primarily to acquire fixed assets or for refunding purposes. Capital stock is usually considered a capital liability, although technically it represents ownership and hence not the claim of a creditor. See also LIABILITY.

capital movement. The liquidation of capital investments of one kind and the reinvestment of the realized capital funds in investments of another kind; or the liquidation of investments in one place and reinvestment of proceeds elsewhere. The term is used particularly in describing the capital movements, as thus defined, from one nation to another.

capital rent. A price paid for the use of improvements permanently attached to the land. The concept is a hypothetical one inasmuch as the improvements cannot be used apart from the land on which they rest. The term is used when it is desired to separate ORDINARY RENT into two parts: GROUND RENT and capital rent. See RENT.

capital stock. The permanently invested capital of a corporation contributed by the owners either at or subsequent to the time the corporation is organized. Capital stock is divided into *shares*, each share representing a proportionate ownership in the corporation. Shares are issued in the form of a *stock certificate* which is usually transferable only by indorsement. Shares of the capital stock may be assigned a PAR VALUE, in which case they are called *par-value stock;* or the shares may be issued without par value, in which case they are called *no-par-value stock.*

Capital stock is frequently divided into classes with different rights and privileges accorded each class. *Common*, *equity*, or *ordinary stock* enjoys exclusive claim to the net assets and to the profits of the corporation if no other class of stock is issued. *Preferred stock*, if issued, takes precedence over the common stock according to whatever terms are determined upon. Usually it is accorded a prior claim on the net assets and a specified amount of the profits. Such stock is also known by the terms *prior* or *preference stock.*

Sometimes a certain class of stock is itself divided. Thus, the preferred stock may be divided into "first," "prior," or "class A" preferred stock and "second" or "class B" preferred stock, the rights and privileges of each being still more closely defined. These subclasses are called *classified stock.* The term *debenture stock* is very seldom used in the United States. When used it has indicated a class of stock enjoying some right or privilege over some other class of stock.

Special rights and privileges accorded or denied a stock, and special liabilities attached to it or from which it is free, are frequently indicated in the name of the stock or in the terms used to describe it. An *assessable stock* is a stock subject to an assessment if the financial affairs of the corporation make such an assessment necessary. The term *callable preferred stock* indicates that the corporation issuing the stock reserves the right to buy it back from the owners at its option. It is frequently stipulated that when such stock is repurchased a premium shall be paid for it. *Convertible stock* is stock which grants the owner the privilege of exchanging it for some other issue either at any time or previous to some fixed date and in accordance with specified terms. The term *cumulative stock* indicates that if the dividends are not paid in any one year, they become a liability of the corporation and, if conditions permit, will be paid during some subsequent year. *Full-paid stock* is stock the full amount of the par value of which has been paid to the corporation issuing it. The term *guaranteed stock* indicates that dividends on the stock are guaranteed by some corporation other than the one responsible for the issue of the stock. *Nonassessable stock* is stock free from all liability of assessments. The term *noncumulative stock* indicates that dividends not paid one year do not become a liability of the company and hence will not be paid during any subsequent year. *Paid-up stock* is the same as full-paid stock, defined above. *Participating preferred stock* is a preferred stock which, in addition to the privileges accorded it as such, participates, together with other stock, in profits usually above a specified sum. *Part-paid stock* is stock only a part of the par value of which has been paid the corporation. *Redeemable preferred stock* is the same as callable preferred stock, defined above.

Other terms applicable to stocks indicate more general characteristics, some of which have little to do with the actual worth of the stock to an investor. An *active stock* is one that is bought and sold continuously on the market in fairly large volume. A *barometer stock* is a stock the market price of which is said to indicate the general condition of the market. The term *bonus stock* refers to the particular stock certificates which are given free to an investor in consideration of the purchase of some other issue. Bonus stock also refers to the particular stock certificates which are issued in return for services rendered such, for example, as those performed by a promoter. *Clearinghouse stock* is stock which is handled by the clearinghouse of the New York Stock Exchange. *Curb stock* is stock which is listed on the American Stock Exchange. *Donated stock* is stock which is given the corporation by the owners, usually to allow the corporation to resell it in order to raise cash capital. The terms *full stock* and *half stock* indicate that the par value of a stock is $100 and $50 respectively. An *inactive stock* is one which is bought and sold relatively infrequently. *International stock* is a term used to indicate that the stock of a corporation located in one country is bought and sold on the security exchanges of another country. A *listed stock* is one accepted for trading on any recognized stock exchange. *Management stock* is stock with special voting rights. It is issued for the purpose of giving management complete control over the affairs of the corporation. The term is also used to indicate simply the stock held by the management of a corporation. A *nonclearinghouse stock* is one not handled by the clearinghouse of the New York Stock Exchange. *Original-issue stock* refers to the particular certificates which are issued to the initial subscribers to the capital stock of a corporation. *Potential stock* is the unissued portion of the authorized capital stock of a corporation. *Premium stock* is stock which commands a premium in the form of an extra fee if it is borrowed for trading purposes. *Quarter stock* is stock the par value of which is $25. A stock issued for some particular purpose such as the payment of a stock dividend is occasionally called *special stock*. It is sometimes accorded some right or privilege over other classes of stock. *Treasury stock* is stock which has been issued and subsequently reacquired from the owner by the corporation originally issuing the stock. *Unissued stock* is the same as potential stock, defined above. *Unlisted stock* is a stock not traded on any recognized stock exchange. *Watered stock* is stock the book value of which is materially in excess of the amount of money that could be paid to the owners at any time if the corporation were liquidated.

capital-stock tax. A tax imposed as a percentage of either the market or par value of the capital stock of a corporation. A capital-stock tax, levied by the United States government in 1916, was repealed in 1926. Many of the states of the United States, however, impose such a tax. See also TAX.

capital surplus. See explanation under SURPLUS.

capitation tax. See POLL TAX.

captive mine. A coal mine owned by a company that itself uses the entire, or almost the entire, output of the mine.

Caribbean Commission. Representatives of Caribbean governments, including Puerto Rico, organized in 1942 but known since 1961 as the Caribbean Organization. It seeks to expand commercial and social relations in the Caribbean area.

car loadings. The number of freight cars loaded during a specified period. The figure is frequently used as an index of general business activity.

cartel. A contractual association of independent business organizations, located in one or more countries, formed for the purpose of regulating the purchasing, production, or marketing of goods by the members. Because such activities have a tendency to restrict markets and fix prices, cartels in the United States are sometimes considered to violate antitrust statutes. See also COMBINATION.

Carter* v. *Carter Coal Co. See BITUMINOUS COAL CASES.

cash. See CURRENCY.

cashier's check. A check issued by a bank and usually signed by its cashier. See also CHECK.

caste system. The separation of different groups in society by rigid social and other barriers, usually originating in political or religious differences. The term should be distinguished from the term *class* which suggests social mobility and differences of economic origin.

casualty insurance. A generic term applicable to various kinds of insurance other than life, fire, and marine. For example, liability, title, credit, and explosion insurance all fall within the category of casualty insurance. See also INSURANCE.

casual workers. Temporary workers who acquire no seniority rights with a company and no permanent affiliation with a labor union. In a CLOSED SHOP, casual workers are issued permit cards by the union.

caveat emptor. Let the buyer beware.

caveat venditor. Let the seller beware.

ceiling prices. See explanation under PRICE CONTROL.

cement case. A case, *Cement Mfrs'. Protective Assn.* v. *United States*, 268 U. S. 588 (1925), in which the Supreme Court of the United States greatly weakened earlier decisions such as the one in the LINSEED OIL INDUSTRY CASE (*q.v.*) invalidating the exchange of price and other related trade information among enterprises in an industry on the ground such exchange violated the antitrust statutes. In this case, the court held that agreements by members of a trade association to exchange pertinent trade information might facilitate more efficient commercial operations and that there was no necessary tendency for such information to lessen competition.

Cement Mfrs'. Protective Assn.* v. *United States. See CEMENT CASE.

Census, Bureau of the. The chief statistical agency of the United States government. It is responsible for the decennial census embracing population and other important statistics and publishes numerous reports, tabulations, and current bulletins on almost every phase of national life. The bureau is a part of the Department of Commerce.

central bank. A bank which exists primarily for public fiscal purposes, which is controlled in whole or in part by the government, and which turns over a large proportion of its profit to the government either directly or in the form of a tax. A central bank is usually charged with the responsibility of maintaining an adequate liquid reserve against the nation's bank credit, controlling the importation and exportation of money or precious metals, and providing a sound note issue. It also acts as fiduciary agent for the government and as a banker's bank. The Bank of England and the United States FEDERAL RESERVE BANKS may be considered central banks. See also BANK.

central reserve cities. A term often used to identify a number of large cities of the United States, certain banks in which, prior to the establishment of the FEDERAL RESERVE SYSTEM, served as depositaries for the legal reserves or part of the legal reserves of correspondent banks; that is, rural banks and banks in smaller cities.

central reserve city bank. A MEMBER BANK of the FEDERAL RESERVE SYSTEM located in New York or Chicago and so designated by the Governors of the Federal Reserve System. For the purpose of determining BANK RESERVE requirements on demand deposits and time deposits, the Federal Reserve System identifies three classes of banks: (1) central reserve city banks; (2) *reserve city banks,* which include member banks in large cities other than New York and Chicago; and (3) *country banks.*

certificate. An instrument giving formal assurance of the existence of some fact or set of facts. Such an instrument is used as evidence of some right or obligation. Many kinds of certificates are in common use. For some of the more important kinds see ARTICLES OF INCORPORATION, CERTIFICATE OF BENEFICIAL INTEREST, CERTIFICATE OF DEPOSIT, CERTIFICATE OF INDEBTEDNESS, CERTIFICATE OF ORIGIN, CERTIFICATE OF PUBLIC CONVENIENCE AND NECESSITY, VOTING-TRUST CERTIFICATE. See also CAPITAL STOCK.

certificate of beneficial interest. A document which identifies an owner's interest in the assets and earnings of a business enterprise. Such certificates may be issued to stockholders when the stock of a corporation is surrendered to a trustee or trustees. They also serve as evidence of interest in a MASSACHUSETTS, or *common-law,* TRUST.

certificate of deposit. A document showing that a deposit has been made in a bank.

certificate of incorporation. See ARTICLES OF INCORPORATION.

certificate of indebtedness. Documentary evidence of a short-term debt. Such certificates are sometimes issued by a government to raise funds to meet current expenses.

certificate of origin. A document which identifies the place of origin of imported goods. Such a document is usually required by customs officials.

certificate of public convenience and necessity. A license to operate issued by a state public-utility commission to a private business affected with a public interest.

certified check. A check bearing the indorsement of a bank guaranteeing its payment. See also CHECK.

certified public accountant. A degree or title conferred upon an accountant under the laws of a state of the United States. It indicates that the holder has met the state's legal requirements for the practice of the profession of accountancy and testifies to his competence in installing accounting systems and in making audits and related reports. See also ACCOUNTANT.

chain banking. Direction of the policies and operations of a group of banks by some one bank or other organization which has acquired its control or influence by a system of interlocking directorates, majority stock ownership, or some other means, the various banks in the group being apparently autonomous and independent of one another. Also called *group banking*.

chain store. One of a number of retail stores, all owned and managed by one company.

chain-store tax. A progressive tax levied by many of the states of the United States on chain stores when the number under one management exceeds a certain maximum. The tax is usually levied in the form of a fee exacted to obtain a LICENSE. See also CHAIN STORE, PROGRESSIVE TAX, TAX.

chamber of commerce. See explanation under BOARD OF TRADE. See also UNITED STATES CHAMBER OF COMMERCE.

chapel. As applied to labor organizations in the printers' trade, a division of a local labor union composed of those members who are employees of one particular printing establishment.

charta partita. An agreement for the leasing of a ship or a part thereof for a definite length of time or for a specific voyage.

charter. 1. As applied to corporations, a document, issued by authority of a government, evidencing the creation of the corporation. Such a charter may consist of a special document, usually issued only when the corporation is authorized by special act of the legislature, or it may consist, for all practical purposes, of the approved and recorded ARTICLES OF INCORPORATION together with the general corporation laws of the government involved. 2. The fundamental statute of some public body, for example, the charter of the UNITED NATIONS.

Chartism. An English reform movement (1840–48) which sought to achieve its objectives by legislation. A parliamentary petition drafted by the leaders of the movement took the form of a charter identifying the principal desired reforms. These included universal adult male suffrage, vote by ballot, equal electoral districts, annual meetings of Parliament, payment of salaries to members of the House of Commons, and abolition of the property qualification for membership in that body. The movement disintegrated after 1848, but many of its objectives were later incorporated in the programs of the developing co-operative and trade-union organizations.

chattel. Almost any kind of personal property; this may include an interest in real estate which is less than a freehold, as a lease.

chattel mortgage. Personal property earmarked as security for a debt or other obligation and pledged in such a way that if the debtor fails to meet the terms of the contract, the creditor can take possession of the property. See also MORTGAGE.

cheap money. A term used to describe a condition when the general price level is high. At such a time a relatively small quantity of goods or services exchanges for a relatively high quantity of money; hence, money is cheap, or its value low, compared with the value of goods and services. The term is also used to indicate low interest rates. See also MONEY.

check. A written order usually issued by a depositor of a bank authorizing that bank to pay a specified sum of money to some person named in the order. See also CASHIER'S CHECK, CERTIFIED CHECK, COUNTER CHECK, TRAVELER'S CHECK.

check credit. A service offered by some banks whereby a client or customer is granted a certain amount of credit for consumer purchases, draws checks against this credit from time to time, and repays the bank periodically.

check currency. See explanation under DEPOSIT CURRENCY.

checkoff. As applied to labor relations, the deduction by the employer of labor-union dues and assessments from the pay of the workers and the payment of such deductions directly to the union by the employer. The arrangement may be a *voluntary checkoff*, in which case the deductions are made only from the pay of those workers who authorize such deductions, or the arrangement may be a *compulsory checkoff* — sometimes called *automatic checkoff* — in which case the workers have no choice in the matter. See also LABOR-MANAGEMENT RELATIONS ACT.

checkweighman. A worker in a coal mine who weighs the coal produced by each miner, a practice required when miners are paid according to the number of tons of coal they individually produce.

chemurgy. The application of chemistry to the industrial utilization of organic raw materials, particularly farm products.

Chicago Board of Trade. A produce exchange organized in 1848, and the leading grain market in the United States. The board is organized as an incorporated association of grain dealers. It supplies the physical facilities, and drafts and enforces the rules under which the trading takes place.

***Chicago, Milwaukee and St. Paul Railroad Co.* v. *Minnesota*.** See *Stone* v. *Farmers' Loan and Trust Co.*

child labor. As determined by the Fair Labor Standards Act passed by Congress in 1938, generally the gainful employment of children under 16 years of age. The act declares such employment unlawful. In the case of six particularly hazardous occupations this law raises the age barrier to employment to 18. Certain exceptions are made in nonmining and nonmanufacturing industries. Moreover, children employed in agriculture during the time they are not legally required to attend school, children engaged in theatrical productions, and those employed by their parents are exempt from the provisions of the law. Child labor is variously defined in the statutes of nearly all of the states of the United States, the minimum age beyond which the employment prohibitions of such laws are inapplicable varying usually between 14 and 18. See also Child-labor cases, Labor.

child-labor cases. 1. *Hammer* v. *Dagenhart.* A case, 247 U. S. 251 (1918), involving the first serious attempt by Congress to prohibit child labor in the United States. The legislation under review denied transportation in interstate commerce to the products of establishments which employed children under certain ages. In its decision the Supreme Court of the United States declared that the legislation violated the Constitution because it was not a bona fide attempt to regulate transportation among the states but an attempt to control the conditions of employment and manufacture within the states. Authority to control the latter, said the court, did not belong to Congress but was within the police power of the states. 2. *Bailey* v. *Drexel Furniture Co.* A case, 259 U. S. 20 (1922), involving a second attempt by Congress to prohibit child labor in the United States. Under review in the instant case was a federal tax of 10 per cent of the net profits of any establishment which had employed children under certain ages. In a decision holding the measure invalid, the Supreme Court of the United States refused to regard the authorized tax as a bona fide one. The court decided it to be a regulatory and prohibitory measure which, if allowed, might open the way for congressional invasion, ostensibly under the taxing power, of all the powers reserved to the states under the 10th Amendment of the federal Constitution. The decisions in both this and the first child-labor case have been impliedly

if not explicitly overruled in later cases where the Supreme Court has supported federal legislative regulation of the employment of minors. See especially *United States* v. *Darby Lumber Co.*

chrematistic. Having to do with the acquirement of WEALTH. Originally, as used by the Greek writers, *chrematistike* meant the science of SUPPLY in contrast to *oeconomia*, from which the word "economy" is derived, which meant the science of household management. A distinction was thus drawn between those activities devoted to the pursuit of PROFIT and those devoted to the acquisition of the necessities of life, the distinction being set forth in Aristotle's *Politics*, Book I, Chaps. VIII–XI. See also POLITICAL ECONOMY.

Christian Socialism. As used in the United States and England, a term applying to a movement started in England about 1850 which protested against the hardships suffered by the working classes at that time and devoted itself chiefly to their welfare. Charles Kingsley and Frederick Maurice were prominent Christian Socialists. At one time the movement fostered small self-governing workshops which were not successful; later it applied itself to the co-operative movement. Christian Socialism, unlike UTOPIAN SOCIALISM, based its program upon definite religious convictions. See also SOCIALISM.

circular letter of credit. See explanation under LETTER OF CREDIT.

circulating capital good. A capital good which, in the course of production, is destroyed by a single use. The term is used in contradistinction to FIXED CAPITAL GOOD. Coal used to generate power in a factory is an example. See also CAPITAL GOOD.

circulating medium. Any medium of exchange which has general acceptance and passes from person to person without indorsement. Ordinarily, the recognized medium of exchange is MONEY.

Civil Aeronautics Board. An independent administrative agency of the United States government which grants authorization to carriers to engage in interstate and foreign air transportation, regulates rates and services of air carriers, and investigates civil aircraft accidents, making recommendations to the administrator of the FEDERAL AVIATION AGENCY in the interests of increased safety.

civil corporation. A corporation created exclusively for business purposes. See also CORPORATION.

class. See explanation under CASTE SYSTEM.

Classical school. A school of economic thought that originated in England with Adam Smith's *Inquiry into the Nature and Causes of the Wealth of Nations* (1776) and which included the writings of such English economists as David Ricardo, Thomas R. Malthus, and John Stuart Mill, as well as the French economist Jean Baptiste Say. In the writings of the Classical economists, man's self-interest is assumed, and man's economic behavior is generalized in the form of principles or laws which are believed to be universally applicable. For example, the general principle that both individuals as such and society as a whole prosper most without government intervention in economic life is indicated in one form or another in the writings of the Classical school. A belief in economic freedom and private property, therefore, is one of its fundamental conceptions. Classical doctrines were used by a group known as the *Manchester school* to support certain reforms, notably the repeal of the CORN LAWS. During recent years the doctrines have been either materially modified or abandoned. Also called *economic liberalism, Individualist school, Liberal school, Orthodox school.* See also SCHOOLS OF ECONOMIC THOUGHT.

classified stock. See explanation under CAPITAL STOCK.

classified tax. A tax system in which property is classified according to its nature and purpose, different tax rates being applied against each class, and some classes being exempted altogether from taxation. See also TAX.

class price. A relatively high price charged to a buyer because he is willing and able to pay it and is ignorant of the fact that the same article can be bought at a lower price elsewhere. See also IMPERFECT COMPETITION, PRICE.

class struggle. A doctrine of Marxian socialism which asserts that modern industrial society is characterized by an inevitable and constant struggle between the capitalistic or ownership class, on the one hand, and the proletariat or propertyless class, on the other, until such a time as the capitalistic class is overthrown.

Clayton Act. An act of Congress, 1914, which aims to prevent monopolies by prohibiting combinations of corporations that control so large a proportion of an industry as to lessen competition. The act specifically prohibits: (1) price discrimination; (2) tying clauses in contracts; (3) interlocking directorates under conditions that lessen competition; and (4) the holding of the stock of one corporation by another when by so doing competition is lessened. The act states that because human labor is not a commodity, labor organizations are not to be considered conspiracies in restraint of trade and are therefore exempt from the operation of antitrust laws.

clean bill. See explanation under BILL.

clearing agreement. An agreement between two or more nations to buy and sell goods and services among themselves according to specified rates of exchange. Payments are made by buyers in the buyers' home currency, balances being settled, at stipulated periods, among the central banks of the nations which are parties to the agreement. See also EXCHANGE CONTROL.

clearinghouse. 1. An association of banks, within a given area, through which claims, arising through the issuance of checks and various forms of commercial paper, are settled. 2. An organization associated with the New York Stock Exchange through which delivery of shares bought and sold on the exchange is effected.

clearinghouse agent. A bank which is a member of a clearinghouse and which accepts the checks of another bank, not a member, for settlement through the clearinghouse. Sometimes called *redemption agent*. See also CLEARINGHOUSE.

clearinghouse stock. See explanation under CAPITAL STOCK.

clearings. Checks, promissory notes, and other such instruments presented by a bank to the clearinghouse for collection. Also called *bank clearings*. See also CLEARINGHOUSE.

close corporation. A corporation the stock of which is held by relatively few persons and which usually is not bought and sold in the open market. See also CORPORATION.

closed-end investment trust. An INVESTMENT TRUST that sells a DEFINITIVE quantity of CAPITAL STOCK and normally acquires ownership of this stock again only through retirement. The stock may be bought and sold through the regular market channels. See also OPEN-END INVESTMENT TRUST.

closed mortgage. A mortgage used as collateral security for a loan of a fixed amount. The mortgage in question, therefore, cannot be used as security for additional loans of any kind. The term is used in contradistinction to an OPEN MORTGAGE. See also MORTGAGE.

closed shop. A shop in which only union workers are employed and in which only union members are accepted for employment. See also UNION SHOP.

closed union. A labor union that either accepts no new members or else imposes regulations which make it very difficult for new members to qualify for admission. See also LABOR UNION.

cobweb chart. A graphic representation of the conditions that may exist in a competitive market when the sale of a perishable GOOD, requiring a period of time to produce, is confined to a short seasonal DEMAND, but enjoys a fairly constant demand from year to year during that season. The seasonal sales period is too short and the time required for production too long to permit changes in the SUPPLY by any producer after sales have begun. Each year, therefore, the supply depends upon the MARKET PRICE of the previous

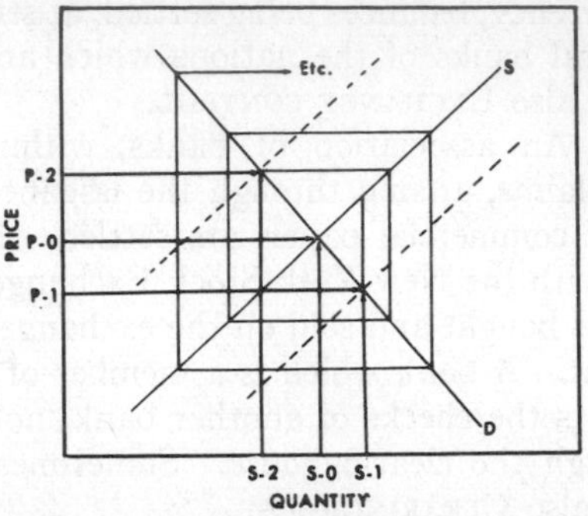

year. This tends to cause price oscillations from year to year, a relatively high price and short supply alternating with a relatively low price and plentiful supply. The appended diagram shows a cobweb chart. *P*-o and *S*-o represent a theoretical price and supply, respectively, around which actual prices and supply fluctuate. *S*-1 shows a relatively plentiful supply, the price during the previous season presumably having been profitable. But with the supply at *S*-1, the price at *P*-1 is relatively low. The following year, therefore, the supply drops to *S*-2, but the price advances to *P*-2. Theoretically, the price oscillations tend to widen as time goes on.

code. As applied to machine data processing, a system of numbers, letters, or other symbols which, when expressed in perforations in cards or tape or electrical charges on magnetic tape, will actuate a machine, causing it to manipulate data in accordance with some prearranged plan.

codes of fair competition. Regulations applying to specific industries, compiled by trade associations under authority of the NATIONAL INDUSTRIAL RECOVERY ACT of 1933, and having to do with maximum hours of employment, minimum wages, and, in many cases, the control of prices. When approved by the President of the United States, these codes had the authority of law governing the industries to which they applied. The codes became inoperative after the National Industrial Recovery Act was declared unconstitutional on May 28, 1935. See also SCHECHTER CASE.

codetermination. As used in Germany (*Mitbestimmung*), the policy of having equal representation of STOCKHOLDERS and LABOR UNIONS on the board of DIRECTORS of INDUSTRY, especially in coal and steel. The claim is made that the plan can be traced back to the Weimar Republic following World War I when labor representatives were placed on the board of some corporations and granted the privilege of participating in the formation of policies having to do exclusively with working conditions. It is said that equal representation was permitted by the British occupation authorities in certain new Ruhr steel corporations organized in 1946, and that the plan was subsequently extended to coal corporations. Early in 1951 a strike of some 750,000 coal- and steelworkers in the Ruhr was threatened if the plan was not continued. In April, 1951, a bill was passed by the *Bundestag* making the continuation of codetermination mandatory.

coefficient of acceleration. See explanation under ACCELERATION PRINCIPLE.

coefficient of correlation. See explanation under SCATTER CHART.

coefficient of cross-elasticity. The relationship, expressed arithmetically, between a percentage change in the price of a particular commodity or service and the resultant percentage change in the sales of a substitute or competitive commodity or service. The generalized equation is:

$$CC = \frac{\dfrac{P_a}{\Delta P_a}}{\dfrac{Q_b}{\Delta Q_b}} = \frac{P_a \times \Delta Q_b}{\Delta P_a \times Q_b}$$

when

CC = coefficient of cross-elasticity,
P_a = average price of commodity a,
ΔP_a = absolute change in price of commodity a,
Q_b = average quantity of commodity b,
ΔQ_b = absolute change in the sales of commodity b.

Example:

10 = original price of commodity a.
16 = new price of commodity a.
100 = original sales of commodity b.
110 = new sales of commodity b.

$P_a = 13$. $Q_b = 105$.
$\Delta P_a = 6$. $\Delta Q_b = 10$.

$$\frac{13 \times 10}{6 \times 105} = \frac{130}{630} = 0.206.$$

coefficient of elasticity. In the case of DEMAND, the arithmetical relationship between the percentage change in the quantity of a COMMODITY or service bought and the percentage change in the PRICE; in the case of SUPPLY, the relationship between the percentage change in the quantity offered and the percentage change in the price.

The generalized equation is:

$$C = \frac{\frac{\Delta q}{Q}}{\frac{\Delta p}{P}} = \frac{P \times \Delta q}{Q \times \Delta p}$$

when

C = coefficient of elasticity,
P = average price,
Q = average quantity,
Δp = absolute price change,
Δq = absolute quantity change.

Example:

10,000 units demanded at price 50.
20,000 units demanded at price 30.

$P = 40.$ $\Delta p = 20.$
$Q = 15,000.$ $\Delta q = 10,000.$

$$C = \frac{40 \times 10,000}{15,000 \times 20} = \frac{400,000}{300,000} = 1.33.$$

If the coefficient of elasticity is more than unity, the demand (or supply) is said to be *elastic;* if less than unity, it is said to be *inelastic;* if just unity, it is said to be *unitary*. If the demand (or supply) curve is vertical, the coefficient of elasticity is zero; if horizontal, it is infinity. See also ELASTIC DEMAND, ELASTIC SUPPLY.

coefficient of variation. A statistical measure of the relative dispersion, variability, or scatter in a FREQUENCY DISTRIBUTION (*q.v.*) obtained by dividing the STANDARD DEVIATION (*q.v.*) by the ARITHMETIC MEAN (*q.v.*) and multiplying the result by 100.

coin. A piece of metal or alloy identified by certain designs or marks and issued by the government to be used as money. See also MINOR COIN, MONEY, SUBSIDIARY COIN, TOKEN COIN.

coinage. The manufacture of coins for use as money. See also FREE COINAGE, GRATUITOUS COINAGE.

coinsurance. A term referring to a clause frequently inserted in a fire-insurance policy, and sometimes made mandatory, to the effect that, in the event of loss to the insured, the liability of the company issuing the policy is limited to a certain per cent of the total loss occasioned by the fire. See also INSURANCE.

collateral. Property, or evidence thereof, deposited with a creditor to guarantee the payment of a loan.

collateral trust bond. See explanation under BOND.

collective bargaining. As applied to employer-employee relations, the meeting in good faith of employers with representatives of their employees for the purpose of discussing and ultimately agreeing upon wages, hours of employment, working conditions, and the like. "Good faith," according to the NATIONAL LABOR RELATIONS BOARD, consists of "a forthright candid effort to reach a settlement."

collective ownership. The ownership of goods by the public as a whole, or by a group of persons, no specific proportion of ownership being assigned to individuals. For example, public parks, roads, and buildings are owned collectively by the people generally as members of a political community.

collectivism. A politico-economic system that places considerable economic power in the hands of the central government. Such power may be exercised through outright government ownership, as in the case of SOCIALISM or COMMUNISM, or it may take the form of such a large degree of ECONOMIC PLANNING that FREEDOM OF CONTRACT is sacrificed even though PRIVATE PROPERTY is maintained in full or in part. See also ECONOMIC SYSTEM.

collector of internal revenue. The person in charge of one of the district offices of the Internal Revenue Service of the United States Treasury. His title is now (1964) "director." To facilitate the collection of internal revenue, there are 58 district offices in the United States.

collector of the customs. An official of the United States Treasury who is responsible for the collection of import duties at a port of entry. See also DUTY, PORT OF ENTRY.

***Collector* v. *Day*.** A case, 11 Wallace 113 (1870), in which the United States Supreme Court upheld the exemption of the salary of a state judicial officer from federal taxation and, impliedly, the exemption of any other state instrumentality from such taxation. The ruling complemented that in *MCCULLOCH* v. *MARYLAND* (*q.v.*) in which federal instrumentalities were exempted from state taxation. Both decisions have been at least partially overruled. See FEDERAL TAX IMMUNITY CASE (*Helvering* v. *Gerhardt*) and STATE TAX IMMUNITY CASE (*Graves* v. *New York* ex rel. *O'Keefe*).

Colombo Plan. A British Commonwealth plan for the industrial and general economic development of the countries of Southeastern Asia, so called because it was first broached at a Commonwealth conference held in Colombo, Ceylon (January, 1950). The plan was formally put into effect on June 30, 1951, for a 6-year period, but in 1955 was extended for 4 years and in 1959 extended again to 1966. Membership in the plan, limited originally to Britain, Australia, Canada, Ceylon, India, New Zealand, and Pakistan, was subsequently extended to include some 15 Southeast Asia nations. By the middle of 1959, the six major creditor states, namely the United States, Britain, Canada, Australia, New Zealand, and Japan, had made available more than $6 billion. The major national governmental contribution had come from the United States. It is estimated that since the start of the plan, some $40 billion in technical aid has been made available to the Colombo Plan nations through various donor governments, private financing, and international development agencies such as the International Bank for Reconstruction and Development.

colonial bond. See explanation under BOND.

colonial system. Regulations and practices, largely exclusive and discriminatory in nature and common during the 17th and 18th centuries, by means of which a state possessing colonies managed them in such a way as to enhance its power and wealth.

column diagram. See explanation under FREQUENCY DISTRIBUTION.

combination. In the case of business organization, any temporary or permanent unification of separate establishments or enterprises. The motives prompting such unification are numerous and varied. The more important ones are a desire to lessen competition, to lessen costs through large-scale production and centralization of management, or to provide large amounts of capital for some venture. Also called *consolidation.* For some of the more important kinds of combination see AMALGAMATION, CARTEL, HOLDING COMPANY, MERGER, POOL, SYNDICATE, TRUST. See also COMBINATION IN RESTRAINT OF TRADE, FORMS OF BUSINESS ORGANIZATION, MONOPOLY.

combination in restraint of trade. Any agreement between two or more persons which attempts to restrict competition. The agreement may take the form of a CARTEL, POOL, HOLDING COMPANY, or some other organizational device. It may attempt price fixing, the creation of a MONOPOLY, or resort to some other device to reduce competition.

combination rate. As applied to railway traffic, a rate charged for carrying freight between two points not on the same railroad which is the sum of all the local rates between the point of origin, the junction points of the two or more railroads, and the point of destination. A combination rate is used when no JOINT RATE exists. See also LOCAL RATE.

commerce. The buying and selling of commodities or services, particularly on a large scale, nationally or internationally. See also INTERSTATE COMMERCE, INTRASTATE COMMERCE.

Commerce, Department of. One of the 10 major administrative units of the federal government, which received its present title in 1913 when activities affecting the interests of labor were taken from it and set up within the separate Department of Labor (*q.v.*). It exerts jurisdiction over the census, patents and copyrights, the Coast and Geodetic Survey, the Weather Bureau, the Bureau of Standards, and various other units having to do with the promotion of foreign and domestic commerce and economic development.

commercial bank. A bank, the principal function of which is to receive deposits subject to check, and to make short-term loans to its customers. Besides these primary banking functions a commercial bank performs a variety of incidental functions. It keeps the community supplied with the kinds of currency most in demand, acts as a collection agent for promissory notes, drafts, and similar COMMERCIAL PAPER, and transmits funds to distant points upon request. It may offer its vaults for the safekeeping of valuables, offer interest for TIME DEPOSITS, and perform the functions of a TRUST COMPANY. Commercial banks may be NATIONAL BANKS, or STATE BANKS. All national banks are commercial banks, but not all state banks are commercial banks. See also BANK.

commercial credit. Short-term loans furnished a business undertaking for temporary needs. See also CREDIT.

commercial credit company. A company engaged in certain specialized forms of financing, particularly the purchasing of accounts receivable, the extension of credit to retail dealers, and the discounting of installment accounts. In the automobile business, for example, dealer purchases from manufacturers are frequently settled in cash by a commercial credit company in return for a trust receipt signed by the dealer. As the cars are sold, the dealer settles with the credit company. Promissory notes of consumers who purchase on the installment plan are discounted by such companies. Also called *discount house* and *finance company*.

commercial paper. One of various types of short-term negotiable instruments, particularly a promissory note, which calls for the payment of a specific amount of money at a given time.

commercial policy. Governmental policies relating to the industrial and commercial welfare of the nation. The term applies particularly to public policies to control or encourage foreign trade, investment and shipping, and the maintenance of facilities in foreign countries to aid business interests.

commercial revolution. The expansion of European commerce from the Mediterranean to the Atlantic and throughout the globe following the age of discovery with the geographical explorations of the 15th and 16th centuries and the establishment of new trade routes.

commercial treaty. An agreement between two or more countries setting forth the conditions under which the nationals of one country, party to the agreement, may do business in the other contracting country or countries. For example, a commercial treaty may set forth tariff privileges, terms on which property may be owned, or the manner in which claims may be settled.

commission. 1. As applied to commercial transactions, compensation to a broker or agent for conducting some business project for another person. The term infers that the payment is a percentage of some amount involved in a transaction. 2. A public regulatory body.

Commissioner of Customs. The officer in charge of the Bureau of Customs of the United States Treasury. He is responsible for the enforcement of customs regulations and regulations applicable to maritime commerce.

commissioner of deeds. 1. A local officer in the United States who usually resides in a state other than the one in which he receives his appointment and whose function it is to administer oaths and to take acknowledgments to be used in the state from which he received his appointment. Unlike a NOTARY PUBLIC, he has no authority to PROTEST negotiable instruments. 2. An appointive officer having similar duties in New York City.

Commissioner of Internal Revenue. The head of the Internal Revenue Service of the Department of the Treasury of the United States. He has general supervision over the determination, assessment, and collection of all internal revenue taxes.

Committee for Economic Development. An organization of American businessmen created in 1942 to plan for maximum employment and production in the period following World War II. The committee has published various statements relating to national economic policy and many research reports relating to such subjects as taxes, employment, wartime controls, agriculture, and world trade. The committee was reorganized on a permanent basis in 1948.

commodity. Any article of commerce or trade that can be transported. The term is often used instead of the singular for "goods," because "good" has other common meanings, and a specialized meaning in economics such as ECONOMIC GOOD.

commodity agreement. An agreement, usually made between nations, covering the production and distribution of commodities, existing quantities of which exceed normal world demands. Such an agreement may include provisions for the control of production, exports, and prices, the creation of reserve stocks, and means of expanding existing markets.

Commodity Credit Corporation. A public corporation of the United States government, with an authorized and paid-in capital of $100,000,000, attached to the Agricultural Marketing Service of the Department of Agriculture. It provides the necessary financial services for carrying forward public price-support activities with respect to certain agricultural commodities, including governmental lending, purchase, sale, storage, transport, and subsidization of such commodities.

commodity dollar. A dollar which, ideally, always has the same exchange value in terms of commodities. The purpose of such a dollar would be to do away with wide fluctuations in the general PRICE LEVEL. Many devices have been proposed to create a commodity dollar, but up to the present time the idea of such a dollar has not been realized in practice. Also called *neutral money.* See also COMPENSATED DOLLAR.

commodity exchange. An association of traders providing an organized market for the buying and selling of certain commodities. The commodities dealt in are not brought to the market place; their existence is attested by documents which identify the amounts and quality. Much of the trading on the commodity exchanges is for HEDGING purposes, involving purchases and sales for future delivery. Commodity exchanges exist for wheat, cotton, sugar, corn, coffee, and other products that can be accurately classified as to standards of quality.

Commodity Exchange Authority. An administrative unit set up within the United States Department of Agriculture in 1947 to carry out the provisions of the Commodity Exchange Act of 1922 regulating practices on certain COMMODITY EXCHANGES.

commodity paper. Drafts, promissory notes, or other similar commercial paper representing a loan and secured by order bills of lading or warehouse receipts as collateral. In case the loan, represented by the commodity paper, is not paid at maturity, the creditor, usually a bank, may secure the goods, sell them, and apply the proceeds to the amount of the loan. See also ORDER BILL OF LADING.

commodity standard. A monetary system in which some commodity, other than a precious metal, is accepted as standard money. The difficulty of convertibility and portability, and the absence of stability of value and homogeneity of the commodity itself make a commodity standard impracticable in a modern economy. See also MONETARY SYSTEM, STANDARD MONEY.

commodity theory of money. The assertion that the value of money is determined by the value of the commodity of which it is composed or which it represents. When the MONETARY UNIT is defined in terms of gold, according to this theory, the value of money is determined by the supply of gold and the demand for gold arising by virtue of its use in manufacture and the arts, and there exists at all times a definite exchange ratio between gold and other commodities whether the gold is in the form of BULLION, COINS, or REPRESENTATIVE MONEY. According to this theory, when, in 1934, the gold content of the United States dollar was reduced from $25\frac{8}{10}$ to $15\frac{5}{21}$ grains $\frac{9}{10}$ fine, prices should have advanced proportionally. They did not, and it is generally conceded today that the value of money is not determined by so simple a formula.

common carrier. An individual or company engaged in the transportation of goods or persons in return for a fee, such service being available at uniform rates to all persons. Telephone and telegraph companies are not common carriers, although they may be subject to the same rules as those governing common carriers.

common-law trust. See explanation under MASSACHUSETTS TRUST.

Common Market. See EUROPEAN ECONOMIC COMMUNITY.

common stock. See explanation under CAPITAL STOCK.

common trust. Two or more relatively small trust funds combined for economy in administration. See also TRUST, TRUST FUND.

***Commonwealth* (*Mass.*) v. *Hunt*.** See *COMMONWEALTH* (*PA.*) v. *CORDWAINERS*.

***Commonwealth* (*Pa.*) v. *Cordwainers*.** The first recorded labor case in the United States, tried before the Mayor's Court in Philadelphia, Pa., March, 1806. Eight bootmaker defendants, who had previously participated in a STRIKE, were charged with the offense of combining and conspiring to raise wages. It was the law, rather than the facts, upon which the court was called to decide, the decision hinging on whether or not the English doctrine of common-law conspiracy was applicable in the state of Pennsylvania. The court accepted the English doctrine, and the defendants were convicted, fined, and committed to jail pending the payment of the fines. Subsequent cases, for example *Commonwealth* v. *Hunt* [Mass. (1842)], modified the decision that concerted action through labor organizations violated common-law doctrines of conspiracy, and paved the way for the acceptance of LABOR UNIONS as a legitimate instrument of economic action by workmen.

communism. Government or community ownership of all wealth. Communism abolishes the concept of private property. Production by individuals is ideally in accordance with capacity, and consumption is in accordance with need. The term is sometimes used to describe the contemporary economic system of Soviet Russia where private property in all capital goods has been abolished but has been retained in various types of consumer goods. Soviet theoreticians, however, usually refer to this system as SOCIALISM and suggest that actual communism is a condition to be achieved in the vague and indefinite future. The term is also used to suggest social revolution by force. See also ECONOMIC SYSTEM.

community-property principle. The principle, derived from Spanish law and now (1963) accepted in more than a dozen states of the United States, that husband and wife create a community estate in the property accumulated by them, and that they have an equal interest in such estate as long as the marital relationship endures. In the states where this principle governs, it is therefore permissible for husband and wife to divide equally the total of their joint income for tax purposes, each being regarded as having an equal share in such income. Revision of federal revenue laws in 1948 authorized the application of the community-property principle to joint income-tax returns of husband and wife throughout the United States.

company. An association of persons organized for the purpose of carrying on some commercial or industrial activity. A company may be a CORPORATION or a PARTNERSHIP, or it may assume some other FORM OF BUSINESS ORGANIZATION. Companies are frequently designated by some descriptive title indicating the nature of their business or their relation to some other company, such as insurance company, operating company, parent company, and the like.

company store. A retail store owned and operated by an enterprise for the use of its employees and conducted as an adjunct to its regular business.

company town. A community located on property owned in whole or in major part by an industrial or similar concern and inhabited chiefly by that concern's employees. A company town is controlled in many of its corporate activities by whatever policies the concern may pursue.

company union. A labor union, the membership of which is made up of workers employed by one company only and which is usually not affiliated with any other labor union or group of unions. See also LABOR UNION.

comparative advantage. The condition which exists when one nation or region can produce each of two products at less cost than some other nation or region, and the relative saving in the case of one of these products is greater than in the case of the second. The nation or region thus favored is said to enjoy an *absolute advantage* in the case of both products over the nation or region not so favored and to enjoy a comparative advantage in the case of the product where the relative saving is greater. For example, nation A can produce both sugar and automobiles at less cost than can nation B. Nation A thus has an absolute advantage over nation B in the case of both of these products. But the relative saving of nation A over nation B in the production of automobiles is greater than the saving which nation A enjoys over nation B in the case of sugar. Hence nation A has a comparative as well as an absolute advantage over nation B in the production of automobiles.

The term "comparative advantage" may also be employed to mark the fact that in the less favored of two nations or regions, the cost of production of one commodity is less than that of another. In the above example, nation B is at an absolute disadvantage vis-à-vis nation A in the production of both sugar and automobiles. But it is also true that within nation A, the production of sugar is relatively cheaper than the production of automobiles, and in this somewhat negative sense, nation B is said to have a comparative advantage in the production of sugar. The distinction is significant because, in view of these internal circumstances, nation A might find it profitable to concentrate its productive resources on automobiles and import sugar from nation B despite the fact that sugar as well as automobiles can be produced cheaper in nation A than in nation B. Sometimes referred to as *comparative costs.*

comparative costs. See COMPARATIVE ADVANTAGE.

compensated dollar. A proposal once advocated by certain American economists to create a commodity dollar by constantly varying the gold content of the STANDARD MONEY dollar according to fluctuations in the general PRICE LEVEL. In the event of a marked advance in the general price level, the gold content of the standard money dollar would be increased, thus making it possible to offer more gold for commodities, but with fewer dollars since each dollar would contain more gold. Conversely, in the event of a marked decline in the general price level, the gold content of the standard money dollar would be decreased, thus making it possible to offer less gold for commodities, but with more dollars since each dollar would contain less gold. According to the proposal, this procedure would keep prices, or the number of dollars exchangeable for commodities, more or less constant, although the dollars would contain a larger or smaller quantity of gold at one time compared with some other time. See also COMMODITY DOLLAR.

compensatory duty. 1. A duty sometimes levied on imported manufactured articles in order to offset the increased costs of a domestic manufacturer of similar articles when such costs are attributable to a tariff on the raw materials used by such domestic manufacturer. The plan has been used intermittently, for example, in the application of United States' duties on wool and woolen cloth. In 1861 the duty on wool was 3 cents a pound. On the assumption that it takes about 4 lb. of wool to produce 1 lb. of cloth, a compensatory duty of 12 cents a pound was placed on woolen cloth. At that point the domestic producer of wool cloth could compete with imported cloth on equal terms. Such additional duty as was imposed on wool cloth at that time was for the benefit of merchants dealing in this commodity. **2.** A duty on an imported commodity designed to offset an excise tax placed on the same commodity when produced in the importing country. Also called ***countervailing excise duty.*** See also CUSTOMS DUTY.

compensatory fiscal policy. Procedures for the collection of PUBLIC REVENUE, regulation of government expenditures, and management of the NATIONAL DEBT designed to influence directly or indirectly the general level of economic activity and particularly inflationary or deflationary tendencies in the economy. The attempt to check INFLATION by heavy taxation and concomitant retirement of bank-held government bonds is a case in point. Also called ***functional finance.***

compensatory principle of money. As applied to bimetallism, the assertion that the ratio between the mint and market values of two metals in a bimetallic monetary system will be maintained through the normal operation of the forces of supply and demand. Thus, a high market demand and an augmented market value for one metal will be offset through fewer deliveries to the mint and more to the market. Conversely, a low market demand and a declining market value for one metal will be overcome through fewer deliveries to the market and more to the mint. See also BIMETALLISM.

compensatory principle of taxation. See BENEFITS-RECEIVED PRINCIPLE OF TAXATION.

compensatory spending. See explanation under DEFICIT FINANCING.

competition. The condition that exists in a market when there are an indeterminate number of traders all dealing in the same product and when no one trader can demand or offer a quantity sufficiently large materially to affect the market price. This condition is frequently referred to as *free competition*, ***perfect competition***, or ***pure competition.*** As thus defined the term is subject to certain qualifications for which see IMPERFECT COMPETITION, MONOPOLISTIC COMPETITION, and OPEN COMPETITION. See also CUTTHROAT COMPETITION, DESTRUCTIVE COMPETITION.

competitive socialism. A proposed ECONOMIC SYSTEM that would abolish PRIVATE PROPERTY in the FACTORS OF PRODUCTION while theoretically retaining FREEDOM OF CONTRACT.

composite commodity standard. A proposed monetary system in which the value of the monetary unit would be defined in terms of a selected number of commodities called a "composite commodity unit" instead of in terms of one or more precious metals. See also MONETARY UNIT.

composite demand. The total demand for a product or service originating in an indefinite number and variety of wants, all of which can be satisfied by that particular product or service. The demand for day laborers, for example, may originate in agricultural production, construction work, or a large number of other activities. See also DEMAND.

composite supply. An indefinite number and variety of goods each of which is capable of satisfying a specific want. Transportation requirements, for example, can often be satisfied by busses, railroads, streetcars, or some other means of conveyance. See also SUPPLY.

composition. An agreement between a debtor and a creditor wherein, for proper consideration, the creditor agrees to accept part of the amount due him in satisfaction of the whole.

compound duty. A tariff duty consisting of a specific duty to which is added an ad valorem duty. See also AD VALOREM DUTY, CUSTOMS DUTY, SPECIFIC DUTY.

compound interest. Interest calculated on a principal sum and also on all accumulated interest earned by that principal sum as of a given date. See also INTEREST.

Compromise Tariff. The United States Tariff Act of 1833. It provided for a gradual reduction of all duties exceeding 20 per cent ad valorem. So called because the purpose of the act was to conciliate Southern opposition, particularly that of South Carolina where the tariff law of 1828 (TARIFF OF ABOMINATIONS) had been declared null and void because it was considered discriminatory toward Southern producers.

comptroller. Usually the executive head of the accounting staff of a large corporation or governmental agency.

Comptroller of the Currency, Office of. A unit of the Department of the Treasury of the United States which supervises the operations of all NATIONAL BANKS. Under the NATIONAL BANK ACT of 1863, which created this office, the Comptroller must report directly to Congress.

compulsory checkoff. See explanation under CHECKOFF.

concession. A grant of land or other property for some specific use, or the right to the use of, or access to, all or a portion of some land or other property made either by a government or a private agency. Thus, a government may grant land to a private company for the construction of a canal or the building of a railroad, or the management of a county fair may grant an individual the right to operate a lunch counter on the fairground.

conciliation. As applied to labor relations, the appointment of a third party, in the event of a labor-management dispute, who attempts to settle the dispute by suggesting various ways in which the differences might be resolved but who has no authority to compel a settlement.

condemnation. 1. The determination by a public authority that a certain property is unfit for use. Thus, a ship or a tenement house may be condemned as unsafe. 2. The acquisition of private property by public authority under the power of EMINENT DOMAIN (*q.v.*). See also EXCESS CONDEMNATION. 3. An official declaration that certain property is forfeited to the state because of a violation of law.

conditional indorsement. An indorsement which contains some condition affecting the indorser's liability. See also INDORSEMENT.

conditional sale. A sale made with the understanding that title to the property sold will not pass to the buyer until payment of the sale price is made, or, conceivably, until some other condition has been met.

confirmed letter of credit. See explanation under LETTER OF CREDIT.

confiscation. Seizure of private property by the government, without compensation to the owner.

Congress of Industrial Organizations. A federation of labor unions in the United States. Organized in 1935 it was affiliated with the AMERICAN FEDERATION OF LABOR as the Committee for Industrial Organization; 2 years later it took its present name and became an independent organization. On December 5, 1955 it merged with the AFL to form the AMERICAN FEDERATION OF LABOR AND CONGRESS OF INDUSTRIAL ORGANIZATIONS (*q.v.*).

consent decree. A means of settling certain cases in equity by agreement of the parties in court. This means of settlement has been extensively used by the antitrust division of the United States Department of Justice. A party against whom an antitrust suit is pending offers to introduce reforms satisfactory to the Department of Justice which, instead of proceeding with the contemplated suit, accepts the offer. The agreement takes the form of a judicial decree.

conservation. As applied to natural resources, care and preservation in such a way as to prolong their use or make for their most effective use.

conservator. 1. In the United States, an official appointed to administer the affairs of a national bank which is in unsound condition or which is being liquidated. 2. An official charged with the protection of a legally incompetent person, or one who enforces certain statutes in the public interest.

consignee. A person who receives a consignment. The person who makes the consignment is the consignor. See also CONSIGNMENT.

consignment. 1. Goods shipped by one person to another. 2. Goods shipped on condition that they will be paid for when sold.

consol bond. See explanation under BOND.

consolidated bond. See explanation under BOND.

consolidation. See COMBINATION.

conspicuous consumption. The use of consumer goods in such a way as to create a display for the purpose of impressing others rather than for the satisfaction of a normal consumer demand. See also CONSUMPTION.

constant costs. Costs which, under a given set of conditions, remain the same, per unit of product, despite an increase in the total production. Handicraft articles made by individual craftsmen complete from beginning to end are subject to constant costs. See also COST.

consul. A government official stationed in a foreign country who cares for the commercial interests of the citizens of his own government and protects the interests of its seamen and its traveling nationals. In the United States Foreign Service consular officials rank as follows: ***consul general***, ***consul***, ***vice-consul***, and ***consular agent***.

consular agent. See explanation under CONSUL.

consular invoice. An invoice which has been stamped by a consul of the nation for which the goods represented on the invoice are destined. Such an invoice is frequently required for customs or statistical purposes. See also INVOICE.

consul general. See explanation under CONSUL.

consumer co-operative. A form of membership business organization, usually incorporated, created by consumers to meet their own needs. It is controlled by consumers by virtue of the regulation that each of them, as a member, has one vote. Each consumer member, moreover, participates in the benefits resulting from the enterprise through a plan of rebating to members, in proportion to their purchases, such excess of income over expenses as may be authorized by the membership.

consumer credit. Credit extended to consumers for the purchase of consumer goods and services. Consumer credit may be extended by means of charge accounts, an installment purchase plan, or through money loans. See also CREDIT.

consumer economics. In the broadest sense of the term, a study of economics considered from the standpoint of the consumer. Much the same range of subject matter is involved as in the case of the more formal study of economics, but some problems, for example those involving credit terms and consumer purchasing, are stressed, and other problems are given more cursory treatment. See also ECONOMICS.

consumer good. An economic good which is used directly in the satisfaction of human desires. The term is used in contradistinction to CAPITAL GOOD. The distinction is one of use. An automobile used by an individual for pleasure is a consumer good. The same automobile used in a business for delivery purposes is a capital good. When used for pleasure it is satisfying a human desire directly. When used for delivery service it is being used intermediately for the creation of additional wealth for its owner. It should be noted, furthermore, that the distinction between consumer goods and capital goods is not one of durability. Coal used by the manufacturer is a capital good, although it is spent with one use. The automobile mentioned above, when used for pleasure, is a consumer good even though it may yield satisfaction over a long period of time. On the other hand, a capital good in the form of a steam locomotive is relatively lasting, while a consumer good in the form of bread on the dining-room table is destined to be short-lived. Consumer goods are frequently classified according to their durability as: (1) durable, (2) nondurable, and (3) semidurable. See also ECONOMIC GOOD.

consumers' capital. See explanation under CAPITAL GOOD.

consumer sovereignty. The conception that consumers control economic life. If prices are higher than consumers will pay, demand will slacken and prices will fall; if prices are low, consumers will buy and thereby provide an incentive to producers to satisfy consumer wants at a profit. If a product is no longer wanted, producers will cease making it, and if a demand arises for a new product the prospect for profits will cause it to be produced. In such ways, according to this conception, the consumer is the ultimate ruler of economic life through his control of the market.

consumption. The utilization of services or material goods for the gratification of human desires. As thus defined "consumption" means the destruction of UTILITY and is one of the main topics customarily included in the study of ECONOMICS. In popular parlance "consumption" may also mean the use of goods and services for productive purposes as, for example, when it is said that raw materials are consumed in the finished product. See also CONSPICUOUS CONSUMPTION, INDUCED CONSUMPTION, UNPRODUCTIVE CONSUMPTION.

consumption tax. See CUSTOMS DUTY, EXCISE TAX.

continental bill. See explanation under BILL.

contingent asset. An amount on a book of ACCOUNT which may become an asset at some future time if conditions regarded as currently uncertain are fulfilled. See also ASSET.

contingent duty. See explanation under COUNTERVAILING DUTY.

contingent fund. See explanation under FUND.

contingent liability. An amount which may become a liability at some future time if certain specified events transpire or certain circumstances develop. See also LIABILITY.

continued bond. See explanation under BOND.

continuous market. A market in which a price for a commodity or stock is constantly established, thus enabling purchases and sales to be consummated at any time.

contract. A legally binding agreement between two or more parties in which, for a consideration, one or more of the parties agree to do or not to do a certain thing.

contract clause. A clause in the Constitution of the United States which specifies that no state may pass any law impairing the obligation of contracts.

contract labor. The practice of bringing persons from a foreign country under agreement to work for a particular employer. Contract labor is forbidden in the United States. See also LABOR.

contract rent. Payment for the use of land arrived at through the process of bargaining. The term is used to establish the fact that the actual rent paid, or contract rent, may differ from ECONOMIC RENT although the former always tends to approximate the latter. See also RENT.

contract research. An agreement to conduct, for a fee, some investigation of a scientific nature, often involving experimentation in some area of knowledge, the object being to discover new facts or procedures or to revise old ones. Most United States military research is carried on by contract with private firms. Universities often maintain institutes or departments which conduct research of various kinds for business establishments and governments.

Contract Settlement Act. An act of Congress, 1944, which established a procedure for adjusting claims against the United States government arising out of the government's termination of contracts made with suppliers during World War II. The act provided for an Office of Contract Settlement to adjust terminated contracts, according to policies and procedures prescribed by its director. The latter was assisted by a Contract Settlement Advisory Board and by an Appeal Board. Since 1949 the functions of the director, Advisory Board, and Appeal Board have been lodged in the GENERAL SERVICES ADMINISTRATION.

contract system. As applied to penal institutions, a contractual arrangement between a government and a private employer for the latter's use of convict labor. Work is done in the prison with materials furnished by the employer; supervision is provided by the prison authorities. Because of opposition by LABOR UNIONS and by employers competing with prison-made products, as well as agitation for more humanitarian and scientific correction methods, the contract system has been practically abolished in the United States, fewer than 1 per cent of convicts now being thus employed. See also CONVICT LEASE SYSTEM, PUBLIC WORKS AND WAYS SYSTEM, STATE USE SYSTEM.

contributory negligence. A common-law conception that carelessness on the part of an employee absolves the employer from responsibility in the event of an accident resulting in an injury to the employee. This has been modified in most states of the United States by WORKMEN'S COMPENSATION LAWS.

contributory pension. A pension for the benefit of employees, contributions to the cost of which are made by both the employer and the employees. See also PENSION.

control. Public regulation of some phase of economic life. There are many kinds of controls. Some of the more important are CREDIT CONTROL, EXCHANGE CONTROL, PRICE CONTROL, STANDBY CONTROLS.

controlled economy. An economy which is extensively regulated by government. Such an economy does not necessarily involve government ownership of the means of production, but it may embrace a certain amount of economic planning by government and a variety of public controls over such matters as credit, production, foreign trade, and the disposition of the labor force. Also called *directed economy*, *statism*.

controlling account. An account appearing in a general ledger summarizing detailed accounts carried in some other ledger. Thus, the general ledger may carry an accounts-receivable page showing the total of the balances in the customers' or accounts-receivable ledger. See also ACCOUNT.

controlling company. See HOLDING COMPANY.

conventional tariff system. A system of tariff duties which depends upon agreements with other nations and which is subject to change, therefore, as the agreements with the other nations are revised and altered. The term is used in contradistinction to AUTONOMOUS TARIFF SYSTEM. See also TARIFF.

conversion price. The price applicable to the stock of a corporation for which the holder of a convertible bond of the same corporation may exchange such bond. The conversion price is usually indicated at the time the bond is issued and may differ from the market price of the stock at the time the right of conversion is exercised. See also BOND, PRICE.

convertible bond. See explanation under BOND.

convertible money. Money which is redeemable in the standard money of the nation. See also MONEY, STANDARD MONEY.

convertible stock. See explanation under CAPITAL STOCK.

convict labor. See explanation under STATE USE SYSTEM.

convict lease system. A contractual arrangement between a government and a private employer for the latter's use of convict labor at so much per head, the private employer supplying materials, tools, food, housing, and supervision, as well as guards to preserve order and to prevent escape. The government is thus relieved of all financial responsibility for the penal population so engaged. Serious abuses developed under the system, and it has now been abolished in all states of the United States. See also CONTRACT SYSTEM, PUBLIC WORKS AND WAYS SYSTEM, STATE USE SYSTEM.

***Cooley* v. *Board of Wardens*.** A case, 12 Howard 299 (1851), in which the United States Supreme Court established the principle that states of the United States may make local regulations, such as pilotage regulations, affecting interstate and foreign commerce which are valid until such time as Congress chooses to supersede them.

cooling-off period. A provision in a labor agreement or a requirement of law that a specified interval of time shall elapse before any overt action is taken by either party to a labor dispute. The purpose is to provide time for amicable adjustment before resorting to economic pressure such as a strike.

co-operative bank. A bank organized on the plan of a consumer co-operative. In Massachusetts BUILDING AND LOAN ASSOCIATIONS are called co-operative banks. See also BANK, CONSUMER CO-OPERATIVE.

co-operative commonwealth. A society, the economic life of which is conducted entirely by consumer co-operatives. See also CONSUMER CO-OPERATIVE.

Co-operative Marketing (Capper-Volstead) Act. An act of Congress, 1922, which exempted bona fide co-operative associations from the operation of the federal antitrust statutes. The act encouraged farmers, ranchers, and growers to combine in such associations for the purpose of obtaining more efficient distribution of their products.

***Coppage* v. *Kansas*.** A case, 236 U. S. 1 (1915), in which the Supreme Court of the United States held invalid, as a deprivation of contractual liberty protected by the due process clause of the 14th Amendment, a Kansas statute which attempted to outlaw the so-called yellow-dog employment contract. In such a contract a person agrees that, if employed, he will not join a labor union and that he may be dismissed if he subsequently joins a union or is found to belong to a union. The decision in this case is almost identical with that of the earlier case of *ADAIR* v. *UNITED STATES* (*q.v.*), and the reasoning is similar. Legislation outlawing yellow-dog contracts has since been sustained by the courts.

copyright. An exclusive right conferred by a government upon a person or organization, for a term of years, to reproduce a literary or artistic creation, including a book, map, article, drawing, chart, photograph, or musical composition. The right thus granted may be enforced in the courts. In the United States the term of a copyright (1964) is 28 years with the right of renewal for the same length of time.

corner. As applied to stock-market trading, the possession of all or the major part of the available supply of a security. The object of a corner is to profit by advancing the price. The term has a similar meaning in the commodity markets.

corn laws. A term usually applying to the British regulations covering trade in grains, in force from 1436 to 1846. Heavy import duties were levied on grain imports for home consumption as long as the domestic price remained below a stipulated figure. Agitation against such regulations became particularly intense after 1837, and led to repeal of the laws. See ANTI-CORN-LAW LEAGUE.

Coronado case. A case, *United Mine Workers* v. *Coronado Coal Co.*, 259 U. S. 344 (1922), in which the United States Supreme Court ruled that where damages may be assessed against a labor union because of the operation of the Sherman Antitrust Act, a suit for recovery will be directly against the labor union. This decision thus changed the old common-law rule that a union was a partnership, that liability attached only to each individual member, and that when suit was brought it had to be brought against each member as an individual.

corporate stock. 1. The shares of the capital stock of a corporation.

See also CAPITAL STOCK. 2. The term is sometimes applied to the debt, or part of the debt, of New York and a few other cities in the United States which is held in the form of long-term municipal bonds secured by a SINKING FUND. See also BOND.

corporation. A body, created by law and consisting of one or more persons, which, within the scope of its charter, is treated in many respects as a natural person. Thus, a corporation, normally, may own property, incur debts, and sue and be sued in a court of law. There are many types of corporations, each type or class of corporation being governed by laws which normally apply only to that class. Occasionally referred to as *incorporation*. For some of the more important kinds of corporations see AGGREGATE CORPORATION, CIVIL CORPORATION, CLOSE CORPORATION, ECCLESIASTICAL CORPORATION, ELEEMOSYNARY CORPORATION, LAY CORPORATION, LIMITED-DIVIDEND CORPORATION, MUNICIPAL CORPORATION, PRIVATE CORPORATION, PUBLIC CORPORATION, QUASI CORPORATION, QUASI-PUBLIC CORPORATION, SOLE CORPORATION, WESTERN HEMISPHERE TRADE CORPORATION. See also FORMS OF BUSINESS ORGANIZATION.

corporation income tax. A tax levied upon the earnings of corporations. In the United States the rate of the tax increases as the volume of earnings increases. See also INCOME TAX.

correspondent bank. In the United States, a bank that carries on continuing mutually advantageous business and financial relations with a bank in some other locality. Although the advent of the FEDERAL RESERVE SYSTEM has reduced the role of correspondent banks, particularly in the matter of clearing checks, they still perform some collection services for one another, exchange information regarding local conditions, and, on occasion, lend and borrow surplus funds.

cost. As used in theoretical economics, the total payments made by an enterprise for capital, land, and labor, including management. These payments are made in the form of interest, rent, wages, and salaries. In most productive enterprises some proportion of each of these is absorbed in the cost of raw materials, hence the term *material cost* is commonly used. The total costs of an enterprise are frequently divided into VARIABLE COSTS and FIXED COSTS, the former necessarily increasing as production increases, the latter remaining constant or more nearly constant. In contrast to total costs, UNIT COST refers to the cost of a single unit of the product. As production increases the unit cost may remain constant, decrease, or increase. See CONSTANT COSTS, DECREASING COSTS, INCREASING COSTS. See also BULK-LINE COSTS, JOINT COSTS, MARGINAL

COST, OPPORTUNITY COST, SUNK COST, USER COST.

cost accounting. A system of ascertaining the total cost of a finished product. Individual items making up the total cost include raw material, labor applied directly to the raw material, and a proportionate amount of FIXED COSTS allotted to a finished unit of the product.

cost-of-living adjustment. A term designating an arrangement, included in some important labor contracts since 1948, whereby wages are increased or decreased in the same proportion as increases or decreases in an appropriate index of prices reflecting the living costs of the workers affected.

cost-of-production theory of value. The theory that makes the value of a product depend upon the amount of labor and the amount of time necessary to produce it. The theory is more comprehensive than the LABOR THEORY OF VALUE in that it includes in the value of the finished product the productive efficiency contributed by capital as well as the contribution of labor. The theory was set forth by David Ricardo in the early part of the 19th century. See also VALUE.

cost-of-service principle of taxation. The principle that taxes should be levied upon individual taxpayers on the basis of the cost to the government of the services rendered those individual taxpayers. The principle is quite impossible of application except in the case of charges for postal or electric power and light services, which are in the nature of prices rather than taxes. The cost of police or fire protection supplied one individual taxpayer may be much greater or less than the same services supplied some other taxpayer, but to determine just how much greater or less and to calculate the taxes accordingly is generally considered to be impracticable.

cost plus contract. A contract which, instead of setting a fixed selling price, permits the seller to charge whatever his costs may be plus a fixed percentage of that cost.

Council for Economic Mutual Assistance. An intergovernmental organization to counter the Marshall (European Recovery) plan, establishment of which was announced January 25, 1949. Consisting of Soviet Russia and various satellite countries, it is supposed to promote exchange of experience in the economic field, and the rendering of mutual assistance as respects technical knowledge, raw materials, foodstuffs, machinery, equipment, etc.

Council of Economic Advisers. A division of the executive office of the President of the United States, established under the authority of the Employment Act of 1946 to assist in the preparation of the

President's annual economic report to Congress and to recommend to the President measures and policies to promote the economic well-being of the nation. See also EMPLOYMENT ACT OF 1946.

counter check. A form of receipt for cash supplied by a bank to depositors who, having executed and signed it, use it to withdraw funds from their accounts in the bank supplying the receipt. A counter check is not negotiable. See also CHECK.

counterfeit money. Money made to resemble legal money and passed as such with the intent to defraud. Such actions are universally considered criminal. See also MONEY.

counterpart fund. A sum, in local currency, which each European country participating in the EUROPEAN RECOVERY PROGRAM was required to set aside to offset internally the gift of dollars made to that country by the Economic Cooperation Administration of the United States Government. With the consent of the latter body the sum thus set aside, roughly the equivalent of three-fourths of the dollar value of the United States gift to the country in question, was subsequently released to that country for internal investment in public works or for other approved purposes.

countervailing duty. A duty levied by an importing country as a protective surtax to offset an EXPORT BOUNTY paid by the exporting country. The term is also applied to a tariff duty levied on imported goods when the country of origin levies duties on similar goods imported by it. Such a duty is sometimes called a *contingent duty*. See also CUSTOMS DUTY.

countervailing excise duty. See COMPENSATORY DUTY.

country bank. See explanation under CENTRAL RESERVE CITY BANK.

county agent. An individual employed jointly by the Department of Agriculture of the United States, a state LAND-GRANT COLLEGE, and a county government to make available to farmers and their families the results of agricultural research adapted to local needs and conditions, to encourage improved practices in farm operations and home maintenance, and to act as a source of help and guidance to the local farmers in their relationships with the various agricultural credit and operational services available to them. County agents are now stationed in nearly all the agricultural counties in the United States, the men being known as *county agricultural agents* and the women as *home-demonstration agents*. In addition there is frequently a 4-H Club agent who carries on educational and recreational activities among the farm youth.

coupon bond. See explanation under BOND.

covenant. An agreement between two or more persons, or one of the stipulations in such an agreement.

craft guild. A medieval association of artisans that enjoyed a virtual monopoly in the production of articles identified with its craft. The guild maintained certain standards of quality in the output of its members and sought to guarantee standards of workmanship and to preserve its monopoly by appropriate regulations concerning apprenticeship and admission to its ranks. See GUILD.

craft union. A labor union composed of workers in one skilled trade or in two or more closely allied skilled trades. Also called *horizontal labor union.* See also LABOR UNION.

credit. 1. A promise of future payment in kind or in money given in exchange for present money, goods, or services. See also BANK CREDIT, COMMERCIAL CREDIT, CONSUMER CREDIT, INVESTMENT CREDIT, RESERVE BANK CREDIT, STORE CREDIT. 2. An entry on the right or credit side of an account in a DOUBLE-ENTRY system of BOOKKEEPING. See also ACCOUNT.

credit bill. See explanation under BILL.

credit card. A document indicating that the person to whom it is issued is entitled to credit. Credit cards are frequently issued by companies to their customers gratuitously. Similar cards are issued by finance companies to whom bills are sent for purchases of goods or services from any of a large number of suppliers, one consolidated monthly charge being made to the person to whom the card is issued. An annual fee is charged by the finance company for such service.

credit control. Any policy designed to expand or contract credit, such a policy being applied by government, banks, or other appropriate agencies according to the economic conditions that obtain at any particular time. Credit may be controlled to a certain extent by changing the REDISCOUNT RATE, or by lowering or increasing the requirements for BANK RESERVES. An advance in the rediscount rate of the federal reserve banks in the United States, for example, may discourage loans because of the higher interest charges, and this contracts credit. Conversely, a reduction in the rediscount rate may encourage loans and thus expand credit. Likewise, higher bank reserves may discourage loans and contract credit, whereas lower bank reserves may encourage loans and expand credit. Such credit policies affect the volume of DEPOSIT CURRENCY; and the volume of deposit currency, in turn, affects the PRICE LEVEL, this being governed in part by the volume of currency in circulation. Hence, credit control may be regarded as one means of controlling prices. See also CONTROLS, PRICE CONTROL.

Crédit Mobilier. In the United States, a joint-stock company organized in 1863 in Pennsylvania, originally for the purpose of conducting a general credit and contract business. It was reorganized in 1867 under this name for the specific purpose of building the Union Pacific Railroad. Charges of corruption among its officers and of alleged bribes offered to members of Congress by representatives of the company brought about its collapse.

credit money. See FIDUCIARY MONEY.

creditor. One to whom a debt is owed.

creditor nation. A nation whose international trade and finance is such that the total amount owed to its government, private business, and banking interests from foreign sources exceeds the sum owed to foreign creditors. In other words, a nation which regularly enjoys a creditor position in its BALANCE OF PAYMENTS.

credit rating. A rating given a business establishment by a mercantile agency indicating that establishment's record of performance in meeting its financial obligations and its ability to meet such obligations in the future.

credit theory of the business cycle. The theory that the volume of economic activity is primarily dependent upon the ebb and flow of bank credit. According to this theory, expansion of bank credit inflates prices, enhances business activity, and expands employment. When, on the other hand, prudence and the canons of safe banking policy dictate retrenchment, the economy enters upon a deflationary phase to the accompaniment of falling prices, declining business activity, and decreased employment. See also BANK CREDIT, BUSINESS CYCLE.

credit union. A co-operative organization which makes small loans to its members for personal needs. Shares in the organization are usually sold for about $5, and members may buy as many shares as they wish. Applications for loans are considered by a designated committee. Most credit unions are chartered under state laws; others are chartered by the federal government under the provisions of the Credit Union Act of 1934. See also CONSUMER CO-OPERATIVE.

Crime of 1873. A derogatory term applied to the action of the United States government, taken in 1873, to discontinue the free coinage of silver dollars. The term did not come into use until some time after that event. At the time the silver dollar was discontinued as standard money, silver was undervalued at the mint, and none of that metal was being delivered for coinage. After 1873, however, during a period of depression and falling prices, a strong agitation developed for legislation which would increase the money in circulation. It was then that the action of the government in demonetizing silver some years earlier was termed the "Crime of 1873."

critical material. See explanation under STRATEGIC MATERIALS.

crop insurance. Insurance against loss of certain crops owing to unavoidable hazards. In the United States such insurance is provided by the FEDERAL CROP INSURANCE CORPORATION, and applies to 10 individual crops as well as a combined crop-protection plan. Nearly one third of the nation's agricultural counties now (1964) participate in the crop-insurance program.

cross-elasticity. The effect of a change in price of one commodity or service on the sales of a substitute commodity or service. For example, an increase in the price of fuel oil might engender an increase in the sales of coal. For examples of commodities that have such a competitive effect, see COMPOSITE SUPPLY. See also COEFFICIENT OF CROSS-ELASTICITY.

cross of gold. A phrase used by William Jennings Bryan (1860–1925) at the Democratic National Convention held at Chicago in 1896. The GOLD STANDARD versus BIMETALLISM or the FREE COINAGE of silver at fixed ratios with gold was the political issue at the time. A faction in the Democratic party, under the leadership of David B. Hill of New York, was opposed to FREE SILVER but was voted down after Bryan had delivered the oration in which he said in part, "You shall not press down upon the brow of labor this crown of thorns. You shall not crucify mankind upon a cross of gold."

cross picketing. Picketing by two or more rival unions, each claiming to represent the employees of the establishment being picketed. See also PICKETING.

cross-rate. The rate of exchange between two CURRENCIES calculated by reference to the rates of exchange between each and a third currency. For example, in April, 1952, CABLE TRANSFERS for pound sterling were quoted at $2.8079 in New York, and equivalent transfers for the Mexican peso were quoted at $0.11569. The cross-rate between pound sterling and the Mexican peso was, therefore, 1 pound sterling for 24.271 Mexican pesos, as contrasted with the par rate established by the INTERNATIONAL MONETARY FUND of 24.220.

crude birth rate. See explanation under BIRTH RATE.

crude death rate. See explanation under DEATH RATE.

culture lag. The condition which exists when changes in ideas and practices pertaining to political, social, and economic life fail to keep pace with physical changes in the environment caused by mechanical invention, technological innovation, depletion of essential natural resources, or similar circumstances.

cum rights. A term describing corporate stock offered with the privilege of purchasing a limited number of shares of a new issue of such stock. STOCK RIGHTS (*q.v.*) are offered to stockholders of record as of a certain date. A person buying the stock of the corporation before this date will therefore receive the stock rights. Stock offered at that time is said to be offered "cum rights." The term is used in contradistinction to EX RIGHTS.

cumulative dividend. A dividend which, if not paid, becomes a liability of a corporation and must be paid in subsequent years before any dividends are paid on the common stock. Sometimes called *accumulative dividend.* See also DIVIDEND.

cumulative stock. See explanation under CAPITAL STOCK.

cumulative voting. As applied to corporate elections, a method of voting which permits each stockholder as many votes as the number of shares of stock he holds, as shown on the records of the corporation, multiplied by the number of directors to be elected. The stockholder may group, or cumulate, his votes and cast them all for one candidate, or he may distribute them among two or more candidates.

curb exchange. The name, previous to 1953, of the American Stock Exchange operating at 86 Trinity Place, New York, N. Y. It was originally organized before the Civil War, and for many years conducted its trading in the open street—hence the term. In 1921 the curb exchange opened its own building.

curb stock. See explanation under CAPITAL STOCK.

currency. Anything that serves as a medium of exchange whether of general or limited acceptability. Hence, besides *cash* or MONEY, this term includes checks drawn on bank accounts, postal money orders, express checks, and other similar instruments which, while not enjoying the general acceptability of money because they usually require identification of maker or indorser, are nonetheless important as media of exchange in the business world. Indeed it is by means of bank checks rather than money that most business transactions are carried out. See also DEPOSIT CURRENCY.

currency bond. See explanation under BOND.

current asset. An asset which is temporary in character and hence will be transformed or converted into cash within a relatively short period of time, usually a year. In financial statements current assets are usually listed according to the degree of liquidity; for example, cash, BILLS RECEIVABLE, ACCOUNTS RECEIVABLE, and INVENTORY. See also ASSET.

current liability. A liability which is due within a comparatively short length of time. See also FLOATING DEBT, LIABILITY.

current ratio. In a BALANCE SHEET, the proportion of total CURRENT ASSETS to total CURRENT LIABILITIES. If the current assets are $6,000 and the current liabilities $4,000, the current ratio is 1½ to 1. Current ratio is frequently used as one test to determine CREDIT RATING.

Current Tax Payment Act. An act of Congress, 1943, which requires certain employers to deduct legally stipulated percentages from the gross total of employees' wages and salaries at the time such wages or salaries become due and payable, and to remit the amounts deducted to the Internal Revenue Bureau of the United States Department of the Treasury. The deductions thus made on behalf of any employee constitute a credit against that employee's federal income-tax liability and are considered as such when the employee executes his formal tax return for any tax period. The deductions are sometimes improperly called a *withholding tax.* Actually, they are simply a means of keeping tax payments current; that is, of collecting a tax liability as soon as it becomes such.

current yield. The annual return on an investment expressed as a percentage of the principal sum. Thus, if the return is $20 per annum on an investment of $1,000, the current yield is 2 per cent.

custodian account. An arrangement whereby a bank, in return for a fee, provides for the safekeeping of securities and the collection of income and principal therefrom. The bank also executes purchase and sales orders as directed by the owner of the securities, rendering him an account of all transactions and providing him with such other services as may be called for in the custodian agreement.

customhouse. The building where import and export duties are paid. If located in a seaport, vessels are entered and cleared at the customhouse.

customs. See CUSTOMS DUTY.

customs broker. An individual, licensed by the Treasury Department of the United States who, in return for a fee, handles for importers the details of clearing goods through the customs.

Customs, Bureau of the. A service of the Department of the Treasury of the United States which administers the affairs of the department in relation to the importation and exportation of merchandise into and out of the United States. Its principal responsibilities are the assessment and collection of import duties, the prevention of smuggling, and the enforcement of various regulations affecting vessels used in foreign trade.

customs duty. A tax levied upon goods transported from one political jurisdiction to another. In the United States the term refers particularly to a tax levied on imported goods. It is sometimes referred to as a *consumption tax.* For particular kinds of customs duties see AD VALOREM DUTY, ANTIDUMPING DUTY, COMPENSATORY DUTY, COMPOUND DUTY, COUNTERVAILING DUTY, DIFFERENTIAL DUTY, RETALIATORY DUTY, SPECIFIC DUTY. See also DUTY, TARIFF.

customs union. An agreement between two or more political jurisdictions to abolish customs duties and other trade restrictions among themselves, and to adopt a common policy regarding trade with political jurisdictions outside of the union. Sometimes referred to as *tariff union.*

cutback. As applied to labor relations, the laying off of workers because of a sudden cessation of work.

cutthroat competition. Intense competition which results in losses and which is often intended to eliminate one or more business rivals, the losses being recouped later by relatively high prices. Such competition, when entered into with an intent to create a monopoly or from sheer malice, may be illegal. Also called *rate war.* See also COMPETITION.

cybernetics. The study of control and communication functions in animals and in mechanicoelectrical systems. The term was first used in 1947 by Norbert Weiner, Professor of Mathematics, The Massachusetts Institute of Technology, and by Dr. Arturo Rosenblueth, then of Harvard Medical School. It is derived from the Greek word meaning "steersman" and from the Latin corruption of that word meaning "governor."

cyclical fluctuations. More or less periodic variations in a time series caused by forces generating a BUSINESS CYCLE. There are various statistical methods for estimating cyclical fluctuations in a time series. The appended diagram shows an estimate of the extent to

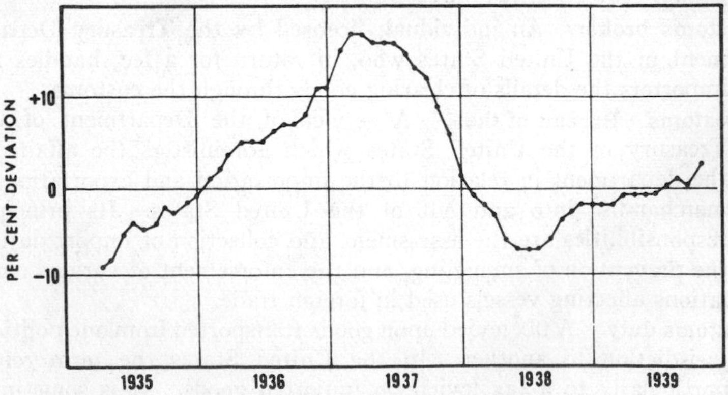

which BANK DEBITS in the United States, outside of New York City, between 1935 and 1939, inclusive, reflected the minor business cycle recorded for those years. The curve may be computed by calculating the SECULAR TREND using the LEAST-SQUARES METHOD, ascertaining the SEASONAL FLUCTUATIONS, and correcting the trend values accordingly. The results are then subtracted from the original data and the differences are expressed as percentages of the corrected trend values. The curve is finally smoothed by means of a five-item MOVING AVERAGE. For the original data, see TIME-SERIES CHART.

cyclical unemployment. Unemployment attributed to the deflationary phase of a business cycle. See also BUSINESS CYCLE, UNEMPLOYMENT.

D

Danbury Hatters' case. A case, *Loewe* v. *Lawlor*, 208 U. S. 274 (1908), in which the United States Supreme Court ruled that a general boycott instituted by a labor organization against the product of an employer prevented him from engaging in interstate commerce and was therefore a violation of the Sherman Antitrust Act. The decision thus applied the Sherman Act to the activities of labor organizations when such activities affected directly and substantially the flow of commerce between the states. The provisions of the Clayton Act subsequently modified this ruling.

Dawes plan. A plan, put into effect in 1924, designed to make possible the payment of reparations owed by Germany to the Allied nations under the terms of the Treaty of Versailles. The plan included: (1) progressively higher payments by Germany each year for a period of 5 years and payments thereafter on the basis of a prosperity index; (2) stabilization of German currency and a balanced budget; (3) a foreign loan to Germany; (4) international control of Germany's financial affairs; and (5) the eventual withdrawal of Allied troops from occupied German territory. The plan was named for General Charles G. Dawes, chairman of the reparations committee that formulated the plan. In 1929 it was superseded by the YOUNG PLAN.

days of grace. See GRACE PERIOD.

Dayton-Goose Creek Ry. Co. v. United States. A case, 263 U. S. 456 (1924), in which the United States Supreme Court upheld the so-called "recapture provisions" of the Transportation Act of 1920.

These stipulated that half the earnings in excess of a fair return be set up as a separate fund by each railroad and the other half be remitted to the Interstate Commerce Commission for its general railroad revolving fund. The court stressed that the recapture provisions constituted the heart of a plan for the general betterment of the railroads which Congress had set up in the act and pointed out that what was recaptured was not a taking of property since the railways were entitled only to a fair return and not to the excess. The court also rejected the argument that the recapture provisions interfered with the power of the states to fix returns on intrastate commerce, asserting that, in the Transportation Act, Congress had to treat the railways of the country as a unit and that, in so doing, its power extended to the necessary incidental control of intrastate commerce.

deadheading. 1. As used in the transportation industry, the movement of empty cars, busses, or trucks to a given destination, or the practice of furnishing free transportation to employees of a transportation company. 2. As applied to labor relations, the promotion of a junior employee in preference to another who has seniority rights but is deemed incapable of filling the higher position satisfactorily.

dead rent. A fixed annual sum paid for a mine or a quarry, in addition to payment of royalties which vary in amount according to the yield. See also RENT.

dead time. Time lost through no fault of the employee and for which he is usually paid at the full rate. Time lost because of machine breakdowns or delays in delivery of material are examples.

dear money. A term used to describe a condition when the general price level is low. At such a time a relatively large quantity of goods or services exchanges for a relatively small quantity of money; hence, money is dear, or its value is high compared with the value of goods and services. The term is also used to indicate high interest rates. See also MONEY.

death rate. The number of deaths per 1,000 persons in any given area during the period of a year. This is called the *crude death rate.* If corrections are made to allow for differences in the composition of the population, for example the number of people in various age groups, the crude death rate becomes a *refined death rate.* The number of deaths per 1,000 children 1 to 10 years of age would be a refined death rate.

death sentence. As applied to legislation regulating public-utility companies, a provision of the PUBLIC UTILITY HOLDING COMPANY

ACT, passed by Congress in 1935, which required individual holding companies in the public-utility field to simplify corporate structures by eliminating, not later than 1938, complicated networks of subsidiary and operating companies servicing extensive geographical areas.

debasement. As applied to coinage, the reduction of the amount of precious metal contained in the standard MONETARY UNIT.

debenture bond. See explanation under BOND.

debenture certificate. A customhouse document authorizing a rebate on duties paid on imported goods which are destined to be exported. A debenture certificate may also authorize the payment of money granted as a BOUNTY to an exporter of certain domestic goods.

debenture stock. See explanation under CAPITAL STOCK.

debit. An entry on the left or "debit" side of an account in double-entry bookkeeping.

Debs case. A case, 158 U. S. 564 (1895), growing out of the Pullman Strike of 1894. Because of alleged interference by strikers with the United States mails and interstate commerce, the United States secured a writ from the federal circuit court in Chicago enjoining the strikers from interfering with these federal interests. Eugene Debs, as leader of the strikers, refused to obey the injunction, was subsequently held in contempt, and punished by fine and imprisonment. On Debs' appeal to the Supreme Court, that body declared that the federal government could use the entire strength of the nation to protect its interests, and that this broad authority included the lesser authority of securing injunctive relief from the courts. The decision was a factor in the subsequent demand of organized labor for a statute which would restrict the courts' power to issue injunctions in labor disputes and to try persons without a jury in cases of contempt. This demand led to the enactment in 1932 of the ANTI-INJUNCTION ACT.

debt. Whatever is owed to one person or organization by another. The obligation may involve money, goods, or services. See also FLOATING DEBT, FUNDED DEBT, NATIONAL DEBT, PRIVATE DEBT, PUBLIC DEBT.

debt limit. As applied to public finance, a constitutional or legislative provision sometimes imposed upon a state or a municipal government limiting its authority to borrow funds to a certain specified sum, to a fixed per cent of the assessed value of the taxable property within its jurisdiction, or in some other manner restricting its borrowing capacity.

debt monetization. The procedures by which United States government SECURITIES, representing the NATIONAL DEBT, are made to increase the CURRENCY in circulation. Debt monetization occurs in several ways: (1) DEPOSIT CURRENCY is credited to the government by certain COMMERCIAL BANKS in payment for government securities purchased by them; (2) CHECKS in payment of government securities purchased by the FEDERAL RESERVE BANKS in OPEN-MARKET OPERATIONS are deposited in federal reserve banks to the credit of MEMBER BANK RESERVES, which adds to the capacity of member banks to create deposit currency or to draw FEDERAL RESERVE NOTES; (3) the PROCEEDS of LOANS, secured by government securities, made to member banks by federal reserve banks are credited to member bank reserves, which also adds to the capacity of member banks to create deposit currency or to draw federal reserve notes; (4) the amounts represented by the limited quantity of government securities that the federal reserve banks purchase directly from the United States Treasury are credited to the government's deposit account.

These operations are affected by: (1) legislation by the Congress and regulations by the Board of Governors of the FEDERAL RESERVE SYSTEM which determine BANK RESERVES; (2) legislation by the Congress establishing the ratio of GOLD CERTIFICATES to federal reserve bank deposits and federal reserve notes issued; (3) the policy pursued by the United States Treasury in reference to STERILIZED GOLD; and (4) the policy of the government relating to the national debt, especially the kind of securities (short- or long-term, degree of NEGOTIABILITY, etc.) in which the debt is expressed.

debtor. One who owes a debt.

debtor nation. A nation whose international trade and finance is such that the total amount which its government, private business, and banks owe to foreign creditors exceeds the sum due from foreign debtors. In other words, a nation which chronically has a debtor position in its BALANCE OF PAYMENTS.

debt service. Payment of the interest on a debt and of such installments of the principal as are legally due. Normally, the term is used in connection with a public debt. See also DEBT.

decentralization. As applied to industry: (1) the establishment of factories away from large cities and at some distance from one another—the policy applying to a single company or to an industry in general; (2) a technique of organization in large business enterprises whereby units of the business representing separate products, common functions, or stages of process are given a large measure of autonomy, only general guidance and major decisions affecting the enterprise as a whole being reserved for central management.

decile. See explanation under QUARTILE.

declining-marginal-efficiency-of-capital theory. The theory emphasized by Keynesian economists that when, at a given rate of consumption, more and more productive plant and equipment are established, the rate of return on new and existing capital equipment declines. Also referred to as the *falling-rate-of-profit theory.* See also MARGINAL EFFICIENCY OF CAPITAL.

decreasing costs. Costs which, under a given set of conditions, decrease, per unit of product, as the total production increases. The savings brought about by mass production, by interchangeable parts, and by division of labor have resulted in a condition of decreasing costs. See also COST.

decreasing returns. See DIMINISHING RETURNS.

dedication. A voluntary gift of private property to some political jurisdiction; for example, a right of way or a park. The owner thereby relinquishes forever the right to the property in question.

deductive method. A process of logical reasoning starting with a premise generally accepted as true and arriving at one or more conclusions based on such a premise. This method was widely used by the CLASSICAL SCHOOL and later challenged by the HISTORICAL SCHOOL. The usefulness of the method depends upon the validity of the basic assumptions, and many times these have been found to be faulty. When properly used, however, it has a recognized place in scientific investigation.

deed. A written document setting forth an agreement, particularly an agreement involving the transfer of property, the document being duly signed, sealed, and delivered. Commonly the term refers to a document transferring the ownership of real property.

defalcation. Misappropriation of money or property, especially by an agent or officer holding such money or property in trust.

Defense Production Act. An act of Congress, 1950, which authorizes STAND-BY CONTROLS for the nation's economy. The President is permitted to use these controls at his discretion. Imposition of selective PRICE CONTROLS was made contingent upon the simultaneous establishment of WAGE CONTROLS in those industries producing the commodities directly affected by the price controls. On a stand-by basis, the act authorized consumer and real-estate CREDIT CONTROLS, the requisitioning of materials and property essential for national defense, reduction in the civilian use of critical materials, potential measures against hoarding, and the RATIONING of consumer goods. Some of these powers were placed in effect during the late summer of 1950. Since 1953 their administration has been confined chiefly to the Business and Defense Services Administration of the Department of Commerce.

deferred annuity. An annuity which begins only after a specified period of time has elapsed following its purchase or other arrangements for its payment. Deferred annuities are often provided for in life-insurance policies. See also ANNUITY.

deferred bond. See explanation under BOND.

deferred demand. Demand necessarily postponed because of a scarcity of goods and services. See also DEMAND.

deferred income. See UNEARNED INCOME.

deficit. A deficiency usually expressed in money. On books of account it is the amount necessary to balance an asset and liability statement when the liabilities exceed the assets.

deficit financing. Large-scale expenditure of borrowed funds to meet some unusual or emergency situation requiring such expenditure or making such expenditure desirable. The term is used popularly to describe a governmental policy of alleviating a business depression by heavy expenditure of funds secured by expanding the public debt. This is often called *compensatory spending* because it is argued that the policy of government borrowing and spending may increase general purchasing power to such an extent as to compensate for the decline of private borrowing and spending to which the depression may be attributed.

definitive. A term used to denote a permanent stock certificate or bond issued to replace an existing document because of some change in the corporation involved, particularly a change affecting the corporation's financial structure.

deflation. A decrease in the general price level. Deflation may occur when the quantity of MONEY or DEPOSIT CURRENCY in circulation is small compared with the quantity of goods and services offered, or when fear of the future or some other cause curtails consumer spending materially, thus reducing the velocity of circulation. See also DISINFLATION.

deflationary gap. A statistical phrase denoting the amount by which the theoretical volume of spending necessary to maintain full employment or to absorb all available goods and services at prevailing prices exceeds actual private spending and government expenses.

degressive taxation. A form of PROGRESSIVE TAXATION in which rates increase as the base amount taxed increases, but in which each addition to the tax rate is less than the preceding one. A tax system in which a rate of 1 per cent is applied to a base of $1,000,

$2\frac{1}{2}$ per cent to a base of $10,000, $3\frac{3}{4}$ per cent to a base of $100,000, and $4\frac{1}{4}$ per cent to a base of $1,000,000 is an example. It might be said that, in a completely degressive tax, each addition to the tax rate, being less than the preceding one, might conceivably always approach zero but never reach it. For all practical purposes, however, a tax that proceeds as described above, even though a constant rate is applied after a certain limit in the base has been reached, is a degressive tax.

del credere agreement. An agreement sometimes entered into by exporters with an agent in a foreign country. Such an agent guarantees payment for goods shipped to a buyer and receives an extra commission for this service.

delinquent tax. A tax that remains unpaid after the date when payment is due. In most cases penalties are imposed for short- and long-term delinquency. In the case of a delinquent property tax, the resulting tax lien on the property in question may, after a prescribed interval, be foreclosed and, through such proceedings, the property may revert to the taxing authorities. See also TAX.

demand. 1. The quantity of an economic good that will be bought at a given price at a particular time. Demand in this sense is sometimes called *market demand.* For example, if at a particular time 100 units of an economic good can be sold at $5 and 200 units at $4, it is said that the market demand for the good is 100 at $5 and 200 at $4. 2. The term may also be defined as the quantity of an economic good that will be bought at all possible prices at a particular time, often referred to as the total, or *schedule, demand.* In the following table the schedule demand for a good is indicated for various prices at two different periods:

Price	First-period Demand	Second-period Demand
$5	100	200
4	200	300
3	300	400
2	400	500
1	500	600

It will be noted that, during the interval between the first and second periods, the total or schedule demand increased; that is, there was an increased demand for the good at all prices. These two schedule demands are represented by lines a — a′ and b — b′ in the appended diagram.

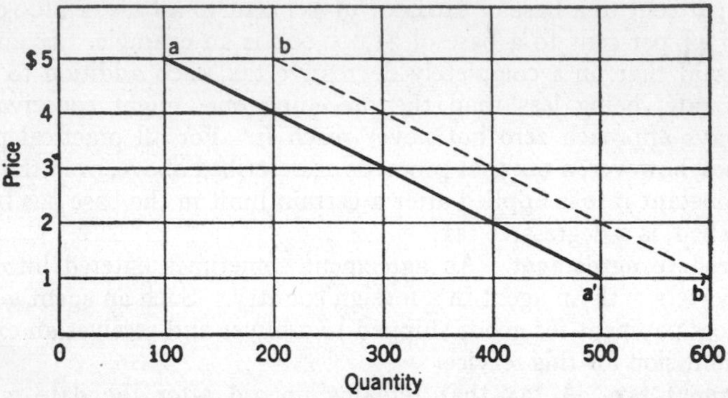

See also COMPOSITE DEMAND, DEFERRED DEMAND, DERIVED DEMAND, EFFECTIVE DEMAND, ELASTIC DEMAND, INELASTIC DEMAND, JOINT DEMAND, POTENTIAL DEMAND, REPLACEMENT DEMAND.

demand-and-supply curves. A graphic representation of the maximum buying and minimum selling prices offered and acceptable to traders in a specific commodity at a particular time and place, and the resulting market price. In the appended graph, which indicates a market price of 12, the horizontal axis represents quantities, and the vertical axis, prices, as follows:

Quantity Demanded	Prices	Quantity Offered
5	10	1
4	11	2
3	12	3
2	13	4
1	14	5

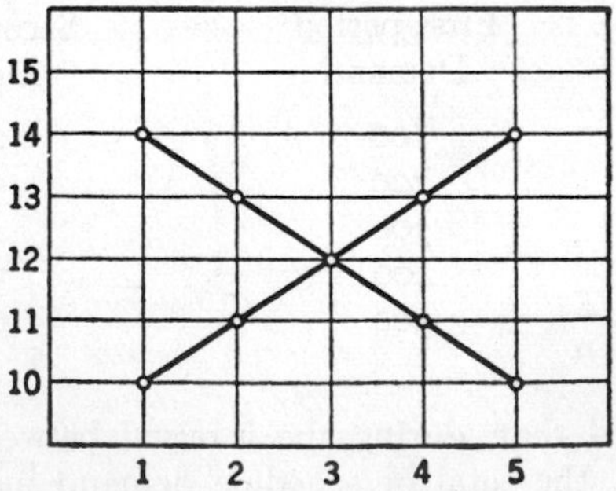

demand bill. See explanation under BILL.

demand deposit. A bank deposit subject to withdrawal at any time. See also BANK DEPOSIT.

democratic socialism. A somewhat vague term by which is meant a policy of reconciling a modified degree of socialism, particularly national economic planning and some nationalization of industry, with parliamentary political processes and the maintenance of traditional civil liberties.

demonetization. **1.** The removal of certain currency from circulation. **2.** The discontinuance of the monetary unit of a nation the value of which was previously defined in terms of a precious metal. The STANDARD MONEY made of that metal is then said to be demonetized, but it may continue to circulate as FIDUCIARY MONEY.

demurrage. A charge made by a transportation company for holding freight cars or lighters beyond a stipulated period while being unloaded.

denominational value. The face value of coins, paper money, and securities of various kinds. See also PAR VALUE, VALUE.

department. For official and other agencies in which "department" is the first word of the title, see under descriptive title of agency, e.g., AGRICULTURE, DEPARTMENT OF.

depletion allowance. A deduction from taxable income derived from a WASTING ASSET. The Internal Revenue Code of the United States permits the calculation of depletion allowances either on the basis of a percentage of the gross income from the property in question, or on a per unit-of-product basis. Depletion differs from DEPRECIATION in that the asset subject to depletion cannot be replaced. Thus a mine or an oil field cannot be replaced in the sense that a factory or a machine can.

depositary. A person or establishment entrusted with the safekeeping of money, valuable papers, or property. The term usually refers to a bank, a trust company, or a safe-deposit vault. It may also refer to a warehouse. For depositaries of United States government funds, see GENERAL DEPOSITARY, LIMITED DEPOSITARY, SPECIAL DEPOSITARY.

deposit currency. The proceeds of a bank loan which have been credited to a depositor's account and made subject to withdrawal by check. The effect of many such transactions is to supplement money with "check" or "deposit currency" and thereby expand greatly the amount of currency in circulation. Loans creating such "deposit currency" are secured by the borrowers' resources or particular securities deposited as collateral, and the repayment of the loan has the effect of retiring the deposit currency which it created. See also CURRENCY.

deposit insurance. Insurance against the loss of deposits in a bank. Such insurance, up to $10,000, is provided in the United States in member banks of the Federal Reserve System and in some approved nonmember state banks. The insurance is afforded by the FEDERAL DEPOSIT INSURANCE CORPORATION established by authority of the BANKING ACT of 1933. The corporation's original capital was subscribed jointly by the United States government and the federal reserve banks. Additional funds are obtained through assessments on the insured banks amounting to $\frac{1}{12}$ of 1 per cent annually of their total deposits. See also INSURANCE.

deposit slip. A printed form supplied by banks to their depositors and filled in by them when making deposits. The form provides spaces for recording the amount of bills (paper money), specie, and the amount of each check.

depreciation. A decrease in value because of wear and tear through use, action of the elements, inadequacy, accident, or obsolescence.

depression. A period of low business activity when prices are low, purchasing power sharply curtailed, and unemployment high.

derivative deposit. A bank deposit created by a loan or by the deposit of funds in anticipation of the repayment of a loan. Some writers do not include within the meaning of the term deposits made in anticipation of the payment of a loan. As defined, the term distinguishes all credits to a deposit account which are directly offset on the bank's books of account by an asset such as a United States bond or a promissory note. Thus, deposits are derivative whether just created by a loan and as yet unused, or, having been used, are replaced by funds held on deposit and earmarked for the payment of the loan. See also BANK DEPOSIT, DEPOSIT CURRENCY.

derived demand. The demand for a commodity which grows out of the desire to satisfy the demand for some other commodity. The demand for a house, for example, may create a demand for lumber, bricks, and many other things needed to build the house. See also DEMAND.

descriptive economics. Economic studies which explain and describe existing economic phenomena without necessarily attempting to make logical deductions as to their cause and effect. See also ECONOMICS.

descriptive labeling. See explanation under GRADE LABELING.

desterilized gold. See explanation under STERILIZED GOLD.

destructive competition. Competition that forces prices to so low a level that satisfactory service or commodities cannot be offered the public, and sufficient revenue cannot be realized by the competitors properly to maintain their properties. Destructive competition is likely to develop when there are only a few competitors, when their fixed expenses are high compared with their variable expenses, and when a slight reduction in the selling price will attract a large volume of business. Such conditions exist frequently in local public-service companies and often lead to a NATURAL MONOPOLY (*q.v.*). See also COMPETITION.

devaluation. As applied to a monetary unit, a reduction in its metallic content as determined by law. In 1934, for example, the gold content of the United States dollar was reduced from 25.8 to $15\frac{5}{21}$ grains $\frac{9}{10}$ fine. The term may also apply to the lowering of the value of one nation's currency in terms of the currencies of other nations. Such values or exchange rates are often determined arbitrarily irrespective of whatever actual values exist, and may, therefore, be changed at will.

devise. A gift of real property provided for in a will.

diagonal expansion. Expansion of a business establishment by developing new products which can be manufactured by using the equipment ordinarily employed in the production of an established product or which contain much the same raw materials as the established product. The discovery of by-products is frequently the cause of diagonal expansion.

differential duty. A duty of different amounts imposed upon identical commodities according to the source of those commodities or according to some other factor unrelated to the nature of the commodities themselves. Sometimes called *discriminating duty* or *preferential duty*. See also CUSTOMS DUTY.

diffusion theory of taxation. The theory that the burden of any kind of tax is ultimately distributed throughout the population by means of price changes or by some other method of passing a tax, in whole or in part, on to other persons, by the person who actually pays it to the government.

digital computer. An electronic device which, through a system of multitudinous electrical switchlike devices, manipulates data in accordance with a prearranged program, permitting or preventing the passage of various combinations of electrical charges to which meanings have been assigned. Computation is usually accomplished by the automatic conversion of decimal notation to some version of BINARY NOTATION (*q.v.*) which uses only the two digits, 0 and 1. An open switch represents 0, and a closed switch represents 1. Repeated electrical impulses open and close these switches. At any particular time, then, these switches represent some combination of zeros and ones, or a binary number which the machine automatically reconverts to the decimal system. Similarly, in manipulating logical data, an open switch represents "no" and a closed switch represents "yes." Switches wired in series represent "and"—no current can flow unless all are closed. Two switches wired in parallel represent "or"—if either is closed, current can flow. Digital computers are usually linked with other machines. Input machines feed information and instructions into the computer by means of punched cards or punched or magnetic tape. Output machines record the results by means of an electrical typewriter or some similar device. Collectively, the machines are called an *electronic data-processing system.*

diminishing productivity. See explanation under DIMINISHING RETURNS.

diminishing returns. The condition which exists when, in successively applying equal amounts of one or two factors of production (land, labor, or capital) to the remaining factor or factors, an added application yields a lesser increase in production than the application just preceding. The condition may be illustrated by the following table.

Land and Capital Constant

Labor (Number of Men)	Total Production (Bushels)	Production Increase (Bushels)
1	10	10
2	21	11
3	32	11
Point of Diminishing Returns		
4	42	10
5	51	9
6	59	8

Sometimes the term is restricted to cases where land is the constant factor. The term *diminishing productivity* is then used to describe cases where capital or labor is the constant factor. In any case there is some ideal relationship among the factors of production that will produce optimum returns. See also PROPORTIONALITY,

diminishing utility, law of. See explanation under MARGINAL UTILITY.

Dingley Tariff. The United States Tariff Act of 1897. It increased protective rates, removed raw sugar from the FREE LIST, and reincorporated the RECIPROCITY PRINCIPLE.

direct cost. See VARIABLE COST.

directed economy. See CONTROLLED ECONOMY.

direct financing. Raising capital by a direct appeal to investors, without resort to underwriting. See also UNDERWRITING.

director. As applied to business corporations, one of the stockholders who is elected to serve on the managerial board, called the *board of directors*, of the corporation.

director of internal revenue. The person in charge of one of the district offices of the Internal Revenue Service of the United States Treasury. To facilitate the collection of internal revenue, there are 58 (1964) district offices in the United States.

direct production. The satisfaction of a human want without the intervention of capital goods of any kind. The construction of shelter from stones, snow, or the boughs of trees without the use of tools is direct production. The term is used in contradistinction to INDIRECT, *roundabout*, or *capitalistic* PRODUCTION. See also PRODUCTION.

direct strike. A strike by employees against their own employer because of allegedly unsatisfactory wage scales or other grievances. See also STRIKE.

direct tax. A tax, the burden of which cannot be easily shifted or passed on to some other person by the person on whom it is levied. The term is used in contradistinction to INDIRECT TAX. It is usually very difficult to determine when a tax is direct. A tax on a mortgage, for example, may seem to be a direct tax but might conceivably be shifted to the borrower in the form of a higher interest rate. Personal income, inheritance, and poll taxes are fair examples of direct taxes. See also TAX.

disability benefits. Payments made to assist those who have become partly or totally incapacitated as a result of accident or illness or other cause. Most states of the United States have long had provision for WORKMEN'S COMPENSATION. Under the federal government's social-security legislation, states with an appropriate plan may receive federal assistance in making "public assistance payments" to incapacitated persons. Such assistance may be extended to needy disabled persons 18 years of age or over on the same basis that aid is extended to the needy aged, to the blind, and to needy and dependent children. Some private companies have agreed in labor contracts to provide disability benefits for their employees.

discount. 1. A deduction made from a debt or charge, such as an amount deducted from a bill for prompt payment. 2. The amount deducted from the face value of a promissory note or similar commercial paper for cashing it previous to the date of maturity. **3.** The difference between the face value of a bond and the market price when the face value is the higher.

discount house. See COMMERCIAL CREDIT COMPANY.

discounting the news. An explanation frequently given for an advance or decline in security prices preceding good or bad news. Presumably a sufficient number of traders anticipate the news and make decisions which are reflected on the security markets before the news becomes generally public.

discount market. An indefinitely defined financial center where individuals, banks, and financial institutions of various kinds buy and sell commercial and financial paper. For example, a time DRAFT (*q.v.*), accepted by a bank, is considered a prime bill for funds seeking short-term employment and hence can be converted into cash immediately at a discount from its face value when offered in the discount market. See BILL.

discretionary trust. See GENERAL MANAGEMENT TRUST.

discriminating duty. See DIFFERENTIAL DUTY.

discriminatory taxation. Taxation designed to favor certain industries. Excise taxes on margarine, for example, have been used to protect dairy interests. Likewise, special taxes on corporations, chartered outside a state in which they are doing business, have benefited local industry, and special taxes on CHAIN STORES have benefited independent merchants.

disguised unemployment. The condition said to exist in a densely populated country with a nonmonetary, peasant economy when, with no change in production techniques, a material reduction in the agricultural working force would cause no reduction in the total volume of farm output. Although no one is idle, large numbers are engaged in tasks that could be equally well performed by fewer workers. Technically expressed, the MARGINAL PRODUCTIVITY (*q.v.*) of labor is zero.

dishoarding. Taking something out of storage and putting it to use; for example, taking money from a safe-deposit box and investing it. The term is often applied to the act of reducing a stock of goods that was intended, when accumulated, to exceed normal future needs.

disinflation. A term recently coined to indicate a planned reduction in the general PRICE LEVEL, so administered that the economy is benefited by increased purchasing power and not harmed by drastic DEFLATION.

disinvestment. A diminution of CAPITAL GOODS. The term is used to designate either an absolute diminution in the total supply of capital goods such as occurs when producers fail to renew worn-out items or when INVENTORIES are reduced, or a diminution in a particular stock of capital goods caused, for example, by the sale of a capital item. It is sometimes called *negative investment.*

dismal science. A term of derision applied to political economy by Thomas Carlyle.

dismissal wage. A sum of money paid to an employee who is dismissed from employment. The payment may be made in one lump sum or at intervals over a period of time. Also called *severance wage* and *terminal wage.* See also WAGE.

disposable income. The income remaining to persons after deducting personal taxes and all other payments to the government.

dissaving. Expenditure in excess of income.

distribution. 1. The apportionment of the total income of society among the factors of production. As thus defined, distribution is one of the main topics customarily included in the study of ECONOMICS. Among the subjects included under "distribution" are INTEREST, PROFIT, RENT, and WAGES. Sometimes called *functional distribution.* See also FACTORS OF PRODUCTION. 2. The apportionment of the total income of a society among individuals. Sometimes called *personal distribution.* 3. The diffusion of commodities through the ordinary channels of trade. Also called *physical distribution.*

disutility. The ability of a good to cause discomfiture or pain. For example, while one increment of a commodity, such as water, may save a life, and successive increments may satisfy wants ranging in intensity from the more to the less essential, a time arrives when an added increment is not wanted, and after such a point has been reached, further increments may cause distress or disutility.

diversification. As applied to the purchase of securities, the investment of a capital sum in various kinds of securities, in different localities, and in different industries, in order to minimize risk.

dividend. A payment to the stockholders of a corporation from earnings. See also ACCUMULATED DIVIDEND, CUMULATIVE DIVIDEND, EX DIVIDEND, OPTIONAL DIVIDEND, SCRIP DIVIDEND.

divisional bond. See explanation under BOND.

division of labor. A plan of production whereby each of several workers, in succession, performs only one or a very limited number of operations on a product until it is finally completed. See also LABOR.

documentary bill. See explanation under BILL.

dole. Relief in cash or IN KIND given by a government body to unemployed workers or to families in needy circumstances.

dollar deficit. See DOLLAR GAP.

dollar exchange. Bills of exchange drawn for a specified number of United States dollars whether actually paid in dollars or in the equivalent in other currency. The term is also used to indicate the condition which exists when the dollar is used as the basis of exchange in place of the pound sterling or some other national MONETARY UNIT.

dollar gap. In any given period, the amount by which imports from the United States into any foreign area, and other dollar debits in such area, exceed that area's exports to the United States and other dollar credits. Also called *dollar deficit.*

domestic bill. See explanation under BILL.

domestic industry. See HOUSEHOLD SYSTEM.

domestic system. An economy prevalent in the 16th and 17th centuries in which merchants supplied materials and sometimes tools and machines to workers who produced goods at home and turned the finished products over to the merchants. Also called *home industry.*

donated stock. See explanation under CAPITAL STOCK.

double budget. A popular term for any plan to segregate capital and nonrecurring items in a budget from recurring items of income and expense. Such a plan was recently advocated for the United States federal budget. See also CAPITAL BUDGET.

double entry. A system of bookkeeping which provides two entries, a debit and a credit, for each transaction. Debit entries record increases of assets or of expenses or reductions of liabilities or of income; credit entries record increases of liabilities or of income or reduction of assets or of expenses. In double-entry bookkeeping the sum of the debits must always equal the sum of the credits. See also BOOKKEEPING.

double liability. The liability assumed by a stockholder of a corporation when the stock that he owns may be assessed up to an amount equal to its face value to pay the debts of the corporation. See also LIABILITY.

double standard. See BIMETALLISM.

double taxation. The levy and collection, within one fiscal period, of two taxes both of which are calculated on the same tax base. Double taxation may occur because two competing tax jurisdictions assess the same tax base, or because the same tax jurisdiction assesses the same tax base twice. In the United States the first condition exists when both federal and state taxes are imposed upon estates and inheritances or upon incomes. The second condition may be said to exist when federal income taxes are levied upon corporation profits, once when earned by the corporation in question, and again when received by the stockholders in the form of dividends. The result of such double taxation is the same as though one tax were imposed equal in amount to the two that are imposed. A levy on the same tax basc by state and federal governments, though double taxation in fact, is not so recognized in legal theory because the taxing authorities are constitutionally separate and independent entities. The term is often used to indicate an alleged injustice as, for example, when a person living in one state owns property in another and is compelled to pay taxes on the property to both states, one of them claiming jurisdiction over the property because of the property's situation, the other because of the residence of the owner of the property. Such situations, which create double taxation within the United States, may also exist internationally and result in double taxation by the action of two or more sovereign states.

down period. A period in which a factory is shut down for repairs and maintenance.

downtown. A term used to designate, rather indefinitely, the relatively old, main business district of any sizable town or city. Originally used only when referring to a generally recognized business center in a specific town or city, the term has become generalized, particularly when differentiating older business centers from new SHOPPING MALLS located on the outskirts of the more populous areas.

Dow theory. A method of determining major trends in stock prices, but not their extent or duration. The theory was developed by Charles H. Dow.

draft. A written order for a definite sum of money, originating with a creditor and naming a debtor, customarily forwarded to a bank for collection. Upon receipt of a draft, the bank presents it to the debtor for approval. If approved, the order is then called an ACCEPTANCE and is executed by the bank, the original document being returned to the debtor as a receipt. *Sight drafts* are payable at once. *Time drafts* are payable at some future time specified on the document.

drawback. A refund made for duties or internal taxes collected on imported goods which, not being intended for domestic consumption, are reshipped to other nations.

drayage. A charge made for carting goods from one place to another.

drummer. A salesman, usually one who solicits trade for a merchant by showing samples; so called because he "drums up" trade.

dry farming. In general, all phases of land use under semiarid conditions. Water is brought to the semiarid regions by irrigation, and various methods of conserving moisture are used. For example, the moisture may be allowed to accumulate one season for use during the following one. Thus, a crop is produced every other season.

dual pay system. A method of computing the wages of employees in transportation companies by the mile and also by the hour, the employee being entitled to receive wages according to whichever calculation yields him the greater sum.

dummy incorporators. Usually at least three persons who, in the course of the formation of a new corporation, act temporarily as the incorporators and directors, later resigning and assigning their interest to the real owners. The practice is one of convenience to the real owners as it relieves them of the necessity of attending personally to all the details necessary to the formation of a new corporation.

dumping. Selling a product in a foreign market below the price for which the same product is sold in the domestic market. This practice may be pursued by a monopoly when a large volume of production materially lessens the unit cost of the product, and when, because of the large production, the price of the product would be materially reduced if sold entirely in the domestic market. By restricting the supply offered in the home market and thus gaining the maximum price on that part of the supply, the producer may sell the balance of the supply abroad at a lesser price and still gain larger gross sales and conceivably more profits than he would gain if the entire supply were sold at home. The term is also used to indicate the practice of promiscuous price cutting to dispose of INVENTORIES. See also MONOPOLY.

duopoly. The condition that exists when only two producers offer identical or nearly identical products. Although there is some element of COMPETITION in the fact that neither producer controls the entire supply, and the action of one producer can materially influence the other's price, the resulting situation approximates a MONOPOLY and is sometimes called a *partial monopoly.* An OLIGOPOLY results in a similar situation although it is less monopolistic. See also MONOPOLISTIC COMPETITION.

duosony. The condition that exists when there are only two buyers for identical or nearly identical products offered by numerous producers. See also MONOPOLISTIC COMPETITION.

***Duplex Printing Co.* v. *Deering*.** A case, 254 U. S. 443 (1921), in which the Supreme Court of the United States implied that provisions of the Clayton Antitrust Act, which purported to remove labor activities from the operation of the Sherman Antitrust Act, were largely illusory. The court held that the Clayton Act merely restated existing law on the subject; that it was merely "declaratory of the law as it stood before."

Dutch auction. An auction in which the seller offers goods at a relatively high initial price and then successively lowers his prices until the goods are sold.

duty. A tax imposed on the importation, exportation, or consumption of goods. In the United States the term has come to mean a CUSTOMS DUTY. See also TAX.

dynamic economics. See explanation under GENERAL EQUILIBRIUM.

E

eagle. As applied to money, a United States $10 gold coin, first placed in circulation in 1794. None was coined between 1805 and 1837. In 1933 all gold coins were required to be surrendered to the United States Treasury in return for other forms of money. The $20 gold coin was called a double eagle, the $5 gold coin a half eagle, and the $2.50 gold coin a quarter eagle.

earmarked gold. Gold owned by the central bank of one country and stored in the central bank of another country. Such gold is not considered a part of the monetary reserve of the country where it is stored but is held subject to ultimate disposition by the owning central bank.

earned income. Income which is received in return for services rendered or as the result of trading or some other similar business transaction. The term is used in contradistinction to UNEARNED INCOME. See also INCOME.

earned surplus. Profits of an enterprise that remain undistributed and which have been gained through the regular operations of the enterprise in question. See also SURPLUS.

earning asset. A term applied to certain interest-bearing investments held by the United States federal reserve banks. Such investments may include the secured notes of member banks, notes discounted for member banks and for other federal reserve banks, various acceptances, and, under certain conditions, United States bonds, certificates, and notes. See also ASSET.

earning-capacity standard. As applied to the valuation of a corporation's capital assets, the fixing of their value by finding a principal sum which, at an assumed rate of interest, will yield an amount equivalent to the earnings of the corporation. Virtually identical with CAPITALIZED-VALUE STANDARD. See also VALUATION.

easement. Any one of a number of rights which may be possessed by one person in the real property of another.

Eastern States Retail Lumber Assn. v. United States. A case, 234 U. S. 600 (1914), in which the Supreme Court of the United States, relying on its ruling in the DANBURY HATTERS' CASE (*q.v.*), declared that a black list of certain wholesalers, circulated among retailers to persuade them not to deal with the black-listed wholesalers, was a conspiracy in restraint of interstate commerce and thus came within the interdiction of the Sherman Antitrust Act.

ecclesiastical corporation. A corporation created for religious purposes and consisting usually of churchmen or ecclesiastical persons. See also CORPORATION.

econometrics. Economic measurement for the purpose of testing and developing economic theory. See also ECONOMICS.

economic. A term applicable to any action or process which has to do with the creation of goods or services designed to satisfy human wants. More specifically the term is used to characterize the production of goods and services by the most effective means and in accordance with existing technical knowledge.

Economic and Social Council. An agency of the United Nations which deals with economic, humanitarian, educational, and related functions entrusted to the United Nations, and which co-ordinates the activities of various specialized agencies such as the INTERNATIONAL LABOR ORGANIZATION and similar bodies. See also UNITED NATIONS.

Economic Commission for Asia and the Far East. An organization created by the ECONOMIC AND SOCIAL COUNCIL of the UNITED NATIONS to further economic reconstruction in Far Eastern areas. At its first session in June, 1947, steps were taken to ascertain the essential reconstruction needs of the countries in question. Consideration was given to the training of administrators and technical personnel, and an examination was made of the obstacles to the free exchange of goods among the countries falling within the Commission's geographical jurisdiction.

Economic Commission for Europe. An organization created by the ECONOMIC AND SOCIAL COUNCIL of the UNITED NATIONS in 1947 to further the economic reconstruction of Europe and to strengthen economic relations among European countries and between those countries and the rest of the world. The commission succeeded the Emergency Economic Committee for Europe and was authorized to absorb the activities of the European Coal Organization and the European Central Inland Transport Organization. The first session of the commission was held at Geneva during May, 1947.

economic determinism. The idea that social evolution is the result of economic forces.

economic friction. The condition that obtains when obstacles of a social or psychological nature prevent the normal operation of economic forces. Custom, prejudice, likes, and dislikes are examples of such obstacles.

economic good. Anything external to man that is inherently useful, appropriable, and relatively scarce. The term is used in contradistinction to FREE GOOD. Economic goods may be either material or immaterial. Thus, the services of a teacher or lawyer are considered economic goods quite as logically as the books that they use. As thus defined the term is more comprehensive than the term WEALTH, the latter, as defined in this dictionary, being restricted to material economic goods. See also CAPITAL GOOD, CONSUMER GOOD, GOOD, IMPROVED GOOD, PUBLIC GOOD, REPRESENTATIVE GOOD.

economic harmonies. The forces that contribute to the welfare of society as a whole when each individual pursues his own self-interest. According to Adam Smith such forces were supernatural. Thus, he says that man is "led by an invisible hand to promote an end which was no part of his intention."

economic imperialism. The extension of the sovereignty or influence of a nation over foreign territory and peoples for the purpose of obtaining raw materials, creating markets for finished products, or seeking profitable investment opportunities.

economic independence. See ECONOMIC SELF-SUFFICIENCY.

economic interpretation of history. History written from the point of view that economic conditions and events exert a predominant influence in shaping mankind's institutions and civilizations. See ECONOMIC DETERMINISM.

economic law. A generalization expressing a constant relationship among particular economic phenomena. Because of the complexity of such phenomena and the impossibility of isolating the effects of any one economic force from the effects of multitudinous other such forces operating in society, economic laws are either very general in scope as, for example, the law of SUPPLY AND DEMAND or GRESHAM'S LAW; or they are generalizations expressing varying degrees of probability. The term is often misused, being applied to some popular nostrum or unproved assertion or to some generalization to which there are many obvious exceptions.

economic liberalism. See CLASSICAL SCHOOL.

economic man. A hypothetical man moved only by economic motives. This was a concept created by the English economists of the Classical school and subject to criticism because of the broad generalizations based upon this restricted premise. The German Historical or Realist school of economic thought particularly opposed the concept as devoid of any practical application. See also CLASSICAL SCHOOL, HISTORICAL SCHOOL.

economic mobilization. Any effort to focus the productive energies of a nation upon some major objective such as national defense or the successful prosecution of a war. The effort may be voluntary in some respects. Normally, however, the government must intervene with legislation affecting production, credit, prices, employment, etc.

economic nationalism. See SELF-SUFFICIENT NATION.

economic planning. Any attempt to exercise forethought with reference to an economic operation and to anticipate the scope, character, and results of such an operation. Currently the phrase signifies governmental direction of economic activity. It may imply determination by some supreme governmental authority of both the kind and quantity of economic goods to be produced in a nation. It may also be used to indicate some measure of foresight and action exercised by the government in a capitalistic society particularly to offset disastrous depressions. The construction of public works to provide employment, the reduction of taxation to increase private purchasing power, or the use of the public debt to influence credit are examples of such limited planning.

economic rent. A theoretical amount paid for the use of land, representing the difference in the productivity of one plot of land and the productivity of the poorest land similarly situated and used for the same purpose, the assumption being that equal increments of capital and labor have been expended on each. Thus, if the poorest land can produce 25 bu. of grain per acre, and a better piece of land can produce 50 bu., the economic rent for the better land, in terms of money, is 25 times the market price of the grain per bushel. "Productivity" may also be expressed in different degrees of fertility, in varying distances to market, or, particularly in the case of urban land, in relative desirability of location, either for business or for living purposes. Also called the *Ricardian theory of rent.* See also RENT.

economic royalist. A man of wealth; a member of the plutocracy President Franklin D. Roosevelt used the term in a disparaging sense in his 1936 acceptance speech in which he identified men of wealth as opposed to his policy of improving the economic status of the rank and file.

economics. That body of knowledge which treats of the creation and appropriation of goods and services for the satisfaction of human wants. Some authorities emphasize the social aspects of such activities by including in the definition of economics the communal problems or social phenomena involved in the process of getting a living. Economics customarily includes the topics CONSUMPTION, DISTRIBUTION, EXCHANGE, and PRODUCTION. A few of the more important main divisions and approaches to the subject are APPLIED ECONOMICS, AGRICULTURAL ECONOMICS, CONSUMER ECONOMICS, DESCRIPTIVE ECONOMICS, ECONOMETRICS, INSTITUTIONAL ECONOMICS, INTERNATIONAL ECONOMICS, MACROECONOMICS, MATHEMATICAL ECONOMICS, MICROECONOMICS. See also ECONOMIC SYSTEM, SCHOOLS OF ECONOMIC THOUGHT.

economic sanctions. Coercive measures of an economic nature adopted in international affairs to enforce collective decisions or to compel a refractory nation to abide by international law. Article 16 of the Covenant of the League of Nations imposed obligations upon member nations to adopt coercive measures, including the economic boycott, to prevent aggression. In 1935 economic sanctions in the form of an arms embargo, financial embargo, and trade restrictions were imposed by the League upon Italy in an unsuccessful attempt to prevent that nation's invasion of Ethiopia. Article 41 of the United Nations Charter also anticipates the use of economic sanctions.

economic self-sufficiency. The production within a particular geographical area of everything that is consumed within that area. The area may be a farm, a community, a nation, or any other limited territory. Complete self-sufficiency is impossible, even for countries of considerable territorial extent and diversified resources, except on the basis of a relatively low LEVEL OF LIVING. Also referred to as *economic independence*.

economic system. The nature of economic life as a whole, proposed or actual, with particular reference to the ownership and use of property and the extent of government regulation and controls. For the different kinds of existing economic systems and some of the important ones proposed, see ANARCHISM, CAPITALISM, COLLECTIVISM, COMMUNISM, FASCISM, SOCIALISM, SYNDICALISM. See also ECONOMICS.

economic union. An agreement between two or more nations involving the pursuance of common economic policies in such matters as customs duties, fiscal and monetary regulations, internal taxation, and related subjects.

economic warfare. Economic activities designed to embarrass an enemy in time of war; for example, acquiring control of the supply of essential materials in neutral countries, bringing pressure upon those countries to restrict their trade with the enemy, or blockading the enemy territory to prevent the entrance of essential supplies.

economic wealth. See explanation under WEALTH.

economy of abundance. The condition that exists when the price structure and general purchasing power are such as to keep the productive facilities of an economy operating at capacity. Occasionally the term is used to describe a hypothetical condition when all wants are satisfied.

economy of scarcity. The condition that exists when purchasing power, available at prevailing prices, is insufficient to keep the existing productive facilities for consumer goods working at capacity. Occasionally the term is used to describe the fact that, in a price economy, goods are necessarily distributed according to ability to pay, there never being enough goods or ability to acquire them to satisfy all wants.

Edge Act. An act of Congress, 1919. It amended the FEDERAL RESERVE ACT so as to permit federal incorporation of organizations desiring to engage in international banking operations. Such organizations are sometimes called *Edge banks.*

Edge banks. See explanation under EDGE ACT.

educational tariff. A system of tariff duties that protects a new home industry, presumably until that industry is able to compete on equal terms with imported products. See also INFANT INDUSTRY, TARIFF.

effective demand. The desire to buy coupled with the ability to pay. When the word "demand" is used in economic writings, effective demand is usually assumed. See also DEMAND.

efficiency engineer. One whose profession it is to study production methods and controls with a view to eliminating waste and establishing more effective procedures.

elastic demand. Demand which increases or decreases in relatively large volume as prices increase or decrease. In general the demand for luxuries is elastic. See also COEFFICIENT OF ELASTICITY, DEMAND.

elastic money. Money the quantity of which can be increased or decreased as general economic conditions may require. In the United States FEDERAL RESERVE NOTES may be regarded as an elastic money. Their issue is related to the volume of REDISCOUNTS. Federal reserve notes are retired when the issuing bank deposits them with the FEDERAL RESERVE AGENT, and when so deposited they cannot be reissued except upon compliance with the conditions of an original issue. See also MONEY.

elastic supply. Supply which increases or decreases in relatively large volume with a relatively slight change in price. See also COEFFICIENT OF ELASTICITY, SUPPLY.

electronic data processing. The manipulation of information by machines capable of performing various sequences of logical and arithmetical operations through the use of vacuum, gas, or phototubes and other devices governing the behavior of currents of free electrons. See ANALOG COMPUTER, DIGITAL COMPUTER.

electronic data-processing system. See DIGITAL COMPUTER.

eleemosynary corporation. A corporation conducting charitable or alms-giving activities exclusively. See also CORPORATION.

eligible paper. As applied to sec. 13 of the FEDERAL RESERVE ACT of 1913, PROMISSORY NOTES, BILLS, and other SECURITIES acceptable for REDISCOUNT or for COLLATERAL LOANS at the FEDERAL RESERVE BANKS.

embargo. Any prohibition imposed by a government upon commerce or freight. In 1807, for example, the United States government restricted the carrying of goods, destined for foreign ports, to certain approved ships. The term may also be applied to the refusal of transportation companies to accept or move freight in case of a strike or because of undue traffic congestion.

embezzlement. Appropriation for personal use of property belonging to another. It differs from theft in that the misappropriated property is legally in possession of the guilty party, whereas in theft its possession is acquired illegally.

eminent domain. The right of a government, apart from its taxing power and police authority, to appropriate private property for the use of the public upon the payment of proper compensation ascertained according to law.

emolument. Remuneration in the form of a salary, fee, or perquisite of some kind.

Empire preference system. A term applied to the international trade policy of Great Britain in granting certain concessions to imported Empire-produced goods. The traditional free-trade policy of Great Britain was abandoned in 1932 with the adoption of an extensive tariff schedule and, in the case of some imports, of a quota system. The policy of Empire preference was greatly extended following the Ottawa conference held during the same year. See also OTTAWA AGREEMENTS.

Employees' Compensation, Bureau of. A unit of the United States Department of Labor which administers WORKMEN'S COMPENSATION LAWS for the benefit of the federal government's civilian employees and for certain private employees, particularly those engaged in maritime pursuits.

employers' associations. Various kinds of local, state, and national organizations of employers, designed to promote their joint interests in matters other than those having to do with any particular trade or business. Employers' associations sometimes seek to resist the policies and activities of labor organizations in one way or another. Other associations attempt to further the principle of COLLECTIVE BARGAINING. Some carry on propaganda campaigns by means of advertising, newspaper articles, and even textbooks. Employers' associations should not be confused with TRADE ASSOCIATIONS (*q.v.*).

employers' liability insurance. Insurance covering employers' liability occasioned by industrial accidents to their employees. See also INSURANCE.

employers' liability laws. See WORKMEN'S COMPENSATION LAWS.

employment. Engagement in an occupation, business, trade, or profession.

Employment Act of 1946. An act of Congress, February 20, 1946. Its purpose is to maintain high levels of employment and production. To secure these ends the act directs the President to make an annual report to Congress on the general economic condition of the nation and include in such report his recommendations for remedial legislation. To assist the President in preparing this report and to provide him with expert advice on economic conditions, the act set up a COUNCIL OF ECONOMIC ADVISERS (*q.v.*).

Employment Security, Bureau of. A unit of the United States Department of Labor which supervises the payment of federal grants-in-aid to such states as establish acceptable UNEMPLOYMENT-INSURANCE plans. It also supervises public employment agencies and provides appropriate statistical data.

emporium. A commercial center, place of trade, or store where a variety of merchandise is sold.

enclosures. See explanation under AGRICULTURAL REVOLUTION.

end money. A reserve fund set aside for use in the event that the actual costs of a project exceed estimates. The term is used with particular reference to the production of motion-picture films.

endogenous change. As applied to economics, an alteration in economic life due to a cause that is in itself essentially economic in character. OVERPRODUCTION owing to lack of PURCHASING POWER is a case in point. See also EXOGENOUS CHANGE.

endorsement. See INDORSEMENT.

endowment fund. See explanation under FUND.

endowment plan of life insurance. A plan according to which a life-insurance company agrees to pay a stipulated sum of money upon the death of an insured person or when he reaches a certain age, usually 65 or 70 years, in return for a fixed annual premium for a maximum number of years, usually from 15 to 30 years. See also LIFE INSURANCE.

end product. The product that results after a series of changes in form or assembly, and which is then ready for use directly or indirectly to satisfy a human want.

Engel's law. The assertion that the lower the family money-income, the greater the percentage of that income spent for food; and that the percentage of family income spent for food is therefore the best measure for determining levels of living. Engel's law has frequently been interpreted to include other types of expenditure, but there is some question as to the validity of this broader interpretation.

entail. A legally prescribed order of succession applied to inherited lands. The owner of the land at any particular time is not permitted to change the order, or to terminate it by sale or by any other of the usual means of transferring title.

entrepreneur. A person who, in the course of production, assumes the responsibilities of organization, management, and risk.

entrepreneurship. See MANAGEMENT.

equalization fee. A fee collected from some or all of the beneficiaries of a project the proceeds of which are apportioned among those who benefit the least. The term is applied particularly to a provision in the MCNARY-HAUGEN BILL, twice vetoed by President Coolidge, 1927, which proposed, through an equalization fee, to compensate farmers for losses sustained from dumping surplus products aboard.

equalization of assessments. The adjustment of assessed valuations of real properties over a considerable area such as a county or a state with a view to establishing a more equitable division of the total tax burden within the area. See also ASSESSMENT.

equation of exchange. A mathematical expression of the modern version of the QUANTITY THEORY OF MONEY. As formulated by Irving Fisher, the equation is: $P = \frac{MV + M'V'}{T}$. P represents the general PRICE LEVEL, or the average price of all goods and services exchanged within a given period of time. M represents the amount of MONEY IN CIRCULATION, and M' the amount of money substitutes, such as CREDIT, in circulation during the same period of time. V represents the velocity of money circulation, and V' the VELOCITY OF CIRCULATION of money substitutes during the period, that is, the number of times that a unit of money or a money substitute changes hands. T represents the volume of trade, or the total number of units sold during the period. This is frequently called the *cash-transactions* type of equation because involved in the velocity of circulation is the CURRENCY turnover among all individual spenders, and included in the volume of trade are all the units sold even if sold over and over again in the course of their progress toward final CONSUMPTION.

In contrast to the above cash-transactions type of equation, the income-flow type limits V to EXCHANGES of finished products involving both money and money substitutes, and T to units which constitute only final goods and services. M represents both money and money substitutes in use. The income-flow equation thus indicates the income VALUE of money in contrast to the transaction value of money. It may be written: $P_y = \frac{MV_y}{T_y}$, the y distinguishing it from the cash-transactions type of equation shown above.

Another version of the equation of exchange is the cash-balance type. This is similar to the income-flow type except that there is a different measure for velocity. Velocity is measured by the average length of time that cash balances — both money and money substitutes — are held idle. It may be indicated by K, and expressed as a period of time, usually a fraction of a year. Thus if $K = \frac{1}{12}$, cash balances are being held in sufficient volume to purchase goods and services for $\frac{1}{12}$ of a year, or 1 month. There is a reciprocal relationship between K and the V used in the other two equations. When K is high, V is low because currency is being held idle and not circulated. Conversely, when K is low, V is high because currency is being circulated instead of being held idle. The cash-balance type of equation thus indicates the value of money in terms of the demand for, and the supply of, cash balances. It may be written: $P_y = \frac{M_y}{KT_y}$.

equimarginal principle. See MARGINAL RATE OF SUBSTITUTION.

equipment trust bond. See explanation under BOND.

equitable asset. An asset in the hands of an executor of an estate that can be used for the payment of a debt only through the operation of an equity court; traditionally, an asset which, under common law, could not be used in payment of certain obligations. The term is used in contradistinction to LEGAL ASSET. See also ASSET.

equity. 1. The net value of a property obtained by subtracting from its total value all liens or charges against it. The term is frequently applied to a common stock because the common stock of a corporation represents such assets as remain after all obligations of the corporation have been met. 2. Also a system of law developed by the English courts of chancery.

equity trading. The practice of increasing the earnings of an enterprise by borrowing funds at a rate of interest less than the rate of profit which can be earned by such borrowed funds when applied to the normal operations of the enterprise. A corporation may, for example, be assured of a 6 per cent return on any and all funds invested or applied to its operations. Its existing capital and surplus amount to $100,000 and its total profit would thus be $6,000. But if it can borrow $100,000 at 4 per cent, total profit can be increased by an additional 2 per cent on the amount borrowed, or $2,000.

Erdman Act. An act of Congress, 1898. It provided for the conciliation of labor disputes between the railroads and such of their employees as were engaged in the operation of interstate trains. The act also made it a misdemeanor for any employer to require an employee to agree not to become a member of a labor union. This latter provision was declared unconstitutional by the Supreme Court in 1908. See also *ADAIR v. UNITED STATES.*

escalator clause. 1. A clause frequently inserted in leases during a period of public rent control, allowing the landlord to raise the rent under certain legally recognized conditions. 2. Generally, any clause in a contract which permits a change upward in the obligations incurred, in case certain events transpire, for example, a clause in a labor-management contract which calls for an increase in wages as the cost-of-living index advances or because of some other circumstance.

escape clause. A clause in a labor contract permitting employees in an establishment making the contract with a labor union about 15 days in which to resign from the labor union before the provisions of the contract requiring union membership go into effect.

Esch-Cummins Act. An act of Congress, 1920. It provided for the division of the country into railroad rate districts and for the establishment of rates that would make it possible for the railroads, collectively in each district, to earn a fair return. It provided for the disposition of earnings in excess of a FAIR RETURN and for the valuation of all railroad properties. The act also permitted the consolidation of railroads under certain conditions. Also known as the *Transportation Act* of 1920. See also RECAPTURE OF EARNINGS.

escrow. Property placed by one person in the hands of a second person, usually a trust company, for the delivery to a third person upon the fulfillment by the latter of certain specific obligations.

essential industry. A term used in the United States during World War II to indicate an industry considered necessary to the successful prosecution of war.

estate. Specifically, the nature and extent of a person's interest in real property. The term is frequently broadened, however, to include personal property.

estate tax. A tax, usually progressive in character, levied upon the gross estate of a deceased person previous to its division. The term should not be confused with an INHERITANCE TAX. See also TAX.

Euclid* v. *Ambler Realty Co. A case, 272 U. S. 365 (1926), in which the United States Supreme Court established the constitutionality of comprehensive zoning ordinances; that is, legislation restricting the use of land in designated areas for business, industrial, or residential purposes.

Euromarket. See EUROPEAN ECONOMIC COMMUNITY.

Euromart. See EUROPEAN ECONOMIC COMMUNITY.

European Coal and Steel Community. An essentially supranational arrangement entered into by Belgium, France, (West) Germany, Italy, Luxembourg, and the Netherlands on September 10, 1952, designed to create a single market for coal and steel comprising the six participating states. The agreement envisaged the eventual elimination of tariffs and other trade restrictions among the participants, as well as the abrogation of private cartels, marketing agreements, national subsidies, and legally established wage and price levels applicable to the industries in question, and the establishment of a common customs frontier.

European Economic Community. An association of 6 European countries, created January 1, 1958, for the purpose of eventually abolishing tariff barriers within their borders, establishing common import duties for products originating elsewhere, and establishing other common economic policies believed to be of benefit to the members. The association is composed of Belgium, France, (West) Germany, Italy, Luxembourg, and the Netherlands. On January 1, 1959, the first planned tariff reduction of 10 per cent was put into effect among the participants. Also known as *Common Market, Euromarket, Euromart.*

European Free Trade Association. A trade association composed of Austria, Britain, Denmark, Norway, Portugal, Sweden, and Switzerland, established between December 29, 1959, and January 4, 1960, when the pact was signed in each nation's capital. The object of the association is "to strengthen the economies of its members by promoting expansion of economic activity." A 20 per cent reduction of internal import duties on certain commodities took effect July 1, 1960. The Association plans to eliminate all internal import duties by 1969. Also known as the *Outer 7*.

European Monetary Agreement. An arrangement made by the OEEC states in December, 1958, following the expiration of the EUROPEAN PAYMENTS UNION and the attainment of currency convertibility among 10 of the more important OEEC members. Special agreements were made for the eventual liquidation of existing debit balances incurred under the EUROPEAN PAYMENTS UNION. Subscriptions, largely on a stand-by basis, were made to a new European Monetary Fund, to finance temporary clearing of debit balances, and provision was made for the eventual clearing of all debit balances in gold, or the equivalent, in order to prevent the accumulation of excessive balances in favor of a particular country, such as developed under EPU, that of Germany having amounted to approximately $1 billion vis-à-vis other OEEC states in December, 1958.

European Monetary Fund. See EUROPEAN MONETARY AGREEMENT.

European Payments Union. An organization composed of the United States and 17 European nations which participated in the EUROPEAN RECOVERY PROGRAM. It was set up at the council meeting of the Organization for European Economic Cooperation (OEEC) in Paris, July, 1950. Its purpose was to provide a clearing agency for the trade balances of the European members, to stimulate multilateral trade and discourage bilateralism. Operations were suspended in December, 1958, when EPU was replaced by the new arrangements developed under the EUROPEAN MONETARY AGREEMENT (*q.v.*).

European Recovery Program. A plan for the economic rehabilitation of Europe, first outlined by General George C. Marshall (1880–1959), American Secretary of State, at Harvard University on June 5, 1947. The plan called for a survey of Europe's resources and needs by the European countries themselves, definite procedures for co-ordinated self-rehabilitation, and a detailed report to the United States setting forth the assistance needed. The plan envisaged American financial aid either as a loan or gift or both, provided that the European nations made effective use of existing resources and sought to overcome political divisions and trade barriers. The program was officially terminated in 1951, but aid was continued under different labels. Also called the *Marshall Plan*. See ORGANIZATION FOR ECONOMIC COOPERATION AND DEVELOPMENT.

ever-normal granary. See explanation under AGRICULTURAL ADJUSTMENT ACT (second).

excess condemnation. The acquisition by public authority of private real property under the power of eminent domain when the need is not essential or imminent or where condemned property exceeds actual need; for example, the acquisition of property for aesthetic purposes. Excess condemnation is illegal in most of the states of the United States. See also CONDEMNATION, EMINENT DOMAIN.

excess-profits tax, general. A tax designed to reduce the profits made by virtue of abnormal consumer demands, particularly in wartime. In the United States the first general excess-profits tax was enacted in 1917 and repealed in 1922. An excess-profits tax was again enacted in 1940, materially amended in 1941, 1942, and 1944, and repealed as of Dec. 31, 1946. See also TAX.

excess reserves. Bank reserves in excess of those legally required. See also RESERVES.

exchange. The acceptance of one thing for another. Exchange is one of the main topics customarily considered in ECONOMICS. Among the subjects included under this main topic are CREDIT, FOREIGN EXCHANGE, MARKETS, and MONEY. See also PECUNIARY EXCHANGE.

exchange control. Government regulations relating to the buying and selling of foreign exchange. During recent years such regulations have taken many forms. For some of the more common, see ASKI TRADING SYSTEM, BLOCKED EXCHANGE, CLEARING AGREEMENT, EXCHANGE STABILIZATION FUND, MULTIPLE CURRENCY SYSTEM, RATIONING OF FOREIGN EXCHANGE, STERLING BLOC. See also CONTROL, FOREIGN EXCHANGE.

exchange rate. A price of one national currency in terms of another. Thus, at any time, a BILL OF EXCHANGE, payable in some foreign currency, may cost a few cents more or less per dollar depending upon whether or not the United States dollar is at a premium or at a discount in terms of that currency. The exchange rate may be fixed by the nation involved, or it may be the rate on a free or uncontrolled international market. See also MINT PAR OF EXCHANGE, OFFICIAL EXCHANGE RATE, PAR EXCHANGE RATE.

exchange stabilization fund. In the United States, a fund created by the profits which accrued to the government from the devaluation of the dollar in 1934. The fund was used to buy and sell foreign exchange and thereby promote a more stable equilibrium between the value of the dollar and foreign currencies. See also DEVALUATION, EXCHANGE CONTROL, GOLD RESERVE ACT.

excise tax. Generally, any tax levied internally upon some phase of the production and distribution of goods or services, but occasionally applied to a CUSTOMS DUTY. Also called *consumption tax*, *internal revenue tax*. See also IMPORT EXCISE TAX, TAX.

ex dividend. Without dividend. When a dividend is declared by the board of directors of a corporation, it is declared payable to stockholders of record as of a certain future date. Stock sold between the declaration date and the date of payment is sold ex dividend because the owners at the time the dividend was declared will receive the dividend. See also DIVIDEND.

executive. Any person or body carrying on administrative work involving forethought and planning, and considerable discretion as to ways and means by which such work shall be accomplished.

executive trade agreements. See RECIPROCAL TRADE AGREEMENTS.

executor. A person named in a will to carry out its provisions.

ex officio. Literally, by virtue of an office. The term is used to identify certain duties or prerogatives which fall to the holder of an office by virtue of his office, but which are not a part of the regular duties of such office. Thus, the president of a corporation, by virtue of his office, may be chairman of the board of directors.

exogenous change. As applied to economics, an alteration in economic life due to a cause that is essentially noneconomic in character. A scarcity of wheat because of a drought is a case in point. See also ENDOGENOUS CHANGE.

expediter. In industry, one whose duty it is to see that the proper materials are in the designated places at the right times, and that deliveries are made in accordance with prearranged time schedules.

expendable. Usable to the point of total destruction in the ordinary course of service.

explicit. See IMPUTED.

explicit interest. See LOAN INTEREST.

export. To ship merchandise abroad, particularly to foreign countries; hence, merchandise so shipped.

export association. See explanation under WEBB-POMERENE ACT.

export bounty. A government subsidy paid on certain exports in order to develop an industry or to increase the nation's foreign trade. See also BOUNTY.

Export-Import Bank of Washington. A public corporation created by executive order of the President of the United States February 2, 1934, and given a statutory basis in 1945. The bank makes or guarantees loans to encourage trade between the United States and its insular possessions and with foreign countries. See also BANK.

export license. Authority from a government to export a specific quantity of a particular commodity. Such authority must often be secured when governments place limited EMBARGOES or related restrictions upon exports.

expropriation. The exercise of the sovereign right of a government to appropriate individual property rights. Normally, this is done with compensation to existing owners, as under EMINENT DOMAIN, but it may and does take place without compensation.

ex rights. A term describing corporate stock offered without the privilege of purchasing a limited number of shares of a new issue of such stock. STOCK RIGHTS (*q.v.*) are issued to the stockholders of record as of a certain date. A person buying the stock of the corporation after this date will not receive the stock rights. The stock is therefore offered ex rights. The term is used in contradistinction to CUM RIGHTS.

extended. A term applied to an obligation when a period of time for its settlement beyond the date of its maturity has been granted. The term *overextended* is frequently used to indicate liabilities high in proportion to current assets.

extended bond. See explanation under BOND.

extension bond. See explanation under BOND.

extensive cultivation. The use of relatively small amounts of capital and labor on relatively large amounts of agricultural land.

external national debt. That portion of the national debt owed to nonresident foreign creditors. External national debt is usually made payable in the currency of the country of the creditor, as to both interest and principal. At the present time none of the debt of the United States or of the states and their subdivisions is external, although external public debt has been contracted in the past. See also NATIONAL DEBT.

extractive industry. 1. An industry which takes materials from the earth or water directly and thereby depletes the natural resources. 2. An industry which produces or uses extracts; for example, the tanning or dyeing industries.

extrapolation. A method of estimating an unknown value that is either higher than the highest or lower than the lowest known value in a series of numbers. For example, from the present record of population growth in the United States, an estimate might be made of the population, say 10 years hence.

F

Fabian socialism. A term generally applied to a school of socialism which supports socialistic doctrines but rejects the concept of class struggle. Fabian socialists believe in bringing about the socialist state by evolution and compromise with other political parties working for reform. The term was originally applied to the members of the Fabian Society, organized in England in 1889. See also CLASS STRUGGLE, SOCIALISM.

factor. As used in commerce, a firm or other organization which, under a continuous contract with a client, purchases his accounts receivable, with or without recourse, advances funds on open credit or on the security of inventories or fixed assets, and offers auxiliary services in such areas as marketing, sales analysis, and management. Before 1930, factoring was confined largely to the textile industry where it was customarily combined with selling services. Currently, it is being used by an increasing number of concerns in various lines of business.

factorage. The commission received by a FACTOR (*q.v.*).

factor cost. A term used by the United States Department of Commerce to indicate the MARKET PRICE of a commodity less all items in its cost other than those of the FACTORS OF PRODUCTION employed in its manufacture. INDIRECT TAXES, for example, such as EXCISE TAXES and SALES TAXES, not being payments for any specific factor of production, are excluded from the concept of factor cost. Likewise, DEPRECIATION and business TRANSFER PAYMENTS, not being essential payments for a factor of production, are excluded. DIRECT TAXES, on the other hand, are part of factor costs. SOCIAL INSURANCE contributions, for example, are a direct consequence of the employment of the labor factor. The NATIONAL INCOME is computed on a factor-cost basis. Factor cost is also a useful index to resource distribution in the economy, the total of such costs for each industry indicating the extent to which the available factors of production are absorbed by that industry.

factor reversal test. A method for determining the mathematical validity of an INDEX NUMBER (*q.v.*) constructed on the basis of a WEIGHTED AVERAGE. Separate index numbers are computed for the value change and for the quantity change from the base period to some other period designated hereafter as the first time period, and these are multiplied one by the other. If the product equals the ratio of the total values (that is, the sum of all the quantities times the prices) in the first time period to the total values in the base period, the index is considered a valid one mathematically. FISHER'S IDEAL INDEX meets this test. See also TIME REVERSAL TEST.

factors of production. The various agents, broadly classified, that combine to produce additional wealth. LAND, LABOR, and CAPITAL are generally recognized as factors of production. Frequently a fourth, called MANAGEMENT, is added. Also called *agents of production.*

factory system. An economy in which workers are brought together under one roof and supplied tools, machines, and materials with which they work in return for wages.

faculty principle of taxation. See ABILITY-TO-PAY PRINCIPLE OF TAXATION.

fair, international trade. A special market or trade exhibition usually arranged under public or semipublic auspices at which manufacturers and traders display their products in an endeavor to stimulate sales. Fairs, which attracted traders from a relatively wide area, were popular during the Middle Ages. They provided an important large-scale market. As business grew and markets became more numerous and continuous, however, fairs declined. Since World War II there has been a revival of fairs in important trade centers in Europe and North America, but they serve chiefly as international exhibitions of wares rather than markets.

Fair Deal. A term used by President Truman to characterize the program presented in his message to the 81st Congress on January 5, 1949. The program included higher taxes, inflation curbs, and various measures which the President had proposed earlier, but which had been rejected or ignored by the 80th Congress.

fair-employment practices legislation. Statutes such as the New York State Ives-Quinn bill (1945) which created a permanent special state commission charged with the task of eliminating discrimination in employment because of race, creed, color, or national origin. A federal statute barring such discrimination in interstate commerce has frequently been advocated but has not yet (1963) been enacted.

Fair Labor Standards Act (Wage and Hour Law). An act of Congress, 1938, which established for most employees engaged in or producing goods for interstate commerce a minimum hourly wage of 30 cents and provided for one and a half times the regular hourly rate for hours worked in excess of 40 per week. The act also prohibited the employment of children under 16 years of age (with certain exceptions) in establishments producing goods for interstate shipment, and regulated HOME WORK in specified industries. The amended act, effective January 25, 1950, established a minimum hourly wage of 75 cents, reduced somewhat the number of employees covered, and tightened the provisions against the employment of children. Other amendments have since raised the minimum hourly rate. Also known as *maximum-hour legislation.* See also *United States* v. *Darby Lumber Co.*

fair labor standards case. See UNITED STATES v. DARBY LUMBER CO.

fair return. A reasonable rate of return on invested capital. In determining rates charged the public by transportation and public-utility companies, consideration is given to a fair return as thus defined. This often necessitates placing a value on the CAPITAL ASSETS. See also VALUATION.

fair-trade practices acts. Statutes of various states of the United States permitting *resale price agreements* in which the retailers are required to maintain specified prices on certain commodities. Such agreements were originally held invalid by the courts as, for example, in the BEECH-NUT PACKING CASE; but state legislation subsequently validated them, and Congress passed the MILLER-TYDINGS ACT (*q.v.*) in 1937 to exempt such agreements from the provisions of the SHERMAN ANTITRUST ACT. In May, 1951, in the Schwegmann case (*Schwegmann Brothers* v. *Calvert Distillers Corp.*, 341 U. S. 384), the United States Supreme Court held that the Miller-Tydings Act affected only those retailers who signed price agreements and did not control the action of nonsigners who were presumably free to "cut" prices. To remedy this loophole thus revealed for nonsigners, Congress passed the McGuire Act (July, 1952). Because of adverse judicial decisions in various states and the unsympathetic attitude of the federal courts, many manufacturers, finding it impractical to enforce minimum resale prices, began gradually, after 1958, to abandon "fair-trade" pricing.

falling-rate-of-profit theory. See DECLINING-MARGINAL-EFFICIENCY-OF-CAPITAL THEORY.

family industry. See HOUSEHOLD SYSTEM.

Fansteel case. A case, *National Labor Relations Board* v. *Fansteel Metallurgical Corp.*, 306 U. S. 240 (1939), in which the Supreme Court of the United States ruled that sit-down strikers were not entitled to reinstatement in their former positions of employment, under the terms of the Wagner National Labor Relations Act. The decision explained that to reinstate the strikers would encourage the use of force instead of legal means in seeking remedies for disputes.

farm bloc. A term sometimes used to identify those senators and representatives in the United States Congress who represent agricultural regions and consistently support measures favorable to the agricultural interests.

Farm Credit Administration. An independent agency of the executive branch of the government, the general purpose of which is to provide a comprehensive credit system for agriculture, including long-term, intermediate, and short-term credit to farmers and to farmers' organizations. The Farm Credit Administration conducts its operations through four local credit agencies, viz. a FEDERAL LAND BANK, a FEDERAL INTERMEDIATE CREDIT BANK, a production credit corporation, and a BANK FOR CO-OPERATIVES, which are located in one city in each of the 12 farm-credit districts into which the United States is divided. Necessary co-ordination is secured through the farm credit board of each district, members of which are ex officio directors of each of the four credit institutions located in the district.

Farmers Home Administration. **A unit of the Department of Agriculture of the United States created in 1946 to take over the functions previously exercised by the Farm Security Administration and the Emergency Crop and Feed Loan Division of the Farm Credit Administration. The Farmers Home Administration provides certain types of credit to farmers who cannot obtain loans through the ordinary channels at prevailing rates and terms.**

Farmers Union. See NATIONAL FARMERS UNION.

farm price supports. Subsidies paid, under certain conditions, to producers of specified farm products when the market price falls below the per cent of AGRICULTURAL PARITY (*q.v.*) currently guaranteed by law. The Agricultural Adjustment Act of 1938 authorized such payments when the market price fell below 75 per cent of parity. Farm price supports during World War II were based on 90 per cent of parity. The Agricultural Act of 1948 continued supports at this level, with some modifications after 1950, but indicated a program of flexible and lower price supports. This program was put into effect with price supports guaranteeing 75 to 90 per cent of parity for basic agricultural commodities. Acceptance of a MARKETING AGREEMENT is a requirement for receiving farm price-support payments.

farm surpluses. **Under federal farm legislation, products purchased by the United States government, or taken as security for agricultural loans, in order to maintain prices prescribed by law. The products are stored in government depositaries awaiting eventual disposal. Some of the products involved are: wheat, cotton, corn, potatoes, rice, peanuts, butter, cheese, turkeys, dried eggs, milk, fruit, peas, and beans.**

fascism. **In its economic aspects, a plan by which the institution of private property and the private production of goods and services is retained but is made subject to extensive control by government, particularly as respects management and new capital expansion. Under fascism, moreover, labor loses its freedom to organize and bargain collectively, these activities falling under the direct control of the state. See also ECONOMIC SYSTEM.**

favorable balance of trade. A condition said to obtain in the international trade of a given country when the money value of its merchandise exports exceeds the money value of its merchandise imports for a particular period of time. The term originated in the theory of MERCANTILISM (*q.v.*) and should not today be considered synonymous with "desirable balance of trade." Also called *active trade balance*. See also BALANCE OF TRADE.

featherbedding. As applied to labor relations, labor-union rules allegedly made to provide easy jobs or to require that more workers be assigned to a given task than necessary.

Federal Advisory Council. A body of 12 advisers, representing each of the 12 federal reserve districts of the United States, which makes recommendations to the Board of Governors of the Federal Reserve System on matters within that board's jurisdiction and on general economic and business conditions.

federal aid. Any grant of money made by the federal government to the states of the United States, or to the political subdivisions of the states, to finance in whole or in part local projects or activities that have been duly approved.

Federal-Aid Highway Acts. Various acts of Congress including those of 1916 and 1921 which have authorized the expenditure of federal funds to assist the states in the construction of main trunk and tributary highways. In 1956 the federal government entered upon an ambitious program for the construction of a system of so-called "interstate highways" and for this purpose the receipts of certain special federal tax revenues, particularly taxes upon certain fuels and commodities used in transportation, are being used to defray the cost of this program. The administration of the federal government's responsibility under these various acts, formerly vested in the Public Roads Administration, is now the responsibility of the Bureau of Public Roads in the Department of Commerce.

Federal Aviation Agency. An independent administrative agency of the United States government which promulgates safety regulations for air commerce, including the development of air traffic regulations and the administration of air traffic control of civil and military air operations within the United States. The agency carries on research and development programs aimed to further the safety and efficient operations of civil and military aviation, and is responsible for the establishment and operation of air navigation facilities to further that end.

Federal Credit Union Act. An act of Congress, 1934, which provided for federal incorporation of co-operative credit unions, and provided, originally, for their supervision through the FEDERAL DEPOSIT

INSURANCE CORPORATION. Subsequently, supervision was transferred to the Bureau of Federal Credit Unions, now (1964) a program bureau of the SOCIAL SECURITY ADMINISTRATION. Balances maintained in the credit unions are not insured by the Federal Deposit Insurance Corporation.

Federal Crop Insurance Corporation. A public corporation, operating under the United States Department of Agriculture, which insures growers of certain staples against loss from natural and other hazards. See CROP INSURANCE.

Federal Deposit Insurance Corporation. A public corporation created by the United States government in 1933 to insure deposits in banks and thereby protect depositors against loss in case an insured bank fails or suspends payments to depositors. Deposits up to $10,000 are insured in all banks which are members of the FEDERAL RESERVE SYSTEM and may be insured in other banks if the application of such banks for insurance is approved by the board of directors of the corporation. In carrying on its activities the corporation sometimes acts as RECEIVER of closed banks and may purchase bank assets or make other disposition of the property of closed banks in order to conserve the assets.

Federal Farm Loan Act. An act of Congress, 1916. It divided continental United States into 12 districts and provided for a FEDERAL LAND BANK in each district and for the organization of NATIONAL FARM LOAN ASSOCIATIONS.

Federal Food, Drug, and Cosmetic Act. An act of Congress, 1938. It extends and supplements previous federal consumer legislation, particularly the PURE FOOD AND DRUGS ACT OF 1906, which the new act replaces. It provides somewhat more effective regulations for identifying the quality and composition of packaged goods and more adequate safeguards against the misuse of dangerous drugs. Some of the regulatory provisions of the earlier legislation are extended to include cosmetics.

Federal Home Loan Bank Act. An act of Congress, 1932. It provides for a system of regional banks to serve as a source of credit for member home-financing and thrift institutions. See also FEDERAL HOME LOAN BANK SYSTEM.

Federal Home Loan Bank Board. Since 1955 an independent agency in the executive branch of the United States government. It supervises the administration of the FEDERAL HOME LOAN BANK SYSTEM and the FEDERAL SAVINGS AND LOAN INSURANCE CORPORATION.

Federal Home Loan Bank System. A system of 11 regional banks created under the authority of the Federal Home Loan Bank Act of 1932 to provide a source of credit for the banks' member home-financing and thrift institutions. Every FEDERAL SAVINGS AND LOAN ASSOCIATION is required to become a member of its regional federal home loan bank. Other eligible member institutions are building and loan and savings and loan institutions, homestead associations, savings and co-operative banks, and insurance companies. Each member institution subscribes to the capital stock of its regional federal home loan bank. The federal home loan banks may issue bonds, debentures, or other obligations when permitted to do so by the FEDERAL HOME LOAN BANK BOARD.

Federal Housing Administration. A unit of the United States HOUSING AND HOME FINANCE AGENCY which insures private lending institutions against loss on loans secured by residential mortgages and on loans advanced for repairs, alterations, and improvements which may be secured by collateral.

federal intermediate credit bank. One of a series of 12 banks authorized by Congress in 1923 to provide short-term credit for farmers and ranchers. To this end each bank may make loans to, or rediscount paper for, agricultural credit and loan associations, banks for co-operatives, or state or national banks having an agricultural constituency. Funds for such operations are derived from the sale of collateral trust debentures to the public. The 12 banks are part of the machinery of the FARM CREDIT ADMINISTRATION. See also BANK.

federal land bank. A bank administered by the Farm Credit Administration of the United States. Its primary purpose is to provide long-term, first-mortgage loans to farmers, and with certain limitations, to livestock corporations. There are 12 federal land banks, one in each farm credit district. The loans are negotiated through NATIONAL FARM LOAN ASSOCIATIONS. Operations of the land banks are financed principally from the sale of Consolidated Federal Farm Loan Bonds to the investing public. See also BANK.

Federal Mediation and Conciliation Service. An independent agency, created by the Labor-Management Relations (Taft-Hartley) Act of 1947. It offers its conciliation services in any important labor dispute affecting interstate commerce or may intervene in any labor dispute upon request of either party. It replaced the Conciliation Service of the Department of Labor.

Federal National Mortgage Association. A unit of the United States HOUSING AND HOME FINANCE AGENCY which assists veterans and others to acquire homes by purchasing eligible mortgages and selling these to institutional and other investors.

Federal Open Market Committee. A committee which regulates the open-market operations of the federal reserve banks. It is composed of the Board of Governors of the Federal Reserve System and five other members chosen annually by the boards of directors of certain specified federal reserve banks. See also OPEN-MARKET OPERATIONS.

Federal Power Act. An act of Congress, 1935, which includes the provisions of the Federal Water Power Act of 1921 and amendments thereto. This consolidated legislation provides for extension of authority on the part of the FEDERAL POWER COMMISSION to improve the navigability of rivers, develop and utilize federal water-power resources, and to regulate the rates, services, and various activities of public utilities engaged in the interstate distribution of electric power.

Federal Power Commission. An independent agency of the United States government, organized in its present form in 1930, to improve navigation and develop water power on navigable waters subject to federal jurisdiction, and on federally owned power sites licensed by the commission for private exploitation; to regulate private utility companies in furnishing gas or electricity interstate; and to control the issuance of securities by such utility companies.

Federal Prison Industries, Inc. A special public corporation of the United States Department of Justice in charge of vocational training and industrial enterprises in federal penal and correctional institutions.

Federal Reserve Act. An act of Congress, 1913. It created the Federal Reserve System and changed banking in the United States from a decentralized system to one relatively centralized.

federal reserve agent. The person appointed by the Board of Governors of the Federal Reserve System to serve as chairman of the board of directors of a federal reserve bank. As agent, such appointee maintains a local office for the Board of Governors in the bank where he serves as chairman of the board.

federal reserve bank. A bank chartered and supervised by the United States government, which acts as a source of credit and as a depositary of reserves, and which performs other services for national and other banks that are members of the FEDERAL RESERVE SYSTEM. There are 12 federal reserve banks, one in each of 12 federal reserve districts into which the nation is divided. The capital stock of each federal reserve bank is owned by the member banks in its district. National banks are required by law to be members; other banks may be members upon approval of an application. In respect to many of their activities, the federal reserve banks are supervised by a Board of Governors of the Federal Reserve System with headquarters in Washington, D. C., and this board is assisted by a FEDERAL ADVISORY COUNCIL which meets in Washington, D.C., at least four times a year. See also BANK.

federal reserve bank float. CREDIT extended by FEDERAL RESERVE BANKS on uncollected deposits. The federal reserve banks do not give immediate credit for CHECKS, DRAFTS, etc., deposited. Credit is given, however, at the end of a period estimated to be sufficient to effect collection even though actual collection has not been made at that time.

The financial statements of the federal reserve banks reflect federal reserve bank float in the difference between the balance of uncollected items and the balance of deferred availability items.

federal reserve bank note. A form of United States paper money. Before 1935, federal reserve bank notes were issued by the federal reserve banks and were secured dollar for dollar by United States bonds and TREASURY NOTES authorized to be used for that purpose. No such bonds or treasury notes have been issued since 1935. The federal reserve bank notes are therefore being retired from circulation.

federal reserve city. A city in which one of the 12 principal federal reserve banks is situated. These cities are (1964) Atlanta, Ga.; Boston, Mass.; Chicago, Ill.; Cleveland, Ohio; Dallas, Tex.; Kansas City, Mo.; Minneapolis, Minn.; New York, N. Y.; Philadelphia, Pa.; Richmond, Va.; San Francisco, Calif.; and St. Louis, Mo.

federal reserve note. A form of paper money in circulation in the United States. Federal reserve notes are issued by the federal reserve banks and are secured partly by GOLD CERTIFICATES and partly by commercial and other paper.

Federal Reserve System. A system of federal reserve banks, one in each of 12 federal reserve districts of the country, 24 branches, a Board of Governors, a Federal Open Market Committee, a Federal Advisory Council, and member banks which include all national banks in the United States and such state banks and trust companies as have voluntarily applied to the Board of Governors for membership and have been admitted to the system. See also FEDERAL RESERVE BANK, OPEN-MARKET OPERATIONS.

federal savings and loan association. A private savings institution chartered and supervised by the FEDERAL HOME LOAN BANK BOARD. It makes loans secured by first mortgages on residential property located within a 50-mile radius of the institution and sells investment share certificates in units of $100 for cash or on the installment plan. These and similar bodies organized under state law are popularly known as *savings and loan associations.*

Federal Savings and Loan Insurance Corporation. A PUBLIC CORPORATION of the United States government, administered by the FEDERAL HOME LOAN BANK BOARD, which insures the safety of deposits in all FEDERAL SAVINGS AND LOAN ASSOCIATIONS and such state-chartered savings and loan associations as apply for insurance and are approved. The corporation guarantees the safety of investments and credited earnings up to $10,000 for each investor in an insured institution.

Federal Security Agency. An administrative agency of the United States government, created in 1939 and superseded in 1953 by a Department of Health, Education, and Welfare, the major responsibilities of which are to promote general welfare in the fields of health, education, and social security. The operating units of the Department are: Public Health Service, Office of Education, Social Security Administration, Office of Vocational Rehabilitation, Food and Drug Administration, and Saint Elizabeth's Hospital.

federal tax immunity case. A case, *Helvering* v. *Gerhardt*, 304 U. S. 405 (1938), in which the Supreme Court of the United States reversed the old rule that the salaries of state employees were immune from federal taxation and sustained the application of the federal income-tax law to the salaries of employees of the Port of New York Authority.

Federal Trade Commission. An independent, quasi-judicial agency of the United States government, created in 1914, which, under various statutes, is charged with the responsibility of discouraging unlawful conspiracies or combinations in restraint of interstate commerce and preventing unfair or deceptive acts or practices in the pricing, advertising, and distribution of various commodities and services. In carrying out these responsibilities, the commission may, under certain circumstances, act directly, or it may institute proceedings in the courts.

Federal Trade Commission Act. An act of Congress, Sept. 26, 1914, which established the FEDERAL TRADE COMMISSION (*q.v.*) and empowered it to prevent unfair methods of competition, boycotts, and price-fixing arrangements. The act was amended by the WHEELER-LEA ACT (*q.v.*) which authorizes the commission to control false advertising of foods, drugs, and other commodities and to prevent unfair or deceptive trade practices.

fee. A payment for particular services or for a privilege. For example, a payment to a physician for professional services, payment to a government agency for a license, or a sum paid for admission to a museum.

fellow-servant doctrine. A common-law doctrine that reduced an employer's responsibility for an injury to an employee if that injury could be shown to have been caused by the act of another employee. WORKMEN'S COMPENSATION LAWS have generally modified this doctrine.

feudal system. The system of political, social, and economic relationships which existed in Europe and elsewhere during the Middle Ages, from approximately the 9th to the 14th or 15th centuries. The system was characterized by the existence of manors ruled by lords and worked by vassals who received protection and subsistence in return for their labor and service.

fiat money. Inconvertible paper money in support of which there is no reserve of specie. Governments issuing such money usually give it the quality of full legal tender. See also MONEY.

fiat standard. See MANAGED MONEY.

fidelity bond. A contract in which one person guarantees a second person against defalcation by a third person holding a position of trust. Fidelity bonds sometimes name a position of trust instead of identifying the person holding that position; but this simply means that any person holding that position is covered by the fidelity bond.

fidelity insurance. A type of insurance by which an employer protects himself against financial loss due to the dishonesty of an employee. *Also called suretyship insurance.* A FIDELITY BOND is the instrument of such insurance. See also INSURANCE.

fiduciary. A person who holds property in trust. Guardians and trustees act in the capacity of a fiduciary.

fiduciary money. Money not fully secured by gold or silver. Thus defined, fiduciary money in circulation in the United States in 1964, and not called for redemption, consists of federal reserve notes, United States notes (greenbacks), and all coins. The meaning of the term is sometimes interpreted to include all money not fully secured by gold. Regarded thus, all money in general circulation in the United States today (1964) is fiduciary money. Sometimes called *credit money*. See also MONEY.

fiduciary standard. A monetary system in which the monetary unit is defined in terms of paper money. The latter is made full legal tender but is not redeemable in any precious metal or other commodity. Also a monetary system based on a precious metal and the coinage thereof, but in which the face value of the coins is very little more than a substance on which to stamp an arbitrary value.

fifo. A method of inventory and cost-of-sales valuation in which the individual items of an inventory are valued according to the cost of the most recent acquisitions, the cost of articles sold or used being valued according to the cost of earlier acquisitions. It is assumed that the first items purchased or produced are the first items sold. The costs of articles sold or used, therefore, are not current costs but those of an earlier date, whereas the costs of the items remaining in the inventory are current costs. The term is an abbreviation of "first in, first out." See also LIFO.

final utility theory of value. The theory that explains value on the grounds of final or marginal utility. Thus, a product like water, although a prime necessity of life, is low in value because the quantities available are normally without limit for all practical purposes. Diamonds, on the other hand, although of little functional use, assume a high value because their quantity is limited. See also MARGINAL UTILITY, MARGINAL UTILITY SCHOOL, VALUE.

finance bill. See explanation under BILL.

finance company. See COMMERCIAL CREDIT COMPANY.

Financial (International) and Development Affairs, Office of. A unit of the Department of State of the United States, having to do principally with investments and surplus property abroad and lend-lease transactions. Its functions have been absorbed and extended by various successor agencies, the most recent (1964) being the Agency for International Development.

financial investment. Expenditure for ownership, part ownership, or other interest in some existing capital asset or assets, for example, the purchase of a SEASONED SECURITY on the stock market. The term is used in contradistinction to REAL INVESTMENT.

financial statement. See BALANCE SHEET.

fine. 1. As applied to precious metals, a term meaning pure metal. 2. A penalty imposed by a magistrate upon an offender, requiring him to pay a certain sum of money to the government. The payment may be in place of, or in conjunction with, other forms of punishment.

fink. A member of a labor union who reports to his employer on the activities of the union and his fellow employees. When discovered, a fink is usually expelled from the union. The Labor-Management Relations (Taft-Hartley) Act of 1947, however, permits unions to expel members only for failure to pay union dues or fees.

first-lien bond. See explanation under BOND.

fiscal. Having to do with money and credit, particularly public finance. For certain uses of the term see FISCAL MONOPOLY, FISCAL YEAR.

fiscal monopoly. A government monopoly conducted for revenue purposes. Commodities such as salt and tobacco, for example, are sometimes reserved for sale by the government, the profits derived therefrom being used for public purposes. See also MONOPOLY.

fiscal policy. The policy pursued by government in connection with legislation or administrative practices relating to taxation, the public debt, currency, public appropriations and expenditure, government funds, and similar matters; particularly the intended effect of such legislation and administrative practices upon private business and the economy of the nation at large.

fiscal year. Any 12 months selected as an accounting period. A fiscal year may or may not correspond with the calendar year. The fiscal year of the United States government, for example, ends June 30 of each year.

Fisher's ideal index. An INDEX NUMBER (*q.v.*) compiled by a formula devised by Irving Fisher (1867–1947), American economist, and independently by others, the formula being designed to construct an index number free from the bias inherent to some extent in index numbers compiled by other methods. The formula is:

$$\sqrt{\frac{\Sigma p_1 q_0}{\Sigma p_0 q_0} \times \frac{\Sigma p_1 q_1}{\Sigma p_0 q_1}}$$

when

p_0 = price at base period,
q_0 = quantity at base period,
p_1 = price at first time period,
q_1 = quantity at first time period.

Commodity	Price, 1941	Quantity, 1940	Price times quantity	Price, 1941	Quantity, 1941	Price times quantity
A	$8.00	9	$72.00	$8.00	8	$ 64.00
B	9.00	8	72.00	9.00	9	81.00
C	1.00	90	90.00	1.00	1,000	1,000.00
Totals			$234.00			$1,145.00

Commodity	Price, 1940	Quantity, 1940	Price times quantity	Price, 1940	Quantity, 1941	Price times quantity
A	$9.00	9	$81.00	$9.00	8	$ 72.00
B	2.00	8	16.00	2.00	9	18.00
C	0.10	90	9.00	0.10	1,000	100.00
Totals			$106.00			$190.00

For tests to determine the mathematical validity of an index number, see FACTOR REVERSAL TEST, TIME REVERSAL TEST.

An example showing how an index number may be calculated from the formula follows:

$$\sqrt{\frac{234}{106} \times \frac{1,145}{190}} = \sqrt{2.2075 \times 6.0263} = \sqrt{13.303} = 3.65.$$

In customary usage, 365 per cent is said to be the price index number for 1941.

five percenter. A popular term, used in a disparaging sense, to identify persons who, for a fee of 5 per cent or more, use their alleged influence with public officials to secure federal government contracts for their business clientele.

five-twenty bond. A popular term applied to certain United States bonds issued from 1862 to 1865. They were redeemable after 5 years, payable in 20 years, and yielded 6 per cent interest. See also BOND.

fixed asset. An asset of such nature that the owner can use it repeatedly. Machinery, buildings, and land are examples. See also ASSET.

fixed capital good. A capital good which is relatively durable. The term is used in contradistinction to CIRCULATING CAPITAL GOOD.

fixed cost. A cost which does not necessarily increase or decrease as the total volume of production increases or decreases. Interest on borrowed capital, expenses of maintenance, and fire insurance are examples. Also called *indirect*, *overhead*, and *supplementary cost*. See also COST.

fixed investment trust. An investment trust that confines its purchases to a fixed list of securities acquired at the time of its organization. Sometimes called *nondiscretionary trust*. See also INVESTMENT TRUST.

fixed liability. A liability, also known as *long-term liability*, which is not due for at least a year from the time it is incurred. See also FUNDED DEBT, LIABILITY.

fixed shift. In an enterprise where a 24-hour interval is divided into two or three shifts or working periods, the practice of keeping the same employees on a particular shift instead of interchanging employees in such a way that over a period of time they will have taken a turn on each of the shifts. See also SHIFT.

flexible schedule. As applied to labor relations, a plan by which the number of hours of employment per day or the number of work days per week may be varied, provided such variations do not exceed the maximum period of employment fixed by law or in a labor contract for a given interval of time.

flexible tariff. A tariff system which permits administrative officers or a tariff commission a measure of discretion in fixing the amount of a customs duty when temporary or abnormal conditions change the competitive relationship between foreign and domestic products. A flexible tariff has been applied particularly for the control of DUMPING. See also TARIFF.

flight of capital. See explanation under FLIGHT OF THE DOLLAR.

flight of the dollar. A popular phrase to indicate the purchase of foreign securities with dollar exchange, the real purpose being to escape the adverse consequences of INFLATION, DEVALUATION, or some related economic circumstance. Under similar conditions the same trend could affect the CURRENCY of any country. A more generalized phrase is *flight of capital.*

floating asset. See QUICK ASSET.

floating debt. A debt consisting of short-term obligations. The term is used in contradistinction to long-term or FUNDED DEBT in the United States. It is frequently applied to that part of the PUBLIC DEBT held in TREASURY BILLS or other short-term obligations. The difference between a floating debt and a funded debt is not always clearly distinguishable. See also DEBT.

floor trader. A member of an organized stock exchange, not a broker, who buys and sells on his own account, executes his own orders on the floor of the exchange, and who may act in the capacity of a dealer or jobber in securities.

flow chart. A graphic device displaying a hypothetical movement of money, goods, credit, or some other element in the economy from one point to another. The following diagram is an example of a

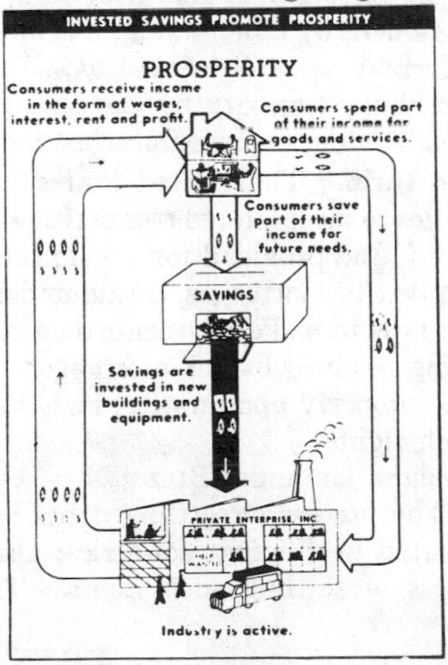
INVESTED SAVINGS PROMOTE PROSPERITY
PROSPERITY
Consumers receive income in the form of wages, interest, rent and profit.
Consumers spend part of their income for goods and services.
Consumers save part of their income for future needs.
SAVINGS
Savings are invested in new buildings and equipment.
PRIVATE ENTERPRISE, INC.
Industry is active.

flow chart. It represents an imaginary movement of money from productive units to ultimate consumers and from thence back to: (1) productive units and (2) savings, and from savings back to productive units in the form of investments.

fluid savings. Savings that have not been invested or spent. See also SAVING.

Food and Agriculture Organization of the United Nations. An official organization of the United Nations consisting (1964) of representatives of some 112 states. By serving as a CLEARINGHOUSE and making appropriate recommendations to member states, the organization hopes to raise nutritional and living standards, better the conditions of rural populations, and promote more efficient and orderly production of food and agricultural staples throughout the world. See also UNITED NATIONS.

food stamp plan. A public subsidy plan, applied for a time in the United States, under which foods declared surplus by the government were distributed to the needy, especially to persons on public relief. By purchasing, at designated retail outlets, stamps of one color which could be exchanged for any kind of food, the qualified customer received stamps of another color, roughly equivalent to half the value of the purchased stamps. These free stamps were exchangeable for commodities declared surplus, the exchange being based on prevailing market prices. All stamps were made redeemable at face value through the banks, the government providing the necessary funds to redeem the free ones.

forced loan. A loan made because of some exigency; for example, a loan that cannot be collected at maturity and which is therefore renewed, or the payment by a bank of an OVERDRAFT which is later converted into a formal loan. See also LOAN.

forced sale. A sale made necessary by the action of a creditor; for example, a sale made under compulsion of FORECLOSURE.

Fordney-McCumber Tariff. The United States Tariff Act of 1922. It raised many duties to meet altered competitive conditions abroad, due to World War I, and provided for a FLEXIBLE TARIFF.

foreclosure. As applied to mortgages, a sale under a judgment held when a mortgagor fails to make payments on a mortgage, the right of redemption being retained by the mortgagor. If the mortgagor fails to redeem the property upon notice, he is forever barred from exercising any such right.

foreign bill. See explanation under BILL.

foreign exchange. The process of settling debts between persons or establishments located in different countries; also the instruments used in the process of settling such debts. These instruments, known as BILLS OF EXCHANGE, are claims for payment in a foreign currency. Any person owing money abroad may buy such exchange and use it to settle his obligation. The foreigner to whom the obligation is owed and who receives the purchased bill may cash it and receive the currency of his own country. The buying and selling of bills of exchange establishes a price for them in the currency of each country whose nationals are involved in exchange transactions. See also EXCHANGE CONTROL.

foreign-trade zone. An area in or adjacent to a port of entry, for storing and transshipping imported goods to foreign ports without payment of duties and without the intervention of customs officials, except under certain conditions. In the United States foreign-trade zones are operated as a public utility by private corporations under the supervision of the Foreign-Trade Zones Board of the Department of Commerce. Also called *free port.*

forms of business organization. The various ways in which business enterprises may be organized; for example, CORPORATION, INDIVIDUAL PROPRIETORSHIP, PARTNERSHIP. See also COMBINATION.

form utility. Satisfaction of a human desire as the result of the alteration of the shape, structure, or composition of some good. When goods are manufactured, a form utility is created. Wood made into a desk is an example. See also UTILITY.

Fort Knox. A United States Army reservation in Kentucky where the federal government maintains guarded underground vaults for COINS and BULLION. The bulk of the gold at Fort Knox is held as security for GOLD CERTIFICATES in the possession of the FEDERAL RESERVE BANKS, or the equivalent, that is, gold-certificate credits to the federal reserve banks on the books of the treasury. The gold stock also includes EARMARKED GOLD, gold held to secure GREENBACKS, gold held on account of the EXCHANGE STABILIZATION FUND, and gold in the treasury's general fund. See STERILIZED GOLD.

forward exchange. A foreign bill of exchange bought or sold at a stipulated price and payable at some future date. By purchasing or selling forward exchange, an importer or exporter can protect himself against the risk of exchange fluctuations. See also BILL OF EXCHANGE.

forwarding agent. A person or business concern whose function it is to collect merchandise and to ship or deliver it as directed.

Fourierism. See PHALANSTERY.

fractional money. In the United States, all coins having a value of less than $1. See also MONEY.

fractional reserves. See explanation under ONE HUNDRED PER CENT RESERVE SYSTEM.

frame of reference. As applied to the social sciences, limits of related thoughts, attitudes, meanings, and similar concepts within which some given intellectual activity takes place.

franchise. A special privilege conferred by government; for example, the privilege of operating an omnibus service on the streets of a city. The term is sometimes used to indicate a privilege granted by a private organization as, for example, the grant of exclusive territory to a sales agent by a private corporation.

franchise tax. A tax levied on some special privilege extended by the government to a private enterprise. See also TAX.

franking. The privilege granted by the United States government, chiefly to congressmen and administrative departments of the government, of sending material through the United States mails free of charge.

Frazier-Lemke Act. An act of Congress, 1935. It established a MORATORIUM on farm mortgage foreclosures, permitting the owners to pay rent for a 3-year period.

free banking system of New York. A system established in 1839 in New York State, authorizing the issuance of bank notes backed by approved securities deposited with the state government. A similar plan was later applied to the NATIONAL BANKS. See also BANK NOTES, NATIONAL BANK ACT.

free capital good. A capital good which can be used for a variety of purposes. The term is used in contradistinction to SPECIALIZED CAPITAL GOOD. See also CAPITAL GOOD.

free coinage. A regulation by which the government is obligated to accept for coinage unlimited quantities of a specified metal or metals under conditions prescribed by law. The term should not be confused with GRATUITOUS COINAGE. See also COINAGE.

free competition. See COMPETITION.

freedom of contract. The right of an individual to enter into such contractual relations as he considers to his own best interests, subject only to regulations imposed by law. The word "liberty" in the "due process clause" of the 14th Amendment to the Constitution of the United States has been interpreted to include the right of freedom of contract as thus defined.

free enterprise. See CAPITALISM.

free good. Anything external to man which is inherently useful and which is in such bountiful supply that as much of it as is desired can be had without conscious effort. The term is used in contradistinction to ECONOMIC GOOD. Fresh air, climate, and sunshine are examples of free goods. It should be noted, however, that indispensability is not necessarily an attribute of a free good. Water in cities, for example, although indispensable, is not a free good because its distribution requires conscious effort. Nor are things that are distributed gratuitously designated as free goods if conscious effort on the part of someone is necessary to acquire them. See also GOOD.

free list. As applied to a customs tariff, a list of goods not liable to the payment of duties.

free market. A market in which buyers and sellers are at liberty to trade without restrictions as to prices or quantities, and in which there is no compulsion either to buy or to sell.

free port. See FOREIGN-TRADE ZONE.

free silver. The free coinage of silver. See also FREE COINAGE.

free trade. As applied to international trade, the absence of export and import duties and of regulations which are clearly designed to reduce or prevent such trade.

frequency curve. See explanation under FREQUENCY DISTRIBUTION.

frequency distribution. A classification of statistical data into class intervals according to size or magnitude with the number of items (frequency) applicable to each class interval. Sometimes called *frequency table.* The following is a frequency distribution of the weekly earnings of 200 employees.

Class Interval	Frequency
40–40.99	5
41–41.99	8
42–42.99	20
43–43.99	30
44–44.99	50
45–45.99	40
46–46.99	25
47–47.99	12
48–48.99	5
49–49.99	5

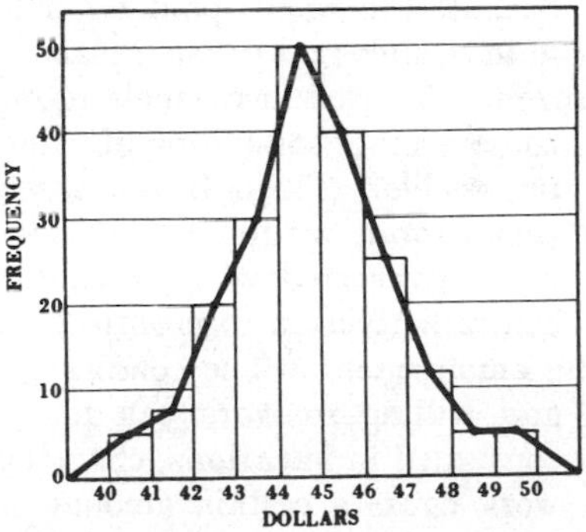

When displayed graphically, using the X axis for class intervals and the Y axis for frequencies, a frequency distribution is called a *column diagram* or *histogram.* When the midpoints of the class intervals at the various frequency levels are joined with straight lines, the resulting broken line is called a *frequency polygon.* A histogram and a frequency polygon derived from the above frequency distribution are shown in the appended diagram. A frequency polygon is customarily made more regular or smoothed out either by inspection or mathematically, as, for example, by a MOVING AVERAGE. The resulting curve is called a *frequency curve*. Frequency distributions are used extensively in economic analysis, as, for example, in comparing one array of statistics with another. The characteristics of a frequency distribution are described by various statistical measurements, the more commonly used of which are as follows. Calculated averages measuring central tendency: ARITHMETIC MEAN, GEOMETRIC MEAN, HARMONIC MEAN. See also WEIGHTED AVERAGE. Positional averages measuring central tendency: MEDIAN, MODE. Measurements showing absolute dispersion, variability, or scatter: MEAN DEVIATION, PROBABLE ERROR, QUARTILE DEVIATION, RANGE, STANDARD DEVIATION. Measurements showing relative dispersion: COEFFICIENT OF VARIATION. For other measurements, see KURTOSIS, SKEWNESS. See also NORMAL CURVE OF DISTRIBUTION.

frequency polygon. See explanation under FREQUENCY DISTRIBUTION.

frequency table. See explanation under FREQUENCY DISTRIBUTION.

frictional unemployment. Unemployment caused by imperfections in the technical functioning of the labor market. Lack of information regarding where work is available, inability to get there, or time consumed in changing jobs are causes of frictional unemployment. See also UNEMPLOYMENT.

fringe benefit. Compensation received by employees other than regular wages for time actually spent on a job. Examples of fringe benefits are wages paid for holidays and vacations, or sums paid in insurance and pension plans.

frozen. As used in business terminology, the word suggests that the conversion of something of value into money is difficult or virtually impossible. Thus, frozen assets or capital are assets or capital that cannot readily be converted into money, or at least cannot be so converted without considerable loss. The term is used in contradistinction to LIQUID. See also ASSET, CAPITAL.

full employment. The condition which exists when all who are able and willing to work can find remunerative employment. Time consumed in vacations, changing jobs, and similar periods without work cause a certain amount of unemployment at all times. As long as this does not exceed 3 to 4 per cent of the labor force, however, full employment is said to exist.

full-paid stock. See explanation under CAPITAL STOCK.

full stock. See explanation under CAPITAL STOCK.

function. As applied in economic analysis, a variable the value of which depends upon another variable. Thus, the increase of a sum of money at a fixed rate of interest is a function of time. The general mathematical expression for a functional relationship is $y =$

f(*x*), meaning that *y* is a function of *x*.

functional distribution. See explanation under DISTRIBUTION.

functional finance. See explanation under COMPENSATORY FISCAL POLICY.

functions of money. The various ways in which money may be used, or the service it renders in the economy. The use of money as a medium of exchange is the principal function. It is also used as a standard of value; that is, as a means of measuring and of comparing values when no exchange is made or contemplated. Further, money is used as a standard of deferred payments when an obligation is assumed at one time to be paid at some future date. It is used as a means of storing value when received as the result of a sale and not immediately used for a purchase. Finally, it is used as a reserve against various forms of currency such as DEPOSIT CURRENCY and thus performs an important function in the creation of credit.

fund. Money, or its equivalent, set aside for a specific purpose the nature of which is usually indicated in the name of the fund. Examples: *contingent fund*, one for use in a contingency; *endowment fund*, a fund the principal of which remains intact, only the interest being used.

fundamental disequilibrium. A term used in Art. IV, sec. 5 of the Articles of Agreement of the INTERNATIONAL MONETARY FUND to indicate a substantial and persisting variation between the PAR EXCHANGE RATE of a national currency and its PURCHASING-POWER PARITY (*q.v.*) with the currencies of other nations. For example, in June, 1949, the British pound was valued at $4.03, but British wholesale prices had risen approximately 6 per cent during the previous year, while prices in the United States had declined in like proportion. Hence, a commodity which cost $20.15 in the United States and £5 in Britain in 1948, in 1949 cost $18.94 in the United States and £5, 6s in Britain. The change placed traders in Britain at a disadvantage because importers in the United States and other HARD MONEY nations tended to reduce their British purchases. With the consent of the International Monetary Fund, the pound sterling was accordingly devaluated from $4.03 to $2.80, the devaluation being in excess of the actual disparity in the purchasing power of the two currencies, presumably to avoid another devaluation of the pound at a later date.

funded debt. 1. A debt represented by a formal written agreement between the borrower and a trustee for the lenders, in which the borrower agrees to pay stipulated amounts at specified times and places until the debt is extinguished. The agreement may, and usually does, provide for some sort of security for the debt. 2. A debt created by the sale of an issue of long-term securities, the proceeds from which have been used to liquidate one or more issues of short-term securities. See also DEBT.

funding. The process of converting short-term or floating indebtedness into securities representing a more permanent loan; for example, the conversion of notes into bonds.

futures. 1. As applied to international trade, the purchase or sale of foreign exchange on the basis of a rate quoted as of some future date. See also FOREIGN EXCHANGE. 2. As applied to trading on the commodity exchanges, see explanation under HEDGING.

G

gain sharing. A bonus system according to which additional wage increments paid to workers for increased production become progressively smaller as production increases.

Gantt chart. A device which displays in graphic form various production data essential to managerial operations. For example, it can show a comparative record of production planned with production completed at any particular time, or a comparative record of the accomplishments of employees with established standards or with each other, or the comparative periods of idleness and activity of machines. The chart was developed by Henry Laurence Gantt (1861–1919), an American management engineer.

garnishment. An order by a court of law requiring an employer to pay part or all of the wages of a debtor employee to a court officer for the benefit of a creditor.

General Accounting Office. An independent agency of the United States government, charged with the responsibility of settling all claims in favor of or against the federal government, and investigating all matters relating to the collection, disbursement, and use of public funds. The agency was created by the BUDGET AND ACCOUNTING ACT of 1921. Its executive head is the Comptroller General.

General Agreement on Tariffs and Trade. See explanation under GENEVA TRADE CONFERENCE.

General Assembly of the United Nations. One of the principal organs of the United Nations. It consists (1964) of 113 nations which have equal voting power. The General Assembly examines and makes recommendations on policies relating to maintenance of peace and the promotion of general welfare. It receives reports from all other agencies of the United Nations and exercises a degree of supervision over most of their activities. Regular meetings are held annually, and special meetings may be called when necessary. See also UNITED NATIONS.

general depositary. A member bank of the Federal Reserve System that is authorized, under specified conditions, to accept deposits from the United States Treasury to be credited to the general account of the Treasurer of the United States. See also DEPOSITARY.

general equilibrium. As applied to theoretical economic analysis, the conception of a balance among interdependent economic forces, each activated by individual decisions based upon SELF-INTEREST. Assuming free COMPETITION, PRIVATE PROPERTY, and FREEDOM OF CONTRACT, forces of SUPPLY and DEMAND acting upon ECONOMIC GOODS are held to be equated at prices that offer the greatest number of traders maximum satisfactions and that are mutually consistent with one another in that respect. A price change in one commodity or service may engender price changes in innumerable other directly and indirectly related commodities and services with resulting maladjustments, but equilibrium, in the sense described, tends eventually to be restored. Actually, general equilibrium is never absolute in a developing economy because of changes in consumer demands and dispositions to spend, save, and invest; new technological developments; shifting competitive relationships; depletion of existing and discoveries of new NATURAL RESOURCES; and other similar factors. The concept is supplementary to that of *partial or particular equilibrium* which considers the economics of specific economic goods. The study of general equilibrium, considered in the light of the effects of change-producing factors on the economy as a whole, consequent disequilibriums, and the processes by which simultaneous adjustment tends to restore a new equilibrium, is called *dynamic economics*, as opposed to *static economics*, which might be defined as the study of a particular economic relationship under certain prescribed conditions assumed to be constant.

general equilibrium theory of international trade. An explanation of the conditions giving rise to international trade, the condition being, fundamentally, a difference in exchange ratios obtaining in the trading nations. Thus, if two commodities x and y exchange in the ratio of 3 to 1 in nation A, and 2 to 1 in nation B, commodity x will be exported from nation A to nation B. Differences in exchange ratios are caused, according to the theory, by varying conditions of supply and demand in the nations concerned. Conditions of supply depend upon natural resources and the natural aptitudes and acquired skills of the people, or other factors that establish ABSOLUTE OR COMPARATIVE ADVANTAGE in production; demand depends upon tastes expressed in buying dispositions as well as upon a nation's purchasing power, this being influenced, in turn, by the distribution of the NATIONAL INCOME. The theory holds that equilibrium prevails when the value of the exports just equals the value of the imports. The theory is an extension of the concept of GENERAL EQUILIBRIUM to international trade.

general management trust. An investment trust that purchases all classes of securities. Sometimes called *discretionary trust.* See also INVESTMENT TRUST.

general property tax. See PROPERTY TAX.

General Services Administration. An independent agency of the United States government, created in 1949 by the Administrative Services Act of that year and amendments thereto. The agency assumes certain functions formerly performed by the Bureau of Federal Supply, the Office of Contract Settlement, the Federal Works Agency, the National Archives Establishment, and related bodies. Its purpose is to act as a procurement, supply, and maintenance body for the real and personal property and nonpersonal services of other governmental agencies.

general strike. Work stoppage in all industries everywhere. The concept of the general strike is somewhat indefinite. The term is frequently used to designate a strike only in certain strategic industries or a general work stoppage in a certain geographic area. It may and sometimes has been directed against government. See also STRIKE.

general tariff. See SINGLE-SCHEDULE TARIFF.

genetic industry. An industry engaged directly in increasing the supply of some form of plant or animal life. Farming and cattle raising are examples.

Geneva Trade Conference. A conference of representatives of 23 states held at Geneva, Switzerland, in 1947. As a result of many bilateral negotiations by participating states, a multilateral agreement, called the *General Agreement on Tariffs and Trade*, was signed, reducing DIFFERENTIAL DUTIES, IMPORT QUOTAS, and other trade restrictions. The conference also developed a draft charter for the proposed INTERNATIONAL TRADE ORGANIZATION (*q.v.*).

gentlemen's agreement. As applied to industry, an informal, often a mere verbal, agreement between two or more industries to divide markets, maintain prices, restrict output, or engage in other related practices designed to reduce competition. Such agreements are now generally outlawed.

geometric mean. A calculated average computed by first finding the product of the numbers to be averaged and then finding whatever root of this product is indicated by the total quantity of numbers to be averaged. The mathematical formula is:

$$M_g = \sqrt[n]{a_1 a_2 a_3 \cdots a_n}$$

when

$$M_g = \text{the geometric mean,}$$
$$a_1, a_2, a_3 \cdots a_n = \text{the numbers to be averaged.}$$

In contrast to the ARITHMETIC MEAN, the geometric mean is suitable for averaging ratios. It is therefore frequently used in the computation of INDEX NUMBERS that record ratios of change in prices and other data. Its advantage for such use can be illustrated in the following frequently cited example:

Commodity	Price First Year	Price Second Year
A	100	1,000
B	100	10
Arithmetic mean	100	505
Geometric mean	100	100

In the first case it would seem that there had been a substantial increase in prices from the first to the second year. In the second case the two changes, being equal ratios in opposite directions, have canceled each other. See also MEAN.

George-Deen Act. See explanation under SMITH-HUGHES ACT.

George-Ellzey Act. See explanation under SMITH-HUGHES ACT.

George-Reed Act. See explanation under SMITH-HUGHES ACT.

German Alliance Insurance Co. v. Lewis. A case, 233 U. S. 389 (1914), in which the Supreme Court of the United States construed a state statute (Kansas), regulating the rates of fire-insurance companies, as consistent with the due process clause of the 14th Amendment. The court's decision was based on the theory that the fire-insurance business was semimonopolistic in character, that it affected the public welfare so vitally as to require regulation, and that, in effect, the business presented a justification for public regulation no different than is presented by transportation, grain elevators, and other enterprises held to be clothed with a public interest and hence subject to public control.

Gibbons v. Ogden. A case, 9 Wheaton 1 (1824), in which the Supreme Court of the United States was called upon for the first time to outline generally the boundaries of the commerce power of Congress under the Constitution. Speaking through Chief Justice Marshall, the court declared that the power over foreign and interstate commerce was a regulatory power; that it comprehended every species of commercial intercourse between the United States and foreign nations; that, in the case of commerce among the several states, the regulatory power of Congress did not stop at the external boundary line of any state of the Union but was applicable within the interior of a state; and that this power embraced every commercial transaction that was not carried on wholly within the boundaries of a single state. The decision also specifically included navigation within the term "commerce."

G. I. Bill of Rights (Servicemen's Readjustment Act). An act of Congress, 1944, which, with subsequent amendments, provides allowances to veterans while unemployed and allowances for subsistence and tuition while attending school or college, and guarantees loans for the purchase of homes, farms, and businesses.

gift tax. In the United States, a tax levied upon the value of a gift after certain specified exemptions, the rate of the tax increasing as the amount of the gift increases. Under federal law an individual may give away $30,000 (1964) during his lifetime which is tax free to both donor and recipient. In addition he may make gifts to individuals not exceeding $3,000 (1964) to any one person in any one year. This is also tax free for both donor and recipient. See also TAX.

gilt-edge security. A security in which the factor of risk is reduced to a minimum; for example, a United States government bond. See also SECURITY.

Glass-Steagall Act. See BANKING ACT.

going value. The anticipated exchange value of some good or service or of some enterprise predicated on the assumption that existing economic conditions are inherently relatively stable, and on the further assumption that market conditions will not be adversely influenced by important technological changes, panics, wars, or some other unforeseen circumstances. See also VALUE.

gold bond. See explanation under BOND.

gold-bullion standard. A monetary system in which the monetary unit is defined in terms of gold, that metal being accepted by the mint at a stipulated price, but not for coinage. All forms of money are redeemable in gold bullion, but redemption can be demanded only for relatively large amounts at one time. When money can be redeemed in gold bullion only for export purposes, the system is sometimes called the *international gold-bullion standard*. See also MONETARY SYSTEM.

gold certificate. A form of United States paper money, representing gold bullion and fully secured thereby, in circulation from 1865 to 1933. Since 1933, gold certificates have been issued in revised form only to the federal reserve banks for reserve purposes. The only gold certificates in circulation (1964) are those which have been lost or are being illegally hoarded.

gold clause. A term used in the United States to identify a clause in a contract which defines a money obligation in terms of a dollar of a specified weight and fineness of gold. In February, 1935, the United States Supreme Court delivered opinions in certain cases involving contractual obligations containing gold clauses. The court upheld the power of Congress, previously exercised, to invalidate the gold clauses of private contracts. See also DEVALUATION, GOLD-CLAUSE CASES.

gold-clause cases. Cases in which the Supreme Court of the United States passed upon the power of Congress to abrogate the gold clause in private and public contracts; that is: (1) upon the power of Congress to require a private creditor to accept existing legal tender in payment of a contractual debt even though the contract called for payment in gold of a certain weight and fineness; and (2) to require holders of United States bonds to accept payment in existing legal tender even though the bonds called for payment of gold of a certain weight and fineness. In *Norman* v. *Baltimore and Ohio R.R. Co.*, 294 U. S. 240 (1935), the court held that Congress could abrogate the gold clause in private contracts on the theory that the terms of any such contract are always potentially subject to regulation by the constitutional power of government, including the established constitutional power of Congress to control the currency. On the issue of the government's refusal to honor the gold clause in its own bonds the court, in *Perry* v. *United States*, 294 U. S. 330 (1935), held that Congress was controlled by its own promise to pay which it had given under its constitutional authority to borrow on the credit of the United States, and that hence it could not dishonor its pledges to its creditors. At the same time the court could find no actual contractual damages resulting to the holder of the gold bonds from the government's decision to pay in existing legal tender and consequently refused to sustain the bondholder's plea for payment in gold or its equivalent. See also GOLD CLAUSE.

gold-exchange standard. A monetary system that permits the redemption of its money in bills of exchange on some gold-standard country in which bank deposits are carried, these being regarded a part of the monetary reserves of the monetary system in question. In this way, it is possible, if the GOLD STANDARD (*q.v.*) is maintained anywhere, for a nation, not itself on the gold standard, to keep its money on a par with gold without maintaining at least the full amount of gold reserves usually required to attain that end. By pursuing the same plan of redeeming its money in BILLS OF EXCHANGE (*q.v.*), a nation can keep its money on a par with the money of some other nation even though neither is on the gold standard. Also called *indirect foreign-exchange standard* and *irredeemable foreign-exchange standard*. See also MONETARY SYSTEM.

gold points. In exchange transactions between traders in gold-standard countries, the rate immediately above and below the mint par of exchange value of gold at which it becomes as cheap to export or import gold and pay for its transportation as to buy or sell bills of exchange; hence, the limits in terms of gold beyond which the price of bills of exchange will not fluctuate. See also BILL OF EXCHANGE, MINT PAR OF EXCHANGE.

Gold Reserve Act. An act of Congress, 1934. It authorized the DEVALUATION of the dollar by from 50 to 60 per cent at the discretion of the President, and ordered the acquisition by the Treasury of all gold held by the federal reserve banks in return for GOLD CERTIFICATES. It abolished the coinage of gold and prohibited the redemption of money in gold. An EXCHANGE STABILIZATION FUND was created out of the premium resulting from the dollar's devaluation.

gold settlement fund. A fund in gold or gold certificates placed on deposit with the Treasury at Washington by the 12 federal reserve banks for clearing purposes, each bank being required to contribute not less than $1,000,000, although in practice the contributions are much greater. Each FEDERAL RESERVE BANK acts as a clearing agency for its member banks and every 24 hours reports by telegraph to the Treasury at Washington its debits and credits against the other 11 reserve banks in the system. These reports are consolidated and appropriate debits and credits entered against each bank's share in the gold settlement fund. If at any time the credit balance in the fund of any reserve bank falls below the established minimum, additional resources must be supplied the fund by that bank. The arrangement makes possible the settlement of balances among the various reserve banks with a minimum of transportation of actual money from one part of the United States to another.

gold standard. A monetary system which defines the monetary unit in terms of gold of a certain weight and fineness, permits the free and unlimited coinage of gold, makes gold coins legal tender, permits them to circulate freely, and maintains the value of all other forms of money at a par with gold coins. See also MONETARY

SYSTEM, STANDARD MONEY.

Gold Standard Act. An act of Congress, 1900, which defined the United States dollar as $25\frac{8}{10}$ grains of gold $\frac{9}{10}$ fine, provided that all forms of United States money should be maintained at parity with the gold dollar, created a reserve fund of approximately $150,000,000 in gold for the redemption of United States notes and treasury notes, and specified other regulations for the maintenance of a gold reserve.

Gompers* v. *Bucks Stove and Range Co. A case, 221 U. S. 418 (1911), in which the Supreme Court of the United States established, among other things, that when a labor boycott causes a substantial reduction of the movement of goods in interstate commerce, a violation of the Sherman Act is indicated. The decision of the court in the DANBURY HATTERS' CASE (*q.v.*) was thus strengthened.

good. Anything external to man either material or immaterial that satisfies a human desire. It should be noted that, unlike the use of the term in popular speech, there is no legal, moral, or ethical connotation in its technical use. A dangerous and harmful drug may satisfy a human desire; so may fresh air. This technical use of the term, of course, in no way justifies the illegal or condones the immoral or unethical. It simply delineates, in part, the scope of economic study. Goods are generally divided into FREE GOODS and ECONOMIC GOODS.

good will. As used in an asset and liability statement, the value imputed to a name or reputation. Presumably an established name or favorable reputation assures a certain amount of continuing business which a new establishment would not enjoy. This probability of continued business is an asset, and its value is recorded in a good-will account.

grace period. A period of time — usually 3 days — after a debt falls due, during which the debtor may occasionally be permitted to delay fulfillment of his obligation without incurring a penalty or other liability. Commonly referred to as *days of grace*.

graded tax. A system of local taxation so designed as to impose an increasingly heavy burden upon land values and a decreasing burden upon improvements. Either the assessed valuation or the tax rate may be used to effect the differential. The object of such a tax is to encourage building and to discourage the holding of unimproved land over a long period of time. See also TAX.

grade labeling. The labeling of consumer goods in accordance with certain standards, presumably established by an authoritative body. A term, letter, or number is used to designate a certain quality, size, or other characteristic essential in judging the product and the price asked for it. The term is used in contradistinction to *descriptive labeling* which, presumably, describes a product but without reference to any recognized authoritative standards.

Grain Futures Act. An act of Congress, 1922, which provides for federal supervision and regulation over operations in grain futures. See also HEDGING.

Grain Standards Act. An act of Congress, 1916, which standardizes grades for grains and provides for federal supervision over all grain-inspection systems.

Grange. See NATIONAL GRANGE ORDER OF THE PATRONS OF HUSBANDRY.

Granger cases. See *MUNN* v. *ILLINOIS*.

granger legislation. Laws favoring agricultural interests enacted in many western states of the United States between 1870 and 1890. The laws resulted from the organized efforts of farmers to curb monopolistic and discriminatory practices on the part of railroads, warehouses, grain elevators, and the like, by bringing the rates and services of such enterprises under public control. See also *MUNN* v. *ILLINOIS*.

gratuitous coinage. Under a system of free coinage, a governmental policy of manufacturing metal into coins without cost to the owner of the metal. See also COINAGE, FREE COINAGE.

gratuity. A voluntary payment given usually in return for some service rendered.

***Graves* v. *New York* ex rel. *O'Keefe*.** See STATE TAX IMMUNITY CASE.

graveyard shift. The shift working from 12 midnight until 8 A.M., when three shifts, each working 8 hours, are employed in an enterprise. See also SHIFT.

gray market. Sources of supply where scarce commodities can be purchased for immediate delivery at a premium considerably above the normal market price. Gray-market operators speculate on future demands. The important distinction between their activities and those of BLACK-MARKET operators is that the latter are illegal.

greenbacks. A form of fiduciary paper money, first issued by the United States Treasury in 1862. The original issue was $150,000,000 in United States notes. Succeeding issues increased this amount to $450,000,000. It was expected that the greenbacks would be retired soon after the Civil War, but such plans met with strong opposition. Some greenbacks were retired under the provision of an act of 1875, but more than $346,000,000 worth were left in circulation, and subsequent legislation provided for the constant reissue of greenbacks. In 1900, under the GOLD STANDARD

ACT (*q.v.*), a gold reserve of approximately $150,000,000 was provided to insure the redeemability of the greenbacks.

***Green* v. *Frazier*.** A somewhat novel case, 253 U. S. 233 (1920), in which the Supreme Court of the United States reviewed a series of statutes of North Dakota authorizing that state's government to become the proprietor and operator of a variety of business establishments. These included a bank, warehouses, flour mills, and food-processing and -distributing plants, normally not deemed to come within the scope of governmental enterprise in the United States. The court was petitioned to declare these statutes contrary to the due process clause of the 14th Amendment of the United States Constitution because taxes levied to support the proposed activities and the incidental property which the state might acquire were alleged to be for a nonpublic purpose. In its decision, refusing to interpose any constitutional bar to this collectivistic program, the court gave particular weight to the special character of North Dakota's economy and to the fact that the state's program had the sanction of its constitution, its legislature, and its people.

Gresham's law. The well-known fact that when two or more kinds of money of unequal exchange value are in concurrent circulation, each being available for payments, the one of inferior value tends to drive the one of higher value out of circulation.

gross income. The term may refer to the total receipts of an enterprise or it may refer to the total receipts less certain expenses. Modern income or profit-and-loss statements customarily group expense accounts into certain broad classifications such as cost of goods sold, selling expenses, operating expenses, etc. In such statements the term is frequently used to indicate the amount remaining after the total "costs of goods sold" only has been deducted from the total sales. Other expenses are then deducted until the NET INCOME is finally computed. In the accounts required of some public-utility companies, the term is used to indicate the amount remaining after all the expenses have been deducted except debt charges and a few other items. See also INCOME.

gross interest. A price paid for the use of capital which includes a sum to cover the risk involved and a sum to cover the administration costs incurred in making the loan. The customary price paid for the use of capital is gross interest but is customarily referred to as merely INTEREST. Gross interest may be either LOAN INTEREST or IMPUTED INTEREST.

gross national debt. The total national debt outstanding, including duplications and that part of the debt held by governmental units in trust, in investment, or in sinking funds. See also NATIONAL DEBT.

gross national expenditure. See GROSS NATIONAL PRODUCT.

gross national product. The total value at current market prices of all final goods and services produced by a nation's economy before deduction of depreciation charges and other allowances for business and institutional consumption of durable capital goods. As computed for any given period of time by the United States Department of Commerce, it includes: (1) personal consumption expenditures, that is, both goods and services purchased and income in kind; (2) gross private domestic investments including inventory changes and new dwellings; (3) net foreign investments, that is, the excess accruing to a nation from the operation of international trade and finance; (4) government purchases of goods and services, but excluding financial transfers such as loan collateral and subsidy payments and transactions not related to income or product. Gross national product may also be called ***gross national expenditure.***

gross profit. See explanation under PROFIT.

ground rent. A price paid for the use of land without improvements, including the right to occupy and improve it. See also RENT.

group banking. See CHAIN BANKING.

group life insurance. Life insurance which covers a group of persons, usually at least 50. This type of insurance is frequently used to cover employees of some organization and is normally issued without medical examination. The premiums are usually the same for each class of persons in the group and are paid to the life-insurance company in one lump sum. See also LIFE INSURANCE.

group medicine. Any co-operative or voluntary plan for securing certain medical services to members of a specific group or association, such services often embracing periodic medical examinations as well as medical care in case of illness. Such a plan may take the form of medical insurance for employees placed through an employer, or it may take the form of special arrangements between medical practitioners and particular groups of persons who pay for medical care collectively.

Grundy tariff. See HAWLEY-SMOOT TARIFF.

guaranteed annual wage. See ANNUAL WAGE.

guaranteed bond. See explanation under BOND.

guaranteed stock. See explanation under CAPITAL STOCK.

guaranteed-wage plan. Generally an agreement by which employees are guaranteed a definite period of employment or a specific amount in wages during a specified period of time. In some studies the term is limited to agreements which guarantee a minimum of three months employment during a one-year period, or the equivalent in wages.

guaranty savings bank. A special type of savings bank located in New Hampshire having some features of the mutual type of savings bank and some features of the stock type of savings bank. There are two classes of depositors, regular and special. The regular depositors are paid a stipulated amount of interest; the special depositors are paid all net earnings not held as reserves, in excess of the payments to the regular depositors. It is the feature of having two classes of depositors that distinguishes this type of savings bank from the usual MUTUAL SAVINGS BANK. See also SAVINGS BANK, STOCK SAVINGS BANK.

Guffey Coal Act. An act of Congress, 1937, designed to secure conservation and better utilization of coal and to stabilize the soft-coal industry by the creation of a bituminous coal code. The code aimed to promote fair competition, establish minimum prices, and improve labor relations. Companies subject to the act but refusing to accept the code were subjected to an ad valorem tax on their products. The act expired April 26, 1943.

guild. An association of persons, engaged in some common pursuit or having common interests, formed for mutual aid and protection. The earliest guilds were religious in character. From these, others were derived that developed interests almost wholly secular in nature. See CRAFT GUILD, MERCHANT GUILD.

guild socialism. Social ownership of the means of production, with industrial operations managed by workers organized into associations comparable to medieval guilds. Local guilds would be federated in national guilds, which would be represented in a guild congress. The guild congress would concern itself with the overall direction of industry and would supplement but not replace existing political assemblies. Guild socialist theories were advanced by G. D. H. Cole and other British intellectuals in the early part of the 20th century. See also SOCIALISM.

H

half stock. See explanation under CAPITAL STOCK.

hallmark. An impression made upon gold- and silverware, required by the British public assay office, indicating the degree of fineness of the metals used. The custom was introduced as early as 1300 by the English Guild of Gold and Silver Smiths and was enforced by royal command.

***Hammer* v. *Dagenhart*.** See CHILD-LABOR CASES.

handicraft economy. An economy that appeared with the growth of towns in the 14th and 15th centuries when artisans pursued crafts or trades, usually in their home or small shop, for the purpose of producing goods for the market.

hard money. **1.** Metal coins in contrast to paper money. **2.** A national money with relatively stable value both internally and in international exchange. See also MONEY.

hard sell. Extremely aggressive selling practice. Examples are: constant repetition of a phrase or slogan in a radio or television program; scare headlines or extravagant therapeutic claims in newspaper and magazine advertising; and conspicuous outdoor billboards, obstructing attractive landscape views.

harmonic mean. A calculated average computed by finding the reciprocal of the ARITHMETIC MEAN of the reciprocals of the numbers to be averaged. The mathematical formula is:

$$\frac{1}{H} = \frac{\frac{1}{r_1} + \frac{1}{r_2} + \frac{1}{r_3} \cdots + \frac{1}{r_n}}{N}$$

when

H = the harmonic mean,
$r_1, r_2, r_3, \cdots r_n$ = the numbers to be averaged,
N = the total quantity of numbers.

In economic computation the harmonic mean is used in averaging such data as time rates and rate-per-dollar prices. For example, suppose the average price per unit is required when a commodity sells for 10 for $1.00 in one store, 20 for $1.00 in another store, and 25 for $1.00 in a third store. The arithmetic mean of 10, 20, and 25 is 18.334, the average number of units sold per dollar, and $1.00 divided by 18.334 is 5.454 cents, the apparent price per unit. But if the arithmetic mean of the unit prices is computed (10, 5, and 4 cents), the average price per units is 6.33+ cents. If, however, the harmonic mean of 10, 20, and 25 is computed, the result is 15.797+, the average number of units sold per $1.00, and the unit price is 6.33+ cents, the same as the arithmetic mean of the unit prices. The computation is as follows:

$$\frac{1}{H} = \frac{\frac{1}{10} + \frac{1}{20} + \frac{1}{25}}{3} = \frac{0.1 + 0.05 + 0.04}{3} = \frac{0.19}{3} = 0.0633+.$$

$$\frac{1}{H} = 0.0633+. \quad H = 15.797+.$$

$$\frac{1.00}{15.797} = 6.33+ \text{ cents.}$$

harmonies. As applied to economic theory, the doctrine that economic life is governed by forces that are essentially in accord with one another and that operate to assure the ultimate welfare of mankind. Although these forces are frequently found in apparent conflict owing to temporary disarrangement, harmony is ultimately restored. The idea is found early in the history of economic thought in the concept of the NATURAL ORDER and in more systematic and comprehensive form, although with some contradictions, in Adam Smith's (1723–1790) development of *LAISSEZ FAIRE*. Later pronouncements of the CLASSICAL SCHOOL, notably in the MALTHUSIAN THEORY OF POPULATION, and in the Ricardian theory of rent (ECONOMIC RENT) left the doctrine of harmonies somewhat impaired. It was reasserted by various adherents of the OPTIMIST SCHOOL, especially Henry C. Carey (1793–1879), the American publicist and economist, and Frédéric Bastiat (1801–1850), a French economist. The latter went beyond the original conception in his emphasis upon divine guidance. The present-day theory of GENERAL EQUILIBRIUM may be said, perhaps, to express scientifically the idea inherent in the doctrine.

Hatch Act. An Act of Congress, 1887, which authorized the establishment of agricultural stations in connection with the LAND-GRANT COLLEGES for the purpose of conducting original research in agricultural science. It was supplemented by legislation passed in 1906 and in 1925.

Havana Conference on Trade and Employment. See explanation under GENEVA TRADE CONFERENCE.

Hawes-Cooper Act. An act of Congress, 1929, exempting goods made by convict labor from a ruling of the United States Supreme Court that prevents a state from imposing taxes or police regulations upon goods in interstate commerce as long as such goods remain in the packages in which they were originally shipped. See also ORIGINAL-PACKAGE CASES.

Hawley-Smoot Tariff. The United States Tariff Act of 1930. It raised the rates on more than 1,000 articles, but it contained a provision that permitted the President to alter the rates within limits of 50 per cent on advice of the UNITED STATES TARIFF COMMISSION. The tariff was nicknamed the *Grundy Tariff* after Joseph Grundy, president of the Pennsylvania Manufacturers Association, who was the chief lobbyist.

headright. A grant of 50 acres of unoccupied land to each immigrant, allowed in the 17th century by some American colonies.

head tax. 1. A tax levied upon immigrant aliens entering at any port in the United States. 2. See also POLL TAX, TAX.

Health, Education, and Welfare, Department of. A department of the United States government, created in 1953, the major responsibilities of which are to promote general welfare in the fields of public health, education, and social security. The operating units of the department are: UNITED STATES PUBLIC HEALTH SERVICE, UNITED STATES OFFICE OF EDUCATION, SOCIAL SECURITY ADMINISTRATION, Office of Vocational Rehabilitation, Food and Drug Administration, and St. Elizabeth's Hospital.

health insurance. A system of insurance against financial loss due to illness. Although not uncommon in Europe, there is no compulsory health-insurance system in the United States (1964). Casualty and life-insurance companies offer such insurance, and some protection is afforded limited numbers in the low-income groups by fraternal orders, labor-union benefit funds, employers' relief funds, and the like. See also INSURANCE.

hedging. A method of selling for future delivery, whereby dealers and processors protect themselves against a declining market price between the time they buy a product and sell or process it. For example, a miller, buying a quantity of wheat to convert into flour, will sell a similar quantity of wheat, which he does not own at the time, at the same price or near the same price as the wheat he buys for processing. He will agree to deliver this extra lot of wheat at the time that his flour is ready for market. If at that time, the price of wheat, and hence of flour, has gone down, he will lose on his flour, but he can buy wheat at the current low price and deliver at a profit the order previously sold for future delivery. If, on the other hand, the price of wheat, and hence of flour, has gone up, he will make an extra profit on his flour. This extra profit he will have to sacrifice, however, by purchasing wheat at the current high price in order to make good his contract to sell. In either event his manufacturing profits are protected. Contracts for future delivery are called *futures*.

hedonistic principle. The idea that although every individual wishes to avoid effort, the desire for well-being and wealth stimulates an attempt to attain them however repugnant the effort expended in so doing may be. Sometimes called *law of self-interest*.

***Helvering* v. *Davis*.** See SOCIAL-SECURITY CASES.

***Helvering* v. *Gerhardt*.** See FEDERAL TAX IMMUNITY CASE.

Hepburn Act. An act of Congress, 1906. It provided that rates determined by the Interstate Commerce Commission should become effective within 30 days of their announcement, and should remain in force unless suspended by a court of law; and extended the jurisdiction of the commission to cover pipe lines, and express and sleeping-car companies.

***Hepburn* v. *Griswold*.** See LEGAL-TENDER CASES.

hidden inflation. The condition that exists when, because of deterioration of the quality of a service or the deterioration of the quality or the reduction of the size or content of a product, less value is offered for the same amount of money. See also INFLATION.

hidden tax. A tax of an indirect nature which is incorporated in the price of goods and services and which is therefore not apparent as such when paid. For example, a CUSTOMS DUTY may increase the price of imported products without the consumer being cognizant of how much of the price is due to the payment of those duties. See also TAX.

higgling. The process of bargaining. Buyers attempt to buy at as low a price as possible, and sellers attempt to sell at as high a price as possible. This necessitates a certain amount of bickering or higgling until for any one product in any particular market, a price is established at which trading takes place.

histogram. See explanation under FREQUENCY DISTRIBUTION.

Historical school. A school of economic thought that first came into prominence in Germany during the middle part of the 19th century. It was a reaction against the abstract and deductive methods of the Classical economists. The writers of the Historical school insisted that economists should turn to history to discover the realities of economic life, and emphasized the evolutionary aspect of economic laws. See also SCHOOLS OF ECONOMIC THOUGHT.

hoarding. 1. Deliberate accumulation of goods, currency, or the supply of some service beyond normal needs. Money saved and placed in a safe-deposit box is hoarded. Stocks of goods beyond the normal inventory requirements of a business or beyond the immediate future needs of a household are likewise hoarded. 2. In KEYNESIAN ECONOMICS, the increase of LIQUIDITY PREFERENCE on the part of the public. Since the quantity of money is fixed by the banking system at any particular time, the public cannot hoard money in the sense of accumulating it. This use of the term, therefore, indicates an attempt rather than an accomplishment. Its significance rests in the effect upon the economy of that attempt. See LIQUIDITY-PREFERENCE THEORY OF INTEREST.

hold-back pay. Wages withheld by an employer, usually for the period necessary to calculate the pay roll. Thus, employees may be paid on Saturday for all work up to Thursday night of a given weekly period.

holding company. A corporation which holds a sufficient quantity of the stock of some other corporation to permit it to direct the latter's affairs. Sometimes referred to as a *controlling company.* See also COMBINATION.

holding the line. A phrase frequently employed to indicate various methods used to prevent prices from rising beyond a current level. The freezing of prices, checking of bank credit, the creation of special bank reserves, and the imposition of restrictions on consumer loans are among the measures commonly used.

Home Building and Loan Association* v. *Blaisdell. A case arising out of state mortgage-moratorium laws passed during the depression of the 1930's. The United States Supreme Court ruled, 290 U. S. 398 (1934), that such laws, extending a mortgagor's right to redeem foreclosed property beyond the time limit stipulated when the mortgage was made, were a proper exercise of the state's police power required by the circumstances of an economic emergency and that the laws did not violate the contract clause (Art. I, sec. 10) of the Constitution.

home economics. A general term covering a large variety of subject matter, including household skills such as cooking, sewing, child care, budgeting, and consumer purchasing for the home, and sometimes training for gainful employment in certain special fields such as dietetics.

home industry. See DOMESTIC SYSTEM.

Homestead Act. An act of Congress, 1862. It granted 160 acres of public lands free to settlers after 5 years of residence or at $1.25 per acre after 6 months of residence.

homestead-aid benefit association. See BUILDING AND LOAN ASSOCIATION.

homework. As applied to some industries, the practice of supplying materials to workers so that they perform certain operations in the production of a commodity at home. Such workers are generally paid on a piecework basis.

Hoosac Mills case. A case, *United States* v. *Butler*, 297 U. S. 1 (1936), in which the Supreme Court of the United States invalidated the first Agricultural Adjustment Act. The court asserted that, under the federal Constitution, the government had no power to enforce commands on the farmer to secure compliance with the price and production-quota objectives of this statute, regulation of agriculture being outside the scope of the delegated power of Congress and reserved, by the 10th Amendment of the Constitution, to the states. As a consequence, the court continued, Congress could not secure compliance of the farmer through the use of the taxing and appropriatory power. In the court's opinion this meant that the processing tax, provided for in the act, was not a bona fide revenue measure but part of a plan of regulation, itself unconstitutional, and that the appropriation of the proceeds of this tax could not be sustained under the general welfare clause of the Constitution since the phrase "general welfare" did not comprehend the use to which these proceeds were to be put. See AGRICULTURAL ADJUSTMENT ACT (first), AGRICULTURAL ADJUSTMENT ACT CASE (second).

Hoover moratorium. A proposal made on June 20, 1931, by Herbert Hoover, then President of the United States, and subsequently ratified by Congress, to the effect that a moratorium of 1 year be declared on all reparation payments from the defeated powers of World War I, and on all intergovernmental debts created by loans made among the Allied and Associated Powers during and immediately after World War I. See INTERALLIED DEBTS.

horizontal expansion. Expansion of a business establishment by absorbing or constructing additional facilities to take care of an increased volume of the activity in which the establishment is already engaged.

horizontal labor union. See CRAFT UNION.

hot money. A term applied to various kinds of money transactions that are illegal, or at least questionable, from the standpoint of the economy as a whole. It is sometimes applied to short-term capital movements from country to country which are independent of the balance of payments arising from the ordinary course of trade. Funds borrowed abroad because of a lower rate of interest than that obtaining in the borrower's own country are a case in point. Such operations are often embarrassing to a country's financial structure because they complicate the problem of maintaining equilibrium in the BALANCE OF PAYMENTS.

hot-oil case. A case, *Panama Refining Co.* v. *Ryan*, 293 U. S. 388 (1935), in which the Supreme Court of the United States invalidated a portion of the National Industrial Recovery Act under which the President had sought to prohibit the movement in interstate and foreign commerce of petroleum or petroleum products in excess of production or marketing quotas fixed by the laws of oil-producing states of the United States. The purpose of the President's action under the law had been to assist in stabilizing production and prices in the petroleum industry. The court ruled that the authority under which the President had acted constituted a delegation of legislative power to the executive and was therefore unconstitutional.

household system. An economy in which the clan, tribe, or family, as an economic unit, produces the goods required for home consumption. Also called *domestic industry, family industry.*

Housing and Home Finance Agency. An independent agency of the United States government, created in 1947, having to do with various phases of national housing. It consists (1964) of the Community Facilities Administration, the Urban Renewal Administration, the FEDERAL HOUSING ADMINISTRATION, the PUBLIC HOUSING ADMINISTRATION, and the FEDERAL NATIONAL MORTGAGE ASSOCIATION.

Housing Expediter, Office of. A special agency, created by Congress in 1946, to promote housing for veterans. A year later this agency was invested with administrative responsibility for federal rent-control legislation. The office was terminated in 1951.

hypothecate. The act of depositing property to secure a loan. The property in question is then said to be hypothecated.

hypothesis. A tentative statement setting forth an apparent relationship among observed facts. See also INDUCTIVE METHOD.

I

idle money. A term usually referring to inactive bank deposits when the ratio between the bank's total reserves and deposits permits of additional loans. Under such conditions the deposits in question are idle in the sense that they do not represent constantly fluctuating balances resulting from active checking accounts, and they are idle also in the sense that they are not used to support bank loans.

illegal strike. 1. Work stoppage by union members not authorized by union officials or voted upon in accordance with union regulations. Sometimes called a *quickie, outlaw,* or *wildcat strike.* 2. Any strike called in violation of the conditions set forth in the LABOR-MANAGEMENT RELATIONS (TAFT-HARTLEY) ACT of 1947. See also STRIKE.

illth. Consumer goods and services that are injurious to the individuals who consume them and to society as a whole.

immigrant remittances. Funds sent by immigrants to their country of origin for the benefit of relatives and friends. Such remittances are an invisible item of trade and have the same effect on the balance of payments of the country from which the remittances are sent as an import of merchandise from the country to which the remittances are sent.

impair investment. An investment which does not create a new capital asset; for example, the purchase of existing securities from other holders, or loans for the purpose of consumption. See also INVESTMENT.

impartial chairman. As applied to labor relations, an arbitrator appointed jointly by labor and management to assist in the settlement of any disputes that may arise in reference to a specific labor contract. See also ARBITRATION.

imperfect competition. The situation said to exist when, because of peculiar conditions of the market or advantages held by certain buyers or sellers, prices can be abnormally influenced by one or more traders. In the retail trade, for example, imperfect competition is the rule because the market is scattered and the buyers cannot always estimate quality accurately. Monopolistic or semi-monopolistic advantages held by certain traders also create imperfect competition. See also COMPETITION.

impersonal account. A ledger account bearing a title which is not a personal name; for example, cash account, bank account, capital account. See also ACCOUNT.

implicit. See IMPUTED.

import. To receive merchandise from abroad, particularly from foreign countries; hence, merchandise so received. See also INVISIBLE ITEMS OF TRADE.

import excise tax. A CUSTOMS DUTY imposed by the United States government and identical with all other such duties except that it is exempt from the provisions of the TRADE AGREEMENTS ACT, which permits the President to alter customs duties as much as 50 per cent. Import excise taxes thus remain fixed unless and until changed by the Congress. They were originally applied to copper, petroleum, coal, lumber, and other important products.

import license. Authority from a government to import a specified quantity of a particular commodity. Such authority must often be secured when imports of specific commodities are subject to an IMPORT QUOTA.

import quota. A specified maximum amount of a commodity permitted to enter a country within a certain period of time.

impost. A tax, especially an import duty.

imprest fund. A definite sum of money set aside for cash expenditures and renewed from time to time to the extent of the exact amount of the signed receipts obtained when the cash expenditures are made. An imprest fund is frequently used for petty-cash expenses and withdrawals. It is easily audited as the sum of the cash on hand and the receipts for payments should always equal the total amount of the fund.

improved good. An economic good (commodity), usually imported, which is eventually processed or assembled in some other product and hence increased in value. See also ECONOMIC GOOD.

imputed. A generic term used in economics to denote an estimated value when no cash payment is made such as would establish an absolute value. For example, an enterprise might calculate imputed interest on its invested capital when no interest as such is paid. Imputed rent might be estimated for a dwelling owned and occupied by the owner. An imputed cost to an INDIVIDUAL PROPRIETORSHIP might be the estimated labor of the proprietor. The term *implicit* is sometimes used in the same sense, in contradistinction to *explicit*, which indicates situations involving a definite payment.

imputed interest. Interest, not involving a cash expenditure, charged for the use of capital goods. When capital is invested in an enterprise, interest on that capital, even though not paid as such in cash, is frequently regarded as a cost of production. This cost is imputed interest, sometimes called *implicit interest.* The term is used in contradistinction to LOAN INTEREST. See also GROSS INTEREST.

inactive stock. See explanation under CAPITAL STOCK.

incentive taxation. Any tax plan which, by modifying the structure of an existing system of taxation, changing its rates, shifting its incidence, or by other appropriate change, is expected to stimulate investment or business activity generally.

incentive wage system. A system of wage payments which provides bonuses for increased production. See also WAGE.

incidence of taxation. The place where the burden of a tax actually rests, irrespective of how or against whom it is formally levied. For example, the incidence of a sales tax almost invariably rests on the consumer, although the seller is the one formally taxed and it is he who remits the tax to the government.

income. 1. As used in theoretical economics, the money return or other material benefits arising from the use of wealth or from the services of free human beings. See also DISPOSABLE INCOME, NATIONAL INCOME, PSYCHIC INCOME. 2. As used in accounting, the term is a broad one indicating, in general, the receipts of an enterprise or of an individual. See also EARNED INCOME, GROSS INCOME, NET INCOME, UNEARNED INCOME.

income and expenditure equation. A mathematical expression of the relation, under conditions of equilibrium, between the national income on the one hand and consumer expenditures and investment on the other. The equation is:

$$Y = C + I$$

when

$$Y = \text{the national income,}$$
$$C = \text{consumer expenditures,}$$
$$I = \text{investments.}$$

This equation is useful because of its implied relation to savings and the general level of economic activity. For if

$$Y = C + I,$$

and

$$S \text{ (savings)} = Y - C,$$

then

$$Y = C + S,$$

and

$$I = S.$$

To maintain the national income, and hence the general level of economic activity, all collective savings must therefore be invested. For conditions under disequilibrium, see PROPENSITY TO INVEST. See also KEYNESIAN ECONOMICS.

income bond. See explanation under BOND.

income statement. See PROFIT-AND-LOSS STATEMENT.

income tax. In the United States, a tax levied upon corporate and individual incomes in excess of specified amounts and less certain deductions permitted by law. See also CORPORATION INCOME TAX, INDIVIDUAL INCOME TAX, TAX.

income-tax case. A case, *Pollock* v. *Farmers' Loan and Trust Co.*, 157 U. S. 429 (1894); 158 U. S. 601 (1895), in which the Supreme Court of the United States held unconstitutional the Income Tax Law of 1894. The issue involved in the court's decision was whether a federal income tax was a direct tax within the meaning of Art. I, sec. 3, of the Constitution which requires that direct taxes be apportioned among the states according to population. The court decided that an income tax was a direct tax, and that since the law of 1894 had not apportioned its burden among the states according to population, the law was void. The decision stimulated agitation for a constitutional change which would make it unnecessary to apportion income taxes, and this agitation culminated in the adoption of the 16th, or "income-tax," Amendment to the Constitution in 1913. In substance this amendment declares that Congress may levy and collect taxes on income from any source without apportioning them among the several states according to population.

inconvertible money. See IRREDEEMABLE MONEY.

incorporation. See CORPORATION.

increasing costs. Costs which, under a given set of conditions, increase, per unit of product, as the total production increases. So far as poorer and deeper mines have to be used to meet a constant or increasing demand, the coal-mining industry may be said to be operating under a condition of increasing costs. See also COST.

increasing misery, theory of. See MARXIAN LAW OF CAPITALIST ACCUMULATION.

increasing returns. 1. Usually the condition which exists as long as each successively applied equal amount of one or two factors of production (land, labor, or capital) to the remaining factor or factors yields a greater increase in production than the application just preceding. This is a common situation before the condition of DIMINISHING RETURNS (*q.v.*) begins to operate. 2. The term is also used to describe the condition that exists when output is increased without adding to any factor of production. Division of labor, or economies brought about by purchasing in large quantities, or increased productivity on the part of labor may bring about increasing returns as thus defined.

increment. An increase, a gain, or something added. See also UNEARNED INCREMENT.

indemnity. 1. As applied to trading, an option to buy or sell a definite quantity of a commodity at a stated price within a specified length of time. 2. A guarantee against possible loss. 3. A payment for damages.

indent. An order from a buyer to a middleman importer to import certain specified goods at a stated price. The importer may accept or refuse the indent within a specified length of time, usually about 6 weeks. The term is sometimes more generally applied to any order for foreign merchandise.

indenture. A formal documentary agreement between two or more persons. So called because of the custom, now obsolete, of placing the copies of an agreement together, before delivery to the interested parties, and tearing an irregular edge on one side. Matching of the edges of any two documents at a later date was considered proof of the identity of the original documents.

indentured servants. Persons who, during the latter part of the 17th century, received their passage to America in return for a definite term of service in the colonies. They also received their maintenance during that period of service.

independent treasury system. A system, begun in 1840, of handling funds and financing the United States government independently of banks. The system was introduced because of the bank panic of 1837, at which time the United States Treasury lost large sums deposited in state banks. The system was temporarily abolished in 1841, re-established in 1846, and finally terminated in 1920. Also called *subtreasury system.*

independent union. A labor union that is not affiliated with a national labor organization. See also LABOR UNION.

index number. A figure which discloses the relative change, if any, of prices, costs, or some similar phenomena between one period of time and some other period of time selected as the *base period.* The latter period is usually assigned the index number of 100. There are numerous methods of calculating an index number. For three commonly used types, see AGGREGATIVE INDEX NUMBER, FISHER'S IDEAL INDEX, RELATIVE-VALUE INDEX NUMBER.

indifference curve. A graphic representation of the various combinations of two commodities or services that will yield equal satisfaction to a given consumer. An indifference curve is shown in the

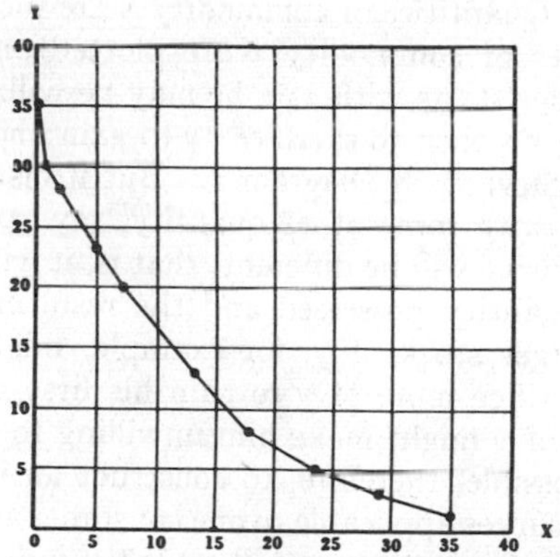

appended diagram. Quantities of commodity *y* are plotted on the *Y* axis, and quantities of commodity *x* are plotted on the *X* axis. The consumer starts with a stock of 35*y*. He sacrifices 5*y* to gain 1*x*. It is a matter of indifference to him whether he has 35*y*, or 30*y* and 1*x*; in other words, 35*y* yields him the same satisfaction as 30*y* and 1*x*. With 1*x* now in his possession, he is willing to sacrifice 2 more of *y* to gain another *x*. It is a matter of indifference to him whether he has 35*y*, or 30*y* and 1*x*, or 28*y* and 2*x*, etc., according to the following *indifference schedule.* The last two columns in this schedule contain the figures plotted on the chart.

Sacrifices of *y*	Gains of *x*	Total stock of *y*	Total stock of *x*
		35	0
5	1	30	1
2	1	28	2
5	3	23	5
3	2	20	7
7	6	13	13
5	5	8	18
3	5	5	23
2	6	3	29
2	7	1	35

See also INDIFFERENCE MAP.

indifference map. A graphic representation of a number of INDIFFERENCE CURVES (*q.v.*). An indifference map is shown in the appended Diagram 1. Quantities of commodity *y* are plotted on the *Y* axis, and quantities of commodity *x* are plotted on the *X* axis. If a given consumer starts with 35*y*, he may be willing to sacrifice 5*y* in order to gain 1*x*, then to sacrifice 2*y* to gain another *x*, as shown in indifference curve *A* in Diagram 1. But if instead of 35*y* the consumer starts with some other quantity, say 50, or 10, or 83*y*, the indifference curve will be different; that is, it will differ according to the initial quantity possessed and the resulting exchange dispositions. A larger stock of *y*, for example, might prompt the consumer to sacrifice more of *y* to gain his first *x*, whereas a smaller initial stock of *y* might make him unwilling to sacrifice even 5*y* for 1*x*. It is possible, therefore, to construct an indefinite number of indifference curves applicable to one consumer and two commodities. A group of these curves on one chart is the indifference map. Each indifference curve, proceeding from left to right, represents a higher scale of satisfactions because of the increased quantities involved.

An indifference map makes it possible to forecast with some degree of accuracy the quantities of each of the two commodities that a consumer will purchase, given the consumer's income and the prices of the commodities. Assume, for example, that the consumer's income is $150 for a given period of time, that the market price of *y* is $7.50 per unit, and the price of *x* is $5 per unit. If the entire income were spent on *y*, 20 items could be bought; if spent on *x*, 30 items could be bought. These quantities are plotted on axis *Y* and axis *X*, respectively, and a straight line is drawn connecting them, as shown in the appended Diagram 2. This straight line shows the various combinations of the two commodities that can be bought with $150 at established prices, regardless of which combinations yield the greatest satisfaction. At point *B*, however, the straight line is tangent to an indifference curve. Point *B* on the indifference curve indicates a combination of the two commodities that will yield at least as much satisfaction as any other combination represented by any other point on that indifference curve. Also, this curve is the farthest to the right of any that can be tangent to the straight line. The possible combinations indicated by this curve, therefore, offer greater satisfactions than those indicated by any curve to the left of it. Hence, point *B* discloses not only the amount of each commodity that can be bought with the stipulated income but also the amount of each that will be bought at that income to yield the maximum amount of satisfaction. The amounts are 8*y* and 18*x*. See also PRICE CONSUMPTION CURVE.

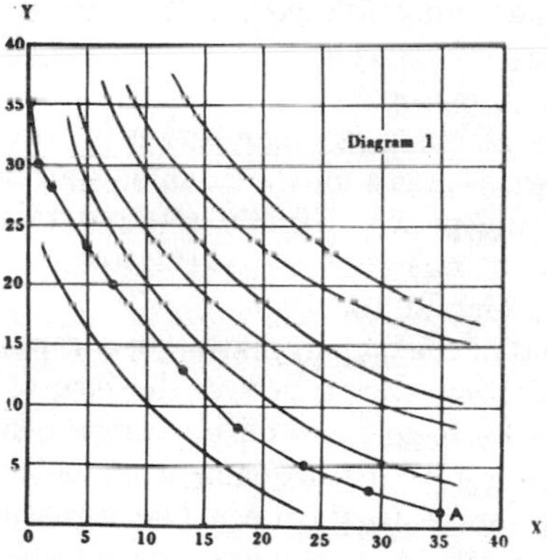

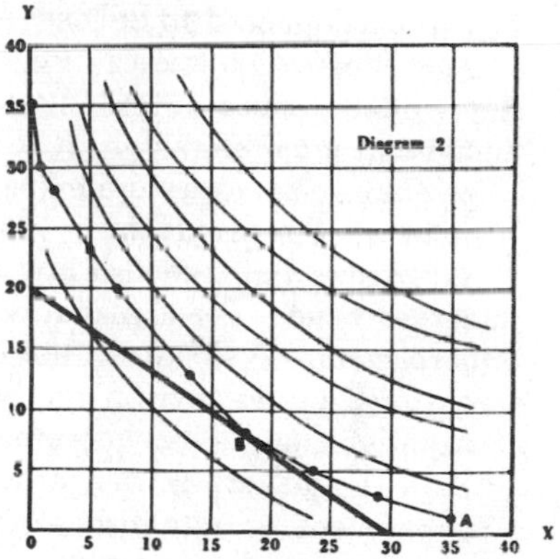

indifference schedule. See explanation under INDIFFERENCE CURVE.
indirect cost. See FIXED COST.
indirect exporting. The process of exporting through a middleman such as an export merchant. Many producers, wishing to reach a foreign market but too small to maintain an export department, use this means of developing their foreign trade.
indirect foreign-exchange standard. See GOLD-EXCHANGE STANDARD.
indirect production. The making of a tool, a machine, or any other kind of capital good that will, in turn, assist in making a product used directly to satisfy a human want. The tool or the machine in question does not directly satisfy the want but facilitates the production of something else that does; in other words, it facilitates

the production of a consumer good. Sometimes called ***roundabout*** or *capitalistic production.* The term is used in contradistinction to DIRECT PRODUCTION. See also PRODUCTION.

indirect tax. A tax, the burden of which can be fairly readily shifted or passed on to someone else by the person who is required by law to pay the tax to the government. The term is used in contradistinction to DIRECT TAX (*q.v.*). Most EXCISE TAXES are indirect taxes. See also TAX.

individual income tax. In the United States, a tax levied upon individual incomes, in excess of a specified minimum amount, less certain deductions allowed by law, the rate of the tax increasing as the amount of the taxable income increases. Both the federal government and many states levy such taxes. See also INCOME TAX.

individualism. As applied to economic life, the enjoyment by individuals and groups of the rights of freedom of contract and private property. The term implies PRIVATE ENTERPRISE and LAISSEZ FAIRE as opposed to COLLECTIVISM and STATE SOCIALISM. See also FREEDOM OF CONTRACT, PRIVATE PROPERTY.

Individualist school. See CLASSICAL SCHOOL.

individual proprietorship. A form of business organization in which one individual owns and manages, assumes all the risks of, and derives all the profits from, an enterprise. Usually referred to as *proprietorship.* See also FORMS OF BUSINESS ORGANIZATION.

indorsed bond. See explanation under BOND.

indorsement. A signature, not that of the maker, drawer, or acceptor, customarily written on the back, but sometimes on the face of a negotiable or similar instrument by means of which a person other than the maker, drawer, or acceptor of the instrument guarantees a payment or establishes transfer of legal title. The signature may be a RESTRICTIVE INDORSEMENT, a QUALIFIED INDORSEMENT, or a CONDITIONAL INDORSEMENT. It may also be a BLANK INDORSEMENT or a SPECIAL INDORSEMENT. Also spelled ***endorsement.***

induced consumption. Increased consumer spending resulting from new CAPITAL FORMATION. Additional employees in the capital goods industries are the first recipients of increased income; as a proportion of these earnings is spent, employees in the consumer goods industries become recipients, resulting in additional consumption, etc. See MULTIPLIER PRINCIPLE.

induced investment. New CAPITAL FORMATION resulting from an increase in the rate of consumer spending. The extent of the new capital formation depends upon such factors as the excess plant capacity (if any) in existence, the amount of capital required to produce one unit of consumer product, individual estimates of the duration of the increased consumer spending, etc. See ACCELERATION PRINCIPLE.

inductive method. As used in economics, a process of logical reasoning, starting with observed facts and arriving at a generalization, setting forth an apparent relationship among those observed facts. Such a generalization is called a HYPOTHESIS; when repeatedly verified by the same method it is called a THEORY. The usefulness of the inductive method depends upon the validity of the basic observations. When properly used, however, it has a recognized place in scientific investigation. Sometimes it is called the *realistic method.*

industrial bank. A financial organization which makes relatively small loans to individuals on terms usually somewhat more liberal than those granted by a COMMERCIAL BANK. These more liberal terms generally provide for weekly or monthly installment payments until a loan is liquidated. See also BANK.

industrial bond. See explanation under BOND.

industrial democracy. A term first used to indicate democratic government within labor unions. More recently, it has come to mean limitation upon the absolute control of management resulting from such practices as collective bargaining, employee stock ownership with full voting rights, and profit sharing. Rather vaguely, the term implies a limited form of socialization.

industrial life insurance. Life insurance issued in policies of small amounts, averaging less than $250, and usually calling for the payment of weekly or monthly premiums by the person insured. See also LIFE INSURANCE.

industrial relations. The relations between employers and employees. Since the beginning of the 20th century the insistent demands on the part of employees for a voice in the determination of wages and working conditions and the growing public control over employer-employee relationships have created a specialized field of study generally known by this term. Referred to also as *labor relations.*

industrial-relations court. A court organized to adjudicate or arbitrate labor disputes. Such a court existed in Kansas between 1920 and 1925 for the settlement of disputes in certain industries. Most of the law establishing the court's jurisdiction was subsequently invalidated by the United States Supreme Court. See *WOLFF PACKING CO.* v. *INDUSTRIAL COURT OF KANSAS.*

industrial research. Research conducted by or in the interests of private industries to discover more efficient methods of production or to develop new and improved products. The term is also sometimes applied to studies having to do with marketing methods, labor relations, and the like.

Industrial Revolution. The conditions which existed during the latter part of the 18th and the early part of the 19th centuries when changes in the techniques of production brought about the replacement of the DOMESTIC SYSTEM by the FACTORY SYSTEM.

industrial union. A labor union, the membership of which is made up of workers from an entire industry. A union of coal miners is an example. Also called *vertical union.* See also LABOR UNION.

Industrial Workers of the World. A revolutionary labor organization founded in the United States in 1904. It is an INDUSTRIAL UNION, including within its membership workers of every trade. Until 1907 the Western Federation of Miners was affiliated with the IWW. Since then the membership has been largely confined to migrant workers.

industry. Productive enterprise, especially manufacturing or certain service enterprises such as transportation and communications, which employs relatively large amounts of capital and labor. The term is often used in a collective sense referring, for example, to the production activities of an entire country or other area. It is also used to identify a special segment of productive enterprise such, for example, as the steel industry. Normally "trading" is not included in the concept "industry," the phrase "commerce and industry" being used if reference is made both to industry as defined above and to buying and selling.

industry-wide bargaining. As applied to labor relations, negotiations carried on between employers and employees with a view to formulating uniform regulations and wage contracts for all workers in an industry, irrespective of the number or location of the different plants or companies concerned.

inelastic demand. Demand which increases or decreases in relatively small volume as prices increase or decrease. In general the demand for necessities is inelastic. See also COEFFICIENT OF ELASTICITY, DEMAND.

inelastic supply. Supply which increases or decreases only slightly despite extensive changes in price. See also COEFFICIENT OF ELASTICITY, SUPPLY.

infant industry. A term applied to newly established or relatively undeveloped manufacturing enterprises in the United States, with particular reference to the argument, especially popular during the latter part of the 19th century, that such industries should be protected from foreign competition by import duties until such a time as they could compete on an equal footing with foreign producers.

inflation. A disproportionately large and relatively sudden increase in the general price level. Inflation may occur when the quantity of MONEY or DEPOSIT CURRENCY in circulation is large compared with the quantity of goods and services offered, or when, because of a loss of confidence in the national money on the part of the public, a general and widespread attempt to convert money into commodities is precipitated. A normal increase in the price level after a period of depression is not generally regarded as inflation. See also HIDDEN INFLATION.

inflationary gap. A statistical phrase denoting the amount by which actual private spending and government expenses exceed the theoretical amount of spending necessary to maintain full employment, or exceed the theoretical amount of spending adequate to absorb all the available goods and services without appreciably raising the price level.

inherent vice. An unperceived defect in goods constituting the cargo of a ship, existing at the time the goods are shipped, which occasions loss or damage to the owner before the cargo reaches its destination. Grain which deteriorates during shipment is a case in point.

inheritance tax. A tax, usually progressive in nature, levied upon the property which individual beneficiaries receive from an estate of a deceased person. The term should not be confused with an ESTATE TAX. See also TAX.

injunction. An order issued by a court of equity demanding that certain activities cease under penalty of contempt of court.

in kind. Value in things, as distinguished from value in money. Thus, payment in kind is payment in produce or commodities.

inland bill. See explanation under BILL.

input and output analysis. An extension of the GROSS NATIONAL PRODUCT showing all transactions of individual enterprises with other firms within a given accounting period, inputs being what a firm buys, and outputs, what it sells. The entries must balance as the total expenditures of all groups equal the total receipts of all groups, and investments equal savings. Input-output calculations have been so extended during recent years as to require the most modern ELECTRONIC DATA PROCESSING.

in re Debs. See DEBS CASE.

inscribed. As applied to certain United States savings notes, the term indicates that the United States Treasury does not keep a record of the names of the owners of the notes as it does in the case of United States registered bonds. Instead, the record is kept by the federal reserve banks and their branches.

insolvent. The condition which exists when liabilities, other than those representing ownership, amount to more than the total assets. Thus, in the statement given below, the liabilities, representing ownership, amount to $400,000. Other liabilities amount to $1,600,000 while the total assets amount only to $1,000,000. An insolvent condition therefore exists.

Assets		Liabilities	
Plant	$800,000	Capital stock	$400,000
Cash	200,000	Accounts payable	600,000
Loss	1,000,000	Bonds	1,000,000
	$2,000,000		$2,000,000

installment bond. See explanation under BOND.

installment buying. Goods or services purchased on terms which call for partial payments at regular intervals over a specified period of time.

institutional economics. An approach to the study of economics which emphasizes the influences of the social environment on man's economic behavior. For example, Thorstein Veblen (1857–1929) argued that, in the course of social evolution, the institution of private property had subordinated the instinct of workmanship to the desire for the accumulation of private property. Accordingly, the struggle for property, prestige, and power tended to overshadow the kind of competition that reduces prices and makes for better quality. This tendency is manifested, according to Veblen, by monopoly, maintenance of price through limitation of production, and the extension of distribution control over wholesale and retail agencies. See also ECONOMICS.

institutionalism. The extension of the authority of public institutions, particularly in the area of social life. See also INSTITUTIONAL ECONOMICS.

instrument. A general term often applied to documents of various kinds; for example, a negotiable instrument or an instrument of credit such as a PROMISSORY NOTE.

instrumental capital. See explanation under CAPITAL GOOD.

insular bond. See explanation under BOND.

insurance. Protection against risk. To secure such protection private contracts are made according to which, for a consideration of a premium paid by one party, called the insured, another agrees to indemnify the insured should he suffer losses specified in the contract. In the United States private insurance contracts are now subject to congressional regulation under the interstate commerce clause. Beneficiaries of various kinds of social insurance provided by a government may or may not make direct contributions for the support of such insurance; when such contributions are made, they are usually supplemented by public funds. There are innumerable kinds of insurance, the names of which are often self-descriptive. For some of the more important kinds of insurance see CASUALTY INSURANCE, COINSURANCE, CROP INSURANCE, DEPOSIT INSURANCE, EMPLOYERS' LIABILITY INSURANCE, FIDELITY INSURANCE, HEALTH INSURANCE, LIFE INSURANCE, OLD-AGE AND SURVIVORS' INSURANCE, REINSURANCE, SOCIAL INSURANCE, UNEMPLOYMENT INSURANCE, USE AND OCCUPANCY INSURANCE. See also INSURANCE CASE.

insurance case. A case, *United States* v. *South-Eastern Underwriters Association*, 322 U. S. 533 (1944), in which the Supreme Court of the United States effectively overruled an earlier decision, *Paul* v. *Virginia*, 8 Wallace 168 (1869), and held that insurance policies which establish contractual relations across state lines must be considered interstate commerce and hence potentially subject to congressional regulation. The case specifically held the Sherman Antitrust Act applicable to interstate insurance business.

intangible asset. As used in accounting, an asset having no material substance and not representing anything material. Good will and patent rights are examples. See also ASSET.

intangible property. 1. A right or interest of some kind; for example, a claim evidenced by ownership of a bond, or an interest in a business indicated by ownership of a share of stock. 2. Any property the value of which cannot readily be obtained by an appraisal. See also PROPERTY.

intensive cultivation. The use of relatively large amounts of capital and labor on relatively small amounts of agricultural land.

Interallied debts. Debts arising out of the network of intergovernmental loans made by the principal Allied and Associated Powers in World War I. France and Great Britain had made loans early in the war to the lesser Allies. The United States later made loans to both France and Great Britain and to other allied states and thus became the principal creditor. Virtually none of the loans has been repaid. See also HOOVER MORATORIUM.

Inter-American Development Bank. The 20-nation American-hemisphere credit agency, established in 1959, to make loans to both public and private agencies. All loans are for developmental purposes in Latin America. Some of these loans may be repaid in the currency of the borrowing state. The new bank's capital is approximately $1 billion.

Inter-American Institute of Agricultural Sciences. A research organization supported by some 19 American republics (1964) which has its headquarters at Turrialba, Costa Rica. It is concerned mainly with research on important tropical industrial and food plants and in the field of animal industry.

Inter-American Statistical Institute. A semiofficial professional organization founded May 12, 1940, to advance statistical science and its practical application among the nations of the Western Hemisphere.

interchangeable bond. See explanation under BOND.

interchangeable parts. The characteristic feature of a system of manufacturing in which any part of a machine can be interchanged with an identical part in any similar machine. Mass production is made possible by this emphasis upon interchangeable parts. Large quantities of individual parts are made with such accuracy and tested with such precision that they can be selected indiscriminately and assembled into a final product.

interest. A sum paid or calculated for the use of capital. The sum is usually expressed in terms of a RATE or percentage of the capital involved, called the *interest rate*. See also ACCRUED INTEREST, CAPITAL, COMPOUND INTEREST, GROSS INTEREST, LEGAL INTEREST, PURE INTEREST, SIMPLE INTEREST. For theories of interest see AGIO THEORY OF INTEREST, LIQUIDITY-PREFERENCE THEORY OF INTEREST, LOANABLE-FUNDS THEORY OF INTEREST, MARGINAL-UTILITY THEORY OF INTEREST.

interest bond. See explanation under BOND.

interest rate. See explanation under INTEREST.

interim bond. See explanation under BOND.

Interior, Department of the. A major administrative unit with a secretary of cabinet rank, created March 3, 1849. Among the more important of its somewhat miscellaneous subsidiary units are the UNITED STATES FISH AND WILDLIFE SERVICE, the Bureau of Mines, the RECLAMATION BUREAU, the NATIONAL PARK SERVICE, the BUREAU OF LAND MANAGEMENT, and the BONNEVILLE POWER ADMINISTRATION.

interlocking directorate. The condition which exists when one person serves as a director of two or more companies. Under federal law in the United States the term applies if each of the companies of which the person is a director has combined capital, surplus, and undivided profits of at least $1,000,000, if all of them are engaged in interstate commerce, and if they are natural competitors. See also DIRECTOR.

intermediate good. See explanation under CAPITAL GOOD.

internal improvement. Some new capital construction of a public nature carried out at public expense. Examples are highways, canals, bridges, or dredged harbors.

internal national debt. That portion of the NATIONAL DEBT owed to persons residing within the nation incurring the debt.

internal revenue. In the United States, federal income from all taxation other than customs duties.

Internal Revenue Service. A branch of the Department of the Treasury of the United States which supervises the assessment and collection of all internal revenue taxes.

internal revenue tax. See EXCISE TAX.

International Bank for Reconstruction and Development. An international credit and development agency created in December, 1945, on the basis of a plan developed a year earlier at the United Nations Monetary and Financial Conference held at Bretton Woods, N. H. By 1964 some 101 nations, including the United States, had become members. With headquarters in Washington, D. C., the bank seeks to promote the rehabilitation and development of member nations. To that end it insures or otherwise guarantees private loans and, when no private source of capital is available, it provides loans on its own resources and credit. In 1960 a subsidiary agency, known as the International Development Association, open to all member countries of the bank, came into being. This allied agency has purposes similar to those of the bank; however, it is chiefly concerned in making so-called "soft" loans to underdeveloped countries to assist them in advancing projects of basic importance to their economic development. See also BANK.

International Chamber of Commerce. A world trade organization established in Paris in 1920 and granted consultative status by the ECONOMIC AND SOCIAL COUNCIL of the UNITED NATIONS in 1946. It acts as a clearinghouse for the exchange of views on international economic policies. Membership, derived from many countries, consists of chambers of commerce, trade and industrial associations, and individual firms engaged in business enterprises.

International Civil Aviation Organization. An international organization which, through an assembly and an executive council, formulates policies and recommends procedures by means of which member states may develop international civil aviation with proper regard for safety standards, efficiency, economy of service, and equality of opportunity. The organization, established on a provisional basis in June, 1945, became a permanent international body on April 4, 1947, when 26 states had ratified the Convention on International Civil Aviation which was drafted at an international air conference held in Chicago in 1944. In 1964 there were 101 members.

International Confederation of Free Trade Unions. An international labor organization established to counter the communist-dominated WORLD FEDERATION OF TRADE UNIONS. When it was organized in London in 1949 its membership included 48 million workers in 53 countries and territories. American participants included the AMERICAN FEDERATION OF LABOR, the CONGRESS OF INDUSTRIAL ORGANIZATIONS, and the United Mine Workers. Permanent headquarters were established at Brussels, Belgium.

International Cooperation Administration. A semiautonomous unit of the United States Department of State, administering the substantial sums voted annually by Congress to strengthen the defenses of nations allied to, or otherwise identified with, the non-Communist West, and to provide economic and technical assistance. Under the Foreign Assistance Act of 1961 it was succeeded by the Agency for International Development (AID).

International Cotton Advisory Committee. An informal group of representatives of the principal cotton-producing countries organized at Washington in 1939, and subsequently largely inactive. A study group, organized to prepare recommendations for reducing cotton surpluses by international agreement, was unable to agree upon a report and dissolved in 1946.

International Court of Justice. A tribunal consisting of 15 judges from various nations, organized under the United Nations Charter to settle legal disputes between nations, when such disputes are submitted to it, and to advise the United Nations on legal questions. All member states of the United Nations are *ipso facto* parties to the court's statute and nonmembers may become parties as determined by the GENERAL ASSEMBLY and SECURITY COUNCIL of the United Nations. The court's permanent headquarters is The Hague, the Netherlands. See also UNITED NATIONS.

international economics. That part of the study of economics which treats of international trade, finance, foreign exchange, and similar subjects. See also ECONOMICS.

international double taxation. See DOUBLE TAXATION.

International Finance Corporation. An international organization open only to member countries of the INTERNATIONAL BANK FOR RECONSTRUCTION AND DEVELOPMENT. Established in 1956, it has an authorized capital of $100 million payable in gold or United States currency. Its aim is to foster the growth of productive private enterprise in so-called underdeveloped areas of the world.

International Finance, Office of. A part of the United States Treasury

Department established in 1947 to advise and assist the Secretary of the Treasury in matters pertaining to foreign financial, monetary, and exchange activities, as well as to governmental loans and assistance programs.

international gold-bullion standard. See explanation under GOLD-BULLION STANDARD.

International Harvester case. A case, *United States* v. *International Harvester Co.*, 274 U. S. 693 (1927), in which the United States Supreme Court enunciated substantially the same doctrine developed in the UNITED STATES STEEL CASE (*q.v.*), viz., that the mere size of a corporation is not prima-facie evidence of violation of the antitrust statutes. The court consequently refused to order the dissolution of the International Harvester Company even though it was a combination of producers of over 80 per cent of the agricultural implements manufactured in the United States.

International Labor Organization. An association of over 100 nations, including the United States, financed by the member governments and set up as an autonomous part of the League of Nations following World War I. Its purpose is to further the interests of labor in the various member nations and particularly to eliminate substandard working conditions and increase social security. In 1947 the International Labor Organization became an affiliated agency of the United Nations.

International Monetary Fund. A fund, plans for which were first elaborated in July, 1944, at the United States Monetary and Financial Conference held at Bretton Woods, N. H. The fund, supported by subscriptions of 91 (1964) member nations, seeks to stabilize international exchange and promote balanced and orderly trade. According to the terms of the Articles of Agreement creating the fund, member nations may obtain foreign currencies under adequate safeguards when needed, thus making it possible for them to correct temporary maladjustments in their balance of payments without currency depreciation and other measures destructive of general international trade and prosperity. The United States became a member of the fund in July, 1945.

International Refugee Organization. A SPECIALIZED AGENCY created by the UNITED NATIONS devoted to the interests of refugees and displaced persons, its primary purpose being to repatriate or resettle such individuals. Operations of the organization began officially in the summer of 1948.

international stock. See explanation under CAPITAL STOCK.

International Sugar Council. An international organization of 21 states created in 1937, to maintain a satisfactory equilibrium between the world production and consumption of sugar. Although inactive during World War II, its secretariat in London has continued to assemble data in preparation for a revised international sugar agreement if and when the commodity again becomes surplus.

International Telecommunication Union. An organization formed in 1932 to regulate telecommunications among the 122 nations constituting the union (1964). It succeeded the International Telegraphic Union, formed in 1865. In 1885 telephone communication was incorporated within the jurisdiction of the union, and in 1906 radio was added. The union has headquarters in Geneva, Switzerland.

International Trade Organization. A proposed international organization to establish standards and develop policies for international trade, intergovernmental trade agreements, and other international economic matters. Plans for this organization were drafted at the GENEVA TRADE CONFERENCE (*q.v.*). These became the basis for the definitive charter of the organization elaborated at the Havana Conference on Trade and Employment, 1947–1948. When formally established, the organization is to be affiliated with the United Nations through that body's Economic and Social Council. At the present time (1964) it seems probable that the establishment of the ITO will be indefinitely postponed.

international union. As used in the United States, a labor union which has members in Canada as well as in the United States. See also LABOR UNION.

international unit. A term sometimes applied to a statistical unit for measuring levels of living in various countries. In using it statisticians sometimes allow it to equal the average purchasing power of one dollar in the United States in the period 1925–1934.

International Wheat Council. A body composed of the major wheat importing and exporting nations which, according to its members, is organized to stabilize prices, provide adequate production and reserves without burdensome surpluses, encourage efficient production and distribution, and promote increased wheat consumption. The council was established in 1942 as an outgrowth of the Wheat Advisory Committee established at London in 1933. In 1962, a price stabilization agreement for wheat and wheat products was reached at Geneva by some 48 states. The U.S.S.R. participated in the conference.

interpolation. As applied to statistics, a method of estimating an intermediate unknown value in a series of numbers by reference to the known values in the series, or by reference to an associated series, the INCREMENTS of which are proportional to the increments of the series for which an intermediate value is desired. For example, the method is frequently used in calculating logarithms. Suppose log 801.4 is desired and log 801.0 is known to be 2.9036, and log 802.0 to be 2.9042, then

$$\begin{array}{lrl} & \log 801.0 = & 2.9036 \\ & \log \underline{801.4} = & \underline{\quad ? \quad} \\ \text{Difference} & 0.4 & \qquad \text{Difference } x \\ & \log 802.0 = & \underline{2.9042} \\ \text{Difference} & = & 0.0006 \end{array}$$

$$\frac{x}{0.0006} = \frac{4}{10}. \quad 10x = 0.0024. \quad x = 0.00024.$$

$$\log 801.4 = 2.9036 + 0.00024 = 2.90384.$$

interstate commerce. Commerce among the various states of the United States. In American constitutional law, this term has been broadened to embrace even the conditions under which goods are manufactured, and almost every incident of their sale and distribution among the states. It also includes the interstate transportation of persons and all instruments of transportation. See also COMMERCE.

Interstate Commerce Act. An act of Congress, 1887, the first of many federal statutes regulating interstate transportation. This original act forbade pools by rail carriers, prohibited special rates, rebates, and other practices considered discriminatory to shippers, and required railways to publish rate schedules. It also created the Interstate Commerce Commission and invested it with limited authority to control abuses among railways. The commission was authorized to require reports from railways, investigate complaints, and to issue cease and desist orders when a violation of law occurred. Many subsequent statutes, the latest being that of 1942, have greatly amended the provisions of the Interstate Commerce Act, enlarged the authority of the commission which it created, and extended its jurisdiction to interstate carriers other than railways. These subsequent statutes or parts of them are often cited as part of the original Interstate Commerce Act. See also INTERSTATE COMMERCE COMMISSION.

Interstate Commerce Commission. An independent administrative agency of the United States government created by Congress in 1887. Under the Interstate Commerce Act of that year and various subsequent statutes, the commission has been authorized to pass upon the rates charged by various interstate carriers including railway, express, motor-coach, and sleeping-car companies, oil pipe lines, and certain interstate and coastal navigation lines. Its activities also include the prescription of uniform statistical and accounting practices among carriers, valuation of certain carrier property, introduction of devices and practices to insure greater safety and convenience for the traveler, the supervision of arrangements for consolidations and pooling arrangements among carriers, and authorization of the issuance of securities by carriers.

interstate trade barriers. State laws in the United States which tend to prevent the unrestricted passage of goods and services from one state to another. Regulations regarding interstate trucking, quarantine laws directed against plant diseases and insects, and DISCRIMINATORY TAXATION have all been used to keep out "foreign" competition; that is, competition emanating from outside the borders of a particular state. Such measures are often defended as inspection or health regulations or as efforts to introduce a degree of equality between the state's taxpayers and nonresidents who use the state's highways and other public works financed by local taxation.

intrastate commerce. In American constitutional theory, commerce deemed to be wholly within the borders of any one of the states of the United States. See also COMMERCE.

intrinsic value. A property or capacity that is assumed to be inherent in an object. Thus it is often said that because bread has a capacity to satisfy hunger, it has an inherent or intrinsic value. From the standpoint of economic analysis, however, if more bread were produced than was wanted, the excess would have little or no value. Modern economics considers, therefore, that the value of any object depends upon its relation to unsatisfied wants rather than upon any inherent quality.

invention. A new and useful art, machine, process, or substance, including a distinct and new form of plant. See also PATENT.

inventory. An itemized list of a stock of goods showing quantities and usually values.

inventory control. The regulation of quantities of materials on hand in such a way as to assure current needs while avoiding excess reserve stocks, the calculation being based on the rate of withdrawals and the time necessary for replacement. In cases where a large number of items are involved, the computation is frequently done by MACHINE DATA PROCESSING.

inventory valuation adjustment. An addition to, or a deduction from, the BOOK VALUES of nonfarm business inventories used by the United States Department of Commerce in computing the NATIONAL

INCOME and the NATIONAL PRODUCT account. Only changes in the physical volume of inventories expressed in terms of current market prices are desired, but, depending upon the method used in valuing inventories of nonfarm enterprises, changes in the total value of those inventories from one accounting period to another may reflect price changes instead of, or in addition to, changes in physical volume. Some adjustment is called for, therefore, in order to isolate the changes in physical volume. Farm income is measured without regard to inventory profits and losses; hence no inventory valuation adjustment is necessary.

investment. The exchange of money for some form of property which, it is expected, will be held over a considerable period of time. Reasonable safety of principal and relative permanency of possession are inferred in the term, as in contrast to SPECULATION. See also AUTONOMOUS INVESTMENT, FINANCIAL INVESTMENT, IMPAIR INVESTMENT, INDUCED INVESTMENT, REAL INVESTMENT.

Investment Advisers Act. An act of Congress, 1940. It gives the SECURITIES AND EXCHANGE COMMISSION power to regulate the activities of INVESTMENT COUNSELORS.

investment banking. The purchase of large blocks of a security by a financial organization, usually known as an investment bank, and the resale of such securities, generally in small blocks, in expectation of a profit. Investment banks are often used in the distribution of new issues of securities. The word "banking," as here used, is misleading in that it suggests the function of deposit. Investment bankers are not permitted to engage in deposit banking. See also BANK.

investment bill. See explanation under BILL.

Investment Companies Act. An act of Congress, 1940. It gives the SECURITIES AND EXCHANGE COMMISSION power to regulate INVESTMENT TRUSTS.

investment counselor. One who for compensation advises on the purchase and sale of securities. Under the provisions of the INVESTMENT ADVISERS ACT passed by Congress in 1940, individuals and firms acting as investment counselors are required to register with the SECURITIES AND EXCHANGE COMMISSION. They are not permitted to charge for their services on the basis of profits gained by their clients or to buy securities from, or to sell securities to, their clients.

investment credit. Long-term loans furnished to a business undertaking for land, buildings, equipment, and other fixed assets. See also CREDIT.

investment portfolio. A list of BONDS, CAPITAL STOCK CERTIFICATES,

PROMISSORY NOTES, and other SECURITIES owned by an institution or by an individual.

investment trust. An institution that invests its capital in securities, such capital being obtained by the sale of its own securities. The income from its investments is used to defray its operating expenses and as a profit to stockholders. Major types of investment trusts in the United States are, according to SECURITIES purchased and sold: GENERAL MANAGEMENT TRUSTS, FIXED INVESTMENT TRUSTS, and SPECIALIZED MANAGEMENT TRUSTS; and, according to organization: CLOSED-END INVESTMENT TRUSTS and OPEN-END INVESTMENT TRUSTS, also called *mutual funds.*

invisible hand. A term used by Adam Smith in setting forth the thesis that when each person acts in his own self-interest, the welfare of society is assured. Hence, according to Adam Smith, society is governed by an "invisible hand" which insures the social welfare, even though individuals seek their own interests. See also ECONOMIC HARMONIES.

invisible items of trade. Items, such as freight and insurance charges and the expenditures of travelers, which, though not recorded as exports or imports, must be considered along with exports and imports in determining the balance of payments between two or more countries. The expenditures of American travelers in England, for example, are equivalent, as far as international balances are concerned, to American imports from England, and, although sometimes referred to as invisible imports, they are not formally recorded as imports. See also BALANCE OF PAYMENTS.

invoice. An itemized list of goods, stating prices and quantities, compiled by a seller and sent to a buyer or consignee. See also CONSULAR INVOICE.

involuntary bankruptcy. See explanation under BANKRUPTCY.

iron law of wages. The theory that wages tend to equal what the worker needs to maintain a bare subsistence level of living. According to this theory, wages temporarily higher than the cost of subsistence will result in an increase in the number of workers; competition will then reduce wages to the subsistence level. Wages less than the cost of subsistence will reduce the number of workers; competition will then eventually advance the wages to the subsistence level. The iron law of wages was formulated by Ferdinand Lassalle, one of the early leaders in the German socialist movement, during the latter half of the 19th century. Sometimes called the *brazen law of wages* and *subsistence law of wages.*

irredeemable bond. See explanation under BOND.

irredeemable foreign-exchange standard. See explanation under

GOLD-EXCHANGE STANDARD.

irredeemable money. Any kind of money that cannot be exchanged for standard money. All money in the United States has been irredeemable since 1933. Also called ***inconvertible money.*** See also MONEY, STANDARD MONEY.

irrevocable letter of credit. See explanation under LETTER OF CREDIT.

irrigation. Bringing moisture to land by means of ditches, piping, or other artificial means.

issue. A block of capital stock, bonds, or other securities sold by a corporation and constituting a part of its obligations.

itemized appropriation. An appropriation which specifies in detail what disposition is to be made of the funds appropriated. The term is used in contradistinction to LUMP-SUM APPROPRIATION. Sometimes called ***segregated appropriation.*** See also APPROPRIATION.

J

jobber. A merchant middleman who buys from an importer or manufacturer or some large wholesaler and sells to retailers.

job evaluation. See LABOR GRADE.

Johnson Act. An act of Congress, 1934. It made illegal the sale in the United States of securities of foreign governments that had failed to pay their debts to the United States government.

joint agreement. As applied to labor relations, an agreement signed by two or more employers and two or more labor unions, or by one employer and two or more labor unions, or by two or more employers and one labor union. See also LABOR UNION.

joint and several bond. See explanation under BOND.

joint costs. The production costs of two or more products which must of necessity be produced together. When cotton is processed, for example, the seeds are separated from the fiber, and the seeds may be used to produce an oil. The production costs of the fiber, therefore, cannot be considered apart from the production costs of the oil. Sometimes referred to as *joint supply.* See also COST.

joint demand. The demand that arises when two or more commodities must be used together, if at all, and hence are wanted simultaneously. The demand for rubber, steel, leather, and many other commodities by automobile manufacturers is a case in point. See also DEMAND.

joint rate. As applied to railway traffic, a single, consolidated rate charged for carrying freight between two points not on the same railroad and arranged by agreement between the two or more railroads carrying the freight from consignment point to destination. When no joint rate exists, a COMBINATION RATE (*q.v.*) is used.

joint return. A combined report of the incomes of husband and wife permitted by the income-tax regulations of the United States and of certain states.

joint-stock company. A form of partnership the members of which are issued shares of transferable stock up to the amount of their investment. Although enjoying a legal personality like a corporation, there are important differences. Unlike a corporation, a joint-stock company can usually sue and be sued only through some designated officer; moreover, unlike stockholders of a corporation who enjoy limited liability, members of a joint-stock company are individually and collectively liable for the debts of the organization.

joint-stock land bank. A bank organized by authority of the Federal Farm Loan Act, 1916. Such a bank issued farm loan bonds to the investing public and made loans to farmers, the loans being secured by farm mortgages. Unlike the FEDERAL LAND BANKS, the joint-stock land banks were not integrated into any unified system. Each bank was responsible for its own securities. They were ordered liquidated in 1933. See also BANK.

joint supply. See JOINT COSTS.

journeyman. A skilled worker who has qualified as such by serving an apprenticeship. See also APPRENTICE.

***Juilliard* v. *Greenman*.** See LEGAL-TENDER CASES.

junior-lien bond. See explanation under BOND.

jurisdictional strike. A strike caused by a dispute between two craft unions, the members of which are employed in some single undertaking. Thus, if carpenters are engaged to hang steel doors, as a part of some construction project, on the ground that the hanging of doors has always been a part of their work, the metal workers may strike because they consider the installation of metal materials wholly within their province. See also STRIKE.

Justice, Department of. A major administrative unit of the federal government, created June 22, 1870, the head of which, the attorney general, has cabinet rank. The department has certain supervisory powers over federal prosecuting agencies and provides representation in courts in cases in which the federal government is a party. It has an ANTITRUST DIVISION which prepares and tries antitrust and similar cases and determines upon appeals in such cases and a Civil Rights Division, established in 1957, to enforce federal election laws and to enforce the rights of citizens guaranteed by the Constitution or federal statue. It also supervises the Immigration-Naturalization Service.

K

kameralism. See CAMERALISM.

key industry. An industry which, because of its size, strategic location, the peculiar importance of its product, or some other characteristic, commands a dominating influence in the particular field of its operations or in the economy as a whole.

Keynesian economics. Economic theories and policies advanced by the British economist, John Maynard (Lord) Keynes (1883–1946) and his followers, or attributed to them. Among the important contributions of the Keynesian school is the view that if savings are not offset by investments in new capital formation, unemployment will follow. It is argued that people decide how much of their savings to spend and how much to save (PROPENSITY TO CONSUME). Then they decide whether to hold their savings in wholly liquid form, as in cash or its equivalent, or to sacrifice complete liquidity for some form of investment (LIQUIDITY PREFERENCE). But such decisions may result in a failure to invest all of the savings. In that event it is held that if the more severe depression phases of the business cycle are to be prevented, if capitalistic economy is not to stagnate, and mass unemployment is not to become chronic, government must stimulate spending or create investments to assure full employment. One of Lord Keynes' major

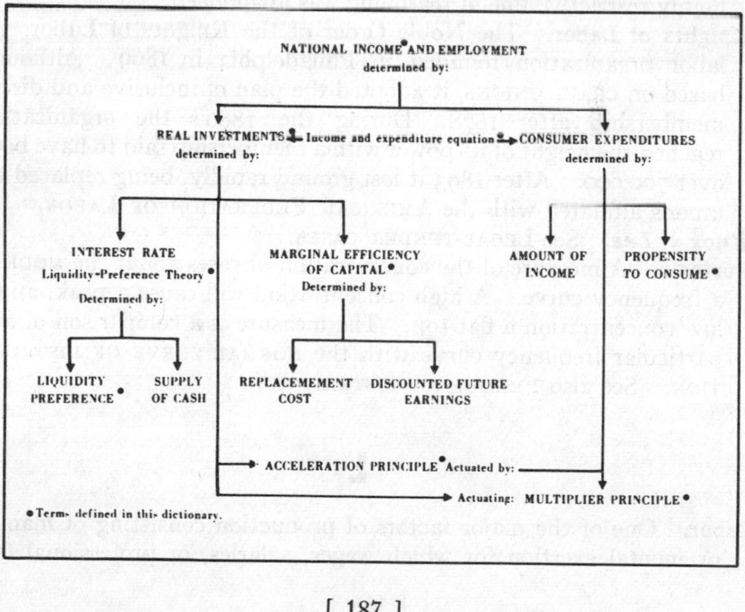

works was *The General Theory of Employment, Interest and Money* (1936). The appended diagram suggests relationships among the more important Keynesian and closely related terms defined in this dictionary. See also SCHOOLS OF ECONOMIC THOUGHT.

Keynes' law of consumption. At every level of income a certain proportion of that income is spent for consumption goods, the proportion decreasing as the income increases. The law was formulated by John Maynard (Lord) Keynes (1883–1946), although others have observed it in human behavior. See also KEYNESIAN ECONOMICS, PROPENSITY TO CONSUME.

kickback. A payment by a worker to his employer or foreman in order to obtain or hold a job.

Knight case. An early antitrust case, *United States* v. *E. C. Knight Co.*, 156 U. S. 1 (1895), in which the Supreme Court of the United States refused to apply the Sherman Act to a merger of four sugar refineries in Philadelphia. The court reasoned that the Sherman Act did not attempt to control monopoly as such but only monopoly in foreign and interstate commerce; that the merger complained of affected manufacture within a single state; and that the incidental results of such merger upon interstate commerce did not change the fact that it was a monopoly of manufacture and not a monopoly affecting interstate commerce which was involved. In later cases, involving application of the Sherman and other antitrust acts, this highly restrictive line of reasoning was abandoned.

Knights of Labor. The Noble Order of the Knights of Labor. A labor organization founded in Philadelphia in 1869. Although based on CRAFT UNIONS, it adopted the plan of inclusive and direct membership after 1878. During the 1880's the organization reached the height of its power with a membership said to have been over 700,000. After 1893 it lost ground rapidly, being replaced by unions affiliated with the AMERICAN FEDERATION OF LABOR.

***Knox* v. *Lee*.** See LEGAL-TENDER CASES.

kurtosis. A measure of the concentration of cases about the MODE of a frequency curve. A high concentration will cause a peak, and a low concentration a flat top. The measure is a comparison of any particular frequency curve with the NORMAL CURVE OF DISTRIBUTION. See also FREQUENCY DISTRIBUTION.

L

labor. One of the major factors of production consisting of manual or mental exertion for which wages, salaries, or professional fees are received. In popular speech the term is generally given a narrower meaning; that is, manual exertion only, or manual workers collectively. For some of the more important uses of the term see CHILD LABOR, CONTRACT LABOR, DIVISION OF LABOR, LABOR GRADE, LABOR TURNOVER, LABOR UNION, LOCALIZATION OF LABOR. See also FACTORS OF PRODUCTION, LABOR THEORY OF VALUE, SURPLUS LABOR AND VALUE THEORY.

labor agreement. See TRADE AGREEMENT.

Labor, Department of. A major administrative unit of the federal government, with a secretary of cabinet rank, created by Congress March 4, 1913, by dividing the erstwhile Department of Commerce and Labor into two separate departments. Among its more important subsidiary units are the WOMEN'S BUREAU and the bureaus of LABOR STATISTICS, EMPLOYEES' COMPENSATION, EMPLOYMENT SECURITY, and LABOR STANDARDS.

labor exchange bank. A term used to denote various schemes advanced during the 19th century for the exchange of commodities on the basis of the amount of labor necessary to create them, and for currency and credit reforms that would do away with the precious metals. Robert Owen, in 1832, arguing that gold and silver create artificial values, established an exchange in London where goods were traded on the basis of the labor hours necessary to produce them. Paper notes were issued for goods delivered, and these notes were accepted for goods purchased, Owen's idea being that such notes should become a common medium of exchange. Josiah Warren in the United States, and Benjamin Mazel in France, experimented with similar plans. In 1848 Pierre Joseph Proudhon proposed that a bank be established in France to convert bills of exchange into a circulating medium, and that such currency be loaned to workers on merchandise collateral. All interest was to be eliminated, according to the plan, fees being charged to cover costs. A refinement of the labor-value exchange idea was introduced in 1871 by Karl Rodbertus, a German socialist, who recognized that different kinds of labor might create different value relationships. Accordingly, he proposed that each industry should establish a working day of a length determined by the amount of physical and nervous energy expended by the workers. Money might then be issued on the basis of a day's labor. Ideas centering around the concept of labor exchange banks were gradually submerged in the growth of socialism.

labor force. As defined by the United States Bureau of the Census, the labor force of the United States consists of all persons 14 yr. of age and over, not housed in an institution, who are gainfully employed and working at their employment, or who are gainfully employed but are temporarily not working, or who are working 15 hr. a week without pay on a family farm or in a family business.

labor grade. The degree of skill and responsibility and the amount of experience or other special qualifications required for a particular job, and the wages paid for that job. In factories requiring a great variety of labor skills, jobs are frequently evaluated by means of a point system, the number of points indicating in general the degree of competency necessary to perform a particular job. Each job is then assigned a minimum and maximum wage. Also called *job evaluation*. See also LABOR.

Labor-Management Relations (Taft-Hartley) Act. An act of Congress, 1947. It amends the NATIONAL LABOR RELATIONS (WAGNER-CONNERY) ACT of 1935 in many important respects. Among its provisions are those outlawing the CLOSED SHOP and imposing regulations upon the UNION SHOP, union welfare funds, and the CHECKOFF system. It specifies procedures for the handling of labor disputes threatening the national health and safety, denies foremen labor unions recognition under the law, and bans strikes by government employees. It also provides for organizational and functional changes in the NATIONAL LABOR RELATIONS BOARD.

labor piracy. Any attempt to win workers away from other employers by offering higher wages or other benefits.

Labor Reform (Landrum-Griffin) Act (1959). New labor legislation, representing a compromise of separate House and Senate measures, signed by President Eisenhower September 14, 1959. The legislation guarantees freedom of speech and a secret ballot to members of unions; limits the tenure of officers; requires periodic financial reports; outlaws secondary boycotts, that is, boycotts of employers doing business with employers against whom employees have a grievance; and establishes certain limitations upon so-called organizational picketing or picketing arising out of a demand for union recognition.

labor relations. See INDUSTRIAL RELATIONS.

laborsaving machinery. Machinery, usually of an automatic or semiautomatic nature, performing operations that would otherwise be performed by hand. The term implies that the labor necessary for the construction, maintenance, and operation or supervision of the machine is less than would be required to produce by hand whatever the machine will produce during its lifetime.

Labor Standards, Bureau of. A major unit of the Department of Labor of the United States which, through appropriate research activities and the collection of necessary statistical data, develops educational, health, safety, and other standards to improve working conditions in industry. It is also concerned with drafting model labor legislation and establishing standards for the effective administration of such legislation. The administration of the child-labor provisions of the FAIR LABOR STANDARDS ACT is entrusted to this bureau.

Labor Statistics, Bureau of. A major unit of the Department of Labor of the United States which compiles and distributes information on subjects concerning labor.

labor theory of value. The theory that the basis of value of an economic good is the amount of human labor expended in producing it. The theory does not deny that UTILITY or the power to satisfy a human want or desire is a basic condition of all value, but it contends that the cause of value, as distinct from the condition, is as above defined. The theory was taught by Adam Smith, and later expounded by Ricardo and others. It was accepted by Karl Marx and expanded into the SURPLUS LABOR AND VALUE THEORY. See also LABOR, VALUE.

labor turnover. The number of employees who leave and the number of new employees engaged to replace them within a given period of time, usually expressed as a percentage of the average number of workers employed by a concern during the period in question. See also LABOR.

labor union. An organization, incorporated or otherwise, consisting of employees. The organization acts in the collective interests of the employees in negotiating with employers, particularly in matters of wages and working conditions. For some of the more important kinds of labor unions see CLOSED UNION, COMPANY UNION, CRAFT UNION, INDEPENDENT UNION, INDUSTRIAL UNION, INTERNATIONAL UNION, MULTICRAFT UNION, NATIONAL UNION, OPEN UNION.

La Follette Seamen's Act. An act of Congress, 1915. It established minimum standards for working conditions of crews on American merchant ships, and regulated their wage scales and the payment of their wages.

laissez faire (*laisser faire, laissez passer*). "Let things proceed without interference." The term originated in France possibly as early as the first half of the 18th century, and was later developed by Adam Smith as a rule of practical economic conduct. He applied the principle of *laissez faire* to foreign trade and advocated the withdrawal of the restrictions imposed by MERCANTILISM. In domestic affairs, too, the principle was expressed in the assertion that the individual is most productive when allowed to follow his own self-interest without external restrictions.

land. One of the major factors of production consisting sometimes of a free good, but usually of a material economic good which is supplied by nature without the aid of man. The term may include not only the earth's surface, both land and water, but also anything that is attached to the earth's surface. Thus, all natural resources in their original state, such as mineral deposits, wildlife, timber, and fish, are land within the technical meaning of the term; so also are sources of energy, outside of man himself, such as water, coal deposits, and the natural fertility of the soil. The technical meaning of the term is so much broader in scope than that usually given it in popular speech that some economists substitute the word *nature*. See also ECONOMIC GOOD, FACTORS OF PRODUCTION, FREE GOOD.

land bank. **1.** An association of landowners in colonial America. Members pledged mortgages on their land to the association and received in return a form of currency called "bills of credit." **2.** A bank organized under the Federal Farm Loan Act of 1916. See also BANK, FEDERAL LAND BANK.

land grant. A gift of public land, often made in the past, by the government of the United States to promote homesteading, to assist education, or to accomplish some other useful purpose.

land-grant bond. See explanation under BOND.

land-grant college. An institution of higher learning that benefited in 1862 from land grants made by the United States government to the states under certain stipulated conditions. See also MORRILL (LAND-GRANT COLLEGE) ACT.

Land Management, Bureau of. An administrative unit of the United States Department of the Interior which enforces federal laws relating to the use and disposition of federal public lands and their resources.

land patent. A legal instrument giving title to the recipient of a land grant. See also LAND GRANT.

Landrum-Griffin Act. See LABOR REFORM ACT.

land tax. See explanation under PROPERTY TAX.

land-value tax. A tax on the value of land exclusive of all buildings and other improvements, the value being the appreciation due to population increase and general economic development of the community for which the landowner, as such, is in no way responsible. It is the UNEARNED INCREMENT, or ECONOMIC RENT, that is taxed in whole or in part. The tax is similar in some respects to a CAPITAL-GAINS TAX except that the appreciation of land value at any particular time is arrived at through APPRAISAL instead of being realized through a sale. See also TAX.

large-scale production. See MASS PRODUCTION.

Latin Monetary Union. An agreement entered into by France, Italy, Belgium, and Switzerland in 1865 according to which the silver content in most of the coins of these nations was reduced. At that time the value of the metal content of the silver coins exceeded their face value, and, in accordance with GRESHAM'S LAW, the coins were disappearing from circulation. By reducing the silver content of the coins, the various governments stopped the tendency of the coins to disappear. Greece joined the union at a later date. The union was dissolved in 1926.

lawful money. In general, any kind of money which has the quality of legal tender. In a more restricted sense, in the United States, any form of money that can be used by the federal reserve banks and, in most cases, by the state banks, as reserves against their deposits. In this latter sense, all United States money is lawful money except federal reserve notes. And federal reserve notes, being full legal tender, are lawful money in the more general sense of the term. See also MONEY.

lay corporation. Any corporation organized for purely secular purposes; hence, any corporation other than an ecclesiastical corporation. See also CORPORATION.

leakage. As applied to economic analysis, an informal term indicating any influence which prevents new CAPITAL FORMATION from exerting its full effect upon the NATIONAL INCOME. According to the so-called MULTIPLIER PRINCIPLE (*q.v.*), the greater the marginal propensity to consume, the greater the contribution of new capital formation to the magnitude of the national income. Leakages decrease this contribution by decreasing the marginal propensity to consume. Examples are: high marginal PROPENSITY TO SAVE, payments on debts, an increase of imports over exports, an increase in the general PRICE LEVEL. See also PROPENSITY TO CONSUME.

lease. A contract for the possession of specified property for the life of the party to whom the property is conveyed or for a period specified in the contract. See also NET LEASE.

least-squares method. A mathematical procedure for computing the average relationship between two variables. Values which express this relationship most accurately are those that total to the minimum sum when the squares of their deviations from the original values of the two variables are added. The equations for obtaining this minimum sum are:

$$\Sigma(y) = Na + b\Sigma(x)$$

and

$$\Sigma(xy) = a\Sigma(x) + b\Sigma(x^2)$$

when

x and y = the variables,
N = the number of pairs of variables,
a and b = constants.

Two equations are secured by substituting the original values of x and y as above indicated. These equations are then solved simultaneously for a and b, the generalized equation for the average relationship being:

$$y = a + bx.$$

The least-squares method is used extensively in economic computations for estimating SECULAR TREND and for calculating the relationship between two or more variables for comparative purposes. For examples, see SCATTER CHART, SECULAR TREND.

legacy. See BEQUEST.

legal asset. An asset in the hands of an executor of an estate that is available to discharge a debt under common law. The term is used in contradistinction to EQUITABLE ASSET. See also ASSET.

legal interest. A rate of interest determined by law which is applied in the absence of any specific agreement. See also INTEREST.

legal person. A term frequently applied to corporations. Because a corporation, as such, is permitted to own property, to sue, to be sued, and to exercise many of the rights accorded to natural persons, it is often referred to as a legal person.

legal reserves. See BANK RESERVES.

legal security. A security which, in the United States, is identified by state and federal laws as a permissible investment for certain fiduciary institutions. See also SECURITY.

legal tender. Money which, according to law, must be accepted in payment of any obligation expressed in terms of money. It should be noted, however, that a seller is under no compulsion to accept legal tender in exchange for his goods if he does not wish to do so.

legal-tender bond. See explanation under BOND.

legal-tender cases. A series of cases, *Hepburn* v. *Griswold*, 8 Wallace 603 (1870); *Knox* v. *Lee* and *Parker* v. *Davis*, 12 Wallace 457 (1871); and *Juilliard* v. *Greenman*, 110 U. S. 421 (1884), in which the Supreme Court of the United States established the constitutionality of the power of Congress to issue irredeemable paper money, such as greenbacks, and make them legal tender. In the first of these cases, that of *Hepburn* v. *Griswold*, the court invalidated provisions of federal statutes, passed during the Civil War, which would have made such paper money a legal tender for debts contracted before the legislation. But in the subsequent cases, this earlier decision was overruled, and the power of Congress to issue paper money and make it a legal tender for any debts, whensoever contracted, was supported without qualification.

***Leisy* v. *Hardin*.** See ORIGINAL-PACKAGE CASES.

Lend-Lease Act. An act of Congress, 1941. It authorized the President to supply munitions to any country, the defense of which was necessary to the defense of the United States, on terms which were deemed satisfactory to him. The act was later amended to include foodstuffs and other products.

letter of credit. A document, usually issued by a bank, in which the issuer agrees to accept drafts, under conditions set forth in the document, to be charged against credit previously established. The main types of letters of credit may be classified according to the extent of the liability assumed by the bank issuing a letter, and again by the use to which the letter is put.

Widely used terms indicating the bank's liability are as follows: *confirmed letter of credit*, a letter in which the payment of all drafts drawn against it is guaranteed; *irrevocable letter of credit*, one that cannot be canceled until a certain stipulated period of time expires; *revocable letter of credit*, one that may be canceled at any time; *straight letter of credit*, one that is confirmed and irrevocable; *unconfirmed letter of credit*, one for which credit has been established, but for which the issuing bank does not itself guarantee payment.

There are also terms indicating the use of letters of credit. A *circular letter of credit* is one not directed to any particular person, concern, or bank. When the beneficiary wishes to use it, he must find some agency willing to negotiate a draft. An *open letter of credit* contains no special stipulations. It is used, for example, when payments are desired without any documents being submitted with the draft drawn against the letter. A *revolving letter of credit* is one in which credit is automatically renewed as drafts are drawn against it. It is used frequently to facilitate payments by purchasing agents traveling abroad. A *traveler's letter of credit* is directed to any one of a number of correspondent banks, a separate list of which is given to the beneficiary. He may then call upon any bank named on the list, identify himself by a signature card given him by the issuing bank, and draw on the credit previously established. A record of the amount drawn is then noted on the letter of credit. See also DRAFT.

letter of lien. A document signed by a buyer, stating that certain goods are held by him in trust for the seller. An agreement of this kind is sometimes used, particularly in foreign trade, to assure the seller that he will be paid for the goods shipped to the buyer. When the buyer pays for the goods, the agreement becomes null and void. Also called *letter of trust.*

letter of marque. A license issued by a government to the owners of private ships in time of war permitting them to attack enemy ships and to seize those ships and such property as may be contained in them. Now virtually obsolete.

letter of trust. See LETTER OF LIEN.

letters patent. In the United States, an instrument which grants some right or conveys some title, and which is issued by one of the states of the United States to a private individual or organization.

level of living. The actual degree of material well-being enjoyed by a person or a group. Also called *plane of living.*

liability. A debt or obligation stated in terms of money. Net worth is a liability because it is an obligation of the enterprise to the owners. Liabilities are a part of a BALANCE SHEET. The other part consists of ASSETS. See also CAPITAL LIABILITY, CONTINGENT LIABILITY, CURRENT LIABILITY, DOUBLE LIABILITY, FIXED LIABILITY, LIMITED LIABILITY.

Liberal school. See CLASSICAL SCHOOL.

liberty bond. A United States government bond issued during 1917 and 1918 to finance American participation in World War I and for loans to nations allied with the United States in that war. See also BOND.

license. A right to engage in certain activities for which permission is necessary. Thus, public authorities may require that a license be secured by those engaged in certain occupations or professions, or an owner of a patent may grant a license for the manufacture of the patented article.

lien. A claim on property to secure the payment of a debt.

life annuity. An annuity which ceases at the death of the person receiving the annuity payments. See also ANNUITY.

life insurance. Insurance which, in return for premiums paid in accordance with the terms of an appropriate contract, provides for a cash payment or the equivalent to beneficiaries named in the contract upon the death of the insured or upon the attainment by the insured of a certain age. There are many varieties of life-insurance contracts. For some of the common varieties see ENDOWMENT PLAN OF LIFE INSURANCE, GROUP LIFE INSURANCE, INDUSTRIAL LIFE INSURANCE, LIMITED-PAYMENT PLAN OF LIFE INSURANCE, TERM PLAN OF LIFE INSURANCE. See also INSURANCE.

lifo. A method of inventory and cost-of-sales valuation in which the individual items constituting the inventory are valued according to the cost of the earliest acquisitions, and the cost of articles sold or used are valued at the cost of the most recent acquisitions. It is assumed that the last items purchased or produced are the first items sold. The cost of articles sold or used, therefore, are current costs, whereas the cost of the items remaining in the inventory are those of an earlier date. The term is an abbreviation of "last in, first out." See also FIFO.

limited depositary. A member bank of the Federal Reserve System that is authorized, under specified conditions, to accept deposits from the United States Treasury to be credited to the official checking accounts of disbursing officers of the government. See also DEPOSITARY.

limited-dividend corporation. A corporation the entire capital stock of which is limited in respect to the payment of dividends. Presumably, after the creation of the necessary and desirable surplus and reserves, such a corporation's prices might be reduced to the point where earnings are just enough to meet the maximum dividend requirements and to maintain reserves. See also CORPORATION.

limited liability. The legal condition which exists when a stockholder cannot be held personally liable for the debts of a corporation beyond the amount that he has already invested in the enterprise. See also LIABILITY.

limited partnership. A type of partnership business organization that limits the personal liability of inactive partners to their investment in the enterprise. See also PARTNERSHIP.

limited-payment plan of life insurance. A plan according to which a life-insurance company agrees to pay a stipulated sum of money upon the death of an insured person in return for annual premiums of a fixed amount from the insured person during a maximum number of years, usually about 30. See also LIFE INSURANCE.

limping standard. A modification of the gold monetary standard according to which certain silver coins are treated as standard money to the extent that they are made unlimited legal tender and are not required by law to be redeemed in gold. See also MONETARY SYSTEM.

line of regression. See explanation under SCATTER CHART.

linseed oil industry case. A case, *United States* v. *American Linseed Oil Co.*, 262 U. S. 371 (1923), involving a situation not unlike that in the LUMBER INDUSTRY CASE (*q.v.*) and a somewhat similar decision by the Supreme Court of the United States. Relying on the antitrust statutes, the court enjoined the practice of the linseed oil industry of exchanging information on prices, sales, and related matters and of requiring individual enterprises in the industry to post bonds to assure their adherence to published price schedules.

liquid. As used in business terminology, the word indicates the relative ease with which something of value can be converted into money. Thus, a liquid asset, or liquid capital, is property that can be converted readily into money without appreciable loss in value. Property which is 100 per cent liquid is cash or its equivalent. The word is used in contradistinction to FROZEN. See also ASSETS, CAPITAL.

liquidation. As generally used in business, the conversion of assets into cash. To liquidate securities, for example, means to sell securities. In terminating a business the term includes not only the process of converting the assets into cash but also the paying of the indebtedness and the distribution among the owners of the business of whatever remains. The term may also refer merely to the process of ascertaining the true values of things.

liquidity preference. The preference exhibited by savers as to the degree of liquidity of their savings; that is, as to whether they prefer to hold savings in completely liquid form, as in cash, or to convert them into relatively less liquid form, as in some investment.

liquidity-preference theory of interest. A Keynesian theory that attributes the rate of interest to the demand and supply of money and money substitutes, the demand being determined by LIQUIDITY PREFERENCE and the supply by banking policy. In the appended diagram a liquidity-preference SCHEDULE is indicated by the solid line AA'. According to this schedule, when the interest rate is high, little cash is demanded by the economy because liquidity preference is weak; when the interest rate is low, more cash is demanded because liquidity preference is strong. The supply curve is indicated in the diagram by the straight line SS'. Demand and supply are equated at the point O, or at y rate of interest. If for some reason liquidity preference strengthens, indicated by the dotted line BB', while the supply of cash remains the same, the interest rate will rise to point x. This new interest rate will, in turn, be effected by the sale of securities in order to realize cash. This will depress security prices and hence advance the interest rate. Conversely, if liquidity preference weakens, indicated by the dotted line CC', while the supply of cash remains the same, the interest rate will decline to point z. This lower interest rate will be effected by a demand for securities in order to invest cash. This will advance the price of securities and hence reduce the interest rate. Changes in liquidity preference can be offset in varying degrees by banking policy which can encourage an increase or a decrease in the supply of cash as liquidity preference strengthens or weakens, respectively. This can be illustrated in the diagram by imagining the straight line SS' moved to the right until point O on that line touches BB', or to the left until point O touches CC'. See also DEPOSIT CURRENCY, KEYNESIAN ECONOMICS.

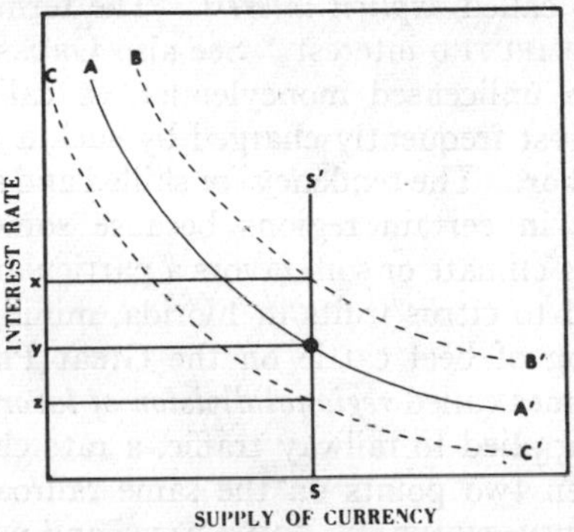

listed security. A security which is admitted by a recognized stock exchange organization for trading on that exchange. See also SECURITY.

listed stock. See explanation under CAPITAL STOCK.

list price. A price, usually published, which makes no allowance for trade or other discounts, rebates, or commissions. See also PRICE.

little steel. A popular term which usually refers to all American steel-producing plants other than those of the United States Steel Corporation.

loan. As generally used in business, a sum of money borrowed from a commercial bank at the prevailing rate of interest. When bonds are sold by a borrower or when a borrower pledges a mortgage as security, the term may be qualified as "long-term loan" or "mortgage loan." The term generally refers to a money transaction, the terms "hire," "rent," or "lease" customarily being used when goods are borrowed. However, the borrowing of a stock certificate to cover SELLING SHORT is a business loan not in terms of money. See also CALL LOAN, FORCED LOAN, MORNING LOAN, TIED LOAN.

loanable-funds theory of interest. The theory that interest rates are determined by the supply of, and the demand for, funds available for lending. The supply of such funds is determined mainly by the extent of savings and the net increase in DEPOSIT CURRENCY; and the demand, by the opportunities for new CAPITAL FORMATION and the desire to increase cash balances. The theory has much in common with the LIQUIDITY-PREFERENCE THEORY OF INTEREST, inasmuch as both recognize the part played by the banking system and the importance of the preference for cash balances for speculation and security purposes.

loaned flat. See explanation under PREMIUM RATE.

loan interest. A price paid by one person to another for the use of capital. Also called *explicit interest.* The term is used in contradistinction to IMPUTED interest. See also GROSS INTEREST.

loan shark. An unlicensed moneylender, so called because of the excessive interest frequently charged by such a lender.

localization of labor. The tendency for skilled and semiskilled workers to congregate in certain regions because some characteristic of nature, such as climate or soil, favors a particular industry or trade. Labor devoted to citrus fruits in Florida, mining in Pennsylvania, and the raising of beef cattle on the Great Plains are examples. This is sometimes called *regional division of labor.* See also LABOR.

local rate. As applied to railway traffic, a rate charged for carrying freight between two points on the same railroad. Other railway rates are: COMBINATION RATE, JOINT RATE, and PROPORTIONAL RATE.

***Lochner* v. *New York*.** A relatively early case, 198 U. S. 45 (1905), in which the Supreme Court of the United States held unconstitutional a state statute (New York) fixing the maximum working day in bakeries at 10 hr. In its opinion the majority of the court suggested that such a statute arbitrarily and unreasonably limited freedom of contract protected by the 14th Amendment to the Constitution of the United States, that it exceeded the police power of the state, and that it was without due process. It was in his dissenting opinion in this case that Mr. Justice Holmes uttered his famous dictum that the 14th Amendment did "not enact Mr. Herbert Spencer's Social Statics," an opinion which presaged a more favorable judicial verdict on regulatory statutes of this type in later cases. See *BUNTING* v. *OREGON*.

lockout. An attempt by an employer in an industrial dispute to bring employees to terms through the economic pressure created by shutting down the operation of a plant or other establishment, thereby denying employment to the workers.

***Loewe* v. *Lawlor*.** See DANBURY HATTERS' CASE.

logistics. Basically, the art of numerical calculation, derived from the Greek *logistikos*. In the 19th century, the word came into use in military terminology referring principally to the quartering, transport, and supply of troops. The meaning has been broadened in current usage to refer to the science and practice of providing the means for the conduct of military operations. It deals with personnel, materiel, facilities, and services and embraces all activities necessary to establish and maintain fighting forces, from the mobilization of the civilian industrial economy to the deployment of men and weapons in combat with an enemy.

London Economic Conference. An international conference held in London from June 12 to July 27, 1933, to consider world monetary and credit policies, the stabilization of world commodity prices, international capital movements, restrictions on international trade, commercial treaty and tariff policies, and the stimulation of production and world trade. It failed in its primary objective of securing agreement to stabilize major national currencies.

long and short haul. A term referring to a practice, once common among American railroads, of charging higher rates between points relatively close together, and served by only one railroad, than between points farther apart but served by competing railroads. The practice is now illegal.

long-term liability. See FIXED LIABILITY.

Lorenz curve. A graphic device, showing cumulative percentage relationships between two variables. It is customarily employed in displaying the extent of equality or inequality in the distribution of money income in an economy. The appended diagram shows a Lorenz curve depicting the distribution of DISPOSABLE INCOME among SPENDING UNITS in the United States for the year 1949 as reported in the *Federal Reserve Bulletin* of August, 1950, as follows:

Total spending units, per cent	Cumulative	Total disposable income, per cent	Cumulative
15	15	2	2
21	36	11	13
23	59	19	32
18	77	21	53
11	88	16	69
8	96	16	85
4	100	15	100

The dotted line represents complete equality; that is, 10 per cent of the spending units receive 10 per cent of the disposable income, 20 per cent of the spending units receive 20 per cent, etc. The broken line represents complete inequality; that is, one spending unit receives 100 per cent of the disposable income. The heavy solid line represents the actual distribution as specified above.

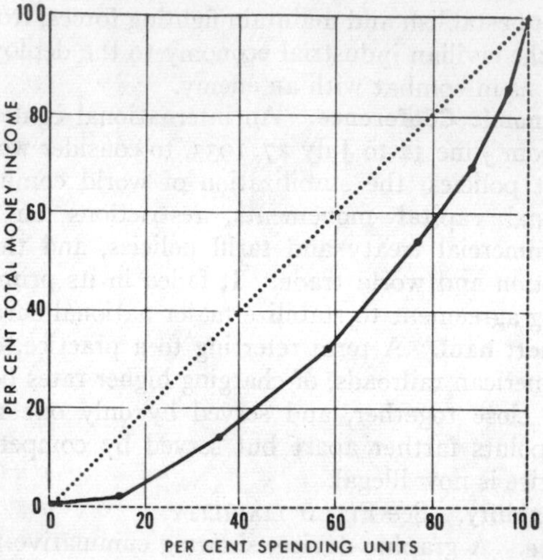

loss leader. A term applied to an article sold in retail trade below cost in order to attract buyers for other merchandise.

lucrative capital. See explanation under CAPITAL.

Luddite. A term applied to certain workmen in England who early in the 19th century conducted a campaign, accompanied in some cases by violence, against the introduction of laborsaving machinery. The term is said to be derived from the name of one Ned Lud who, somewhat earlier, had been particularly aggressive in destroying machines.

lumber industry case. A case, *American Column and Lumber Co.* v. *United States*, 257 U. S. 377 (1921), in which the Supreme Court of the United States held certain practices in the lumber industry to constitute a restraint of trade and a violation of the antitrust statutes. These practices included circularization among various companies in the industry of statistical information on production, sales, and shipments, and requests for curtailment of output to prevent overproduction in the lumber industry.

lump-sum appropriation. An appropriation, especially one by a legislative body for some governmental unit. The appropriation contains no specific instructions as to how the funds appropriated shall be spent. The term is opposed to ITEMIZED APPROPRIATION. See also APPROPRIATION.

luxury tax. A tax imposed upon articles not considered essential to a normal standard of living and usually high in price. See also TAX.

M

***McCray* v. *United States*.** See OLEOMARGARINE CASE.

***McCulloch* v. *Maryland*.** One of the most important cases, 4 Wheaton 316 (1819), ever decided by the Supreme Court of the United States. It involved the constitutionality of the Second Bank of the United States. Chief Justice Marshall, speaking for the court, upheld the constitutional power of Congress to charter such a bank by establishing that this power was derived from other powers expressly confided to Congress by Art. II of the Constitution. He thereby gave judicial blessing to the doctrine that Congress had implied as well as express powers. The Chief Justice also established the principle that no state of the United States might tax the instrumentalities of the federal government, such as the branches of the Bank of the United States at issue in the case, because such a power in the hands of the states might effectively challenge the supremacy of the federal government. Among its other practical effects, this part of the decision resulted in exempting the income of federal bonds from state taxation.

McFadden Act. An act of Congress, 1927. It permits NATIONAL BANKS to establish branches in the communities where their main offices are located, provided the state law accords the same privilege to STATE BANKS.

machine data processing. The automatic or semiautomatic sorting, matching, collating, selecting, computing, printing, or other manipulation of information by machines. See ELECTRONIC DATA PROCESSING, PUNCHED-CARD DATA PROCESSING.

McKinley Tariff. The United States Tariff Act of 1890. It increased the import duties on wool and woolens, higher-grade cottons; other textiles, and many less important items. Some duties were made practically prohibitory. The duty on sugar was replaced by a bounty of 2 cents per pound for 14 years, granted to domestic sugar producers.

McNary-Haugen Bill. A bill which proposed to advance the prices of agricultural products in the domestic market by selling surplus products abroad for whatever they would bring. Farmers suffering losses from such exports were to be reimbursed from fees collected from all beneficiaries of the plan. The bill was vetoed twice by President Coolidge (1927). See also EQUALIZATION FEE.

macroeconomics. Economic studies or statistics that consider aggregates of individuals or groups of commodities; for example, total consumption, employment, or income. The term is used in contradistinction to MICROECONOMICS. See also ECONOMICS.

Maine plan. A plan in operation in the state of Maine to encourage new capital formation undertaken by SMALL BUSINESS. The Maine Development Credit Corporation, authorized by the state legislature, and financed by banks, insurance companies, savings and loan associations, railroads, and others, makes loans for business expansion and improvement programs and for the establishment of new business enterprises.

maintenance of membership. As applied to labor relations, a provision in a labor contract in which the management agrees that union workers must remain in good standing with the union in order to retain their jobs. See also UNION SECURITY CLAUSE.

make-work fallacy. The fallacious belief that accidental or deliberate destruction of wealth or inefficient or uneconomic application of labor is beneficial to the economy because it creates or prolongs employment. For example, when a period of unemployment is expected, workers may deliberately slow down their work in order to make their jobs last longer. They may succeed temporarily in prolonging their period of employment by forcing the employer to pay higher labor costs. If such a situation is continued over a period of time, however, it is evident that the amount of wealth created by the workers would be so reduced that the employer could no longer afford to pay their wages, and unemployment would follow anyway.

Malthusian theory of population. The theory that population increases faster than the means of subsistence. The theory was formulated by Thomas Robert Malthus in an essay published anonymously in 1798 and revised in a second edition published in 1803 under his own name. Malthus claimed that population increased by geometrical progression (1, 2, 4, 8, 16, 32, etc.) while the means of subsistence increased in arithmetical progression (1, 2, 3, 4, 5, 6, etc.). Human beings were destined, therefore, to misery and poverty unless population growth was checked. Population growth might be slowed by what Malthus called preventive checks (moral restraint, late marriages, celibacy). If these were not exercised, positive checks (famines, wars, plagues) would reduce the population to the point of subsistence.

managed money. A monetary system in which an attempt is made by government to regulate the amount of money in circulation in such a way as to accomplish some specified objective such as the stabilization of prices. The paper money under such a system is INCONVERTIBLE; it may or may not be partially secured by coins or bullion. Sometimes called *fiat standard.* See also MONETARY SYSTEM.

management. Often considered one of the factors of production. It involves the organization and co-ordination of the other factors — land, labor, and capital — for maximum efficiency in production. Also called *entrepreneurship.* See also FACTORS OF PRODUCTION.

management science. See OPERATIONS RESEARCH.

management stock. See explanation under CAPITAL STOCK.

Manchester school. See CLASSICAL SCHOOL.

manifest. A complete inventory of the cargo of a ship, together with the value, origin, and destination of each item. The term is also applied to carloads of mixed freight, contents of storage warehouses, and loads on long-distance trucks.

man-land ratio. The quantitative relationship which exists at a particular time and place between the total number of people, the natural resources, the stage of technological development, and the level of living. Thus, as long as the natural resources are sufficient and technological progress continues, population may increase, the standard of living may advance, or both may occur. Should natural resources become depleted, and progress in technological development cease, increased population will cause a decrease in the level of living.

Mann-Elkins Act. An act of Congress, 1910. It gave the Interstate Commerce Commission limited power to regulate the rates and operations of telegraph, telephone, and cable companies. This authority, considerably enlarged, has since been transferred to the FEDERAL COMMUNICATIONS COMMISSION.

manorial system. A medieval system of land tenure the principal feature of which was a large estate owned by a feudal lord and maintained by dependent cultivators who provided services and dues in return for protection and parcels of land used for their maintenance.

manpower control. Direction by the government as to the distribution of manpower available for employment, the purpose being to secure the most effective use of available skills in meeting some major national objective such as production for defense or war.

marginal borrower. A borrower at a given rate of interest who will refuse to borrow if the rate of interest is advanced.

marginal buyer. A buyer at any given price who will refuse to buy if the price is advanced.

marginal cost. Whatever amount the production of one additional unit adds to the total costs of production. If the total cost of producing five units is $100 and the total cost of producing six units is $115, the marginal cost is $15. See also COST.

marginal desirability. See MARGINAL UTILITY.

marginal disutility of labor. The increment of labor effort which just equals the MARGINAL UTILITY to the worker of the compensation received for that increment.

marginal efficiency of capital. A statistical term denoting the discount necessary to equate the expected future earnings derived from the most profitable capital asset that can be added to an existing stock of capital goods, with the COST of reproducing that added capital asset. Thus, if for a given capital asset the replacement cost is $10,000, its life is 5 years, and the annual earnings for those 5 years are, respectively, $2,000, $3,000, $2,000, $2,500, and $2,500, the marginal efficiency of capital is 6.3 per cent. This is computed by means of the following equation:

$$A = 2{,}000(1+i)^{-1} + 3{,}000(1+i)^{-2} + 2{,}000(1+i)^{-3} + 2{,}500(1+i)^{-4} + 2{,}500(1+i)^{-5}$$

when

A = the replacement cost,
i = the marginal efficiency of capital.

The equation is solved by substituting different values for i, tabulating the resulting values of A, and then interpolating. Thus, at i = 5 per cent,

$$\begin{aligned} 2{,}000 \times 0.95238095 &= 1{,}904.76190 \\ 3{,}000 \times 0.90703948 &= 2{,}721.08844 \\ 2{,}000 \times 0.86384760 &= 1{,}727.69520 \\ 2{,}500 \times 0.82270247 &= 2{,}056.75618 \\ 2{,}500 \times 0.78353671 &= \underline{1{,}958.84178} \\ & 10{,}369.14350 \end{aligned}$$

Repeating for 6 per cent and 6½ per cent, the results are:

i, per cent	*A*
5	10,369.14
6	10,086.80
6½	9,946.62

By interpolation for $10,000, i = 6.3 per cent. See also KEYNESIAN ECONOMICS.

marginal land. Land which will just repay the cost of products grown on it at the market prices prevailing for such products.

marginal lender. A lender or investor at a given rate of interest who will refuse to lend or invest if the rate of interest is reduced.

marginal producer. A producer who, at a given market price for his product, is able just to meet his costs of production.

marginal product. Whatever is produced by virtue of the addition of a single increment of a variable factor of production. For example, if 10 bu. of grain are produced on a given piece of land, and a unit of 25 lb. of fertilizer increases the yield to 14 bu., the marginal product is 4 bu.

marginal productivity. The ability of one additional increment of a variable factor of production to increase the total product. The term is generally used in conjunction with some particular factor of production; thus, the marginal productivity of land, labor, capital, or management means, in each case, the ability of one additional increment of the factor in question to increase the total product.

marginal-productivity theory of wages. The theory that wages tend to equal the value of the product that would be lost if one less worker were employed. An employer, it is asserted, cannot afford to pay a worker more than the value of the additional product produced because of that worker. If that amount is acceptable to the worker, he may be employed. And all workers, according to the theory, being interchangeable, the amount paid to the marginal worker will determine the wages of all the workers. The theory assumes perfect competition, complete mobility of labor, and full employment among the workers engaged in any particular kind of work. See also WAGE.

marginal propensity to consume. See explanation under PROPENSITY TO CONSUME.

marginal propensity to save. See explanation under PROPENSITY TO SAVE.

marginal rate of substitution. As applied to consumers, the quantity of one commodity or service that a given consumer feels he must acquire to compensate him exactly for the loss of one unit of some other commodity or service. When applied to money, the marginal rate of substitution is the price that a given consumer may be willing to pay for a specified quantity of some commodity or service. Also called *equimarginal principle.* See also INDIFFERENCE CURVE, MARGINAL UTILITY.

marginal revenue. The amount which the sale of one additional unit of product will add to the total income. If, for example, the total income received from the sale of 30 units is $30, and the total income received from the sale of 31 units is $30.50, the marginal revenue is 50 cents.

marginal seller. A seller at any given price who will refuse to sell if the price is reduced.

marginal trading. See Buying on margin.

marginal utility. The least utility attributed to any one item of a supply of goods. In the diagram shown below, for example, the four vertical lines marked A, B, C, and D represent four items exactly alike. The marginal utility, as long as there are four items, is represented by 1. If one item is removed, leaving only three, the marginal utility is then represented by 2, etc. In general, the greater the number of items, the less the marginal utility. This is sometimes called the *law of diminishing utility*, or the *law of satiety*. The extent to which the marginal utility lessens with each additional item depends upon the individual concerned and the objects considered. Also called *marginal desirability*. See also Utility.

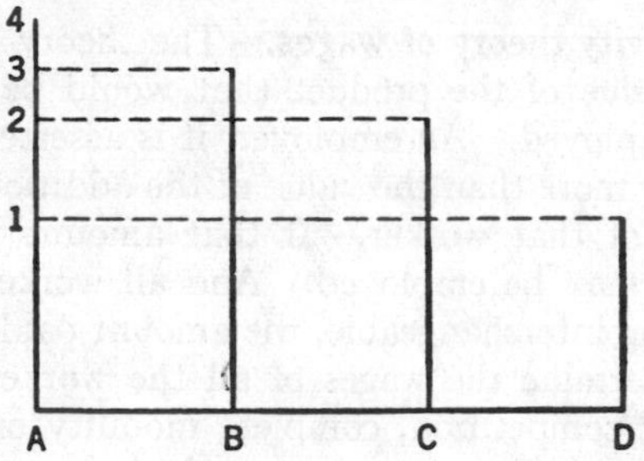

marginal utility school. A school of economic thought developed particularly in the writings of three economists — a German, Karl Menger; a Briton, W. Stanley Jevons; and a Frenchman, Léon Walras — and their followers who, near the last quarter of the 19th century, explained the relationship between desirability and price by reference to the conception of marginal utility. Earlier economists had pointed out the apparent absence of any logical relationship between the usefulness of certain commodities and their prices. Water, for example, was essential to life but virtually free; diamonds, on the other hand, though of relatively little practical use, were very high in price. The writers of the marginal utility school pointed out that, in the case of any one individual, each successive increment of a commodity lessened the subjective value of every increment possessed by that individual. Any one increment of a common substance like water, therefore, would be sacrificed with little or no return despite the fact that water is essential to life itself. But one increment of a rare commodity, like diamonds, would be sacrificed only for a substantial return even though that commodity has no such essential use as water. Also called the *Austrian school* because it was in Austria that the con-

ception of marginal utility first rose to dominance. See also SCHOOLS OF ECONOMIC THOUGHT.

marginal utility theory of interest. The theory that interest rates are determined by the desire of individuals to equalize the MARGINAL UTILITY estimates of their present possessions with the marginal utility estimates of future possessions. For example, under certain assumed conditions, the immediate ownership of a dwelling, when none is possessed, may, for a given individual, offer such a high marginal utility that he is willing to pay a premium for it; that is, he is willing to borrow and pay interest and thus sacrifice the marginal utility of some possession that he might otherwise acquire in the future when the loan must be repaid. Conversely, to another individual the present estimate of the future marginal utility of, say, an automobile may be greater than his estimate of the marginal utility of any immediate new possession or added increment to any present possession. He is therefore willing to lend and thereby receive interest which, together with the return of the principal, will enable him to purchase the automobile at some future time. In those psychological attitudes involving what economists call marginal utility, it is contended, is to be found an explanation for prevailing interest rates. The theory is an amplification of the AGIO THEORY OF INTEREST. See also INTEREST.

margin of cultivation. That stage in the cultivation of land which results in a revenue just sufficient to pay the costs of production. The margin may be extensive or intensive. It is extensive when additional increments of capital and labor are applied to relatively poor land, and intensive when such increments are applied to better grades of land at a point when DIMINISHING RETURNS have set in. See also MARGINAL LAND.

Maritime Administration. An agency of the United States Department of Commerce and successor to the United States Maritime Commission. The administration has numerous and complex duties relating to the construction of merchant ships by the United States government, the leasing and disposal of government-owned ships to private operators, the payment of federal subsidies to privately operated shipping lines, and the administration of regulatory legislation affecting shipping. Its general purpose is to encourage the construction and maintenance of a merchant marine, owned and operated by United States citizens, large enough to carry a substantial part of the foreign commerce of the United States and to provide the navy with necessary auxiliary shipping. Regulation of rates and services has been vested since 1962 in the Federal Maritime Commission.

market. The area within which buyers and sellers are in communication with one another and within which exchanges take place. The communication sometimes takes place face to face, and the market, then, is a very restricted area. On the other hand, the communication may be by telephone, telegraph, cable, or radio, in which case the market may be world-wide. See also BROAD MARKET, DISCOUNT MARKET, MONEY MARKET, NARROW MARKET, OPEN MARKET, RIGGED MARKET.

market demand. See explanation under DEMAND.

marketing agreement. In American agriculture, a system, partly voluntary, partly governmental, of marketing certain farm products in order to increase returns to producers. Authority for such a policy is contained in various laws enacted chiefly since 1937. Some of the commodities affected are dairy products, fats and oils, cotton, grain, fruits, vegetables, sugar, and tobacco. Agreements are made between producers or handlers and representatives of the United States Department of Agriculture. They become valid when approved by two-thirds of the producers representing two-thirds of the products grown, and, when valid, they become mandatory for all producers in a particular production area. The agreements consist of regulations to control the volume of shipments, grades and sizes of product, and adherence to posted prices for a specified length of time.

marketing co-operative. An organization of producers, usually of agricultural products, which markets the combined output of its members and/or nonmember patrons. Although retaining the nonprofit principle by returning to its patrons all authorized surplus of income over expenses, and operating, in most cases, on a one-member–one-vote basis, marketing co-operatives in general do not adhere strictly to the ROCHDALE PRINCIPLES. Many conduct their business virtually on a cost basis; some permit voting on a share basis, limiting the number of shares any one member may own; a few use patronage as a basis for voting rights. In the United States marketing co-operatives have performed a valuable service to farmers by introducing better grading and packaging methods and by improving the quality of the products sold. This, together with more efficient marketing procedures, has, in many cases, materially increased farmers' incomes.

There are about 8,000 marketing co-operatives in the United States, with a combined membership of over $2\frac{1}{2}$ million. They are found among dairy and poultry farmers as well as among producers of fruits and vegetables, grains, livestock, wool, and cotton. They form the largest and most powerful co-operative movement in the United States.

market price. Under conditions of pure competition, the price at which the quantity of a good offered by the sellers just equals the quantity that will be taken by the buyers in a particular market at a specific time. For example, under the conditions noted below, at a market price of 8 cents, the sellers offer 300 and the buyers will take 300. At 9 cents the sellers offer 400, but the buyers will take only 200; hence, the price will be forced down. At 7 cents the sellers offer only 200 while the buyers will take 400, therefore the price will be bid up. At 8 cents equilibrium is established. See also PRICE, PURE COMPETITION.

Prices	Quantities Offered by Sellers	Quantities That Buyers Will Take
10	500	100
9	400	200
8	300	300
7	200	400
6	100	500

markets, law of. The assertion that the greater the number and variety of commodities offered for sale, the greater the market for each one. If, for example, a trader barters his wares, he is more likely to dispose of all that he has if the market offers him an abundance of things and a wide variety in exchange. This is another way of saying that general overproduction cannot occur as long as all human wants are not satisfied. The law was formulated by J. B. Say during the 19th century.

markup. See PRICE SPREAD.

Marshall plan. See EUROPEAN RECOVERY PROGRAM.

Marxian law of capitalist accumulation. A generalization advanced by Karl Marx (1818–1883) and by certain of his disciples to the effect that as CAPITALISM develops, CAPITAL GOODS increase in amount and productivity, ownership becomes concentrated in fewer sources and eventually in the state, and workers become increasingly subject to exploitation and unemployment. During the early stages of capitalist development, according to the argument, surplus value is spent in capital goods rather than in CONSUMER GOODS, and this relative disparity between expenditures on capital, as opposed to consumer goods, continues even as production increases, the trend being aided by the effect of competition. Moreover, so the argument runs, the corporate form of business organization tends to eliminate the small producers in favor of the larger ones. This augments the number of workers and reduces the number of employers. The increase in the amount and concentration of capital goods makes necessary the expenditure of an increasing percentage of money capital on plant, equipment, and raw materials. Increased productivity, on the other hand, decreases the demand for labor. Unemployment results, causing a decrease in the total amount of wages paid. The end result is an accumulation of poverty together with an accumulation of capital goods.

It is predicted that when the process reaches its final conclusion and all industry is in the hands of a few or perhaps only one huge trust, stockholders will be divested of their property in favor of state ownership for the benefit of the workers. Thus, say the proponents of this view, the PROLETARIAT will divest the *BOURGEOISIE* of their property, just as a few centuries ago the *bourgeoisie* allegedly divested the artisans of their tools and established the factory system. Also called *appropriation, law of; increasing misery, theory of.* See also SURPLUS LABOR AND VALUE THEORY.

Massachusetts trust. A business organization which conducts its affairs through a trustee, according to a declaration or agreement of trust. As such, it is neither a CORPORATION nor a PARTNERSHIP. Contributions of capital are made to the trustees who carry on the business, certificates being issued to the contributors as evidence of their contributions, and earnings being paid them as dividends are paid to the stockholders of a corporation. The contributors may enjoy LIMITED LIABILITY, but they have no control over the management of the enterprise. So called because the plan originated in Massachusetts. Sometimes called *common-law trust.* See also TRUST.

mass picketing. Picketing by large numbers before the entrance of the establishment being picketed. It is done for its dramatic effect and sometimes to make entrance to the establishment difficult. See also PICKETING.

mass production. The production of goods in large quantities usually by means of machinery and frequently by means of interchangeable parts and division of labor. Also called *large-scale production.* See also ASSEMBLY-LINE TECHNIQUE, DIVISION OF LABOR, INTERCHANGEABLE PARTS, PRODUCTION.

material cost. See explanation under COST.

mathematical economics. Economic principles and arguments expressed, in part, by mathematical symbols. Use of such symbols is thus a method of economic analysis; it does not constitute a special school of economic thought. The use of graphs and mathematical symbols to supplement an explanation in words is common practice. The use of mathematics as a general tool in economic reasoning is much more limited. See also ECONOMICS.

mature economy. A term used by a few economists to describe the condition of a nation's economy when there is a decline in the rate of population growth and a decrease in the proportion of national income devoted to new capital investment, relatively more national income being spent for consumer goods.

maturity. As applied to securities and commercial paper, the date when payment of the principal is due.

maximum and minimum tariff system. A system of tariff duties which provides two schedules for the same articles, one setting forth maximum and the other setting forth minimum import duties. The system permits the granting of concessions or the imposition of penalties in the course of trade negotiations with foreign nations. See also TARIFF.

maximum-hour legislation. See explanation under FAIR LABOR STANDARDS ACT.

mean. A calculated average. Such averages are computed in various ways, according to the economic or other data under consideration and the object in view. See ARITHMETIC MEAN, GEOMETRIC MEAN, HARMONIC MEAN, MOVING AVERAGE, WEIGHTED AVERAGE. For quadratic mean, see STANDARD DEVIATION.

mean deviation. A statistical measure of the extent of absolute dispersion, variability, or scatter in a FREQUENCY DISTRIBUTION (*q.v.*) obtained by ascertaining the ARITHMETIC MEAN of the total deviations (disregarding plus and minus signs) from a central value such as the MEDIAN (*q.v.*).

Example with median = 2.53 given:

Class interval	Midpoint	Frequency	Deviations from median (disregarding plus and minus signs)	Total deviations (deviations times frequency)
−0.5 to 0.4	0	10	2.53 − 0 = 2.53	25.30
0.5 to 1.4	1	30	2.53 − 1 = 1.53	45.90
1.5 to 2.4	2	40	2.53 − 2 = 0.53	21.20
2.5 to 3.4	3	50	2.53 − 3 = 0.47	23.50
3.5 to 4.4	4	25	2.53 − 4 = 1.47	36.75
4.5 to 5.4	5	8	2.53 − 5 = 2.47	19.76
		163		172.41

$$\text{Mean deviation} = \frac{172.41}{163} = 1.0577.$$

The mean deviation is particularly well suited to economic analysis because, although it is influenced by every value in the series, undue weight is not given to the extremes.

measured day rate. As applied to the compensation of an employee, a daily adjustment of wages based on a record of his previous day's production.

median. As applied to a FREQUENCY DISTRIBUTION (*q.v.*), a positional average, indicating central tendency, secured by designating the midpoint. Its position thus being midway in the frequency distribution, one half of the cases are below it and half above it. Likewise, the value of the median is such that one half of the cases are less than it, and one half are in excess of it. It is calculated by first ascertaining the class interval within which it is located, then finding its value within this class interval by interpolation.

Example:

Frequency distribution

Class interval	Midpoint	Frequency	Cumulative frequency to the third-class interval
−0.5 to 0.4	0	10	10
0.5 to 1.4	1	30	40
1.5 to 2.4	2	40	80
2.5 to 3.4	3	50	
3.5 to 4.4	4	25	
4.5 to 5.4	5	8	
		163	

$$\frac{163}{2} = 81.5.$$

$$81.5 - 80 = 1.5.$$

$$\text{Median} = 2.5 + \left(\frac{1.5}{50} \times 1\right) = 2.5 + 0.03 = 2.53.$$

mediation. A procedure for settling disputes, akin to CONCILIATION but somewhat more formal, often involving the use of a board or commission before which the disputants may appear with their attorneys.

medium of exchange. See explanation under MONEY.

member bank. A term usually applied to a bank which is a member of the FEDERAL RESERVE SYSTEM. See also BANK.

mercantile agency. An organization that supplies information regarding business concerns seeking CREDIT.

mercantilism. The economy prevalent during the 16th and 17th centuries which sought to maintain, by various regulations, an excess of exports over imports and to collect the difference in the form of precious metals for use in increasing the power and prestige of the state. See also SCHOOLS OF ECONOMIC THOUGHT.

merchant guild. Medieval merchant associations that commanded a monopoly of town trade and became closely identified with municipal authority, sometimes to the point of merging with that authority. See also GUILD.

merchantman. A transoceanic or coastwise commercial vessel carrying passengers or freight.

merchant marine. Commercial ships owned and operated either by the government or by the private citizens of a state.

merger. The condition resulting when one corporation buys all of the capital stock of some other corporation or corporations and then dissolves the corporation or corporations thus purchased. The term is also often used interchangeably with AMALGAMATION. See also COMBINATION.

merit rating. As applied to labor relations, a periodic appraisal of an employee's efficiency, responsibility, and other qualifications. The merit rating is frequently used as a basis for wage increases and promotions. It is sometimes considered in determining which employees shall be laid off in the event that a plant is temporarily closed or work becomes slack. Less frequently, it is used by some states to determine workers' unemployment compensation contributions.

microeconomics. Economic studies or statistics that consider particular individuals or single commodities; for example, the demand for wheat or for employment in the automotive industries. The term is used in contradistinction to MACROECONOMICS. See also ECONOMICS.

middleman. A merchant, jobber, wholesaler, or some other such intermediary between the producer and the consumer.

middle way. See MIXED ECONOMY.

milk-control case. A decision of the United States Supreme Court, *Nebbia* v. *New York*, 291 U. S. 502 (1934), upholding a New York State statute which regulated the retail price of milk as consistent with the due process clause of the 14th Amendment of the United States Constitution. Primary significance attaches to this case because the subject regulated, that is, the milk business, does not fall within the category of businesses, such as utilities, which were traditionally considered to be "affected with a public interest" and therefore subject to such regulation as was here attempted. Indeed, the court specifically indicated that in its opinion there existed no particular class of businesses affected with a public interest and suggested that the courts would determine in each case, as it arose, whether circumstances warranted regulation or whether the regulation was arbitrary and discriminatory.

Miller-Tydings Act. An act of Congress, 1937. It permits minimum retail sales prices for trade-marked goods in interstate commerce, when also permitted by state law.

minimum rate. As applied to public-utility companies, the lowest rate that a company is permitted to charge for a specific commodity or service. Minimum rates are established by regulatory commissions. See also PUBLIC UTILITY.

minimum wage. A wage established by law as the lowest which may be paid employees in one or more industries. See also WAGE.

minimum-wage cases. 1. *Adkins* v. *Children's Hospital.* One of the early minimum-wage cases, 261 U. S. 525 (1923), to come before the United States Supreme Court in which that tribunal held unconstitutional a federal minimum-wage act the operation of which was limited to the District of Columbia. Applicable only to women and children in various industries for which a wage board prescribed minimum pay standards, the act was held to establish an uncertain yardstick for compensation and to discriminate arbitrarily against the employer; hence, it was deemed to go beyond the standards of due process prescribed by the 5th Amendment to the Constitution and to be an unreasonable interference with liberty of contract. 2. *West Coast Hotel Co.* v. *Parrish.* A case, 300 U. S. 379 (1937), in which the Supreme Court of the United States ruled that legislative establishment of reasonable minimum-wage rates for women was a proper use of the police power of the state. Earlier minimum-wage decisions, such as the one in the Adkins case above, were thus overruled in recognition of the necessity for a broader interpretation of the police power of the states to meet changing economic needs.

minor coin. A coin made of base metal. See also COIN.

mint. A place where metal is made into coins, usually operated by or under the authority of the government.

mintage. Any charge made by the government for converting bullion into coins.

Mint, Bureau of the. A branch of the Department of the Treasury of the United States having general supervision of the United States mints, assay offices, and depositaries.

mint par of exchange. As applied to the GOLD STANDARD, the ratio between the weights of the pure metal in the MONETARY UNITS of two nations. Thus, before January 31, 1934, when Great Britain and the United States were both on the gold standard, the British gold sovereign contained 113.0016 grains of fine gold, and the United States dollar 23.22 grains. The mint par of exchange was, therefore, 4.8665, obtained by dividing the first figure by the second. Mint par of exchange was self-regulating, the value of gold being maintained by FREE COINAGE and a free market. With the passing of the gold standard, PAR EXCHANGE RATE (*q.v.*) has largely replaced the mint par of exchange.

mint price of gold. The price, determined by law, which the government pays for gold delivered at the mint. In the United States, the dollar is defined by law as $15\frac{5}{21}$ grains of gold $\frac{9}{10}$ fine or 13.714+ grains of pure gold. There being 480 grains to the troy ounce, the mint price of gold is, therefore, $\frac{480}{13.714}$ or $35 per fine troy ounce.

mint ratio. In a bimetallic monetary system, the ratio of weight of one metal in the monetary system to the weight of the other metal in that system. For example, in the American presidential campaign of 1896, the forces supporting Bryan's bimetallic program urged a mint ratio between silver and gold of 16 to 1. See also BIMETALLISM.

Mississippi bubble. A highly speculative trading and financial structure created in France during the early part of the 18th century by John Law, a Scottish economist. After acquiring extensive trading powers over the area drained by the Mississippi, Ohio, and Missouri Rivers, Law succeeded in gaining a tobacco monopoly from the French crown and, later, management of the mint and the privilege of TAX FARMING on condition of assuming responsibility for payment of the French NATIONAL DEBT. These ventures involved the acquirement and consolidation of various trading and financial institutions, in the course of which speculation in the shares of the parent company, the *Compagnie de la Louisiane ou d'Occident*, became rampant. By 1720, however, public confidence began to dwindle, and shareholders began to withdraw their gains. Before the year was over a panic was precipitated by the announcement that the value of BANK NOTES of the Banque Royale, one of Law's financial institutions, would be gradually reduced. This resulted in the suspension of payments by the bank, the removal of Law from office, and his secret escape from the country.

mixed economy. An economic system in which can be found some of the characteristics of both CAPITALISM and SOCIALISM as well as some measure of CONTROL and regulation by the central government. See also ECONOMIC SYSTEM.

mode. As applied to a FREQUENCY DISTRIBUTION (*q.v.*), a positional average, indicating central tendency, secured by designating the most common measure or value. As such, it is the point on the X axis corresponding to the maximum ordinate. It can be derived only approximately from a frequency distribution. The class interval with the greatest frequency is selected. This is called the *modal class.* The equation for the mode is then:

$$Mo = l + \frac{f_2}{f_2 + f_1} \times i$$

when

Mo = mode,
f_1 = frequency of class next below the modal class,
f_2 = frequency of class next above the modal class,
i = class interval,
l = lower limit of modal class.

Example:

Class Interval	Frequency
−0.5 to 0.4	10
0.5 to 1.4	30
1.5 to 2.4	40
2.5 to 3.4	50 *
3.5 to 4.4	25
4.5 to 5.4	8

* Modal class.

$$Mo = 2.5 + \frac{25}{25 + 40} \times 1 = 2.5 + 0.385 = 2.885.$$

modified union shop. A shop in which, upon the consummation of a labor agreement, the status of the existing employees in reference to their labor-union membership, or nonmembership, remains unchanged, but in which new employees are obligated to join the labor union. See also UNION SHOP.

moiety. A term sometimes applied to the share of a fine allotted to an informer.

monetary reserves. The amount of bullion held by the government or by the banks as security for fiduciary or credit money in circulation. For example, the total amount of GREENBACKS in circulation in the United States is secured by about one-half their face value in bullion. See also FIDUCIARY MONEY, RESERVES.

monetary sovereignty. A right, said to inhere in any sovereign nation, to safeguard its economy against severe deflation, unemployment, or imbalance in its foreign payments, despite formal pledges of co-operation which it may have given to such organizations as the INTERNATIONAL MONETARY FUND or the INTERNATIONAL TRADE ORGANIZATION.

monetary system. A general term embracing the policies and practices affecting a particular nation's money. It may include the legal definition of STANDARD MONEY, regulations governing COINAGE and emission of MONEY, MONETARY RESERVES, and LEGAL TENDER, requirements and regulations affecting the value of different types of PAPER MONEY and COINS in terms of the standard money, etc. There are innumerable kinds of monetary systems in use and proposed. For some basic characteristics of the most common see BIMETALLISM, COMMODITY STANDARD, GOLD-BULLION STANDARD, GOLD-EXCHANGE STANDARD, GOLD STANDARD, LIMPING STANDARD, MANAGED MONEY, MONOMETALLISM, MULTIPLE-COMMODITY RESERVE-DOLLAR STANDARD, PARALLEL STANDARDS, POLYMETALLISM.

monetary union. See LATIN MONETARY UNION, SCANDINAVIAN MONETARY UNION, TRIPARTITE CURRENCY AGREEMENT. See also STERLING BLOC.

monetary unit. A specified amount and quality of a commodity selected as standard money and designated by a name. In the case of the United States the commodity selected is gold, and the amount and quality specified is 15⅝⁄21 grains 9⁄10 fine. The name of the unit is the "dollar."

money. Anything generally accepted in exchange for other things within more or less definite areas; hence, a customary medium of exchange. Money is also customarily used as a measure of, and a means of storing, value. Historically, commodities used as money were relatively scarce and universally wanted. Many articles possessing these prerequisites have been used as money, but the precious metals, in addition to these qualities, have been found to possess other characteristics which greatly facilitate their use as money. They are easily recognized, uniform in quality, easily divisible, and they encompass a relatively high value within a small space. An ideal money should also have stability of value in addition to these other characteristics, but no money has yet been devised to meet this requirement satisfactorily. The value of modern coins rests to a large extent upon the credit of the government issuing them, and this is true to an even greater extent of modern paper money. It should be noted that money as here defined is one form of CURRENCY (*q.v.*). Some authorities, however, use the term "money" in the more general sense and the term "currency" in the more restricted sense. See also CHEAP MONEY, COIN, CONVERTIBLE MONEY, COUNTERFEIT MONEY, DEAR MONEY, ELASTIC MONEY, FIAT MONEY, FIDUCIARY MONEY, FRACTIONAL MONEY, FUNCTIONS OF MONEY, HARD MONEY, IRREDEEMABLE MONEY, LAWFUL MONEY, OCCUPATION MONEY, PAPER MONEY, REPRESENTATIVE MONEY, SOFT MONEY, STABLE MONEY, STANDARD MONEY, TILL MONEY.

money capital. See explanation under CAPITAL.

money in circulation. In the United States coins and paper money circulating outside of the United States Treasury and the federal reserve banks.

money market. An indefinitely defined financial center where foreign and domestic BILLS (*q.v.*), foreign currency, and bullion are bought and sold.

money order. An order purchased by a person wishing to make a remittance to some distant point. It is sent to the payee, who may subsequently cash it at the place of payment specifically identified. A money order is usually cashable at any bank, upon identification. Money orders are generally named according to the agency that sells them (bank, express company, postal), according to the means of their transmission (cable, telegraph), or according to their destination (domestic, foreign, international).

money wage. The amount of wages paid in money. The term is used to emphasize the fact that what can be bought with the wages depends upon the PRICE LEVEL. See also WAGE.

monometallism. A monetary system in which the monetary unit is legally defined in terms of but one metal, that metal being accepted in unlimited quantities for coinage and made unlimited legal tender. Also called *single standard.* See also MONETARY SYSTEM.

monopolistic competition. The condition that exists in a market when the operations of one or a few buyers or sellers can materially affect the market price. See also ADMINISTERED PRICE, COMPETITION, DUOPOLY, DUOSONY, MONOPOLY, OLIGOPOLY, POLYPOLY.

monopoly. Usually the condition which exists when there is a single control over all the supply of a product, thus permitting the release of the supply at such a rate as will yield the most profitable price. The monopolist cannot dictate the schedule demand for his product. He can only discover it. But he can dictate the schedule supply. This enables him to offer for sale the particular quantity of his product that, according to the schedule demand, will yield him the most profitable price. This price may be relatively high or low depending upon the nature of the product and the nature of the schedule demand. For some of the more important kinds of monopoly see BUYER'S MONOPOLY, FISCAL MONOPOLY, NATURAL MONOPOLY, PUBLIC CONSUMPTION MONOPOLY, SPECIAL PRIVILEGE MONOPOLY, TRADE MONOPOLY. See also DEMAND, SUPPLY.

monopsony. See BUYER'S MONOPOLY.

moratorium. A period, usually stipulated by law, during which the settlement of debts may be postponed.

more-favorable-terms clause. A clause in a labor contract in which the contracting labor union agrees that it will not grant more favorable terms in any future contracts with competitors of the contracting employer.

morning loan. Unsecured loans made to stockbrokers for whatever amount is necessary to carry on a day's business. This type of loan has replaced the practice of OVERCERTIFICATION (*q.v.*). See also LOAN.

Morrill (Land-Grant College) Act. An act of Congress, 1862. It provided grants of public lands to the states, the revenue from which was to be used for education in agricultural and mechanical arts.

Morrill Tariff. The United States Tariff Act of 1861. Its purpose was avowedly protective. Existing duties were advanced. SPECIFIC DUTIES were restored on raw wool, cotton bagging, and other commodities.

Morris Plan bank. An organization which makes small loans to individuals, generally on the security of two cosigners on the promissory note. See also BANK.

mortgage. 1. A conditional conveyance of property as security for the payment of a debt or the performance of some other obligation. 2. A contract specifying that certain property is hypothecated for the payment of a debt or for the performance of some other obligation. For some of the important kinds of mortgages see CHATTEL MORTGAGE, CLOSED MORTGAGE, OPEN MORTGAGE, PURCHASE-MONEY MORTGAGE. See also HYPOTHECATE.

mortgage bond. See explanation under BOND.

mortgagee. A person who grants a loan secured by a mortgage. See also MORTGAGE.

mortgage-moratorium case. See *HOME BUILDING AND LOAN ASSOCIATION v. BLAISDELL.*

mortgagor. A person who gives a mortgage as security for a loan.

most-favored-nation clause. A provision in a commercial treaty binding the contracting nations to confer upon each other all the most favorable trade concessions that either may grant to any other nation subsequent to the signing of the agreement.

Motor Carrier Act. An act of Congress, 1935, which brings most commercial motor vehicles operating in interstate commerce within the jurisdiction of the Interstate Commerce Commission, and subjects the rate structure and the services of companies operating such vehicles to the commission's regulatory power. See also INTERSTATE COMMERCE COMMISSION.

moving average. A series of averages obtained by selecting a fixed number of successive items in a series, computing the average, then dropping the first item and adding the next succeeding one, computing the average of this second group, dropping the second item and adding the next succeeding one, computing the average of this third group, etc. throughout the series. The following is an example of a three-item moving average:

Items	Three-item moving totals	Three-item moving average
2		
6	9	3
1	15	5
8	12	4
3	12	4
1	15	5
11	24	8
12	27	9
4		

In economic computation, moving averages are frequently used in smoothing out irregular curves.

Mulford* v. *Smith. See AGRICULTURAL ADJUSTMENT ACT CASE (SECOND).

Muller* v. *Oregon. A case, 208 U. S. 412 (1908), in which the Supreme Court of the United States upheld the constitutionality of an Oregon statute limiting the workday of women employed in certain establishments to 10 hours. Apparently the court differentiated this case from the situation in *LOCHNER* v. *NEW YORK* (*q.v.*), decided a few years earlier, because it felt that women were less able to endure sustained labor than men and hence required special protection by law.

multicraft union. A craft labor union, the members of which include workers in several distinctly different kinds of trades and occupations. See also LABOR UNION.

multilateral agreement. An agreement in which more than two parties participate.

multilinear tariff. See MULTIPLE TARIFF SYSTEM.

multiple-commodity reserve dollar. A plan designed to maintain a constant value ratio between gold and other commodities in terms of dollars. It proposes to establish a reserve of selected goods. Money would then be redeemable either in gold or in these reserve goods, and gold and the reserve goods could always be exchanged for dollars. Thus, it is claimed, a constant ratio would be maintained between the value of the commodities, the gold, and the dollar.

multiple currency system. A form of exchange control. It involves the establishment by law of different exchange values for the national currency, the applicable value in any exchange transaction depending upon the type of commodity purchased abroad for which exchange is desired. See also EXCHANGE CONTROL.

multiple expansion of credit. The process by which a loan made by one bank may, in the ordinary course of business transactions, become a deposit in another bank and be used by this second bank as a reserve for another loan. This, in turn, may be deposited in a third bank to serve as a reserve for a third loan, etc., thus multiplying the original credit granted by the first bank. See also CREDIT.

multiple tariff system. A system of tariff duties which specifies different duties applicable to different nations. Also called *multilinear tariff*. See also TARIFF.

multiplier principle. As applied to investments, an explanation, propounded especially by Keynesian economists, as to the way in which an increase or a decrease in new CAPITAL FORMATION can cause cumulative effects in the NATIONAL INCOME through consumer expenditures. For example, assume an increase in new capital formation of $4,000,000. This will normally yield a like increase in the national income in the form of wages, interest, profit, rent, etc. The recipients of this INCOME will spend it according to the existing marginal PROPENSITY TO CONSUME. Assuming this to be 65 per cent, then $2,600,000 will be spent for consumer goods. This will increase the income in the consumer goods industry by that amount. The recipients of that income, in turn, will, according to the assumption, spend 65 per cent of $2,600,000, or $1,690,000. And as this last amount becomes income, 65 per cent of it will be spent, and so on, according to the following table, based on the assumed increase in new capital formation.

Investment, $4,000,000
Marginal Propensity to Consume, 65 per cent

Income	Expenditure
$4,000,000.00	$2,600,000.00
2,600,000.00	1,690,000.00
1,690,000.00	1,098,500.00
1,098,500.00	714,025.00
714,025.00	464,116.25
464,116.25	301,675.56
301,675.56	etc.

Ultimately, the total increase in income will approach $11,428,571, in accordance with the following formula:

$$\frac{I}{1 - R}$$

when

I = the original increase in new capital formation,
R = the marginal propensity to consume.

Applying this to the above example, the results are:

$$\frac{\$4{,}000{,}000}{1 - 0.65} = \frac{\$4{,}000{,}000}{0.35} = \$11{,}428{,}571.$$

The multiplier is the ratio between the increase or decrease in income (Y) and the increase or decrease in new capital formation (I), or, in the above example:

$$\frac{\Delta Y}{\Delta I} = \frac{11{,}428{,}571}{4{,}000{,}000} = 2.8571.$$

A decrease in investments will, of course, have the opposite effect and will decrease the national income. The decrease in the national income from this cause will, it is held, equal the amount of the decrease in new capital formation times the multiplier. See also KEYNESIAN ECONOMICS, LEAKAGE.

municipal bond. See explanation under BOND.

municipal corporation. A corporation organized for the purpose of administering a political subdivision of a state, usually a city, village, or town but sometimes also a county. See also CORPORATION.

municipal socialism. Ownership and operation of local utility services by a municipality. Examples are water supply, gas, or electricity. See also SOCIALISM.

***Munn* v. *Illinois*.** The most important of the so-called *Granger cases* which involved judicial review of the efforts of midwest farming interests in the United States to reduce, through appropriate legislation, the rates charged by railways and warehouses for the transportation and storage of grain and other commodities. This particular case, 94 U. S. 113 (1876), involved an Illinois statute fixing maximum charges for grain storage in elevators, and the principal legal issue was whether such legislation deprived elevator proprietors of their property rights protected by the due process clause of the 14th Amendment of the federal Constitution. The court's decision, upholding the regulatory statute, is noteworthy because it is based on the theory that there are certain businesses, like that of operating a grain elevator, which, though privately owned, are nonetheless businesses in which the "public has a direct and positive interest"; that they are businesses clothed with a public interest and, as such, are amenable to public control. The decision thus became one of the pioneer judicial precedents in the United States validating public regulation of the rates and services of what are commonly known as PUBLIC UTILITIES.

mutual company. Usually a corporation without capital stock, the profits, if any, after deduction of reserves, being distributed among the customers in proportion to the business done with the company. A MUTUAL SAVINGS BANK is a common form of mutual company.

mutual funds. See OPEN-END INVESTMENT TRUST.

mutualism. The economic ideas of Pierre Joseph Proudhon (1809–1865), a French neoanarchist leader, and his followers. Proudhon objected particularly to unearned income payments and value appreciation arising from the private ownership of property. He believed that such payments as rent, interest, and profits were parasitical shares and should be abolished. Services rendered and received would, he argued, then be in balance on the basis of mutual equality.

mutual loan association. See BUILDING AND LOAN ASSOCIATION.

mutual mortgage insurance system. A federal revolving fund available to the FEDERAL HOUSING ADMINISTRATION for insuring mortgages on single and multiple dwelling units, the latter accommodating not more than four families. The maximum insurance which can be issued under this fund is five billion dollars.

mutual savings bank. A savings bank, the depositors of which are the owners, and the net earnings of which are apportioned among the depositors. It is governed by a board of self-perpetuating trustees. See also SAVINGS BANK.

N

narrow market. A period when the volume of trading is limited. The term is usually applied to trading in stocks and bonds but may apply to the market as a whole or to special classes of securities. Sometimes called *thin market.* See also MARKET.

National Advisory Council on International Monetary and Financial Problems. An independent agency of the United States government, created in 1945, to co-ordinate the policies and operations of the representatives of the United States on the INTERNATIONAL MONETARY FUND, THE INTERNATIONAL BANK FOR RECONSTRUCTION AND DEVELOPMENT, and of other governmental agencies in so far as these deal with foreign loans, foreign exchange, or monetary transactions.

National Aeronautics and Space Administration. An independent federal agency, created in 1958, to conduct research into the problems of flight, both within and beyond the earth's atmosphere, to plan and conduct such activities as might be required for the peaceful utilization of outer space, including the creation of space vehicles, and to assist scientists in their research efforts.

National Association of Manufacturers. An organization founded in 1895 and composed of approximately 20,000 manufacturers distributed throughout the United States. It acts as a spokesman for industry before Congress and the administrative agencies of the national government. The association publishes a weekly *N.A.M. News* and occasional booklets relating to a variety of topics.

national bank. An incorporated commercial bank chartered by the government of the United States. See also BANK, COMMERCIAL BANK.

National Bank Act. An act of Congress, 1863, at first called the *National Currency Act.* It established a system of NATIONAL BANKS (*q.v.*). Subsequently, in 1866, a federal tax of 10 per cent on state bank notes drove such notes out of circulation and had the effect of making the national banks the only banks of issue at the time. See also *VEAZIE BANK* v. *FENNO.*

National Bureau of Standards. A unit of the United States Department of Commerce. It has custody of the national standards of physical measurement and conducts research to improve methods of measurement and of testing materials. It develops specifications for the purchase of most supplies for the federal government, and it acts in an advisory capacity to other government agencies on scientific and technical matters.

National Currency Act. See NATIONAL BANK ACT.

national debt. The debt of a central government as distinct from the debts of the political subdivisions of the nation and the debts of private persons corporate and natural. The national debt plus the debts of local governments of a country comprise its PUBLIC DEBT. See also DEBT, EXTERNAL NATIONAL DEBT, GROSS NATIONAL DEBT, INTERNAL NATIONAL DEBT, NET NATIONAL DEBT.

national economy. The economic life of a nation. The term implies that the economic life of a nation forms a unified whole.

National Farmers Union. An organization of farmers, founded in the United States in 1902. It claims a membership representing at least 100,000 farm families, and is officially organized in at least 20 states with local representation in many more. The union sponsors many co-operative business enterprises, offering insurance and dealing in farm supplies, livestock, butter, poultry, grain, and cotton. It endeavors to organize farmers into autonomous groups for the purpose of education in economics, production techniques, and the advantages to be gained through co-operatives. Usually called *Farmers Union.*

national farm loan association. One of many local co-operative associations organized by farmers to secure credit through one of the 12 federal land banks. Land-bank loans are made to individual farmers and cattlemen through one of these farm loan associations. The prospective borrower must secure the association's approval of his proposed loan and its indorsement of the mortgage he offers as security. He must also purchase stock in the association (sometimes directly in the land bank) equal to 5 per cent of his loan, this stock being retired when the loan is repaid. Purchase of the stock makes the borrower a member of the association, and as a member he casts one vote at all stockholders' meetings. Now known as FEDERAL LAND BANK associations.

National Federation of Federal Employees. The first major organization of United States government employees, outside of the postal system, set up in 1917. Certain of its several hundred locals seceded in 1932 when the parent organization left the AMERICAN FEDERATION OF LABOR.

National Grange Order of the Patrons of Husbandry. One of the earliest American farm organizations, founded in 1867. It was originally conceived as a secret organization and has always retained its ritual service. Its object is to improve rural life, foster the processes of democracy, and crystallize an informed public opinion concerning national affairs. It is claimed that there are at least

800,000 dues-paying members, and 8,000 local granges, perhaps half of which own their own halls. These halls are often community centers where regular meetings are held to further the objects of the organization. Popularly known as the *Grange.* Also called *Patrons of Husbandry.*

national income. The total net earnings ascribable to the various factors employed in the production of goods and services in a nation during a particular period. As computed by the United States Department of Commerce, national income includes: (1) all wages and salaries and miscellaneous supplements to wages and salaries, such as employer contributions to pension and workmen's compensation funds; (2) the business operations' income of unincorporated enterprises, capital gains and losses not being considered; (3) corporate earnings accruing to residents, minus intercorporate dividends and plus profits from abroad; (4) loan and imputed net interest from real property and royalties; (5) taxes levied on corporate earnings less any tax refunds for the current period; (6) that portion of the change in value of business inventories which can be counted as current output; and (7) all loan and imputed interest accruing to residents, minus government interest disbursements to corporations, the latter being included in corporate earnings. See also INCOME.

National Industrial Recovery Act. An act of Congress, 1933. It provided for CODES OF FAIR COMPETITION, COLLECTIVE BARGAINING, and other measures designed to promote recovery from the economic depression then in existence. The code provisions of the act were declared unconstitutional by the United States Supreme Court in 1935. See also SCHECHTER CASE.

national industrial reserve. Facilities for the production of aircraft, munitions, chemicals, and ships, administered by the Department of Defense or the GENERAL SERVICES ADMINISTRATION of the United States. In 1960 the national industrial reserve was maintaining 4,403 items in the reserve having an acquisition cost of $31.1 million.

national insurance. See SOCIAL INSURANCE.

National Inventors Council. A special unit of the United States Department of Commerce created in 1940 to evaluate inventions relating to war operations and to submit such evaluations to the appropriate branches of the armed services.

nationalization. Ownership and operation by the central government of a nation of some enterprise previously a private or local-government undertaking. See also PUBLIC OWNERSHIP.

National Labor Relations (Wagner-Connery) Act. An act of Congress, 1935, which guarantees the right of certain employees to full freedom in self-organization and in the designation of representatives of their own choosing for the purpose of collective bargaining, and makes unlawful unfair labor practices which abridge or deny the right of collective bargaining. Its provisions were subsequently (1947) amended by the LABOR-MANAGEMENT RELATIONS (TAFT-HARTLEY) ACT (*q.v.*).

National Labor Relations Act case. A case, *National Labor Relations Board* v. *Jones and Laughlin Steel Corp.*, 301 U. S. 1 (1937), in which the Supreme Court of the United States upheld as constitutional the National Labor Relations Act of 1935 (Wagner-Connery Act) as a valid exercise of congressional power. The court declared that the act, in its provisions for collective bargaining and control over labor relations, sought to reach labor disputes which might burden or obstruct foreign or interstate commerce. In doing so, commented the court, the act "must be construed as contemplating the exercise of control within the Constitutional bounds."

National Labor Relations Board. An independent agency of the United States government, consisting of five members, created by the National Labor Relations Act of 1935 and continued, with certain changes, under the Labor-Management Relations Act of 1947. Among the board's duties are those of conducting elections among private employees to determine what labor organization shall represent them in collective bargaining and to certify labor organizations for collective bargaining. The board also investigates allegations of unfair labor practices by either unions or management; for example, the exaction of discriminatory or excessive fees by unions or employer discrimination against employees for union activity. If such practices are found to exist, the board may issue cease-and-desist orders and petition the federal circuit courts of appeals to enforce them. Responsibility for instituting proceedings against management or labor unions for unfair practices vests in the board's general counsel who is appointed by the President and the Senate for a term of 4 years. See also LABOR-MANAGEMENT RELATIONS (TAFT -HARTLEY) ACT, NATIONAL LABOR RELATIONS ACT.

National Labor Relations Board* v. *Fansteel Metallurgical Corp. See FANSTEEL CASE.

National Labor Relations Board* v. *Jones and Laughlin Steel Corp. See NATIONAL LABOR RELATIONS ACT CASE.

National Mediation Board. An independent agency of the United States government created in 1934 to carry out the provisions of the Railway Labor Act of 1926 and subsequent related legislation.

The board is called upon to promote collective bargaining between labor and management in the nation's interstate railway and air-line systems, and to mediate disputes arising out of existing labor agreements. See also FEDERAL MEDIATION AND CONCILIATION SERVICE.

national minimum. A social-security policy which sets a certain "floor," or minimum, to the level of living. The government attempts to assure this minimum to each individual through social insurance, relief, or some other means of public assistance.

National Monetary Commission. See ALDRICH-VREELAND ACT.

national origin plan. As applied to the immigration policy of the United States, the plan by which the number of immigrants admitted each year from quota countries, other than certain exempt classes, is determined. The number of persons in the United States who were born in a given QUOTA COUNTRY or trace their descent to it is first determined, and the proportion that this number bears to the total United States population is then calculated. This proportion, when applied to the total number of immigrants permitted to enter the United States from all quota countries (approximately 154,000 in 1960), gives the number permitted to enter the United States within a period of 1 year from the quota country under consideration. Thus, if 15 per cent of the American people in 1920 were of a certain nationality by birth or descent, then 15 per cent of 154,000 or 23,100 persons of that nationality would be admitted to the United States in the period of 1 year. Revised immigration quotas were established in 1952 and 1957.

national product. See GROSS NATIONAL PRODUCT, NET NATIONAL PRODUCT.

National Production Authority. A special agency set up in the United States Department of Commerce, 1950, to administer the priorities, allocations, and other controls given the President in the DEFENSE PRODUCTION ACT. It was abolished in 1953.

National Science Foundation. An independent agency of the United States government, created in 1950, to promote education and research in science. The foundation has four separate divisions dealing with medical research, mathematical, physical, and engineering science, biological science, and scientific personnel and education. Its board consists of 24 members chosen from the fields of the basic sciences and appointed by the President with the advice and consent of the Senate.

National Security Council. A division of the Executive Office of the President of the United States, created by the National Security Act, 1947, to integrate civilian and military policies having to do with the nation's defense, thus providing more effective co-operation between the military services and the various other agencies of the national government. It is composed of the President, the Vice President, the Secretary of State, the Secretary of Defense, and the Director of the Office of Civil and Defense Mobilization.

national security exchanges. Security exchanges in the United States registered with the Securities and Exchange Commission in accordance with the provisions of the SECURITIES EXCHANGE ACT of 1934.

National Security Resources Board. A division of the Executive Office of the President of the United States established under the authority of the National Security Act of 1947. The board advised the President concerning the stockpiling and conservation of strategic and critical materials and made recommendations concerning the strategic relocation of industries and services essential to the security of the nation. In time of military emergency the board also developed policies relating to industrial and civil mobilization, the effective use of natural and industrial resources for military and civilian use, and the unification of the activities of various federal agencies. The Board was abolished in 1953.

national union. A labor union whose members are widely distributed throughout the United States, but none of whom resides in a foreign country. See also LABOR UNION.

national wealth. The total money value at any particular time of all the material economic goods possessed by members of a given nation. For many nations the property within the nation owned by foreigners just about balances the property outside of the nation owned by nationals. In such cases the matter of nationality is ignored as it is, for example, in the statistics of the national wealth of the United States issued by the United States Bureau of Census. Where no such balance exists, a distinction may be made between "national wealth" and "wealth within the borders," much of which may be held by nonnationals.

natural capital. See explanation under CAPITAL GOOD.

Natural Gas Act. An act of Congress, 1938, which, as amended in 1942, gives the Federal Power Commission considerable authority over interstate transportation and sale of natural gas. The commission's powers under the legislation include control of rates, the regulation of services, and the investigation of interstate compacts dealing with various aspects of the natural gas industry.

natural monopoly. 1. A monopoly due to natural conditions. For example, the natural conditions may be a peculiarity of soil within a small area enabling the owner or owners of that area to produce a product that cannot be grown elsewhere, or the existence of a limited supply of mineral wealth coming under the control of a single enterprise. 2. A monopoly due to characteristics inherent in the business. The characteristics are usually those which make competition self-destructive and hence incompatible with the public interest. Such conditions have been met by subjecting such businesses to government control as in the case of PUBLIC-UTILITY companies. See also DESTRUCTIVE COMPETITION, MONOPOLY.

natural order. A conception of the physiocrats popular during the 18th century. According to this conception human societies were subject to laws of nature such as govern the physical world. It was necessary, therefore, that all human activities should be brought into harmony with these laws of nature. This, it was held, could be accomplished by seeking the greatest satisfactions with the least sacrifice; and when each member of society thus ordered his activities, the welfare of society as a whole was assured. It was in this conception of a natural order that the term LAISSEZ FAIRE originated. See also PHYSIOCRATS.

natural resources. Wealth supplied by nature. Mineral deposits, soil fertility, timber, potential water power, and fish and wild life are included in the concept. The term "natural resources" is identical with the formal economic concept of LAND.

natural rights. Individual rights which are believed to be beyond the province of the state to deny. The Declaration of Independence of the United States defines such rights as "life, liberty, and the pursuit of happiness."

nature. See LAND.

navicert. A document issued by a belligerent nation permitting specified commodities to be transported overseas by a neutral nation through a blockaded area to a named neutral port of destination. A cargo navicert names the commodities and certifies that the shipment is within the normal requirements of the neutral country to which it is consigned. A ship navicert specifies the cargo carried and certifies that permission has been granted for the vessel to make that specific voyage. The term is an abbreviation of "naval certificate."

near money. LIQUID assets held by individuals and organizations. United States BONDS and various kinds of savings accounts are examples. The concept is significant in economic analysis because the possession of near money may influence buying and saving plans quite as much as does the possession of actual money.

***Nebbia* v. *New York*.** See MILK-CONTROL CASE.

negative investment. See explanation under DISINVESTMENT.

negotiability. The quality possessed by a bank check, promissory note, or other legal instrument of value which permits legal title to it to be transferred from one person to another by INDORSEMENT and delivery, or by delivery without indorsement.

neoclassical school. See CAMBRIDGE SCHOOL.

neoclassical theory of value. The theory which holds that the value of a particular commodity is determined by the interaction between the forces of demand expressed in a demand schedule and the forces of supply expressed in a supply schedule. Value is determined at a point of balance or equilibrium which is the point where the maximum number of exchanges takes place. See explanation under MARKET PRICE. See also VALUE.

net income. As normally used in accounting practice, whatever remains from earnings and profits after all costs, expenses, and allowances for depreciation and probable losses have been deducted. Thus used, the term is usually synonymous with *net profits*.

net interest. See PURE INTEREST.

net lease. A lease requiring the tenant to pay the taxes and insurance and the cost of repairs, maintenance, alterations, and improvements on the leased property. See also LEASE.

net national debt. The total national debt outstanding, less duplications and that part of the debt held by the governmental units in trust, in investment, or in sinking funds. See also NATIONAL DEBT.

net national product. The total value at current market prices of all final goods and services produced by the nation's economy. According to the United States Department of Commerce, it consists of the purchases of goods and services by consumers and the government, net private domestic investments, and net foreign investments. Net national product is the same as GROSS NATIONAL PRODUCT less allowance for depreciation.

net price. The price after all deductions, allowances, and discounts have been made. See also PRICE.

net product. A term used by the PHYSIOCRATS during the middle of the 18th century to indicate the difference between the value of new wealth and the value of the wealth used to create the new wealth. A net product existed, they believed, only in the case of agricultural production, industry being sterile, although essential to the economy. See also *TABLEAU ÉCONOMIQUE*.

net profit. See explanation under PROFIT.

net yield. The annual money income on a bond less the annual amortization if the bond has been purchased at a premium, or plus the computed annual accumulation if the bond has been purchased at a discount. Also called *yield to maturity.* See also AMORTIZATION 2, ACCUMULATION.

neutral money. See COMMODITY DOLLAR.

New Deal. A general term applying to various measures, initiated during the administration of President Franklin D. Roosevelt, to promote national economic recovery and social security in the United States, following the advent of the economic depression of the 1930's. These measures involved industrial recovery, farm relief, direct unemployment relief, control of public-utility holding companies, old-age pensions, and unemployment insurance.

Newlands Act. An act of Congress, 1913. It provided for a mediation board of four full-time members to act upon its own initiative or upon request in the case of disputes between the railroads and their employees. The railroads had urged the creation of a single board to control wages and hours as well as rates and service. The act in question, however, although replacing the mediation and arbitration features of the ERDMAN ACT, gave the newly created mediation board no authority over rates and service.

***New York*, et al., v. *United States*, et al.** A case, 331 U. S. 284 (1947), in which the Supreme Court of the United States sustained an order issued by the Interstate Commerce Commission deducting 10 per cent from certain transportation rates of southern, southwestern, and western trunk-line railroads and adding 10 per cent to the same transportation rates in eastern territory. The court thus sustained the thesis that the INTERSTATE COMMERCE COMMISSION may require adjustments to overcome alleged regional discrimination in certain railroad rates and thereby promote greater equality in the treatment of shippers throughout the United States.

New York Stock Exchange. The principal security market in the United States. It is an unincorporated voluntary organization composed of some 1,375 members and traces its beginning back to 1790. Membership, or a "seat" on the exchange as it is called, is obtained by purchase from a retiring member or from the estate of a deceased member, and upon approval of a committee on admissions.

nominal account. A term used in double-entry bookkeeping to indicate an account which is closed out at the end of an accounting period, and thus not carried over to the new accounting period. Any expense account is an example. See also ACCOUNT.

nominalists. A term sometimes used to identify certain authorities who reserve the term "money" for that which an organized government declares is such. They contend that the basis of money is not the material from which it is made but the legal mandates which establish and regulate its use. Whatever is selected as STANDARD MONEY, therefore, is purely a nominal matter according to this viewpoint — hence the name.

nominal price. A price in name only. The term may imply an amount so small as hardly to justify the term "price," or it may refer to an estimated price for a security or commodity that is not bought and sold often enough to establish a definite market price. See also PRICE.

nominal yield. The rate of return specified on a security calculated on its par or face value. Thus "6 per cent" appearing on a preferred stock certificate the par or face value of which is $100 indicates a nominal yield of 6 per cent of $100, or $6.

nonassented stock or bond. See explanation under ASSENTED STOCK OR BOND.

nonassessable stock. See explanation under CAPITAL STOCK.

nonclearinghouse stock. See explanation under CAPITAL STOCK.

noncontributory pension. A pension for the benefit of employees the entire cost of which is assumed by the employer. See also PENSION.

noncumulative stock. See explanation under CAPITAL STOCK.

nondiscretionary trust. See FIXED INVESTMENT TRUST.

Nonimportation Act. An act of Congress, 1806. It prohibited certain goods originating in any part of the British Empire from entering the United States.

nonimportation agreement. One of numerous agreements, made by American colonials at various times between 1768 and 1774, not to import commodities from England.

noninterest-bearing discount bond. See explanation under BOND.

nonrecourse loans. As applied to the United States government's agricultural policy since 1938, loans made to farmers and ranchers by governmental fiscal agencies on certain surplus commodities, the latter serving as security for the loans. The commodities, in the government's possession, are withheld from the market in order to maintain a higher level of farm prices and protect farm income. The loans cannot be extinguished by the debtor farmer at will but must be liquidated in accordance with the government's market and price policy; hence the designation "nonrecourse" loans.

nonrecurring expense. An expense occasioned by some condition that is not regularly repeated in the ordinary course of business operations. A case in point is a loss by fire or theft.

no-par-value stock. See explanation under CAPITAL STOCK.

normal curve of distribution. A hypothetical frequency curve symmetrical about the maximum ordinate and characterized by certain definite relationships between the ARITHMETIC MEAN and the ordinates at various STANDARD DEVIATION distances from the mean. The diagram below shows a frequency curve with some of these relationships indicated. Also called *normal curve of error* and *probability curve.* See also FREQUENCY DISTRIBUTION.

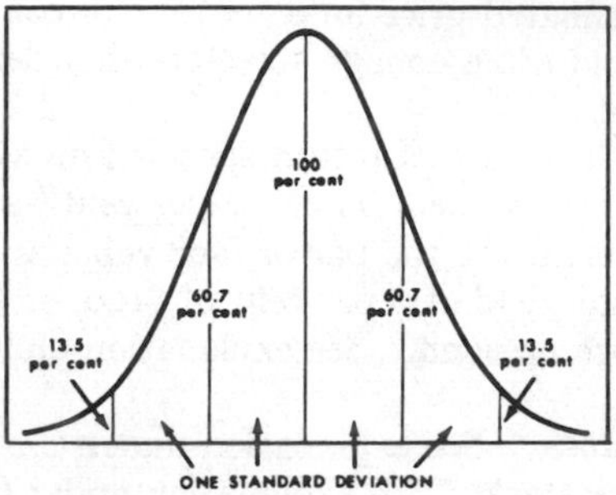

normal curve of error. See NORMAL CURVE OF DISTRIBUTION.

normal price. An equilibrium price to which the market price tends to return after temporary fluctuations either upward or downward. Normal price, therefore, suggests an average price over a relatively long period of time, whereas MARKET PRICE indicates a price at a given moment of time. See also PRICE.

Norman* v. *Baltimore and Ohio R. R. Co. See GOLD-CLAUSE CASES.

Norris-LaGuardia Act. See ANTI-INJUNCTION ACT.

Northern Securities Co.* v. *United States. A case, 193 U. S. 197 (1904), in which the Supreme Court of the United States ordered the dissolution of the Northern Securities Co., a holding company which had been used for the purpose of bringing under single control two of the largest transcontinental railroad systems of the country. The injunction against the holding company was based upon the antitrust provisions of the Sherman Act.

***nostro* overdraft.** Literally, "our" OVERDRAFT. The term sometimes appears on a domestic bank's statements indicating that BILLS OF EXCHANGE have been sold in greater amount than purchased, and that, in consequence, the domestic bank is indebted to some foreign bank or banks to the extent indicated by the overdraft.

notary public. In the United States, an officer appointed under the laws of a state to administer oaths; protest bank checks, promissory notes, and other such papers; and to authenticate copies of documents.

notes payable. See BILLS PAYABLE.

notes receivable. See BILLS RECEIVABLE.

NRA case. See SCHECHTER CASE.

nuisance tax. Any tax the revenue from which does not justify the inconvenience it causes those subject to the tax. See also TAX.

O

obsolescence. The condition of being out of date. Obsolescence is caused by new inventions and improved processes for production or a change in the demand for the things produced. It is not the result of mere age or wear.

occupational level. A vocational grouping based on the existence of some characteristic common to the group. The common characteristic may be the degree of skill required, and the groups may be classified as skilled, semiskilled, and unskilled. Or the character of the work performed may provide the basis of classification. Thus, the United States census makes the following classification: professional, semiprofessional, farmers and farm managers, proprietors and managers, salesmen and saleswomen, craftsmen and foremen, operatives, domestic-service workers, protective-service workers, farm laborers and foremen, other laborers.

occupation money. Money used by military forces in occupied enemy territory. In most cases such money is issued in the MONETARY UNIT of the occupied country and is pure FIAT MONEY. It is used to make local purchases, to pay local labor, and to pay personnel when money that would be accepted locally is required. In the invasion of North Africa during November, 1942, however, the United States used what was known as the *yellow seal* dollar or *spearhead* money, and the British forces used the "military pound" known as the "British Military Authority note." The United States yellow seal dollars were charged against the War Department appropriation, but the British military pound was reported to have been a direct obligation of the British treasury. See also MONEY.

occupation tax. 1. A fee exacted by the government when issuing a license to a person desiring to engage in a certain occupation or profession. 2. Generally, any tax levied upon a particular occupation or calling. Sometimes called *privilege tax.* See also TAX.

odd-lot broker. A stockbroker who buys and sells stock in lots of less than 100 shares.

office. For official and other agencies in which "office" is the first word of the title, see under descriptive title of agency, e.g., HOUSING EXPEDITER, OFFICE OF.

official exchange rate. The price, in terms of its own currency, that the monetary authority of a given nation will pay for the currencies of other nations. This rate may often vary from the FREE MARKET exchange rate.

offsets to savings. Ways of using liquid savings or creating expenditures which are equivalent to such use. For example, savings may be offset directly by investing them in new capital assets, by using them to replace worn-out capital assets, or through payments for increased business inventories. However, if savings remain liquid, they may be offset by indirect means; that is, other economic activities may have the same effect upon the economy as though the savings were actually used as explained above. For example, indirect means of offsetting savings are the creation of government expenses in excess of income, an increase of credit, or an excess of exports over imports. See also SAVING.

offshore oil cases. Two cases, *United States* v. *Louisiana*, 363 U. S. 1 (1960), and *United States* v. *Florida*, 363 U. S. 121 (1960), in which the United States Supreme Court decided that only Texas and Florida had qualified under the terms of a federal statute of 1953 which extended to littoral states on the Gulf of Mexico the right to exploit subsoil mineral wealth, particularly petroleum, both within the traditional 3-mile maritime limit and also up to 10½ miles from the low-tide line, provided such states could prove historic justification for their claim to the more extended area of exploitation. Other littoral states, including oil-rich Louisiana, did not qualify. These were thenceforth restricted to the 3-mile area. In 1947 the Court had declared that the tidal oil-land rights inhered in the national government, but in the aforesaid statute in 1953, Congress had limited this federal authority.

ogive. As applied to statistics, a curve derived directly from a statistical array or obtained from a FREQUENCY DISTRIBUTION by using the *X* axis for class intervals and the *Y* axis for cumulative frequencies. If the ogive slopes upward from left to right it is called a *less-than ogive;* that is, each point on the curve indicates the number of cases on the *Y* axis that are less than the value, or other numerical designation, on the *X* axis. If the ogive slopes downward from left to right it is a *more-than ogive;* that is, each point on the curve indicates the number of cases on the *Y* axis that are more than the value, or other numerical designation, on the *X* axis. The diagram in the middle of the next page shows a less-than ogive in circles and a more-than ogive in dots. Both are derived from the following frequency distribution:

Class interval	Frequency	Cumulative frequencies	
		Less than	More than
1 to 1.9	1	1	40
2 to 2.9	3	4	39
3 to 3.9	5	9	36
4 to 4.9	8	17	31
5 to 5.9	10	27	23
6 to 6.9	7	34	13
7 to 7.9	3	37	6
8 to 8.9	2	39	3
9 to 9.9	1	40	1

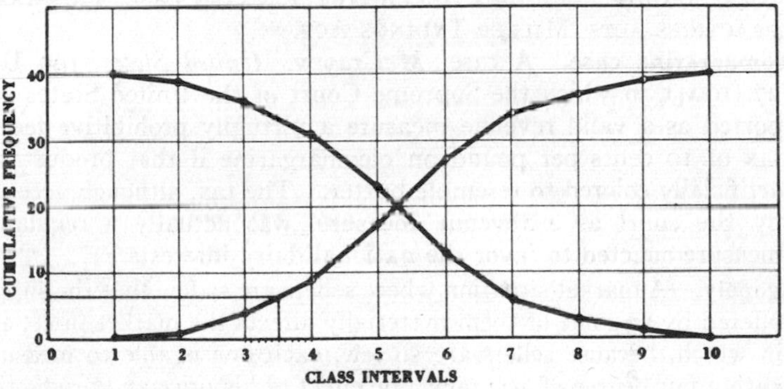

Ogives are sometimes used in economic analysis to approximate values that could otherwise be obtained only by mathematical interpolation. Thus, in the above frequency distribution, if it is desired to know the number of cases at, say, $3\frac{1}{2}$, the number can be approximated at $6\frac{1}{2}$ as shown on the appended diagram.

old-age and survivors' insurance. A nation-wide system of social insurance in the United States, operated by the federal government. It provides old-age benefits of from $10 to $85 per month to insured private employees 65 years of age or over, and guarantees certain payments to the families of an employee in the event of his death at any age. The system is financed by special taxes paid by insured employees and their employers and credited to a fund in the U. S. Treasury. It is administered in accordance

with the terms of the SOCIAL SECURITY ACT of 1935 and amendments thereto. See also INSURANCE.

Old Age and Survivors' Insurance, Bureau of. A former unit of the Social Security Administration which administered the system of old-age insurance and benefits to survivors of those insured. Functions merged (1963) with others under Commissioner for Social Security.

Old Dearborn Distributing Co.* v. *Seagram Distillers Corp. A case, 299 U. S. 183 (1936), in which the Supreme Court of the United States sustained the provisions of so-called "fair-trade" laws in certain states permitting manufacturers and dealers to enter into voluntary resale price-maintenance contracts. Normally, such contracts are limited to branded or trade-marked commodities. The court ruled this practice a legitimate means of protecting the manufacturer's good will. The decision narrowed earlier decisions in which resale price-maintenance agreements were held to violate antitrust statutes. See also BEECH-NUT PACKING CASE, FAIR-TRADE PRACTICES ACTS, MILLER-TYDINGS ACT.

oleomargarine case. A case, *McCray* v. *United States*, 195 U. S. 27 (1904), in which the Supreme Court of the United States supported as a valid revenue measure a virtually prohibitive federal tax of 10 cents per pound on oleomargarine if that product was artificially colored to resemble butter. The tax, although accepted by the court as a revenue measure, was actually a regulatory measure enacted to favor the national dairy interests.

oligopoly. A market situation where sellers are so few that the supply offered by any one of them materially affects the market price, and in which, because sellers are so few, each one is able to measure, with a fair degree of accuracy, the effect of his price and production decisions upon similar decisions by his competitors. Also called *partial monopoly*. See also DUOPOLY, MONOPOLISTIC COMPETITION, POLYPOLY.

one hundred per cent reserve system. A plan that would require commercial banks in the United States to hold the entire amount of their deposits as BANK RESERVES (*q.v.*). Under this system commercial banks would make no loans and therefore would create no DEPOSIT CURRENCY. They might continue, however, as DEPOSITARIES of funds and as mediums for the clearance of checks. The system is opposed to the present arrangement of *fractional reserves*.

one-thousand-hour clause. A clause in the Fair Labor Standards Act of 1938 which permits working hours up to a maximum of 12 hours a day and 56 hours a week, provided, however, the total working hours for any one employee during any 26 consecutive weeks shall not exceed 1,000.

open account. A term usually referring to a manner of supplying credit by charging goods and services to a customer's account, payment for which is to be made at some future time. The account is said to be open until all payments have been received. In bookkeeping any account may be said to be open, however, until it is balanced or closed by an entry which causes the sum of the debits to equal the sum of the credits. See also ACCOUNT.

open competition. A term used to describe a plan whereby members of a trade association exchange statistical information relating to production, stocks on hand, orders, shipments, prices, and other similar data. The United States Supreme Court, in 1921, characterized the term as a "misleading misnomer" in the LUMBER INDUSTRY CASE. See also COMPETITION, OPEN PRICE SYSTEM.

open-door policy. A policy under which a nation opens its foreign trade to foreign nationals on equal terms, the same principle governing any internal commercial or other concessions which it may grant to foreigners.

open-end contract. An agreement whereby a supplier contracts to meet the requirements of a buyer for a specific product during a specified period of time, whatever those requirements may be. No definite quantity being mentioned, the contract is designated "open-end."

open-end investment trust. An INVESTMENT TRUST that sells and redeems its CAPITAL STOCK continuously, selling it at BOOK VALUE plus a sales charge, and redeeming it at book value or at a slight discount. Also called *mutual funds*. See also CLOSED-END INVESTMENT TRUST.

open letter of credit. See explanation under LETTER OF CREDIT.

open market. In general, the condition which exists when trading is not restricted to any particular area or persons; specifically, as applied to securities, a market in which purchases and sales occur outside a formally organized STOCK EXCHANGE.

open-market operations. As applied to the federal reserve banks, the purchase and sale in the open market of various securities, chiefly obligations of the United States, and of bills of exchange and bankers' acceptances of the kinds and maturities eligible for discount by the federal reserve banks. Open-market operations are conducted by the banks subject to the direction of and under the regulations of the Federal Open Market Committee with a view to accommodating commerce and business and to stabilizing the general credit situation of the country. See FEDERAL OPEN MARKET COMMITTEE.

open-market paper. COMMERCIAL PAPER bought by and sold to financial institutions through brokers. For example, instead of borrowing directly from a bank, a business enterprise with a sufficiently high credit standing may issue PROMISSORY NOTES payable to itself and containing a BLANK ENDORSEMENT, thus making the notes negotiable. The notes do not bear interest but are sold at a discount. They usually run from 4 to 6 months, common denominations being from $5,000 to $10,000. The issuer receives the face value of the notes less a discount and commission. The notes may be resold many times before maturity.

open mortgage. A mortgage which, having been pledged as collateral security for a loan, may be increased while serving as such collateral, thereby diminishing the security originally provided for each dollar of the loan. The term is used in contradistinction to CLOSED MORTGAGE. See also MORTGAGE.

open price system. A concerted effort on the part of some or all of the individual units of an industry to keep one another informed concerning the past, present, and future prices of their products. See also OPEN COMPETITION.

open shop. A shop in which employment is offered without reference to membership or nonmembership in a labor union. See also SHOP.

open union. A labor union whose membership is not restricted by prohibitive entrance fees or by race or sex discrimination. See also LABOR UNION.

operating cost. See VARIABLE COST.

operating profit. As used in accounting, an increase in wealth resulting from the regular activities of an enterprise, as distinguished from any activities foreign to that business. For example, income or other gain from financial investments of a mercantile establishment would not be a part of the operating profits of that establishment.

operating ratio. Any one of numerous relationships between various items in a BALANCE SHEET frequently used as an aid in determining CREDIT RATING. For two commonly used operating ratios, see ACID-TEST RATIO, CURRENT RATIO.

operations research. The application of mathematical and logical techniques to certain business problems with the object of discovering a best possible course of action. How to allocate working capital among the various departments of a retail store so as to maximize profits, how to use men and machines in a job machine shop to achieve the highest possible output and the least idle time, or how to manage the routing of freight cars, so as to assure their greatest use, are problems amenable to operations research. The procedure followed is usually to express the problem in the form of a mathematical equation, the solution to which indicates the effectiveness of a given set of conditions. The method may involve a sampling process, the calculation of probabilities, linear programing, or some other such technique. The computations are frequently so involved or so lengthy as to require ELECTRONIC DATA PROCESSING. Sometimes called *management science*.

opportunity cost. The most favorable price that can be commanded by a factor of production which thus tends to become the minimum cost at which that factor can be had by any entrepreneur. Toolmakers, for example, may be able to sell their labor to automobile manufacturers as well as to many other manufacturers. The automobile manufacturers may be willing and able to pay more than the other manufacturers and the latter, in that case, will have to pay the opportunity costs thus set by the automobile manufacturers. See also COST.

Optimist school. The economic ideas of Frédéric Bastiat (1801–1850), a French economist, and Henry C. Carey (1793–1879), an American, and their followers. In general, their writings defended the economic order existing at the time against the attack of socialists and others. The concept of ECONOMIC RENT was questioned, CAPITAL defended, and the MALTHUSIAN THEORY OF POPULATION denied. Rent was regarded as a return from previously invested capital, and income from capital was defended on the ground that it was merely a return on past labor. Proof was lacking, it was said, of any tendency of population to press upon food supply. See also SCHOOLS OF ECONOMIC THOUGHT.

optimum population. As applied to economic life, the number of people within a given area who, with the available capital, equipment, and natural resources, can produce the greatest per capita output.

option. An agreement, often for a consideration, which permits one to buy or to sell something within a stipulated time in accordance with the terms of the agreement.

optional bond. See explanation under BOND.

optional dividend. A dividend which may be paid either in stock or cash, according to the stockholder's preference. See also DIVIDEND.

order bill of lading. A negotiable bill of lading stating that goods are consigned to the order of a specified person who must indorse the bill of lading before the goods may be delivered to the buyer. This form of bill of lading is frequently used when it is agreed that payment shall be made upon delivery. The shipper then consigns the goods to his own order, indorses the bill of lading, and attaches a draft. He then sends these documents to a bank, usually the bank where the buyer has a deposit account. Upon payment of the draft by the buyer, the bank delivers the bill of lading to him, and he may then claim the goods from the transportation company. See also BILL OF LADING.

ordinary asset. As applied to income-tax computations in the United States, the term refers only to an asset regularly bought and sold in the ordinary course of the taxpayer's business. Thus, stocks and bonds would be an ordinary asset to the person who makes it his business to buy and sell such securities for profit, but they would be a CAPITAL ASSET to a person engaged in some other occupation and who bought such securities for income or speculation. See also ASSET.

ordinary bill. Usually a written description of articles sold, with their prices, which is sent to the buyer.

ordinary rent. See explanation under RENT.

ordinary stock. See explanation under CAPITAL STOCK.

Organic school. A term sometimes applied to those who draw an analogy between society and a biological organism. Thus, for example, the railroad system is identified with the arterial and venous system, telegraph wires with the nervous system, the stock exchange with the heart, etc. Such parallels were elaborated in great detail by Herbert Spencer. They are not generally considered of very much scientific value. See also SCHOOLS OF ECONOMIC THOUGHT.

Organization of American States. A regional agency within the UNITED NATIONS, made up of 21 republics of the Western Hemisphere. Its purpose is to maintain the peace and strengthen collaboration among the American states and to defend their sovereignty and independence.

Organization for Economic Cooperation and Development. An organization consisting originally of 17 nations, including (West) Germany, created April 16, 1948, and known until 1960 as the Organization for European Economic Cooperation. It sought to provide an instrument through which the European nations might cooperatively provide their recovery. In 1949 the membership of the organization was increased to 18 nations by the admission of Spain. It continued as an agency of European integration after the suspension of the EUROPEAN RECOVERY PROGRAM (*q.v.*) in 1951 and became an important economic planning body. The organization's headquarters are in Paris. In 1960 it was proposed to extend the planning and developmental activities of the organization, to make the United States and Canada full-fledged members, thus increasing the membership to 20 states, and to change the name to Organization for Economic Cooperation and Development. See BENELUX, EUROPEAN COAL AND STEEL COMMUNITY, EUROPEAN ECONOMIC COMMUNITY, EUROPEAN FREE TRADE ASSOCIATION.

Organization for European Economic Cooperation. See ORGANIZATION FOR ECONOMIC COOPERATION AND DEVELOPMENT.

original-cost standard. As applied to the valuation of a corporation's capital assets, the cost of such assets as computed by the amount paid into the corporation by its stockholders and bondholders when the corporation was organized, or at a subsequent time. See also VALUATION.

original-issue stock. See explanation under CAPITAL STOCK.

original-package cases. Two cases, *Brown* v. *Maryland*, 12 Wheaton 419 (1827) and *Leisy* v. *Hardin*, 135 U. S. 100 (1890), the judicial decisions in which developed the so-called ORIGINAL-PACKAGE DOCTRINE in foreign and interstate commerce. In the first of these cases the Supreme Court of the United States declared that as long as commodities had not been removed from the containers in which they had been imported into the United States, no state of the United States could apply its taxing power or its police regulations to such commodities. In the second case, that of *Leisy* v. *Hardin*, substantially the same decision was made with respect to goods in interstate commerce having a domestic origin. Goods lawfully brought into one state of the United States from another state were held exempt from police or tax regulations of the state of destination as long as such goods remained in their original package and as long as Congress, by its silence, implied that the states were not to interfere with interstate commerce.

original-package doctrine. A ruling established by the Supreme Court of the United States that commodities in foreign or interstate commerce which had not been removed from the containers in which they had been imported or shipped interstate were not subject to the taxing power or police regulations of the states. The doctrine has been modified by Congress, particularly as respects alcoholic beverages and goods made by convict labor. See ORIGINAL-PACKAGE CASES.

Orthodox school. See CLASSICAL SCHOOL.

Ottawa agreements. Agreements comprising a comprehensive system of tariff preferences between Great Britain and most of the dominions, consummated at the Imperial Economic Conference held at Ottawa, Canada, 1932. The agreements were prompted by the abandonment by Great Britain in 1931 and 1932 of its long-established policy of free trade. It was agreed that most products from the dominions concerned would be admitted into Great Britain free of duty for a 3- or 5-year period, depending upon the product in question. In return, the dominions arranged more advantageous preferential duties for a large number of British products.

Outer 7. See EUROPEAN FREE TRADE ASSOCIATION.

outlaw strike. See ILLEGAL STRIKE.

overcertification. A practice, once common among banks, of certifying a stockbroker's check for an amount in excess of his deposit. The practice was usually carried on in conjunction with BUYING ON MARGIN. A broker frequently would not have sufficient funds available with which to purchase the stock that he proposed later to use as security for a COLLATERAL loan. His bank would overcertify his check which would then be used to pay for the stock purchased. The stock would be delivered immediately to the bank where the collateral loan would be consummated. Such a transaction would now be carried out by means of a MORNING LOAN (*q.v.*).

overdraft. The amount by which the face value of a check, acceptance, promissory note, or other similar commercial paper exceeds the funds on deposit to meet it. See also *NOSTRO* OVERDRAFT.

overdraw. The issuance of a bank check for an amount in excess of the deposit in the bank on which the check is drawn.

overextended. See explanation under EXTENDED.

overhead cost. See FIXED COST.

overinvestment theory of the business cycle. See OVERSAVING THEORY OF THE BUSINESS CYCLE.

overlying bond. See explanation under BOND.

overproduction. **1.** More than can be sold at any price. **2.** More than can be sold at a profitable price. Using the term in the sense of the first definition, it is possible to have overproduction in certain specific commodities but not in all commodities at one time, since, for all practical purposes, human wants are without limit. Using the term in the sense of the second definition, it is possible to have overproduction in certain specific commodities as well as general overproduction. See also PRODUCTION.

oversaving. **1.** More liquid savings than can be used in investment opportunities. **2.** The condition said to exist when invested capital, representing savings, produces more goods than can be sold at a profit. See also SAVING.

oversaving theory of the business cycle. The theory which holds that, because of the unequal distribution of the national income, there is so much saving among the higher income groups that those savings, when invested, create more productive capacity than can be permanently and profitably employed. Production thus tends to exceed the ability of the mass of people to buy, prices fall to unprofitable levels, unemployment increases, and depressed conditions prevail until the surplus production is gradually absorbed. See also BUSINESS CYCLE.

over-the-counter market. The purchase and sale of securities outside of the organized stock exchanges.

Owenism. The ideas of social reform advanced by Robert Owen (1771–1858), a British industrialist. Owen maintained that good wages and working conditions were not incompatible with business prosperity — a revolutionary doctrine for the time — and proceeded to demonstrate his contention at New Lanark, Scotland, where he established a model industrial village and pioneered in the establishment of a LIMITED-DIVIDEND CORPORATION. He advocated such reforms as the limitation of employment of children, a system of government factory inspection, and the establishment of an 8-hour working day. In 1839, in Hampshire, England, Owen founded one of his famous villages of co-operation where he proposed to develop a partly industrial and partly farming community and provide for the exchange of products surplus to each group on a mutually advantageous basis. While recognizing innate differences in individuals, Owen believed that character was molded by environmental conditions and social institutions and thus anticipated the materialistic and deterministic views of Karl Marx and the so-called "scientific socialists." See also LABOR EXCHANGE BANK, UTOPIAN SOCIALISM.

ownership utility. See POSSESSION UTILITY.

P

pace setter. As applied to labor relations, a particularly rapid and skilled worker whose production for a specified period of time establishes the basis on which piecework rates are calculated for all workers.

Packers and Stockyards Act. An act of Congress, 1921, which provides for federal supervision and regulation of packing and stockyard companies.

paid-in surplus. Surplus of a business enterprise arising from sources other than profits. For example, paid-in surplus may be acquired from the sale of capital stock at a premium or from donations from stockholders or others. See also SURPLUS.

paid-up stock. See explanation under CAPITAL STOCK.

Panama Refining Co. v. Ryan. See HOT-OIL CASE.

Pan-American Union. The central organ and permanent General Secretariat of the ORGANIZATION OF THE AMERICAN STATES. It acts as adviser to the council of that organization, offers it technical and other assistance, and is the custodian of inter-American agreements.

paper money. Documents issued by the government, or by governmental authority, to be used as money. Paper money may circulate by virtue of a government's mere fiat and nothing else; or it may represent metal coins or bullion, held in some depositary, up to the full amount of the paper's stated value. Between these two extremes, paper money may be secured in numerous ways and to a varying extent. See also CONVERTIBLE MONEY, FIAT MONEY, FIDUCIARY MONEY, IRREDEEMABLE MONEY, MONEY, REPRESENTATIVE MONEY.

parallel standards. A monetary system in which two or more precious metals are coined, but in which the monetary unit is not defined in terms of each metal. There is no fixed ratio, therefore, between the coinage value of one metal and another. The metal content of one kind of coin must be determined, therefore, before its value in terms of another kind of coin can be ascertained. See also MONETARY SYSTEM.

Pareto's law. A controversial generalization of Vilfredo Pareto (1848–1923), Italian sociologist and economist, to the effect that the NATIONAL INCOME tends to be distributed in the same proportion among consumers, regardless of differing institutions and systems of taxation. The universality and inevitability of the law would seem to be subject to serious question today.

par exchange rate. The price of one national currency in terms of another, as established by the INTERNATIONAL MONETARY FUND. The value of the MONETARY UNIT of each member of the fund is expressed in terms of gold, and from the values so expressed the par exchange rates may be obtained. For example, the pound sterling is valued at 2.48828 grams of fine gold, and the United States dollar at 0.888671 gram of fine gold. One pound sterling therefore equals $2.80. Unlike the case of the GOLD STANDARD, gold is here used merely as a unit of measure to avoid the necessity of expressing the value of each currency in terms of every other currency. The gold value assigned to a currency, and hence its par exchange rate with other currencies, is determined by the fund in consultation with the authorities from the nation involved, the usual practice being to accept the valuation suggested by those authorities. For the currencies of nations not members of the International Monetary Fund there is no generally accepted par of exchange. See also MINT PAR OF EXCHANGE.

parity. The condition of being equivalent. The term is used particularly in respect to public price policies for agricultural products, such policies being designed theoretically to equilibrate farm-income standards with the income standards of other sectors of the national economy. The term is also used to describe an exchange rate between the currencies of two countries which makes the purchasing power of one currency substantially equivalent to that of the other currency. See also AGRICULTURAL PARITY, PURCHASING-POWER PARITY.

***Parker* v. *Davis*.** See LEGAL-TENDER CASES.

Parkinson's laws. 1. Work (or at least activity) invariably expands so as to fill the time available for its completion. 2. Expenditure rises to meet income. "Laws" formulated by C. Northcote Parkinson in satirical accounts of business and public administrative procedures.

par-list bank. A bank which, although not a member of the FEDERAL RESERVE SYSTEM, participates in the CLEARINGHOUSE operations of the district FEDERAL RESERVE BANK by paying all CHECKS drawn on it without deductions for service or other fees. MEMBER BANKS are required thus to remit at par. Other banks that agree to do so are placed on a par list published by the Board of Governors of the Federal Reserve System.

partial monopoly. See OLIGOPOLY, DUOPOLY.

partial or particular equilibrium. See explanation under GENERAL EQUILIBRIUM.

participating bond. See explanation under BOND.

participating preferred stock. See explanation under CAPITAL STOCK.

participation certificate. A document which identifies an owner's part interest in some security of large denomination. The security in question can thus be divided to meet the convenience of those with relatively small sums to invest.

partnership. A form of business organization created through a contractual arrangement between two or more individuals, each of whom assumes full personal liability for the debts of the joint enterprise. See also FORMS OF BUSINESS ORGANIZATION, LIMITED PARTNERSHIP, SILENT PARTNER.

part-paid stock. See explanation under CAPITAL STOCK.

par value. As applied to stocks and bonds, the face value, if any, appearing on the stock certificate or on the bond instrument. In the case of stocks a par value is arbitrarily assigned at the time of original issue. Thus, if a corporation plans to raise $1,000,000 by a stock issue, it may issue 10,000 shares at a par value of $100 a share, or it may issue 20,000 shares at a par value of $50 a share.

Par value is not significant and should not be confused with either MARKET PRICE or BOOK VALUE, both of which reflect an important condition. Par value means so little, in fact, that many stocks are issued with no par value. In the case of bonds the par value is usually $1,000. This, too, may be very different from the market price. See also PAR EXCHANGE RATE, VALUE.

par-value stock. See explanation under CAPITAL STOCK.

passbook. A small account book issued by banks to depositors. Deposits and withdrawals are recorded in the book. Although still in use by SAVINGS BANKS, duplicate deposit slips, duly receipted, and monthly statements showing deposits and withdrawals have largely replaced passbooks in COMMERCIAL BANKS.

passive bond. See explanation under BOND.

passive trade balance. See UNFAVORABLE BALANCE OF TRADE.

patent. The right of exclusive proprietorship of an invention granted by a government to a person or organization for a term of years. In the United States (1964) patents are granted for any new and useful art, machine, process, or substance, including distinct and new forms of plants, for a term of 17 years. For designs, patents are granted for terms of 3½, 7, or 14 years. Patent rights may be enforced through the courts.

Patent Office. A major unit of the Department of Commerce of the United States which has charge of all matters pertaining to applications for patents and administers federal trade-mark laws. Through its various examiners and its Board of Appeal, the office passes finally upon the patentability of all inventions which may be submitted to it and determines the question of priority of invention when conflicting claims arise.

paternalism. A term applied to a governmental policy of rendering welfare and protective services to the citizens; for example, supplying jobs to those who are unemployed, providing old-age assistance, or protecting citizens against unfair business practices.

Patrons of Husbandry. See NATIONAL GRANGE ORDER OF THE PATRONS OF HUSBANDRY.

patroon. A title given to any grantee of land in Dutch New Netherlands, now part of New York, who, during the second quarter of the 17th century, established 50 persons over 15 years of age in the colony and received as a reward a grant of 4 miles on the seacoast or 2 miles on a navigable river with no limit toward the interior.

pawnbroker. One who makes small loans secured by personal property or valuable things other than securities.

payee. A person who receives a payment.

payment bill. See explanation under BILL.

Payne-Aldrich Tariff. The United States Tariff Act of 1909. It reduced rates in approximately 584 instances, affecting 20 per cent of the imports, and raised the rates in approximately 300 other instances. It allegedly introduced the principle of imposing such duties as would equalize costs of production at home and abroad, together with a reasonable profit, abandoned the RECIPROCITY PRINCIPLE, and adopted the MAXIMUM AND MINIMUM TARIFF SYSTEM.

payola. A slang term for money, gifts of merchandise, or other things of value offered to public entertainers or others who are in a position to use their calling to direct public attention to the alleged merits of some product or service, the purpose being to increase demand for such product or service. In the case of radio, television, or similar performers, comment on the product or service is ostensibly incidental to a given program or discussion, but is actually aimed at promoting the sale of the product or service in question.

pay-roll tax. A tax imposed upon pay rolls, authorized in the United States by the Social Security Act of 1935 to provide for unemployment insurance and in certain cases by state workmen's compensation legislation. See also SOCIAL SECURITY ACT of 1935, TAX, UNEMPLOYMENT INSURANCE.

peasant movement. A term descriptive of the growing class consciousness and political activity of peasant groups, particularly in eastern Europe. Reforms, following World War I, gave the peasants in many countries ownership of the land they cultivated and the political franchise. The aims of the movement differ from country to country; all such movements, however, maintain a belief in rural life based on small property holdings.

pecuniary exchange. Trade by means of money. The term is used in contradistinction to BARTER. See also EXCHANGE.

pegging. The attempt to keep a market price at a certain figure or very close to that figure by freely buying or selling as circumstances demand.

peg point. A rate of pay for some key operation which serves as a base from which rates of pay for other operations are calculated.

pension. Payments at regular intervals to a person after he has retired from active work. Pensions are created in various ways. Frequently they are derived from a fund made up of contributions by the employer and the employee during the latter's period of employment.

pension pool. A plan whereby private industries in a particular area create a common fund to finance pensions for their employees, permitting the employees to change from one plant to another without losing the pension benefits accumulated previous to such a change.

peppercorn rent. A nominal rent, usually paid in kind, chiefly to give formal recognition to the legal rights of the landlord; so called because during the Middle Ages such rent was often paid in peppercorns. See also RENT.

per capita. By individuals. The per capita national debt, for example, is the total national debt divided by the population.

percentile. See explanation under QUARTILE.

per contra item. As applied to accounting, a balance in one account that is offset by a balance in some other account. For example, in bank statements an item designated as "Customers' Acceptance Liability" will often appear as an ASSET, and an item designated as "Acceptances Outstanding" as a LIABILITY. In this case the customers advance the funds to pay the ACCEPTANCES upon maturity. The asset thus offsets the liability. The bank merely guarantees payment.

per diem. By the day.

perfect competition. See COMPETITION.

peril point. A hypothetical limit beyond which reductions in a United States CUSTOMS DUTY could injure an American industry. The term was applied to legislation in 1949 to extend the TRADE AGREEMENTS ACT. The legislation in question provided that the peril points should be established by the UNITED STATES TARIFF COMMISSION, and that the President should submit specific reasons to Congress if and when any customs duty was reduced below the amount thus established. The peril point provision was eliminated when the Trade Agreements Act was again extended in September, 1949.

permissive wage-adjustment clause. A clause in a labor contract permitting renegotiation of wage rates in case changes in general economic conditions, specified in the contract, such as changes in the cost-of-living index or changes occasioned by technological improvement, should occur during the life of the contract.

permit. Formal authority to exercise some right or privilege. For example, a permit is granted allowing the removal of goods imported into the United States after the duties have been paid.

perpetual bond. See explanation under BOND.

perquisite. Property the title to which is not inherited. The term is commonly used to indicate a gift, bonus, or premium received in addition to a wage or salary.

***Perry* v. *United States*.** See GOLD-CLAUSE CASES.

personal account. A term used in double-entry bookkeeping to indicate an account carried in the name of a person or a company. See also Account.

personal distribution. See explanation under Distribution.

personal finance company. An enterprise which makes a business of lending relatively small sums of money at relatively high rates of interest to individuals for personal needs. In most states such companies must be licensed.

personal property. A right or interest in things other than real property; for example, such things as money, clothing, and household furnishings, as well as bonds, stocks, mortgages, and other evidences of interest or debt. See also Property, Real property.

personal-property tax. See explanation under Property tax.

pet banks. A term used by political opponents of President Andrew Jackson to designate the state banks selected after 1833 as depositaries for federal funds. On President Jackson's orders, such funds had been removed from the Second Bank of the United States, following Jackson's veto of a renewal charter for that institution in 1832. It was claimed, sometimes with justice, that the depositary state institutions were selected with an eye to partisan advantage rather than financial solvency.

petty cash. Money set apart for small cash disbursements. Petty cash is usually handled as an imprest fund.

phalanstery. One of numerous voluntary associations, known as *phalanstère* or *phalange*, envisaged by the French social reformer, Charles Fourier (1772–1837). Each association was to provide housing for approximately 1,600 persons, be economically self-sufficing, and provide maximum opportunity for vocational and professional aptitudes. Fourier's ideas, which greatly influenced the later Marxians, were materialistic, deterministic, irrational, and essentially antistate. Also known as *Fourierism.* See also Utopian socialism.

physical distribution. See explanation under Distribution.

physiocrats. A group of French statesmen and philosophers who, about the middle of the 18th century, made the first systematic attempt to form an economic science on a broad basis. They particularly emphasized land as a source of wealth. See also Schools of economic thought.

picketing. As applied to industrial disputes, the stationing of striking workers at the entrances to factories or other establishments involved in a labor dispute to dissuade workers and others from entering the premises. See also Cross picketing, Mass picketing, Secondary picketing.

piecework. A wage schedule which computes wages by assigning a certain sum for each article produced or each operation completed.

piggyback. 1. As applied to transportation, the carrying of one vehicle by another. Some automobile trucks are so constructed that the bodies can be lifted from the chassis; the bodies are then placed on a flatcar and transported by rail. 2. Two satellites, placed into orbit from a single rocket and separated after an interval of time, each following some predetermined path, are said to be launched piggyback fashion.

pit. A place on the floor of an exchange arranged in broad, circular steps to enable the traders better to see and hear one another. The term is often used in connection with grain trading as in the term "grain pit" which refers to the pit on the floor of the Chicago Board of Trade.

place utility. The accessibility of goods at a place where they are wanted to satisfy human desires. When goods are transported from a place where they are plentiful to a place where they are scarce, a place utility is created. California fruit obtainable in New York is an example. See also UTILITY.

plain bond. See explanation under BOND.

plane of living. See LEVEL OF LIVING.

planning. See ECONOMIC PLANNING.

plantation system. The agricultural system, firmly established in the southern states by 1840, under which a proprietor and his managerial staff, employing the labor of slaves, devoted relatively large acreages to the production of certain staples such as tobacco, cotton, or sugar. The system tended to make small farms uneconomic and actually absorbed many of them.

Plumb plan. A plan proposed during the 1920's for the public ownership of railroads and their operation by the government through representatives of employees and supervising officials.

plunger. Usually a speculator of some kind who takes heavy risks and either profits greatly or loses disastrously.

plutocracy. Rule by the wealthy.

point. As applied to a market price, a specified amount considered as a unit or step in a price advance or decline. In the stock market a point is 1 per cent of $100. In foreign exchange a point is one hundredth of 1 cent. Thus, if the dollar price of pounds sterling changes from $4.8615 to $4.8625, there is said to be a 10-point advance. In commodity markets such as those dealing in cotton, coffee, or sugar, a point is one hundredth of 1 cent per pound. An advance in the price of cotton of ¼ cent would be described as a 25-point advance. See also GOLD POINT.

Point 4 Program. A plan suggested by President Harry S. Truman, in his inaugural address of January, 1949, to share the scientific and technical knowledge and industrial "know-how" of the United States with the economically underdeveloped and undeveloped areas of the world and to promote productive investment in such areas. Funds for the program were to come from the United States and United Nations sources and from the beneficiary countries.

point of ideal proportions. That stage in the operation of a productive enterprise at which the most profitable relative amounts of the FACTORS OF PRODUCTION (land, labor, capital and management) are employed. See also PROPORTIONALITY, LAW OF.

point of indifference. That stage in the operation of a productive enterprise at which the cost of an additional increment of any FACTOR OF PRODUCTION (land, labor, capital, or management) merely equals the money return of the additional product created because of that increment.

political arithmetic. Political economy. The term was used in England during the latter part of the 18th century; for example, *Several Essays in Political Arithmetic* by Sir William Petty (1775).

political economy. Literally, the management of a free commonwealth. The Greek οἰκονομική denotes the management of a household, and πολις, a city as a political unit. For many centuries discussions of production, trade, and finance were inextricably involved in considerations of monetary, fiscal, and commercial policies of governments. The term "political economy," therefore, was descriptive. But during the 19th century such matters began to be discussed more frequently apart from governmental policies, and the term "economics" began to be used. The publication in 1890 of Alfred Marshall's *Principles of Economics* had a great influence in bringing about the change, although the term "political economy" is still frequently used, particularly outside the United States.

Pollock v. Farmers' Loan and Trust Co. See INCOME-TAX CASE.

poll tax. A local tax levied upon all male, and sometimes female, adults. The tax is levied at a certain amount per head and hence is sometimes called a *head tax.* Veterans, paupers, and disabled persons are frequently exempt. Payment of the tax, in some places, is made a prerequisite for voting, obtaining an automobile license, or other privileges. Also called *capitation tax.* See also TAX.

polymetallism. A theoretical monetary system in which more than two metals are made standard money and coined in some definite ratio one to another in the matter of weight and fineness. See also MONETARY SYSTEM.

polypoly. A market situation where sellers are so few that the supply offered by any one of them materially affects the market price, but where, nevertheless, there is a sufficiently large number so that no seller can effectively gauge the possible effect of his price or production decisions upon similar decisions of his competitors. See also OLIGOPOLY, MONOPOLISTIC COMPETITION.

pool. A loose combination of business units for some specific and often temporary purpose. Frequent objectives have been the division of markets, the maintenance of prices, and the combining of selling organizations. Pools were prohibited in the case of railroads by the Interstate Commerce Act of 1887, and in other fields, when in restraint of trade, by the Sherman Antitrust Act of 1890. See also COMBINATION.

population pyramid. A graphic device for displaying the composition of a population according to sex and age groups. The appended diagram shows a population pyramid representing the population of the United States for 1950, as reported in the census returns. The vertical axis is divided according to age groups in 5-year intervals from 0 to 105. The bars extending to the right and to the left from the vertical axis represent the percentage of the total population in the various age groups. The bars to the left represent the male population, and those to the right the female.

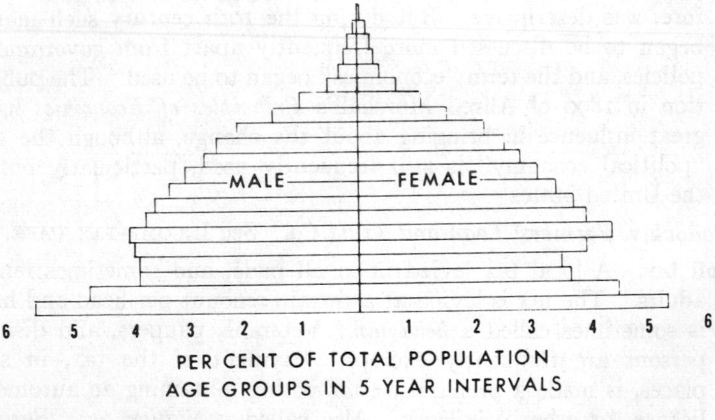

PER CENT OF TOTAL POPULATION
AGE GROUPS IN 5 YEAR INTERVALS

Portal-to-Portal Act. An act of Congress, 1947, which invalidates all claims to portal-to-portal pay not covered specifically in labor contracts, and which places a 2-year limit on claims which might arise under existing federal minimum-wage laws. The act arose from a controversy over lawsuits brought by labor unions to recover back pay for uncompensated time claimed to be due under existing legislation. See also PORTAL-TO-PORTAL PAY.

portal-to-portal pay. Compensation for an hourly rate employee, which embraces not merely the period during which the employee is actually engaged on an assigned task or operation but the entire period during which he is on the employer's premises or during which he is subject to the employer's direction. The term originally applied to coal mines where the portal or mouth of the mine is a definite place. When applied to the buildings and grounds of a factory, the exact point where the employee comes under the direction of the employer cannot be so readily identified. If the employee is ordered to display identification credentials, the place where that order is given may be considered the portal, and compensated time might begin at that point. Or, if the employee arrives in an automobile and is told by a factory guard where to park it, the place where such direction is given might be considered the portal, and compensated time might begin at that point.

port authority. A commission or other agency, usually created by special legislative act and enjoying a legal personality, which is given power to co-ordinate land and water traffic in and about a port. Its power may extend to the construction and maintenance of bridges, tunnels, and other structures essential to the development of the port area. In the United States, because of federal control over navigable waters and because the area of a port may affect the territory of more than one state, the concurrence of Congress and of the legislatures of all states affected is necessary to the creation of such an authority; for example, the Port of New York Authority.

port of entry. In the United States, any place where a customs officer is stationed and authorized to collect duties on imported materials.

Port of New York Authority. See explanation under PORT AUTHORITY.

possession utility. The satisfaction resulting from the actual possession of goods or services. In an exchange between two traders, two possession utilities are created; that is, each trader has greater satisfaction in the thing he received than in the thing he gave in the exchange. Also called *ownership utility*. See also UTILITY.

postal savings. A service offered by the United States Post Office Department which makes it possible for individuals to deposit sums of money in multiples of $5 up to an amount ordinarily not in excess of $2,500, and receive interest at a rate specified by law.

postal savings certificate. A document issued by United States post offices as evidence of deposit in a postal savings account. Such certificates are issued in fixed denominations of $5, $10, $20, $50, $100, $200, $500, and $1,000. See also POSTAL SAVINGS.

postaudit. An audit of the accounts of departments of the government, made at regular intervals to ascertain whether the expenditure of funds has been in accordance with the law.

potential demand. Demand that is expected to become effective at some future time. Such conditions as increased purchasing power, the stimulation of wants, or reduced prices might transform potential demand into EFFECTIVE DEMAND. See also DEMAND.

potential stock. See explanation under CAPITAL STOCK.

poundage. A rate or amount calculated by the pound. Historically, a tax calculated at a certain percentage of the pound sterling.

poverty. A relative term indicating the absence of the comforts of life and an inadequate supply of the necessities. Sometimes the term is defined more precisely as that point at which deprivation makes impossible the maintenance of physical efficiency.

power of attorney. Authority granted to one person by another to act on behalf of the latter. A general power of attorney authorizes the agent to act for the principal in all matters. A special power of attorney limits the agent's acts to specific matters.

preaudit. An audit made by a government official to ascertain whether a contemplated public expenditure is in accordance with the law.

preclusive buying. Buying materials or services for the express purpose of denying their use to a competitor, or similar buying by a belligerent nation in wartime to prevent neutrals from selling goods or services to the enemy.

prefabricate. The production of standardized parts in a factory making possible the construction of a product elsewhere with only assembly operations. Standardized wall, floor, ceiling, roof, window and door sections for houses are frequently produced in a factory and shipped to the construction site where they are assembled to form a complete house.

preference stock. See explanation under CAPITAL STOCK.

preferential duty. See DIFFERENTIAL DUTY.

preferential shop. An establishment in which union employees are granted certain privileges not accorded to nonunion employees. For example, union employees may be the last to be laid off or the first to be re-employed after a layoff. See also SHOP.

preferred stock. See explanation under CAPITAL STOCK.

premium. Generally, an amount paid over and above a given figure. As applied to bond prices, the difference between the face value of a bond and the market price when the face value is the lower. As applied to insurance, a payment for protection against a risk.

premium for risk. The actual yield on an investment less the basic yield prevailing at the time. See also BASIC YIELD.

premium pay. A sum in addition to regular compensation which is paid because of unusual circumstances such as overtime, Sunday, or holiday work; because the work is of a particularly hazardous or unpleasant nature; or because the employee receiving the premium possesses unusual ability or skill.

premium rate. As applied to trading in stocks, an extra charge made under certain conditions by those whose business it is to lend shares of stock for trading purposes. When SELLING SHORT, a person borrows a stock to effect delivery, and this loan is secured by depositing with the lender cash equivalent to the market value of the stock borrowed. The lender usually allows the borrower to deduct interest on this deposit from the fee charged for lending the stock. But if the stock is scarce, a very small amount of interest or perhaps none at all will be allowed. When no interest is allowed, the stock is said to be *loaned flat*. If the stock is particularly scarce, no interest is allowed on the borrower's deposit and an extra or premium rate may be charged in addition to the regular fee.

premium stock. See explanation under CAPITAL STOCK.

prepaid expense. As applied to accounting, payments made for goods or services before the goods are delivered or the services are performed. Such payments are regarded as ASSETS until the goods have been received or the services rendered. At that time the payments in question are charged to an expense account.

prescription. The vesting of title to real property by virtue of long use.

price. Value expressed in terms of money. For common uses of the term see ADMINISTERED PRICE, CLASS PRICE, CONVERSION PRICE, LIST PRICE, MARKET PRICE, NET PRICE, NOMINAL PRICE, NORMAL PRICE, PRICE LOCO, RESERVATION PRICE. See also COMPETITION, MONOPOLY, VALUE.

price consumption curve. A curve placed on an INDIFFERENCE MAP (*q.v.*) indicating the demand by one consumer for a given commodity or service at different prices. In the appended Diagram 1, the price consumption curve is AB, as usual in an indifference map. Various quantities of x are plotted on the X axis. On the Y axis, however, the PURCHASING POWER or cash possessed by the consumer is plotted, and the spaces into which the Y axis is divided represent units of purchasing power. In the appended Diagram 1, an income of $35.00 for a given period of time is assumed. Straight lines are drawn from point 35 on the *Y* axis to each main quantity division on the *X* axis, and prices are assigned for each quantity of *x* that will absorb the entire income if the entire income is spent for *x*. These various quantities and prices are as follows:

Price	Quantity	Income
$7.00	5	$35.00
3.50	10	35.00
2.33	15	35.00
1.75	20	35.00
1.40	25	35.00
1.16	30	35.00
1.00	35	35.00

On each straight line, then, may be plotted all the possibilities of purchasing various quantities of *x* at a specified price and of retaining some quantity of purchasing power or cash. Each straight line, however, is tangent to an INDIFFERENCE CURVE (*q.v.*), shown by dotted lines *a*, *b*, *c*, *d*, and *e* and shown only in part. This point of contact indicates just what quantity of *x* will be purchased at a specified price and just how much purchasing power will be retained by a given individual. The summary of these combinations, indicated by the price consumption curve, is as follows:

Price *x*	Quantity of *x* purchased	Total expended for *x*	Total purchasing power retained	Total income
$7.00	1	$ 7.00	$28.00	$35.00
3.50	4	14.00	21.00	35.00
1.75	12	21.00	14.00	35.00
1.40	20	28.00	7.00	35.00
1.00	30	30.00	5.00	35.00

Diagram 2 shows the above data in the form of a graph representing a schedule demand for commodity *x* on the part of one consumer. By combining such demand curves for all consumers, a generalized schedule demand curve can be obtained. See also DEMAND, DEMAND-AND-SUPPLY CURVES.

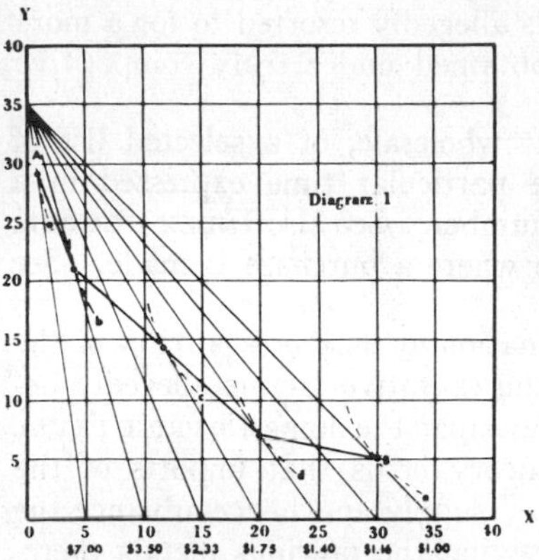

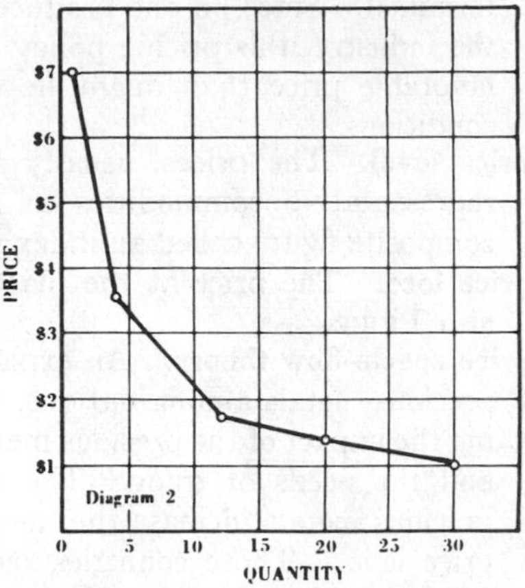

price control. The control or actual fixing of prices by the government. During World War II, for example, the United States government fixed *ceiling* (or maximum) *prices* on many commodities and introduced a RATIONING SYSTEM. The term may apply, however, to any effort by the government to influence the PRICE LEVEL — for example, by means of CREDIT CONTROL; or it may refer to efforts of private organizations to fix prices or to restrict the freedom of the market. Sometimes called *price fixing*. See also CONTROL, PRICE-CONTROL LEGISLATION.

price-control legislation. Legislation which fixes prices for the market, usually by establishing a ceiling or maximum price above which an article cannot be legally sold. Federal legislation of this nature was enacted in the United States to cover rents in the District of Columbia immediately following World War I. In World War II the federal government enacted the comprehensive Emergency Price Control Act of 1942 and established the Office of Price Control to administer it. This act expired on June 30, 1946. Another bill, providing for greatly modified controls to operate for a limited period was then enacted; but all price controls applicable to World War II were discontinued by January, 1948. Price-control legislation was again inaugurated January 25, 1951, following the outbreak of the Korean war, and continued, with various modifications under successive amendments, into 1953. See also RENT CONTROL.

price fixing. See explanation under PRICE CONTROL.

price leadership. The assumption that prices in a given industry are often determined by one, usually the largest, producer and that other producers in that industry tacitly accept the prices thus determined. Since no one producer is able to control the market in the industry, this pricing policy is allegedly resorted to for a more favorable price than might be obtained under truly competitive conditions.

price level. The prices, usually at wholesale, of a selected list of representative commodities at a particular time expressed in a composite figure called an index number. See also INDEX NUMBER.

price loco. The price at the place where a purchase is made. See also PRICE.

price specie-flow theory. An explanation of the DISTRIBUTION of the precious metals among nations, the causative factors allegedly being the impact of the precious metals upon the domestic PRICE LEVEL and the needs of trade. The theory holds that imports of the precious metals increase the money supply and hence advance the price level. Those countries receiving the precious metals therefore become good markets for commodity imports and poor markets for foreign buyers. Hence, they tend to develop an excess of imports over exports, and this eventually reverses their position. The excess of commodity imports is paid for by exporting the precious metals. Other countries which receive the precious metals in turn develop relatively high prices and an excess of commodity imports, and eventually become exporters of the precious metals. Thus, according to the theory, the precious metals tend to be distributed among the nations automatically, in accordance with the needs of trade. The theory, originally formulated by David Hume (1711–1776), a British philosopher and economist, became the basis of the international trade theory of the CLASSICAL SCHOOL. As national monetary supplies became less dependent upon the precious metals and central banking systems exerted an increasing influence upon the price level through the regulation of credit, the price specie-flow theory failed to offer any realistic explanation of distribution of the precious metals among nations.

price spread. The difference between the total cost of producing a particular product and its selling price to consumers. The difference indicates the cost of physical distribution; that is, what it costs to get a product from the place where it is produced or grown into the hands of the person who ultimately uses it, including such profits as are made by middlemen and the retailer. Sometimes called *markup*.

price support. Governmental regulations, usually involving some form of public subsidy or financial aid to producers or distributors, designed to keep market prices from falling below a certain minimum level. In the United States, for example, agricultural prices are maintained by a complex system of outright subsidies, government purchase of commodities at prices higher than the market, or government loans to producers at prices higher than the market. By means of a stabilization fund used to purchase foreign exchange, and other devices, governments also often attempt to check serious declines in foreign-exchange rates.

price system. The system by which the kind and quantity of economic goods produced is determined by the price consumers, collectively, are willing to pay, the actual allocation of those goods being determined by the ability of consumers, individually, to pay the price.

pricing out of the market. A popular phrase to describe a price structure so high that goods cease to sell in their usual market.

primary boycott. See explanation under BOYCOTT.

primary deposit. A bank deposit which is not directly offset on the bank's books of account by an asset such as a United States bond or a promissory note. Thus, a deposit is primary when it is not created by a loan and when it is not earmarked for the payment of a loan already made. See also BANK DEPOSIT, DEPOSIT CURRENCY.

primary money. See STANDARD MONEY.

primary reserves. See explanation under BANK RESERVES.

prime bill. See explanation under BILL.

prime cost. See VARIABLE COST.

prime rate. The interest rate charged business borrowers having the highest CREDIT RATING.

primogeniture. A preference in inheritance given to the eldest son, or sometimes to the eldest daughter.

priority system. See RATIONING SYSTEM.

prior-lien bond. See explanation under BOND.

prior stock. See explanation under CAPITAL STOCK.

private bank. An unincorporated bank which, in the United States, operates under state laws. See also BANK.

private corporation. A corporation created to conduct enterprises for private profit. The term includes quasi-public or public-service corporations. See also CORPORATION.

private debt. The debt of private persons, corporate or natural, as distinct from the debt owed by a government or its subdivisions. The total of the net private debt in the United States in 1962 was approximately 755 billion dollars. See also DEBT.

private enterprise. Economic activities carried on with the expectation of profit by private individuals acting either as individual entrepreneurs or through partnerships, associations, joint-stock companies, or corporations. The term is used to distinguish such activities from economic activities carried on by the government.

privateering. The wartime practice, common in the 17th and 18th centuries, of using private vessels, with government authority, to prey upon the merchantmen of the enemy. See LETTER OF MARQUE.

private property. The exclusive right of a person, natural or corporate, to control and enjoy an economic good, limited by law. In popular speech the term frequently refers to whatever is owned by individuals. See also PROPERTY.

privilege tax. See explanation under OCCUPATION TAX.

probability curve. See NORMAL CURVE OF DISTRIBUTION.

probable error. As applied to a NORMAL CURVE OF DISTRIBUTION, a measure of dispersion, variation, or scatter such as, when pointed off on both sides of the ARITHMETIC MEAN, will provide a space that will include one-half the total number of cases. As such, it is equivalent in value to the QUARTILE DEVIATION, but whereas the quartile deviation is used as a measure of dispersion for irregular frequency curves, probable error is fully applicable only to normal frequency curves. In such a normal curve it may be computed from the STANDARD DEVIATION by multiplying the standard deviation by 0.6745.

The term is misleading, as neither error nor probability is involved. The name is derived from the custom of grouping, in a frequency distribution, measures obtained by various observers of a given astronomical or other scientific phenomenon in order to establish an index indicating the reliability of the observations. See also FREQUENCY DISTRIBUTION.

proceeds. 1. The amount remaining after deducting the discount from the face value of a promissory note or similar commercial paper. See also DISCOUNT. 2. A tax yield after deducting the the costs of collection.

process effects. A term sometimes applied to the increase in consumer spending and private investment resulting directly from the spending on a public-works project.

processing tax. A tax such as the one which, under the terms of the first Agricultural Adjustment Act (1933), was levied upon millers, packers, and other processors of agricultural commodities, the returns from which were used to compensate farmers for the difference between the market price of the unprocessed commodity and the higher parity price authorized by law. The Supreme Court held this processing tax unconstitutional on January 6, 1936, (HOOSAC MILLS CASE) for the reason that it was not a tax as usually defined but a special burden levied upon one class of persons for the benefit of another class, and for the additional reason that this tax allegedly invaded the reserved powers of the states under the 10th Amendment of the Constitution. The second Agricultural Adjustment Act (1938) eliminated the processing tax and drew upon the general revenues of the government for the special financial benefits it provided farmers. See also TAX.

producer co-operative. A group of farmers or industrial workers who pool their capital, apportion their labor according to their individual abilities, and divide their earnings equally. Producer co-operatives in the United States have not proved very successful and are few in number.

producer's capital. See explanation under CAPITAL GOOD.

production. The process of increasing the capacity of goods to satisfy human desires or of rendering services capable of satisfying human desires. In formal economics, of which production is one of the main topics, it is generally recognized that the utility or power of a material good to satisfy a human desire may be increased by the creation of (1) a TIME UTILITY, (2) a PLACE UTILITY, (3) a FORM UTILITY, or (4) a POSSESSION UTILITY. For specific purposes the term is sometimes given a much more restricted meaning. As defined for federal income-tax purposes, for example, the term means "created, fabricated, manufactured, extracted, processed, cured, or aged." In popular speech, too, the term suggests a process of creating or changing the form of something. See also DIRECT PRODUCTION, INDIRECT PRODUCTION, MASS PRODUCTION, OVERPRODUCTION.

production allocation program. Placing production plans for war materials required by the armed forces of the United States with private industry in order that a rapid transition from peacetime to wartime production may be effected in the event of an emergency. The program aims to provide an effective distribution of manufacturing load, to disclose possible shortages requiring remedial action, and to familiarize private management with its potential responsibilities.

production factors. Various indexes which measure production and data closely related thereto. Examples: physical production, number of wage earners, wages paid, productivity per worker. The term should not be confused with FACTORS OF PRODUCTION.

productivity. The amount each worker produces during a given length of time. Productivity depends upon technological developments, capital equipment, organization and management, working and living conditions, and many other factors. Changes in quality are not reflected in the statistical measurements of productivity but might well be considered a part of the general concept.

profit. 1. As used in theoretical economics, the residual share of the product of enterprise accruing to the entrepreneur after all payments for capital (interest), for land (rent), and for labor including management (wages). Also called ***pure profit.*** 2. As used in accounting, a broad term indicating an increase in wealth resulting from the operation of an enterprise. The term ***gross profit*** usually indicates the difference between the selling price and the cost price, such items as selling expenses and operating expenses being customarily deducted from the gross profits in order to arrive at the ***net profit*** or NET INCOME. See also OPERATING PROFIT, WINDFALL PROFIT.

profit-and-loss statement. A condensed account of the operations of a business enterprise over a period of time, usually 1 year. Such an account sets forth the total sales, the cost of goods or services sold, and the gross profit or loss. The expenses of running the business are then listed under general classifications and appropriate entries made to show net operating profit or loss. Other income is subsequently added and other expenses are deducted to show net profit or net loss. Also called ***income statement.***

profit-sharing bond. See explanation under BOND.

program. As applied to machine data processing, a sequence of operations with descriptions, codes, and formats, integrating a system for manipulating and recording information to some desired end.

progressive taxation. A tax system, the rates of which increase as the base amount taxed increases. A rate of 2 per cent applied to a base of $1,000, 4 per cent applied to a base of $10,000, and 6 per cent applied to a base of $100,000 is an example.

proletariat. The wage-earning class.

promissory note. A written promise to pay a specific amount of money to some person at a given place and time with interest at a specific rate, or without interest, as the case may be.

promoter. One who undertakes to launch a new business project, especially one who assumes responsibility for selling a new project's stock or securities in order to obtain necessary capital for the enterprise.

propensity to consume. A Keynesian statistical phrase denoting the relation, expressed as a percentage, between total income and total consumer expenditures. For total income some authorities use NATIONAL INCOME, others GROSS NATIONAL PRODUCT, and still others DISPOSABLE INCOME. The relation is expressed in the equation:

$$P = \frac{C}{Y}$$

when

P = propensity to consume,
C = consumer expenditures,
Y = income.

Thus, in 1950 the gross national product was 282.6 billion dollars, and consumption expenditures were 193.6 billion dollars. Propensity to consume, therefore, was $\frac{193.6}{282.9}$ or 68.4 per cent.

The term "consumption FUNCTION" is frequently used because the percentage expresses a relationship between two variables. When the percentage is calculated on the basis of a specific increase or decrease in income and consumption expenditures compared with the totals of some previous period, it is called the ***marginal propensity to consume.*** The marginal propensity to consume is thus a ratio of change in consumption expenditures to a change in income. For example, the gross national product was 12.9 billion dollars less in 1930 than in 1929, and consumption expenditures were 8 billion dollars less. A marginal propensity to consume of $\frac{8.0}{12.9}$ or 62 per cent is thus indicated.

Occasionally, these terms are used to denote the spending disposition of a single consumer or other individual spending unit.

propensity to invest. A statistical phrase, used especially by Keynesian economists, denoting the relation, expressed as a percentage, between total NATIONAL INCOME and that part of income expended on new CAPITAL FORMATION. Under conditions of equilibrium, propensity to invest is identical with PROPENSITY TO SAVE (*q.v.*), as demonstrated in the INCOME AND EXPENDITURE EQUATION (*q.v.*). But under conditions of disequilibrium the propensity to invest may be greater or less than the propensity to save. Under such conditions, however, income tends to bring savings and investment into balance because if savings exceed investments, income is reduced, and if investments exceed savings, income is increased. See also KEYNESIAN ECONOMICS.

propensity to save. A Keynesian statistical phrase denoting the relation, expressed as a percentage, between total income and that part of the income not devoted to consumer expenditures. For total income some authorities use NATIONAL INCOME, others GROSS NATIONAL PRODUCT, and still others DISPOSABLE INCOME. The relation may be expressed by the equation:

$$S_1 = \frac{Y - C}{Y}$$

when

S_1 = propensity to save,
Y = income,
C = consumer expenditures.

Thus, in 1950 the gross national product in the United States was 282.6 billion dollars, and consumer expenditures were 193.6 billion dollars. Propensity to save, therefore, was $\frac{282.6 - 193.6}{282.6}$ or 31.49 per cent.

When the percentage is calculated on the basis of a specific increase or decrease in the total income and in that part of the income not devoted to consumption expenditures, compared with the totals of some previous period, it is called the *marginal propensity to save.* The marginal propensity to save is thus a ratio of change in savings to change in income. For example, the gross national product was 12.9 billion dollars less in 1930 than in 1929. There was a decrease in savings calculated as follows:

	1929	1930
	(billions of dollars)	
Gross national product	103.8	90.9
Consumer expenditures	78.8	70.8
	25.0	20.1

$$25.0 - 20.1 = 4.9.$$

A marginal propensity to save of $\frac{4.9}{12.9}$ or 37.98 per cent is thus indicated.

Occasionally, these terms are used to denote the savings disposition of a single individual or other saving unit.

property. The right to the future benefits of economic goods — material and nonmaterial — as determined by law. Although, technically, the term means a right or interest in things rather than the things themselves, common usage makes it applicable to the things rather than to the right or interest. See also ECONOMIC GOOD, INTANGIBLE PROPERTY, PERSONAL PROPERTY, PRIVATE PROPERTY, REAL PROPERTY, TANGIBLE PROPERTY.

property account. See REAL ACCOUNT.

property capital. See explanation under CAPITAL.

property tax. Generally, a tax levied on any kind of property. The property may be real, as in the case of lands or buildings, or it may be personal, as in the case of stocks and bonds or home furnishings. Sometimes property is classified for tax purposes. In such cases a *personal property tax* is applied at a rate different from the rate applied to real property. A distinction may also be made in the case of real property, a *land tax* being applied to such lands as are unimproved, as distinct from a *real-estate tax* which may apply to both improved and unimproved land. Often called *general property tax.* See also GRADED TAX, TAX.

proportionality, law of. A term sometimes applied to the relationship between production and the factors of production. It implies that in any enterprise there is some ideal relationship among the factors of production that will produce optimum returns. Also called *law of variable proportions.* See also DIMINISHING RETURNS, FACTORS OF PRODUCTION.

proportional rate. As applied to railway traffic, a special rate applying between two points on the same railroad exclusively for freight originating in or destined for a point on a connecting railroad. Thus, if the regular local rate between point A, located on one of two railroads, and point B, the junction of the two railroads, is 20 cents for 100 lb., and the local rate between the junction point B and point C, located on the second railroad, is 50 cents for 100 lb., the second railroad may establish a proportional rate of 40 cents for 100 lb. between points B and C exclusively for freight originating at point A and destined for point C, or for freight originating at point C and destined for point A.

proportional taxation. Taxation using the same rate regardless of the base amount taxed. A rate of 2 per cent, for example, applied to a base of $1,000, $10,000, or $100,000 would be a proportional rate.

proprietorship. See INDIVIDUAL PROPRIETORSHIP.

prospectus. As applied to securities, a statement, printed or broadcast, which describes a particular security offered for sale.

prosperity. In general, a condition of economic activity with goods plentiful, money circulating freely, and unemployment at a minimum.

protectionism. Advocacy of protective tariffs as a means of developing national wealth and power, a policy supported by such American protectionists as Henry C. Carey (1793–1879) and S. N. Patten (1852–1922). The chief arguments in support of the policy were: (1) encouragement of infant industries; (2) opportunity for the employment of a variety of individual talents through industrial diversification; (3) savings in the cost of transportation; (4) conservation of natural resources for home use; and (5) national power in the form of a self-reliant economy. The infant-industry and national-power arguments received support particularly from the German economist Friedrich List (1789–1846). The other arguments, in English-speaking countries at least, have been rejected with practical unanimity, although in recent years protection has occasionally been defended because, contemporary specialization having made capital and labor less mobile, a liberal trade policy might induce at least short-term unemployment.

protective tariff. A tariff high enough to assure domestic producers against any effective competition from foreign producers. See also TARIFF.

protest. A formal written declaration by a notary public certifying to a demand for payment of some instrument and to the refusal to honor that demand. Checks, for example, drawn on insufficient funds may thus have a protest attached to them when they are returned to the maker unhonored. See also ACCEPTANCE SUPRA PROTEST.

prudent-investment-cost standard. As applied to the valuation of a corporation's capital assets, the original cost of the assets less such of the cost as represents dishonest, wasteful, or imprudent investments. See also VALUATION.

psychic income. Satisfactions, other than material ones, derived from economic activity. The nature, place, or conditions of a person's work, for example, may offer such satisfactions in a high degree; they may transcend the material satisfaction of a higher money income which could be derived from work under less favorable circumstances. See also INCOME.

psychological theory of the business cycle. A theory that explains business cycles largely by ascribing causative factors to mental attitudes and human emotions. General optimism, based upon favorable economic conditions, stimulates economic activity. Over-optimism, it is held, then becomes widespread, and the cycle becomes overdeveloped. When economic disturbances occur, some degree of pessimism is felt, and the turning point of the cycle is reached. This, it is argued, engenders deeper pessimism, and a depression follows. See also BUSINESS CYCLE.

Public Assistance, Bureau of. A part of the federal Social Security Administration, known since 1962 as the Bureau of Family Services. which administers provisions of the SOCIAL SECURITY ACT that authorize grants and other assistance to states of the United States possessing satisfactory plans for assisting the needy aged, the blind, and dependent children.

public bond. See explanation under BOND.

public consumption monopoly. A government monopoly conducted for the purpose of regulating the consumption of certain commodities believed to be harmful; for example, a government monopoly in alcoholic beverages, established primarily for the purpose of limiting their consumption. Such a monopoly, however, is often established for the dual purposes of regulation and revenue, in which case it is partly a FISCAL MONOPOLY. See also MONOPOLY.

public corporation. A corporation organized by the government to facilitate the administration of public affairs. In the states of the United States the charter of such a corporation may be altered or revoked at any time at the will of the legislature unless it enjoys special constitutional protection. See also CORPORATION.

public debt. 1. The debt of any governmental entity. 2. The total governmental debt of any country, including that of the central government and of political subdivisions, as distinct from the debts of private persons, corporate or natural. The debt of the central government as distinct from the debts of the political subdivisions of the nation is usually referred to as the NATIONAL DEBT. See also DEBT.

Public Debt, Bureau of the. A part of the fiscal service branch of the United States Department of the Treasury which administers the national debt. It prepares the papers incident to the offering of a new debt issue, allocates the new issue among potential subscribers, handles the subscriptions, and makes regulations governing transactions in national debt issues already in existence.

public domain. 1. Lands over which a government exercises proprietary rights. 2. The term is also applied to the condition which exists when a copyright or patent right expires and the composition or process involved may be exploited by anyone.

public finance. The financial operations of all levels of government. Such operations include budgeting, taxing, appropriating, purchasing, borrowing, disbursing funds, and regulating the currency.

public good. As applied to economic goods, a commodity or a service supplied gratuitously to individuals by the government. Public fountains, recreation parks, museums, public education, and food distributed to ameliorate distress are examples. The distinction between a public good and a FREE GOOD should be noted. See also ECONOMIC GOOD.

Public Housing Administration. A unit of the United States HOUSING AND HOME FINANCE AGENCY which administers legislation providing for loans and subsidies to local housing authorities to encourage the creation of low-rental dwelling units. It also promotes adaptation and use of wartime and emergency federal housing and other structures as permanent low-rental dwelling units.

public lands. Lands owned by the government; public domain. In the United States the federal government has title to vast tracts included in Indian reservations, national parks and forests, and grazing lands.

public-opinion survey. A method of determining public opinion on specific issues by consulting, in one way or another, a representative cross section of the population. The first periodical service based on the sampling method was established in 1935. Since then numerous such agencies have been organized, some conducting national surveys, some regional, and others, surveys among special-interest groups.

public ownership. Ownership and operation by a government unit of some service or productive enterprise, presumably for the benefit of the citizenry.

public relations. The relations between an individual or a business or other organization and the public. The term implies the deliberate creation of favorable public opinion through publicity, as distinct from advertising.

public revenue. Government income from taxes and from all other sources.

Public Roads, Bureau of. A unit of the Department of Commerce of the United States government which administers federal grants-in-aid to the states for the construction and maintenance of major highways, and co-operates with the Departments of Agriculture and the Interior in the construction of roads in national forests, national parks, and elsewhere.

public-service commission. A regulatory body, found in most of the states of the United States, charged with the responsibility of supervising the operations of public-utility companies and passing upon their rates.

public-service corporation. A private business organization which provides a service of peculiar importance to the public's welfare and convenience. The production of gas or electric power, the operation of a telephone system, and the distribution of water are examples. Public-service corporations frequently operate under a FRANCHISE granting them a monopoly or a partial monopoly. For this and other reasons they are subject to government regulation in various matters, including the rates charged. Also known as QUASI-PUBLIC CORPORATION or PUBLIC UTILITY.

public utility. A private enterprise engaged in production deemed of such importance to the public welfare that many of its activities, including the prices it charges for its goods and services, are regulated by law. See also PUBLIC-SERVICE CORPORATION.

public-utility bond. See explanation under BOND.

Public Utility Holding Company Act. An act of Congress, 1935. It requires public-utility HOLDING COMPANIES to register with the SECURITIES AND EXCHANGE COMMISSION. It also prohibits complicated networks of holding and operating companies by restricting the organizational structure of a holding company, with certain exceptions, to subsidiaries that consist exclusively of operating companies.

public welfare. The well-being of the people as a whole in contrast to the well-being of only a few.

public works. Construction projects designed for public welfare or convenience, carried on by the government with public funds. Highways, canals, bridges, parks, and public buildings are examples. The term refers to public improvements in contrast to mere maintenance activities such as street lighting, disposal of rubbish, grading of roads, and the like.

public works and ways system. The employment of convict labor on public works and highways.

pump priming. Any policy of large-scale public expenditure for public works and other activities, the purpose being to increase employment and purchasing power and raise the level of economic activity during a depression. See also DEFICIT FINANCING.

punched-card data processing. The manipulation of information by automatic and semiautomatic machines actuated by electrical circuits, the manipulation being determined by cards containing perforations to which meanings have been assigned. The processing consists of recording, classifying, computing, and printing information. Recording from primary sources is done on a key punch machine which perforates the cards. A sorter separates the cards into any desired classification. An accounting machine interprets the perforations in the form of numerical or alphabetical characters, performs addition and subtraction, if desired, and prints the results all in accordance with "instructions" given by means of a panel wired for the particular report desired. Various other machines perform such operations as verifying, reproducing, merging, matching, selecting, interpreting, posting, and calculating.

purchase-money mortgage. A mortgage given wholly or in part in lieu of cash for the purchase of tangible property. See also MORTGAGE.

purchasing power. The ability to buy.

purchasing-power parity. In international economics, that rate of exchange between the currencies of two countries, both of which may be on a fiat standard, in which the units of national currency expressed in the exchange rate command equivalent or comparable purchasing power, in terms of specified commodities, in either the domestic or world markets. Assuming relatively unhampered world trade and no arbitrary manipulation of national currency, a purchasing-power parity exchange rate of this sort, once established, is likely to maintain a certain equilibrium. Thus if $1 in the United States has a purchasing power equivalent to the purchasing power of 100 francs in France, the price of franc bills of exchange in New York will be 1 cent per franc and the price of dollar exchange in Paris will be 100 francs to the dollar. If the price of franc bills of exchange should advance, this would tend to discourage French imports into the United States and encourage United States exports to France. This process would, it is said, tend to restore the rate of exchange to its former parity. The same equalizing process would occur, according to the doctrine, only in the reverse direction, if the price of francs in terms of dollars should decline. See also PARITY.

pure competition. See COMPETITION.

Pure Food and Drugs Act. An act of Congress, 1906. It prohibits interstate commerce in adulterated or misbranded foods and drugs. Amendments since 1906 have strengthened the prohibition against false or fraudulent claims on patent-medicine labels, require that the net weight be specified on containers, and establish standards of quality that must be identified on the labels of canned foods. See also FEDERAL FOOD, DRUG, AND COSMETICS ACT.

pure interest. A price paid for the use of capital excluding all sums to cover risk and all other costs incurred because of the loan. Sometimes called *net interest*, or *true interest*. Pure interest is a theoretical concept because all payments for the use of capital include items other than pure interest. See also INTEREST.

pure profit. See PROFIT.

purposive sample. A limited number of observations selected from an entire aggregate of phenomena on the basis of some known attribute. For example, suppose that there is known to be a high correlation between taxable incomes and property valuations, and an estimate of property valuations in a state is desired. A few counties in which the average of taxable incomes is the same as that of the entire state might be selected as a sample. It would then be assumed that the average property valuations found to obtain in the sample would apply to the state as a whole. See also SAMPLING.

put. A privilege accorded a trader, for a fee, to deliver a specified quantity of a given stock or commodity, within an agreed length of time, and receive for it a stipulated price.

Q

quadratic mean. See STANDARD DEVIATION.

qualified indorsement. An indorsement that limits the liability of the indorser to that of a mere assignor thus relieving him from all responsibility in the event of the nonpayment or nonacceptance of the instrument. A qualified indorsement is often indicated by the words "without recourse." See also INDORSEMENT.

quantity theory of money. The assertion that the general PRICE LEVEL depends directly upon the amount of money in circulation. Thus, according to the theory, an increase in the quantity of money in circulation will increase prices, assuming the supply of goods remains constant; conversely, a decrease in the amount of money in circulation will lower prices. One of the oldest definitely postulated economic theories, its first explicit formulation is attributed to John Locke (1632–1704). With some qualifications and additions it became one of the basic tenets of the CLASSICAL SCHOOL. Early advocates of the theory recognized the importance of CREDIT, that is, deposit currency or money substitutes, but paid insufficient attention to the effect of velocity, or the rapidity of money circulation. In its modern form the theory is expressed in various versions of the EQUATION OF EXCHANGE (*q.v.*).

quarter stock. See explanation under CAPITAL STOCK.

quartile. As applied to a FREQUENCY DISTRIBUTION in economic or other analyses, points on the *X* axis which separate the total number of items into four groups of an equal number of items each. There are three quartiles. The second quartile is the same as the MEDIAN. A quartile is found by first ascertaining the class interval in which it is located and then finding its value within that class interval by INTERPOLATION. Example:

Class interval	Frequency	Cumulative frequencies	
		To second-class interval	To third-class interval
−0.5 to 0.4	10	10	10
0.5 to 1.4	30	40	40
1.5 to 2.4	40		80
2.5 to 3.4	50		
3.5 to 4.4	25		
4.5 to 5.4	8		
	163		

First quartile (Q_1):

$$\frac{163}{4} = 40.75.$$

$$40.75 - 40.00 = 0.75.$$

$$Q_1 = 1.5 + \left(\frac{0.75}{40} \times 1\right) = 1.5 + 0.01875 = 1.51875.$$

Third quartile (Q_3):

$$\frac{163}{4} = 40.75.$$

$$40.75 \times 3 = 122.25.$$

$$122.25 - 80.00 = 42.25.$$

$$Q_3 = 2.5 + \left(\frac{42.25}{50} \times 1\right) = 2.5 + 0.845 = 3.345.$$

In a similar manner, frequency distributions may be divided into *deciles* or *percentiles.* The former are points on the X axis which divide the total number of items into 10 groups; the latter into 100 groups.

quartile deviation. A statistical measure of the extent of absolute dispersion, variability, or scatter in a FREQUENCY DISTRIBUTION (*q.v.*), obtained by subtracting the value of the first QUARTILE (*q.v.*) from the value of the third quartile and dividing by 2.

quasi corporation. A term sometimes applied to an unincorporated political subdivision of one of the states of the United States. A New England town, for example, is not incorporated but enjoys practically all the rights and privileges of a municipal corporation. See also CORPORATION.

quasi-public corporation. A private corporation engaged in a business of a public nature such that it must under regulatory legislation serve all who apply for its goods or services. Also called PUBLIC-SERVICE CORPORATION. See also CORPORATION, PRIVATE CORPORATION.

quick asset. Cash, or some other asset which can quickly be converted into cash at approximately its book value. Sometimes called *floating asset.* See also ASSET.

quickie strike. See ILLEGAL STRIKE.

quick ratio. See ACID-TEST RATIO.

quitrent. In the United States a term used to indicate a nominal perpetual rent sometimes made a condition of a conveyance of land. The term harks back to the feudal usage of having a tenant substitute a perpetual money payment to the lord of the manor for all other feudal obligations. See also RENT.

quota country. As applied to the immigration policy of the United States, a country from which the number of persons (other than certain exempt classes) who can enter the United States during a given year is limited by a quota. Quota countries (1964) include virtually all countries except those of the Western Hemisphere. See also NATIONAL ORIGIN PLAN.

quota sample. A limited number of observations selected from an entire aggregate of phenomena by separating the entire aggregate into constituent parts on the basis of some known attribute and selecting a certain number of cases from each part. Quota samples are used extensively in PUBLIC-OPINION SURVEYS. For example, the population (entire aggregate) might be separated into groups according to sex, political party, income status, or some other known attribute, and a number chosen from each group corresponding to the proportion which that group bears to the total aggregate. See also SAMPLING.

R

racism. Belief in the socio-economic, intellectual, and cultural significance of alleged racial differences; justification of a discriminatory policy against any group because of alleged racial difference.

rack rent. Rent, the amount of which equals or nearly equals the entire value of the products produced on the property rented. Hence, in general, an unreasonably high rent. See also RENT.

railroad bond. See explanation under BOND.

Railroad Commission of Wisconsin* v. *Chicago, Burlington and Quincy R. R. Co. See WISCONSIN RATE CASE.

Railroad Retirement Act. An act of Congress, 1935, which, as amended in 1937 and 1946, provides old-age benefits up to $120 a month to aged and disabled railroad employees, and in case of the death of the employee provides survivors' benefits to his family.

Railroad Retirement Board. A board which administers a retirement system and an unemployment insurance and employment service for aged, disabled, and unemployed railroad employees. The board was established by the RAILROAD RETIREMENT ACT of 1935 and was given additional authority by the Railroad Unemployment Insurance Act approved in 1938 and various amendments to that act. It is composed of three members appointed by the President with the advice and the consent of the Senate.

Railroad Unemployment Insurance Act. An act of Congress, 1938, which, with subsequent amendments, insures qualified railroad employees against loss of income because of unemployment due to sickness or inability to find remunerative work.

Railway Labor Act. An act of Congress, 1926, which, with subsequent amendments, governs the relations between the railroads and air lines and their employees. It guarantees employees the right of collective bargaining, provides for labor contracts, and specifies procedures for the settlement of various types of disputes. See also NATIONAL MEDIATION BOARD.

railway valuation case. A case, *St. Louis and O'Fallon Ry. Co.* v. *United States*, 279 U. S. 461 (1929), in which the Supreme Court of the United States invalidated the valuation criteria issued by the Interstate Commerce Commission to be used by that body for rate-making purposes and for determining recapture of railway earnings under existing transportation legislation. See also INTERSTATE COMMERCE COMMISSION, RECAPTURE OF EARNINGS, VALUATION.

random sample. A limited number of observations selected by chance from an entire aggregate of phenomena. In random sampling, each item in the population (the entire aggregate) must have the same chance of being selected for the sample as any other item. This can be accomplished by a blind chance drawing, by the selection of items at stated intervals, or by means of a table of random numbers prepared for such purpose. See also SAMPLING.

range. As applied to a FREQUENCY DISTRIBUTION (*q.v.*), a statistical measure indicating the approximate extent of absolute dispersion, variability, or scatter, obtained by ascertaining the difference between the lower limit of the lowest class interval and the upper limit of the highest class interval. Applied to the original data, the range is the difference between the smallest and the largest items. It is commonly used as a measure of stock-market variations, but, because one unusual item at either extreme can materially affect its value, it is seldom used in economic analysis. For example, see FREQUENCY DISTRIBUTION, which shows a range of 9.99.

rate. A term expressing a fixed relationship between two magnitudes and used as a means of measurement by economists, businessmen, and statisticians. It may be a unit price for a service, e.g., 3 cents per mile; a formula for computing wages, e.g., $1 per hour; a formula for computing taxation, e.g., $10 per $1,000 of assessed valuation; a formula, called *interest rate*, for expressing interest or a discount, e.g., 4 per cent, meaning $4 per $100. In England especially, the term is popularly synonymous with a tax levied by a nonsovereign governmental body.

rate regulation. The determination by a public-service commission or similar authority of the maximum and occasionally the minimum rate which public-utility corporations may charge for their services.

rate war. See CUTTHROAT COMPETITION.

ratio chart. A graphic representation of statistical data showing relative rather than absolute variations. The most common form of a ratio chart is the semilogarithmic type with logarithmic divisions on the *Y* axis and arithmetic divisions on the *X* axis. Thus, equal vertical distances on the *Y* axis indicate equal percentage variations.

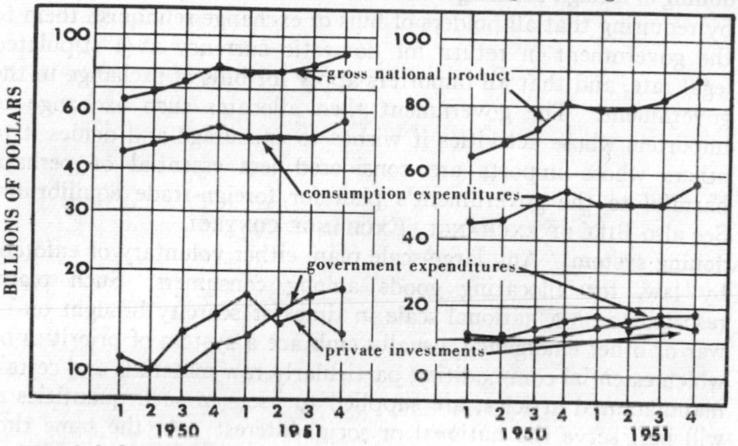

The left-hand section of the preceding diagram shows a ratio chart displaying the following data:

1950	Billions of dollars			
	Gross national product	Government expenditures	Private investments	Consumption expenditures
First quarter	64 +	10	11	44
Second quarter	67	10	10	47
Third quarter	72 −	10	13	50
Fourth quarter	80 +	12	15	54
1951				
First quarter	79 +	13	17	50
Second quarter	79	15	14	50
Third quarter	82	17	15	50
Fourth quarter	88 −	18	13	56

On such a chart, therefore, data representing a time series can be plotted according to absolute values, with the resulting curve representing relative variations.

The right-hand section of the diagram shows the same data plotted on a conventional *arithmetic chart;* that is, one with cross-sectional ruling.

rationalization. As applied to industry, improved methods of an administrative nature which increase efficiency.

rationing of foreign exchange. A means of controlling foreign exchange by requiring that all holders of bills of exchange relinquish them to the government in return for domestic currency at a stipulated legal rate, and that all importers apply for bills of exchange to the government. The government then allocates such exchange to importers whose activities it wishes to encourage and denies it to others whose imports are considered less essential or perhaps harmful to the government's plan for foreign-trade equilibrium. See also BILL OF EXCHANGE, EXCHANGE CONTROL.

rationing system. Any large-scale plan, either voluntary or enforced by law, for allocating goods among consumers. Such plans, resorted to on a national scale in times of scarcity brought on by war or other emergency, usually embrace a system of priorities by which essential commodities, particularly raw materials and certain manufactured articles, are supplied to users in such quantities as will best serve the national or social interest. At the same time the total supply of the necessities of life are distributed among consumers on an equal basis, some form of stamp usually being issued, which the consumer surrenders when purchases are made. Also called *priority system.* See also RATIONING OF FOREIGN EXCHANGE.

raw material. Nonfabricated material used in processing or manufacturing, during the course of which its nature or form is changed. Thus, iron is a raw material used in the production of steel, and steel is a raw material used in the manufacture of automobiles.

real account. A term used in double-entry bookkeeping to indicate an account which is carried over from one accounting period to another. Asset and liability accounts are examples. Such accounts usually bear the title of some sort of property and hence are often called *property accounts.* See also ACCOUNT.

real estate. Land and structures of a permanent nature erected thereon. In general, all immovable things.

real-estate tax. See explanation under PROPERTY TAX.

real investment. Expenditure that creates a new and additional CAPITAL ASSET. Real investments thus result in new CAPITAL

FORMATION. The term is used in contradistinction to FINANCIAL INVESTMENT.

realistic method. See explanation under INDUCTIVE METHOD.

real property. A right or interest in land or whatever is attached to that land in such a way that it cannot be readily moved. The term is used in contradistinction to PERSONAL PROPERTY. See also PROPERTY.

real wage. What the money received as wages will buy. As the general price level advances, a MONEY WAGE will buy less, and as the PRICE LEVEL declines, a money wage will buy more. Real wages may change, therefore, while money wages remain the same. Money wages may be converted into real wages by dividing the money wages by an index number of general prices. Thus if money wages of $1,500 remained the same from 1926 to 1940, and the price index number in 1940 was .80, with 1926 taken as the base period and considered 100, then the real wage value of $1,500 in money wages in 1940 was $1,500 ÷ .80 or $1,875. See also WAGE.

rebate. An amount returned out of a sum already paid, or the equivalent in the form of a deduction or discount.

recapture of earnings. 1. A term descriptive of a clause in the Esch-Cummins Act of 1920. The clause permitted the railroads to apply to their reserves one-half of all earnings in excess of those which the act identified as constituting a fair return on the valuation of the capital assets. The other half of such earnings was made subject to "recapture"; that is, such earnings were to be earmarked by the government for bolstering the weaker railroads. 2. Generally, any policy requiring a public utility to transfer to the government earnings in excess of a return on investment which may be fixed in a statute or a franchise.

receipt. A written acknowledgment that money, goods, or some other property has been received.

receiver. A person usually appointed by a court of law to exercise control over a property or business when, in the interests of justice, it appears necessary to the court that some impartial, qualified person assume such authority. A receiver is appointed, for example, when a company cannot pay its creditors.

receiver's certificate. A short-term note sold by a receiver with the approval of the court which appointed him. The purpose of the sale is to realize immediate funds with which to carry on a business. A RECEIVER of a railroad or other public utility will sometimes issue this form of security in order to keep the business, essential to the public welfare, in operation. A receiver's certificate is usually secured by a first lien upon the property and net earnings of the business in receivership.

recession. As applied to business conditions, a mild tapering off of economic activity, not sufficient to mark a major phase of a business cycle. See also BUSINESS CYCLE.

reciprocal trade agreements. The term usually refers to the trade agreements consummated by the United States Department of State by authority of the Trade Agreements Act of 1934 and amendments. The original act authorized the increase or decrease of existing American duties up to 50 per cent for the purpose of negotiating with foreign countries in the interest of promoting mutually profitable international trade. Also called *executive trade agreements*. See also TRADE AGREEMENTS ACT.

reciprocity principle. The granting of trade, tariff, or other concessions by one nation in return for equivalent concessions from the grantee.

reclamation. **1.** Any method for bringing waste natural resources into productive use. Thus, desert land may be reclaimed through irrigation, forest lands may be restored by artificial planting and seeding, and fields, if not too badly eroded, may be restored through proper methods of cultivation. **2.** A banking term used to indicate a check or other form of commercial paper, the face value of which has been incorrectly recorded in the clearinghouse, and hence awaits reclamation or correction.

Reclamation, Bureau of. A principal bureau of the United States Department of the Interior. It is engaged in irrigation projects, supplying water to arid sections of 17 western states, and in related activities such as construction of dams and reservoirs, power plants, transmission lines, canals, tunnels, and aqueducts. Major projects of the bureau include the Colorado Big-Thompson, the Missouri Basin, the Central Valley, and the Columbia River projects.

Reconstruction Finance Corporation. A public corporation of the United States government organized in 1932 to extend financial assistance to agriculture, industry, and commerce by granting loans or purchasing the obligations of banks, trust companies, railways, building and loan associations, insurance companies, mortgage-loan companies, local government bodies, other federal corporations, and various agricultural credit and co-operative agencies. The capital stock of the corporation was originally fixed at $500,000,000 all of which was subscribed by the United States government through the Secretary of the Treasury. The corporation was abolished in 1957 and its functions were transferred to other agencies.

reconversion. An over-all change in the direction and operation of a nation's economy when, having been modified to meet the exigencies of a major war, it is readjusted to satisfy peacetime needs and objectives. In a more limited sense, the retooling and administrative changes required in a particular industry or other establishment because of a return to normal peacetime market conditions following a period in which a national military emergency had dictated the type and volume of goods and services produced.

recourse. As applied to loans, the right to collect from an indorser or other guarantor in the event the person making the loan fails to pay it.

redeemable bond. See explanation under BOND.

redeemable preferred stock. See explanation under CAPITAL STOCK.

redemption agent. See CLEARINGHOUSE AGENT.

rediscount. The discounting of commercial paper which has been previously discounted. The term usually refers to the common practice of member banks of the Federal Reserve System having a federal reserve bank discount commercial paper which the member banks have already discounted for their customers. A member bank may, for example, discount a depositor's 3-month promissory note for $1,000 at 4 per cent, giving the depositor $990. The member bank may, in turn, request a federal reserve bank to discount (or rediscount) the note at an established rate of 3 per cent, receiving $992.50, thus making a profit of $2.50.

rediscount rate. The rate of interest at which, in the United States, the district federal reserve banks rediscount eligible commercial paper offered by their member banks. The rediscount rate is determined by each federal reserve bank for the member banks in its district, subject to the approval of the Board of Governors of the Federal Reserve System, or the board itself may specify the rate. If rediscounting occurs among the district federal reserve banks the Board of Governors determines the rate.

re-export. The exportation of imported commodities in substantially the same form in which they were originally imported, the interval between importation and exportation being relatively brief. FOREIGN-TRADE ZONES are usually provided by the importing countries for re-export transactions.

referee. 1. A person appointed by a court of law to investigate and to report to the court regarding some controversy involved in a legal action. 2. A person who arbitrates a dispute.

refined birth rate. See explanation under BIRTH RATE.

refined death rate. See explanation under DEATH RATE.

reflation. Inflation or deflation of the currency in order to restore a former price level. See also INFLATION, DEFLATION.

reforestation. The renewal of forests either by artificial or natural seeding. The term should not be confused with AFFORESTATION.

refunding. 1. The substitution of a new issue of bonds for an older issue, or part of an older issue, the purpose of the operation often being to prolong an existing debt or to change, usually to reduce, the interest rate on such a debt. 2. The act of returning a sum of money from an amount already paid.

refunding bond. See explanation under BOND.

regional division of labor. See LOCALIZATION OF LABOR.

regional pension system. See PENSION POOL.

registered bond. See explanation under BOND.

registered coupon bond. See explanation under BOND.

regressive supply curve. A graphic representation of the condition that exists when a commodity or service is offered in increasing quantities as the MARKET PRICE declines. With the *X* axis representing quantity, and the *Y* axis price, the supply curve slopes downward from left to right and is hence called *regressive.* The condition is frequently found in the agricultural economy. Because they are themselves proprietors, farmers can often increase production by working longer hours without additional monetary outlay. Relatively high fixed monetary expenses may make this increased production necessary in the face of declining market prices. See also SUPPLY.

regressive taxation. A tax system, the rates of which decrease as the base amount taxed increases. A rate of 6 per cent applied to a base of $1,000, 4 per cent applied to a base of $10,000, and 2 per cent applied to a base of $100,000 is an example. A tax may be regressive in effect, however, even when the rates are uniform. A sales tax, for example, although applied at a uniform rate, takes a larger percentage of the total income of low-income groups than it takes from the total income of higher income groups.

regulation. As applied to economic life, some measure of governmental control over private enterprise.

reinsurance. A risk insured by one company which is, in turn, partially insured by a second company. The first company thereby reduces its CONTINGENT LIABILITY. See also INSURANCE.

relative-value index number. An INDEX NUMBER (*q.v.*) computed by assigning the index number 100 to each item in a list of figures representing a period of time designated as the base period, finding for each item in each of the other periods under consideration an individual index number or a figure which bears the same relation to 100 that the item in question bears to its corresponding item in the base period, and calculating a GEOMETRIC MEAN of the individual index numbers for each period.

Example:

Base period 1940			1941		
Item	Value	Individual index number	Value	Calculation	Individual index number
A	9.00	100	10.00	x:100::10.00:9.00	111.11
B	5.00	100	4.00	x:100:: 4.00:5.00	80.00
C	7.00	100	9.00	x:100:: 9.00:7.00	128.57
Index number for 1941, geometric mean					104.55

This method provides no logical means for assigning relative importance to the various items constituting the lists of figures. The resulting index numbers, therefore, even though mathematically valid, may fail to disclose the full significance of changes that may have occurred from one period to another. For example, in calculating variations in the cost of living, changes in consumer buying habits will alter the relative quantities of various commodities purchased, and may affect the cost of living quite as much as do price changes. For this reason a WEIGHTED AVERAGE is often incorporated in this method of constructing an index number. In the case of a cost of living index, the weights might logically be the quantities purchased. For tests to determine the mathematical validity of an index number, see FACTOR REVERSAL TEST, TIME REVERSAL TEST.

remonetization. The re-establishment of a coin as standard money after it has been demonetized. See also DEMONETIZATION.

rent. Theoretically, an amount paid for the use of land. In popular usage, however, the term commonly refers to a payment for the use of land as well as the improvements thereon. Such a payment is often designated as *ordinary rent*. Or, in popular usage, the term "rent" may refer to a payment for the use of a CAPITAL GOOD, such as a machine, quite apart from any land. For the more theoretical uses of "rent" see CONTRACT RENT, ECONOMIC RENT. See also CAPITAL RENT, DEAD RENT, GROUND RENT, IMPUTED, PEPPERCORN RENT, QUITRENT, RACK RENT.

rent control. Fixing of rents by the government and other legislation regulating the terms of a lease. Rent control was part of market and price-control legislation enacted by Congress in 1942, following precedents established during World War I. Modified federal rent control was continued for some time after the close of World War II. At the present time (1964), most of the existing rent-control legislation is maintained by state legislation or municipal regulation authorized by the state legislature.

rent-control case. A case, *Block* v. *Hirsh*, 256 U. S. 135 (1921), in which the United States Supreme Court upheld state and federal legislation fixing rents and extending leases at the close of World War I. The wartime housing emergency, said the court, had temporarily clothed the landlord-tenant relationship with a preponderant public interest and, as a consequence, had brought that relationship within the scope of the same sort of regulatory power that government normally exerted over public utilities.

rentier. A person who receives a fixed income from land, stocks, or bonds.

reorganization bond. See explanation under BOND.

reparations. Cash or materials collected from or charged to defeated nations as a war indemnity. The term was used by the Allied and Associated Powers in the Treaty of Versailles following World War I, and has been used after World War II particularly with reference to the collection of war indemnity from current production in occupied Germany.

repatriation. A return to the country of origin. The term is often used to describe the process of liquidating foreign investments and reinvesting the proceeds in the investor's own country.

replacement-cost standard. As applied to the valuation of a corporation's capital assets, the value as determined by the cost of replacing equipment with new models and designs capable of performing operations identical to those performed by the old equipment. See also VALUATION.

replacement demand. Demand for capital goods or durable consumer goods created because of depreciation or obsolescence. See also DEMAND.

representative good. A term sometimes applied to a document which is evidence of the ownership or an interest in the ownership of wealth; for example, a stock certificate, a bond, or a mortgage. Thus, theoretically, a representative good is one kind of ECONOMIC GOOD. See also WEALTH.

representative money. Money fully secured by gold or silver. Thus defined, silver certificates are the only representative money in general circulation in the United States today (1964) and these are being replaced by FEDERAL RESERVE NOTES. GOLD CERTIFICATES, another kind of representative money, are issued by the Treasury to the federal reserve banks, but these banks use them only for reserve purposes. Occasionally the term is used for any kind of money fully redeemable in gold or silver. See also MONEY.

repressive tax. A tax which discourages production and thus reduces potential tax income. See also TAX.

reproduction-cost standard. As applied to the valuation of a corporation's capital assets, the cost, as of a specific date, of reproducing the assets in question less an allowance for depreciation for the period during which the existing assets have been in use. See also VALUATION.

repudiation. As applied to finance, refusal to honor a debt; generally used to describe the action of a government in refusing to pay its debt in whole or in part.

resale price agreements. See explanation under FAIR-TRADE PRACTICES ACTS.

resale price-maintenance cases. See BEECH-NUT PACKING CASE and *OLD DEARBORN DISTRIBUTING CO. v. SEAGRAM DISTILLERS CORP.*

reservation price. The highest offered price at which a seller still refuses to sell. He will sell at any figure above the reservation price. Sometimes the term is used to indicate the minimum price at which a seller will sell. See also PRICE.

reserve bank credit. BANK CREDIT created by the FEDERAL RESERVE BANKS. Reserve bank credit may take the form of: (1) loans to member banks through REDISCOUNT operations based upon PROMISSORY NOTES properly secured; (2) loans to member banks, collateral security being United States BONDS, CERTIFICATES OF INDEBTEDNESS, TREASURY BILLS, TREASURY NOTES; and (3) ACCEPTANCES purchased.

reserve city bank. See explanation under CENTRAL RESERVE CITY BANK.

reserve ratio. The percentage of a bank's total deposits which the bank keeps in liquid assets as a reserve against deposits. Normally the law establishes a minimum reserve ratio for various classes of banks. The higher the reserve ratio, the less opportunity there is for the creation of bank loans through DEPOSIT CURRENCY (*q.v.*). Hence, regulation of the reserve ratio is often suggested as a means of controlling inflation or deflation. See also BANK RESERVES.

reserves. Money or property set aside usually for some specific purpose. For example, it is common business practice to set aside, from each year's earnings, a sum to cover depreciation of certain CAPITAL ASSETS; and banks are required to set aside reserves against deposits. See also BANK RESERVES, EXCESS RESERVES, MONETARY RESERVES, RESERVE RATIO.

restraint of trade. Price fixing, the creation of a monopoly, or practices of a related nature which are designed to hamper the free exchange of goods and services or have the effect of reducing competition.

restrictive indorsement. An indorsement which limits the further negotiability of the instrument indorsed. See also INDORSEMENT.

Resumption Act. An act of Congress, 1875. It provided for the redemption of GREENBACKS in specie and for the gradual reduction of greenbacks in circulation.

retaliatory duty. A customs duty designed to penalize foreign countries for alleged discriminatory trade practices or to coerce them into making trade concessions. See also CUSTOMS DUTY.

returns to scale of plant. The relation between quantity of output of a business enterprise and the quantity of the various FACTORS OF PRODUCTION used in attaining that output. As a given enterprise first begins to expand its activities, assuming that the factors of production are acquired in optimum proportions as needed, output normally increases at an accelerated rate relative to the increments of the factors added. As economies consequent upon DIVISION OF LABOR and other cost-saving methods are exhausted, there follows a period when output increases more or less in proportion to new increments of the factors. As expansion continues, additional increments of the factors may produce a disproportionately low rate of increased output because of lack of intimate firsthand knowledge of operations on the part of management, delegation of responsibilities, inevitable delays in rendering decisions, and, in general, the complicated routine associated with very large organizations.

revalorization. Attempted restoration by government of a former value of a monetary unit.

revaluation. The process of restoring the value of a depreciated currency within a country. The principal methods are to reduce the demand for, or to increase the supply of, foreign BILLS OF EXCHANGE, and to lower the domestic price level by decreasing the credit supply or by other deflationary measures.

revenue. As applied to public finance, the term refers to government income from taxation, duties, etc. According to some authorities, the term may also be applied to government receipts from the sales of stock, land, and other such property, and from fees; hence all PUBLIC REVENUE. The term is less commonly applied to the income of corporations and private individuals.

revenue bond. See explanation under BOND.

revenue expenditure. An amount paid to meet an expense of an enterprise; hence, it is to be distinguished from a capital expenditure which adds to the value of the enterprise.

revocable letter of credit. See explanation under LETTER OF CREDIT.

revolving credit fund. An arrangement whereby a consumer may purchase goods up to a stipulated amount and is given 6 months or more to pay for them, new purchases being permitted as payments for previous ones are made. A revolving credit fund is thus a form of INSTALLMENT BUYING. In recent years such funds have replaced, to a substantial extent, the conventional 30-day retail-store charge accounts in the purchase of soft goods.

revolving fund. A sum of money which is constantly renewed as it is used, either by further appropriations or by income from the activities it finances, thus leaving a balance at all times.

revolving letter of credit. See explanation under LETTER OF CREDIT.

Ricardian theory of rent. See ECONOMIC RENT.

rigged market. The condition which exists when purchases and sales are manipulated to such an extent as to distort a normal supply-and-demand price.

right-to-work laws. Legislation in about one third of the states of the United States which makes it illegal for labor contracts to provide for the establishment of a UNION SHOP (*q.v.*).

risk. The possibility of loss. The term is commonly used to describe the possibility of loss from some particular hazard, as fire risk, war risk, credit risk, etc. It also describes the possibility of loss by an investor who, in popular speech, is often referred to as a *risk bearer*.

risk bearer. See explanation under RISK.

risk capital. See VENTURE CAPITAL.

risk-capital pooling. Augmenting the available volume of venture capital in a particular area, or for any particular constituency of potential borrowers, through the establishment of a fund to which various individuals or institutions, particularly banks, contribute assets or credit. Plans of this sort are occasionally broached especially to help small business. One such, recently suggested in the United States, would establish a special fund or pool of lending capital in each of the 12 federal reserve districts, the capital or credit to be contributed by the member banks of the district. The fund, administered by businessmen rather than by bankers, would provide loans to small businessmen at low rates of interest. The loans might qualify for rediscount by the federal reserve bank of the district and 90 per cent of each loan might be guaranteed by the federal government.

rival demand. See COMPOSITE DEMAND.

rival supply. See COMPOSITE SUPPLY.

Robinson-Patman Act. An act of Congress, 1936. It prohibits those engaged in interstate commerce from either receiving or granting special price or service concessions in the sale of commodities when such concessions substantially lessen competition. Different prices to different customers are permitted when those price variations are caused by genuine differences in production and selling costs, or by efforts to meet some new form of competition. The act authorizes the Federal Trade Commission to determine limits for discounts on quantity sales, a provision designed particularly to prevent abuses by CHAIN STORES.

Rochdale principles. Criteria for conducting a CONSUMER CO-OPERATIVE, generally attributed to Charles Howarth and a group of fellow workers in Rochdale, England, who, in 1844, organized there one of the earliest successful co-operative enterprises. The principles include: (1) granting of one vote only to each member regardless of the number of shares owned; (2) sale of goods for cash and at current market prices; (3) apportioning any income, beyond expenses and RESERVES, pro rata according to the total amount of purchases made; (4) permitting no restrictions on membership; (5) allowing only nominal interest payments on capital invested; and (6) requiring a reserve for educational purposes. See also CONSUMER CO-OPERATIVE.

roll-back. A popular expression denoting a governmental policy of establishing, as the legal price, an earlier and lower price than the existing market price. Normally this is accomplished by a public subsidy to producers or distributors to compensate them for the difference between the higher existing market price and the lower legally fixed price.

rolling stock. The physical property of a railroad that operates on its own wheels on rails. Locomotives, passenger and freight cars, wrecking derricks, etc., are a part of the rolling stock of a railroad.

root-mean-square deviation. See STANDARD DEVIATION.

rotating shifts. In an enterprise where a 24-hour interval is divided into two or three shifts or working periods, the practice of interchanging employees in such a way that over a period of time they will have taken a turn on each of the two or three shifts instead of being confined to a particular shift. See also SHIFT.

roundabout production. See INDIRECT PRODUCTION.

round-of-wage increases. A popular term to identify any one of several periods in which there was a broad advance in the wage level in the United States. For example a so-called "first round" of wage increases occurred between the end of World War II and the autumn of 1946. In 1947 there was a second "round"; in 1948, a third; and in 1949, a fourth. In every "round" the amounts involved in the increase differed widely among occupations, among industries, and, in many cases, even among concerns in the same industry.

royalty. As applied to income, compensation resulting from the use of a patent, copyright, or other property. The royalty is usually a percentage of the sales value of an article or service in the production of which the patent, copyright, or other property has been exploited.

Rubber Study Group. An informal group of representatives of the principal rubber-producing and rubber-consuming countries formed in 1944 to discuss the world position of rubber and to offer the governments of interested states its advice and counsel on issues relating to the rubber industry.

rule of reason. A criterion for judging alleged infringements of the antitrust laws, first adopted by the United States Supreme Court in 1911 in the American Tobacco and Standard Oil cases. Mere size was not to be considered an offense; the intent to restrain trade or to monopolize was set forth as the crucial factor. See also STANDARD OIL CASE.

runaway inflation. Serious and unusually severe INFLATION (*q.v.*).

runaway shop. A business organization that moves from one location to another primarily to escape unionization of its employees or the application of labor laws. See also SHOP.

running cost. See VARIABLE COST.

run on a bank. A sudden demand on the part of a large number of depositors for the withdrawal of their funds on deposit in a bank. Such a run is usually caused by fear that the bank in question is financially unsound.

Rural Electrification Administration. A unit of the Department of Agriculture of the United States which makes loans, preferably to public bodies, co-operatives, and nonprofit and limited-dividend corporations for the construction of rural electric facilities to serve rural people in areas where no central-station electric service is available.

S

sabotage. In industrial disputes, the practice of slowing down production or otherwise making production unprofitable, resorted to by employees who believe they have a grievance against their employer. Sabotage may take the form of merely wasting time, or it may take the form of actual destruction of machinery or of the manipulation of machinery to make it temporarily unworkable or less efficient.

safe-deposit company. Generally, a corporation that provides a vault in which are located safes and other similar receptacles for the custody of securities, important papers, jewelry, and other valuable personal property. The receptacles are rented to users, and access to the vault is provided during certain hours of the day.

safety-fund bank system. A plan put into effect in 1829 by the state of New York whereby all the banks within the state were required to contribute to an insurance fund designed to protect BANK DEPOSITS and to guarantee the redemption of bank notes at par. The plan required of each bank annual contributions equal to $\frac{1}{2}$ of 1 per cent of its capital until such a time as the fund reached an amount equal to 3 per cent of the total banking capital employed in the state. Thereafter, pro rata contributions were required to maintain the fund at this level. The fund was the predecessor of various state and federal schemes to insure bank deposits.

***St. Louis and O'Fallon Ry. Co.* v. *United States*.** See RAILWAY VALUATION CASE.

Saint-Simonians. The followers of Claude Henri de Rouvroy, Comte de Saint-Simon (1760–1825), who is credited with founding French socialism. The movement early took the form of a religious cult, the disciples of which believed that private property was the cause of human exploitation and wished to abolish it. They maintained that, through the laws of inheritance, private property fell into the hands of those incompetent to use it for the benefit of society; hence, the state, they argued, should become the sole inheritor of all forms of wealth.

salary. Compensation for services rendered, paid at fixed intervals. The term implies work of an executive or clerical nature in contrast to manual labor. Occasionally called *stipend.*

sales tax. A tax levied on the sale of goods and services at one or more stages in the process of distribution. The tax may, for example, be levied on the sale of a commodity every time it changes hands. Such a tax is commonly called a *turnover* or a *transactions* *tax.* Or the tax may be levied on the sale of a commodity only upon its transfer of ownership at one particular time. Thus, only the sales of manufacturers may be taxed when those sales represent completed products; only the sales of wholesalers may be taxed when goods pass into the hands of retailers; or only retail sales may be taxed as the goods pass into the hands of consumers. See also TAX.

sampling. A process of inductive mathematical reasoning whereby qualified quantitative generalizations with respect to an entire aggregate of phenomena, having certain characteristics in common, are drawn from a comparatively limited number of observations. There are various methods of sampling and various mathematical techniques for arriving at generalizations. A simple illustration may be cited in the case of a large aggregate such as the price per dozen of grade-A eggs in New York City. Suppose a RANDOM SAMPLE of 1,600 (N) representative prices is gathered, the results are arranged in a FREQUENCY DISTRIBUTION, and the ARITHMETIC MEAN and STANDARD DEVIATION (σ) are calculated at 80 cents and 5 cents, respectively. From this one sample it can be estimated what the standard deviation, called the *standard error of the mean*, would be in a frequency distribution constructed from the means of an indefinite number of samples, such as the above, all containing the same number of items. The generalized equation for the standard error of the mean ($\sigma_{\bar{x}}$) is:

$$\sigma_{\bar{x}} = \frac{\sigma}{\sqrt{N}}$$

and, in the above example,

$$\sigma_{\bar{x}} = \frac{0.05}{\sqrt{1{,}600}} = 0.00125.$$

In a NORMAL DISTRIBUTION, 99.7 per cent of the items fall within three standard deviations of the mean. It may be assumed, then, in this example, that there are 99.7 chances out of 100 that the obtained mean of 80 cents is not more than \$0.00375 (3 × 0.00125) away, plus or minus, from the unknown mean of the total aggregate. See also AREA SAMPLE, PURPOSIVE SAMPLE, QUOTA SAMPLE, RANDOM SAMPLE.

satiety, law of. See explanation under MARGINAL UTILITY.

saving. **1.** Accumulation of wealth through the postponement of consumption. **2.** The economical use of want-satisfying goods. See also FLUID SAVINGS, OFFSETS TO SAVINGS, OVERSAVING.

savings and loan association. See FEDERAL SAVINGS AND LOAN ASSOCIATION.

savings bank. A bank, the principal function of which is to accept time deposits and to invest its funds in such securities as the law permits for such banks. A savings bank may be a MUTUAL SAVINGS BANK, a STOCK SAVINGS BANK, or a GUARANTY SAVINGS BANK. See also BANK.

savings bond. See explanation under BOND.

Say's law. The assertion that the total supply of economic goods must necessarily always equal the total demand for them. The assertion is supported by the argument that goods really exchange for goods, money being merely a medium of exchange. All goods produced, therefore, represent a demand as well as a supply. Hence, any increase in production is an increase in demand, and any general overproduction is impossible. The law is derived from Jean Baptiste Say (1767-1832).

scab. A person who works under conditions contrary to those prescribed by a labor union, or who accepts employment in an establishment where the regular employees are on strike.

Scandinavian Monetary Union. An agreement by Denmark, Norway, and Sweden (1873 and 1875) which provided that the gold and silver coins of any one of these states would be lawful money in all three, and that bank notes issued by any one state would be accepted in the others at par. Difficulties arose during the period of World War I, and in 1924 Sweden withdrew. The Union has not been revived.

scarcity value. Value caused by a demand for a good, the supply of which cannot be increased. Antique furniture is an example. See also VALUE.

scatter chart. A graphic device which displays actual relationships between two variables by spot markings, and usually the average relationship between them by a mathematically constructed curve. In the diagram on p. 296, black dots indicate actual relationships between the GROSS NATIONAL PRODUCT and private domestic investments in the United States for the years 1919 to 1928, inclusive, as shown in the table on p. 295.

The solid line, called the *line of regression*, indicates the average relationship between these two variables during the same period. Its mathematical equation is:

$$y = -2.58 + 0.2029x.$$

The equation is computed according to the LEAST-SQUARES METHOD. The *standard error of estimate* (S_y) measures the significance of this line, that is, the extent to which the spot markings are in close proximity to it. The standard error of estimate is the STANDARD

Year	Billions of dollars	
	Gross national product, x	Private domestic investments, y
1919	77.1	17.2
1920	86.2	18.5
1921	70.3	9.2
1922	72.5	10.3
1923	84.3	15.6
1924	83.4	13.3
1925	90.0	15.3
1926	95.3	16.8
1927	93.5	15.2
1928	95.6	14.9
Number of cases 10 (N)		

DEVIATION (σ) measured from the line of regression. Its value in the present example is 2.17. It may be computed by means of the following equation:

$$S_y^2 = \frac{(\Sigma y^2) - a\Sigma(y) - b\Sigma(xy)}{N}.$$

In the same diagram the dotted lines show the limits of the standard error of estimate. Within these limits are about 68 per cent of the cases, this being the approximate constant proportion of cases within one standard variation plus and one standard variation minus the ARITHMETIC MEAN. The *coefficient of correlation* (r) is an abstract measure indicating the degree of relationship between the two variables. It is used extensively in economic calculations to compare the degree of relationship between one pair of variables with that between another. The coefficient of correlation in the present example is 0.6311. It may be computed from the following equation:

$$r = \sqrt{1 - \frac{S_y^2}{\sigma_y^2}}.$$

Unity indicates perfect correlation; zero indicates the absence of any correlation. A correlation of 0.6311 is considered medium. If calculations similar to the above are made for the gross national product and personal consumer expenditures during the same period, the coefficient of correlation will be found to be 0.9733, a definitely high correlation.

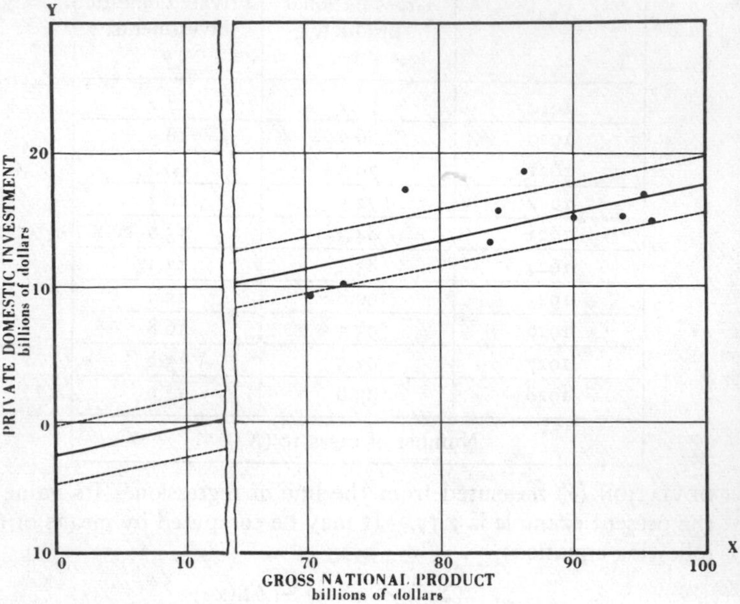

Schechter case. A case, *Schechter Poultry Corp.* v. *United States*, 295 U. S. 495 (1935), in which the Supreme Court of the United States invalidated the National Industrial Recovery Act and the fair-practice codes which that statute authorized. The court held the statute unconstitutional on two principal grounds. These were: (1) that Congress did not establish adequate standards for the code-making authority confided to the President under the law, and thus delegated the substance of legislative power to the President; and (2) that production and trade, which the statute attempted to regulate, are primarily matters of state concern, and their attempted regulation had only an indirect relation to interstate commerce; consequently the regulation could not be justified under Congress' commerce power and constituted, in fact, an attempt to regulate matters reserved to the states under the 10th Amendment. See also *United States* v. *Darby Lumber Co.*

***Schechter Poultry Corp.* v. *United States*.** See SCHECHTER CASE.

schedule. 1. As applied to economic analysis, a list setting forth a series of quantities that depend upon two variables. For example, a LIQUIDITY PREFERENCE schedule sets forth the various quantities of money that are demanded at various interest rates, a PROPENSITY TO CONSUME schedule lists consumer expenditures that are made at varying income levels, etc. Such schedules are customarily shown in the form of a graph with the independent variable, that is, the quantity that increases by increments deliberately determined, plotted along the *X* axis, and the dependent variable plotted along the *Y* axis. For examples, see DEMAND, SUPPLY. **2.** As generally used in industry, the term means a plan for future operations or procedure. Thus, a production schedule sets forth the quantity of goods expected to be manufactured within a certain time, and a sales schedule the quantity to be sold. The term may refer merely to a list of some kind, such as a price schedule.

schedule demand. See explanation under DEMAND.

schedule supply. See explanation under SUPPLY.

school desegregation cases. See *BROWN* v. *BOARD OF EDUCATION OF TOPEKA*.

schools of economic thought. A more or less systematic body of doctrine concerning fundamental aspects of economic behavior developed by certain leading economic theorists and further expounded by their disciples. See CAMBRIDGE SCHOOL, CAMERALISM, CLASSICAL SCHOOL, HISTORICAL SCHOOL, KEYNESIAN ECONOMICS, MARGINAL UTILITY SCHOOL, MERCANTILISM, OPTIMIST SCHOOL, ORGANIC SCHOOL, PHYSIOCRATS. See also ECONOMICS.

scrip. Various kinds of documents indicating that the bearer is entitled to receive something, for example, fractional paper money issued in the past by banks and the government in the United States, or certificates issued by employers and exchangeable for goods at a COMPANY STORE. The term is sometimes applied to CERTIFICATES OF INDEBTEDNESS and to certificates issued provisionally to identify partial payment on a subscription for stocks, bonds, or like instruments. During the depression years following 1929, the term was used to indicate temporary currency used within the boundaries of some communities.

scrip dividend. A corporation dividend paid in the form of a promise to pay at a specified time in the future, or when a specified event transpires, or at the will of the corporation. See also DIVIDEND.

seasonal fluctuations. A characteristic often discernible in a time series wherein, over a period of years, each of the 12 months shows more or less regular variations from the SECULAR TREND. There are various statistical methods of calculating seasonal fluctuations in a time series. The appended diagram shows the general seasonal pattern for BANK DEBITS in the United States outside of New York City for the years from 1935 to 1939, inclusive. The curve may be computed by ascertaining the secular trend according to the LEAST-SQUARES METHOD, finding for each month the percentage that the original data bear to the trend value, calculating the ARITHMETIC MEAN of these percentages by months, and finally adjusting these average percentages to a mean of 100 per cent. For the original data, see TIME-SERIES CHART.

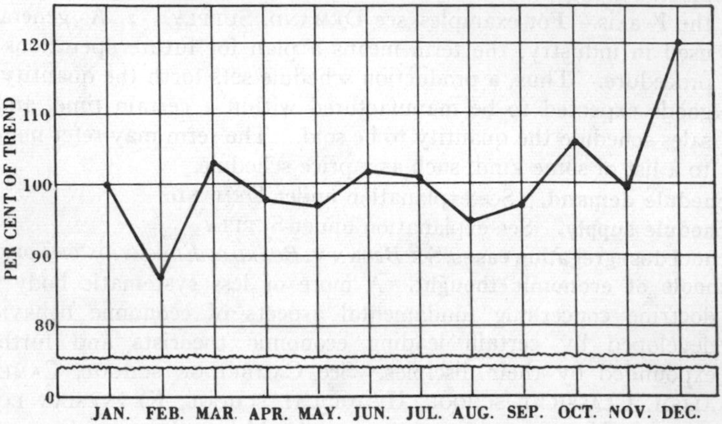

seasonal unemployment. Unemployment caused by seasonal variations in the volume of production of certain industries. The building-construction, clothing, and coal-mining industries, for example, normally maintain full production only during certain seasons of the year. As a rule, therefore, few workers in these industries enjoy full employment the entire year. See also UNEMPLOYMENT.

seasoned security. A security which has a good record of interest or dividend payments, which has been on the market for a period of time, and which has attained a reasonably stable price. See also SECURITY.

seat on the exchange. Membership in a stock exchange organization.

secondary boycott. See explanation under BOYCOTT.

secondary picketing. Picketing of an establishment not directly engaged in a labor dispute but associated in some way with an establishment that is so engaged. See also PICKETING.

secondary reserves. See explanation under BANK RESERVES.

secondary strike. See SYMPATHETIC STRIKE.

secular stagnation. A low level of economic activity over a considerable period of time.

secular trend. Any general tendency of values in a time series to increase or decrease over a period of years. The heavy line in the appended diagram shows the secular trend of BANK DEBITS in the United States outside of New York City from 1935 to 1939, inclusive. There are various methods of estimating secular trend in a time series. The linear curve in the diagram may be computed by the LEAST-SQUARES METHOD, the equation being:

$$y = 16.7386 + 0.3682x.$$

For the original data, see TIME-SERIES CHART.

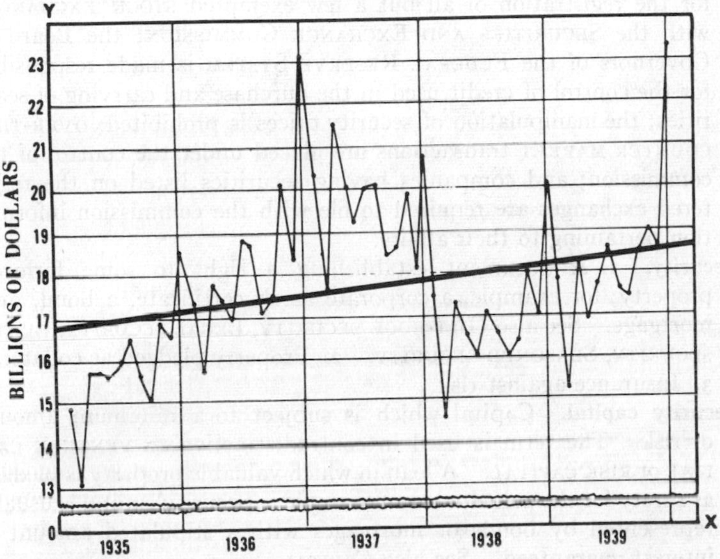

Securities Act. An act of Congress, 1933, designed to protect investors in new issues of securities. The act requires that specific information covering some 32 points on most new security issues be filed with a supervising agency before the securities in question are offered to the public. Those issuing the securities are made responsible for the accuracy and completeness of the information thus disclosed. The act's provisions are intended to secure full and accurate information regarding new security issues for the public; but they do not prohibit speculative issues. The act named the FEDERAL TRADE COMMISSION as the supervising agency, but with the enactment of the SECURITIES EXCHANGE ACT of 1934 the newly created SECURITIES AND EXCHANGE COMMISSION was vested with this authority.

Securities and Exchange Commission. An independent, quasi-judicial agency of the United States government created under the authority of the SECURITIES EXCHANGE ACT of 1934 to administer the provisions of that act, the SECURITIES ACT of 1933, and other comparable legislation. Its primary purpose is to protect the interests of the public and investors against malpractices in the securities markets.

Securities Exchange Act. An act of Congress, 1934, supplementing the Securities Act of 1933. It is designed to protect investors purchasing seasoned securities through brokers. The act provides for the registration of all but a few exempted STOCK EXCHANGES with the SECURITIES AND EXCHANGE COMMISSION; the Board of Governors of the FEDERAL RESERVE SYSTEM is made responsible for the control of credit used in the purchase and carrying of securities; the manipulation of security prices is prohibited; OVER-THE-COUNTER MARKET transactions are placed under the control of the commission; and companies having securities listed on the registered exchanges are required to file with the commission information pertaining to their affairs.

security. 1. A document establishing a right to some form of property; for example, a corporate stock certificate, a bond, or a mortgage. See also GILT-EDGE SECURITY, LEGAL SECURITY, LISTED SECURITY, SEASONED SECURITY. 2. Property pledged as collateral. 3. Insurance against risk.

security capital. Capital which is subject to a minimum amount of risk. The term is used in contradistinction to VENTURE CAPITAL OR RISK CAPITAL. A loan in which valuable property is pledged as surety for the principal is an example. Security capital is usually represented by bonds or mortgages with a stipulated amount of interest guaranteed. See also CAPITAL.

Security Council. One of the two major organs of the United Nations. Its primary function is to preserve the peace of the world, and to that end the Charter of the United Nations permits it to take direct action in the form of diplomatic, economic, and military sanctions if authorized by 7 of the council's 11 members including all of its 5 permanent members, the so-called BIG FIVE. See also UNITED NATIONS.

security exchange. See STOCK EXCHANGE.

segregated appropriation. See explanation under ITEMIZED APPROPRIATION.

seigniorage. A charge made by the government for converting bullion into coins. This charge is sufficiently high to yield a profit. The term is used also to indicate the profit made by marking subsidiary coins at a value higher than the cost of their metal content. Occasionally the term is made synonymous with BRASSAGE.

self-interest. A greater regard for personal welfare than for the welfare of others. The importance of self-interest as an actuating force in human affairs gave rise to the concept of the ECONOMIC MAN used extensively by the CLASSICAL SCHOOL.

self-interest, law of. See HEDONISTIC PRINCIPLE.

self-liquidating. A characteristic of an investment which enables its original cost to be paid from its earnings.

self-sufficient nation. A nation that produces all that it consumes. The attempt to attain such an end is called *economic nationalism.* Modern wants are so numerous that no nation can be absolutely self-sufficient and maintain high levels of living. Self-sufficiency is contrary to the principle of COMPARATIVE ADVANTAGE (*q.v.*) and hence requires the uneconomic production of some things.

sellers' market. The situation which results when, under competitive conditions, the schedules of supply and demand are such that market prices are at a relatively high level, giving the sellers an advantage. In other words, the sellers are disposed to retain their goods and services rather than to sell them at a low price, and the buyers are disposed to acquire the goods and services even if they have to pay a high price. The term is used in contradistinction to BUYERS' MARKET. See also DEMAND, SUPPLY.

sellers seven sale. A stock sold on the floor of a stock exchange with the understanding that delivery will be delayed possibly as much as 7 days, possibly longer, according to whatever time is agreed upon.

seller's surplus. The hypothetical difference between what a seller actually receives for a product and what he would have been willing to sell for if necessary.

selling short. The practice of selling a security that is not owned, but which is borrowed, temporarily, to effect delivery. Short selling is done in anticipation of a decline in the market price. If a decline occurs it may enable the trader to buy the security at a price lower than that for which he sold it, pay the cost of borrowing the security, and make a profit. If the market advances, however, the trader may be forced to buy the security at a higher price than that for which he sold it, and he will have to pay the cost of borrowing the security besides. It is to prevent too great a loss on an advancing market that a STOP-LOSS ORDER is given.

seniority. As applied to labor relations, an employee's length of service in a given establishment. Seniority is often used as a basis for wage rates and promotion.

Senn* v. *Tile Layers Protective Union. A case, 301 U. S. 468 (1937), in which the United States Supreme Court, by upholding a Wisconsin statute which prohibited the issuance of injunctions against "peaceful PICKETING," substantially altered its view in an earlier case [*TRUAX v. CORRIGAN*, 257 U. S. 312 (1921)] that prohibition of the weapon of injunction in certain labor disputes constituted violation of the equal-protection clause of the 14th Amendment. The court attempted to reconcile the two cases by suggesting that the earlier anti-injunction statute tended to legalize militant actions of labor unions which were illegal before the statute was passed, whereas the subsequent anti-injunction statute had no such effect, the picketing in question being "peaceful."

sensitive market. The condition which exists when market prices fluctuate widely in response to good and bad news.

serial bond. See explanation under BOND.

series bond. See explanation under BOND.

Servicemen's Readjustment Act. See G. I. BILL OF RIGHTS.

service utility. Utility created by the rendering of a personal service. The services of a lawyer, physician, or teacher, for example, are service utilities. See also UTILITY.

severance tax. A tax levied on natural resources removed from land or water. See also TAX.

severance wage. See DISMISSAL WAGE.

share cropper. A tenant farmer who, in addition to land and living quarters, receives seed, stock, and implements from the landlord and who shares the crops with the landlord, credits advanced by the landlord being deducted from the tenant's share and occasionally, also, certain charges for maintenance and improvements.

shares. See explanation under CAPITAL STOCK.

share-the-work plan. See WORK-SHARING.

Sheppard-Towner Act. An act of Congress, 1921. It granted federal funds to assist the states in their efforts to promote maternity care and infant welfare.

Sherman Antitrust Act. An act of Congress, 1890, which prohibits combinations or conspiracies in restraint of interstate or foreign trade, and forbids monopoly or the attempt to monopolize. It allows any person injured by another's violation of the act to sue the offending party, and, if the fact of his injury is judicially sustained, to recover three times the amount of the ascertained damage. Federal authorities may resort to the use of injunctions and prosecution to enforce the act.

Sherman notes. See explanation under TREASURY NOTES.

Sherman Silver Purchase Act. An act of Congress, 1890, which provided for the purchase by the Secretary of the Treasury of 4,500,000 oz. of silver each month, and the issuance in payment therefor of treasury notes of full legal tender. The value of the silver purchased under the act was about $50,000,000 per year.

shift. As applied to labor, a period of working time, usually an interval between stipulated hours of a 24-hour day. For example, a day shift may begin at 8 A.M. and stop at 5 P.M., and a night shift may begin at 9 P.M. and stop at 6 A.M. See also FIXED SHIFT, GRAVEYARD SHIFT, ROTATING SHIFTS.

shifting of taxation. The transfer of the incidence of a tax, usually in the course of ordinary business transactions, from the person upon whom the tax has been levied to some other person. See also INCIDENCE OF TAXATION.

shinplaster. A derisive term applied at various times in the United States to depreciated paper currency. After the American Revolution it was applied to Continental paper currency; later, about 1837, to various notes issued by private bankers; and again, during the Civil War, to Confederate currency.

ship broker. An individual who, for a fee or commission, provides vessels with cargoes and shippers with freight space on ships.

shoe machinery case. A case, *United States* v. *United Shoe Machinery Corp.*, 258 U. S. 451 (1922), in which the Supreme Court of the United States declared that tying clauses in contracts, which provided for the leasing and selling of patented or unpatented articles on condition that purchaser or lessee did not deal with competitors of lessor or seller, lessened competition and violated Sec. 3 of the Clayton Act. See also CLAYTON ACT, TIE-IN SALE.

shop. An emporium; also an establishment where a particular kind of work is carried on; for example, a paint shop, a machine shop, or a carpenter shop. In referring to labor relations the term is commonly applied to an individual factory or to an entire enterprise. See also CLOSED SHOP, OPEN SHOP, PREFERENTIAL SHOP, RUNAWAY SHOP, UNION SHOP.

shopping center. See SHOPPING MALL.

shopping mall. A community of retail stores and related establishments devoted exclusively to pedestrian traffic. Shopping malls are frequently found on the outskirts of cities, where spacious automobile parking space is provided adjacent to the mall. In an attempt to meet this suburban competition, however, city merchants have developed shopping malls in downtown districts by prohibiting vehicular traffic on certain city blocks, by providing more sidewalk area, often attractively landscaped, and by eliminating the hazards of street crossing, thus adding to the comfort and safety of shoppers. Merchants in a shopping mall often engage in joint promotional activities such as advertising the mall as a convenient and desirable place to shop. Also called *shopping center*.

Shreveport case. A case, *Houston East and West Texas Ry. Co.* v. *United States*, 234 U. S. 342 (1914), in which the Supreme Court of the United States decided that in order to overcome injurious discrimination to interstate commerce resulting, in certain special situations, from the relation of interstate and intrastate railway rates, Congress, acting through an appropriate authority like the Interstate Commerce Commission, can order the discrimination removed. This order may issue even if it should result in the federal government fixing rates on commerce between points which are wholly intrastate.

shrinkage. The loss in weight or volume of a commodity due to evaporation of moisture or other similar cause.

sight bill. See explanation under BILL.

sight draft. See explanation under DRAFT.

silent partner. A person participating in a business enterprise organized as a partnership, who supplies capital but assumes no active responsibility in the management. See also PARTNERSHIP.

silver certificate. A form of United States paper money, redeemable in silver. Silver certificates originated in 1878 and are now (1964) being replaced by FEDERAL RESERVE NOTES.

Silver Purchase Act. An act of Congress, 1934. It authorized the United States Treasury to purchase silver under certain conditions and up to specified amounts and to issue SILVER CERTIFICATES on the basis of the silver thus purchased. It also authorized the President to require that all silver stocks be delivered to the government and added to the monetary reserves. Subsequently the President ordered that all domestic stocks of silver be delivered to the mint within 90 days. Owners were paid the mint price of $1.29 per fine ounce, less a seigniorage of $61\frac{8}{25}$ per cent.

simple interest. Interest calculated on a principal sum but not on any interest that has been earned by that principal sum. See also INTEREST.

sinecure. A position of value which involves limited or no responsibility and requires little if any labor or active service.

single entry. A general term for all methods of keeping accounts other than double-entry bookkeeping. The term is always used to indicate a method of bookkeeping containing only accounts with persons. See also BOOKKEEPING, DOUBLE ENTRY.

single-schedule tariff. A tariff that specifies only one rate of duty for any given article regardless of the country of origin of that article. There may be exceptions as, for example, when special rates are established in a reciprocity agreement, but such special rates do not constitute a second or supplementary schedule. Also called *general tariff* and *unilinear tariff*. See also TARIFF.

single standard. See MONOMETALLISM.

single tax. Any tax which constitutes a government's sole source of tax revenue. There have been various proposals for supporting a government on a single tax, such as a tax levied on expenses, on houses, on income, or on capital. The term has come to be applied particularly to Henry George's ideas of making a tax on land value the sole source of public revenue. See also LAND-VALUE TAX, TAX.

sinking fund. A fund to which periodical contributions are made for the purpose of ultimately paying a debt or replacing assets of some kind.

sinking-fund bond. See explanation under BOND.

sit-down strike. A strike in which the employees cease work but do not leave the establishment in which they are employed. See also STRIKE.

sixteen to one. The ratio of pure metal in the United States silver dollar to the pure metal in the United States gold dollar as established by Congress in 1834. At that time the pure-metal content of the silver dollar was established at 371.25 grains, and that of the gold dollar at 23.2 grains. In the presidential campaign of 1896 this phrase became the slogan of the Democratic party and its candidate, William J. Bryan, in their effort to remonetize silver at the old rate to gold and re establish bimetallism. See also BIMETALLISM, REMONETIZATION.

skewness. The extent to which a FREQUENCY DISTRIBUTION (*q.v.*) is asymmetric. It may be measured by subtracting the MODE (*q.v.*) from the ARITHMETIC MEAN (*q.v.*) and dividing the result by the STANDARD DEVIATION (*q.v.*), or by the following formula:

$$sk = \frac{q_2 - q_1}{q_2 + q_1}$$

when

q_2 = the difference between the third QUARTILE (*q.v.*) and the MEDIAN (*q.v.*),

q_1 = the difference between the median and the first quartile.

sliding-scale tariff. A system of tariff duties in which the duties vary with the current prices of the articles imported. The duties may be AD VALOREM or SPECIFIC. The usual practice is to reduce the duties as prices rise, and advance the duties as prices decline. See also TARIFF.

slow asset. An asset which can be converted into cash at approximately its book value only after a considerable length of time. See also ASSET.

slowdown strike. A deliberate and purposeful slowing down of production by employees. See also STRIKE.

slum clearance. The razing of old buildings, usually tenements, in congested slum areas and the construction in their stead of modern, low-priced housing and various public works, thereby rehabilitating the entire area. Such operations by private corporations or specially organized housing authorities are frequently encouraged by governments by a promise of tax exemption, tax reduction, or other favors.

small business. According to the United States Census Bureau, all establishments employing less than 100 persons. Other divisions of the Department of Commerce use different criteria in determining what constitutes small business in each of several areas of activity: manufacturers, less than 100 employees; wholesalers, annual sales less than $200,000; retail and service enterprises, annual sales less than $50,000. Others have identified small business: (1) as respects size, not more than $1 million annual sales, $500,000 in total assets, 250 employees; (2) as respects management, independent organization with owner management; (3) as respects financing, stock held by owner-managers; (4) as respects area of operations, local. According to these criteria 95 per cent of the business of the nation is small business, and one half of the nonagricultural employees are employed by small business.

small-loan law. Laws enacted in many of the states of the United States limiting the interest rate usually to 3 or $3\frac{1}{2}$ per cent per month on loans of less than $300 made by finance companies and banks.

Smith-Hughes Act. An act of Congress, 1917, authorizing federal appropriations which are expended by the states under state plans for the promotion of vocational education. The work has been expanded and appropriations increased through the *George-Reed Act*, the *George-Ellzey Act*, and the *George-Deen Act* amended by the *Vocational Education Act* of 1946.

Smith-Lever Act. An act of Congress, 1914. It granted federal funds to the states for aid in agricultural extension work carried on jointly by the United States Department of Agriculture and the state agricultural colleges.

smuggling. The entry into a country of dutiable articles without passing them through the customhouse or submitting them to the revenue officers for examination and the payment of duties.

***Smyth* v. *Ames*.** A relatively early case, 169 U. S. 466 (1898), in which the question of the power of a state legislature (Nebraska) to fix the maximum rates of transportation companies came before the United States Supreme Court under the due process clause of the 14th Amendment, and in which that tribunal effectively annulled maximum rates established by an administrative tribunal, operating under the legislature's authority, because such rates were deemed by the court to be unreasonably low and therefore to constitute a deprivation of the company's property. The court, however, clearly implied that a state legislature, and public-service bodies operating under its authority, might fix rates and that the courts would interpose no objection if they found the rates to be reasonable. The court also laid down certain standards for the evaluation of the property of a public utility which public rate-making bodies might consider in establishing a fair return. The degree of judicial control over the fact-finding activity and the general discretion of public rate-making bodies, evinced in this decision, has since been considerably reduced.

social credit. An economic doctrine which claims that there exists a constant deficiency of PURCHASING POWER in the economic system as now constituted, compensation for which must be provided by CREDIT created by the government. The doctrine was advanced by Major C. H. Douglas, a Scottish engineer, after World War I. The claim of purchasing-power deficiency rests, apparently, upon what is called the "$A + B$ theorem," A and B representing two kinds of costs. A costs are payments for wages, salaries, and dividends within a given enterprise, and B costs are payments made to other organizations, such, for example, as for raw materials and machinery. It is claimed that only A costs, being payments to consumers, create purchasing power. Purchasing power, represented by A, therefore cannot meet total costs, represented by $A + B$. The proposed remedy lies, according to the doctrine, in a system of controlled retail prices consisting of discounts from base prices. Retailers might sell at the discounted price and receive compensation from the government in the form of paper money, or they might sell at the base price and deliver to the consumer SCRIP equivalent to the amount of the discount. The scrip could then be deposited in banks that would, in turn, receive compensation from the government. In either case the government would make up to the consumer the purchasing power which the producer had allegedly failed to pass on to him. In addition, the doctrine proposes a system of national dividends in cash to every citizen, these dividends representing payments for what is conceived to be a new FACTOR OF PRODUCTION, that is, heritage from previous generations. Shortly after World War II the system of social credit was investigated by a committee of eminent economists representing the British Labor Party and was rejected as fallacious.

social insurance. A term embracing various kinds of insurance, usually offered by the government and designed to protect wage earners and those in lower income brackets against various hazards. Unemployment, accident, health, and maternity insurance and old-age pensions are examples. See also INSURANCE.

socialism. A collective system of ownership and operation of the means of production, usually by the government. By "means of production" is meant CAPITAL GOODS (*q.v.*). During the course of the 19th century the terms "socialism" and "COMMUNISM" (*q.v.*) reversed their meanings. Socialism at one time referred to the ideas of certain social reformers who were called Christian Socialists and utopian socialists, some of whom established colonies in America based on principles of communism in various forms. On the other hand, Karl Marx, generally regarded as the architect of modern socialism, at first referred to his program as communism. As the experiments of the above-mentioned social reformers gradually fell into disrepute, Karl Marx and his followers began referring to their program as socialism, and it is by that term that their own program is known today, although in popular speech socialism and communism are very frequently confused. For the more important kinds of socialism see CHRISTIAN SOCIALISM, FABIAN SOCIALISM, GUILD SOCIALISM, MUNICIPAL SOCIALISM, STATE SOCIALISM, UTOPIAN SOCIALISM. See also ECONOMIC SYSTEM.

socialized medicine. See STATE MEDICINE.

social legislation. Laws to improve living conditions and to provide the individual with some degree of security against various hazards such as unemployment, accident, illness, old age, and the like. In the United States various kinds of social legislation have been enacted under the police power of the states and under the taxation, commerce, and other powers of the federal government. See also SOCIAL INSURANCE, SOCIAL SECURITY ACT, OLD-AGE AND SURVIVORS' INSURANCE, UNEMPLOYMENT INSURANCE.

Social Security Act. An act of Congress, 1935, which, with subsequent amendments, provides insurance to certain wage earners for loss of income due to unemployment or old age, and provides protection for their families in the event of death. OLD-AGE AND SURVIVORS' INSURANCE is administered by the federal government. UNEMPLOYMENT INSURANCE is administered under a joint federal and state plan. In addition, the act provides joint federal and state aid to needy old people, dependent children, and blind persons. Federal grants to the states, supplementing state and local funds, are also provided for maternal and child-health aid, and for crippled children and child-welfare services.

Social Security Administration. A branch of the Department of Health, Education and Welfare. It administers federal old-age and survivors' insurance; approves state unemployment-insurance laws, state arrangements for old-age assistance, and aid to dependent children and the blind; and performs other functions involving economic security and related subjects.

social-security cases. Two cases, *Helvering* v. *Davis*, 301 U. S. 619 (1937) and *Steward Machine Co.* v. *Davis*, 301 U. S. 548 (1937), in which the Supreme Court of the United States held constitutional the taxes levied under the SOCIAL SECURITY ACT of 1935 (*q.v.*). The taxes were levied for the maintenance of an extensive system of social insurance for wage earners in the administration of which both the federal and state governments participated. The court declared that such taxes were levied for the general welfare and that the program they financed did not result in coercing the states in violation of the 10th Amendment of the United States Constitution.

social-security tax. A tax levied usually upon employers and/or employees, directly or indirectly, to finance public insurance plans such as the OLD-AGE AND SURVIVORS' INSURANCE system and the UNEMPLOYMENT-INSURANCE system in the United States.

social wealth. All useful things, material and immaterial, free and scarce, enjoyed by a people. The term is broad enough to include such things as the inventive genius of a people, knowledge acquired from the past, climate, and beautiful scenery. Some authorities, however, give this phrase the same narrow economic significance as they give the word WEALTH, and use these two terms interchangeably. Others make social wealth synonymous with NATIONAL WEALTH. See also WEALTH.

social workshop. Historically, an association of workers in the same trade who co-operatively pool their tools and skills and share their earnings in common. Each social workshop was envisaged as a unit. The various units would, it was believed, center about some main establishment, and these main establishments, scattered throughout a nation, would reinforce one another by giving mutual aid and assistance. It was anticipated that an economy, devoid of the evils of COMPETITION, would thus develop. The idea was espoused by Louis Blanc (1811–1882), a French economist and historian, especially during the revolutionary period, 1848–1850. Although not so comprehensive a scheme as others, notably the PHALANSTERY or some aspects of OWENISM, the idea gave impetus to the later establishment of numerous co-operative productive societies. See also UTOPIAN SOCIALISM.

soft money. 1. Paper money in contrast to metallic currency. 2. Any national money which is subject to unusual fluctuations in value, both internally and in international exchange. See also MONEY.

soil bank program. A procedure whereby farmers contract to divert certain lands from the production of unneeded crops to long-range conservation uses. Participating farmers receive advice in the particular conservation practices to be pursued and an annual rent for the unused croplands. The program is administered by the Commodity Stabilization Service of the United States Department of Agriculture.

soil conservation. Any one or all of various methods of preventing soil depletion and of restoring soil productivity. Soil conservationists attempt to replace chemical elements in the soil, lost through cropping or leaching, by the application of chemical or organic fertilizers. They try to correct the breakdown of soil structure by proper methods of tillage and crop rotation, and to lessen erosion of topsoil by terracing, contour cultivation, and other methods.

soil-conservation district. A local public agency established under state law in the United States when a majority of the land users in a given area so decide by vote. It is governed by a board of supervisors usually composed of farmers locally elected. The United States government, through its SOIL CONSERVATION SERVICE, and appropriate state agencies, co-operates with the soil-conservation districts to provide technical help in surveying soil-conservation problems and in devising methods for the better use of the land.

Soil Conservation Service. A unit of the Department of Agriculture of the United States, primarily concerned with the department's soil-conservation program. It seeks to secure such physical adjustments in the use of land as will promote a better balanced agriculture, conserve natural resources, and reduce the hazards of flood.

soil erosion. The carrying away of the topsoil through the action of either water or wind.

sole corporation. A corporation which is composed of only one member. See also CORPORATION.

solidarism. A doctrine of mutual dependence. Those who have prospered owe a debt to others who have contributed toward making their prosperity possible, according to the doctrine; and those who have been less fortunate consequently have a moral and even economically justifiable claim upon the more fortunate. Hence, gratuitous insurance against the risks of life, a minimum level of living, free education, minimum-wage-and-hour legislation, public housing, etc. are supported as measures expressing this sense of social solidarity and social equity. To finance these activities, progressive taxation applied to unearned wealth and larger incomes is advocated. The doctrine is a French version of socioethical economics popular at the end of the 19th century. Its chief proponent was Léon Bourgeois (1851–1925), a French statesman and social philosopher.

solvent. The condition which exists when liabilities, other than those representing ownership, amount to less than the total assets. In the statement given below, for example, the liabilities representing ownership amount to $1,200,000. Other liabilities amount to $800,000, while the total assets amount to $2,000,000. A solvent condition therefore exists.

Assets		Liabilities	
Plant	$1,500,000	Bonds	$ 800,000
Cash	500,000	Capital stock	1,200,000
	$2,000,000		$2,000,000

South Carolina v. United States. A case, 199 U. S. 437 (1905), in which the United States Supreme Court declared that state-owned liquor stores might be taxed by the federal government since the rule exempting state instrumentalities from federal taxation involved only such instrumentalities as were strictly governmental in character and did not embrace proprietary activities.

South Sea Bubble. A highly speculative joint-stock venture undertaken in England at the beginning of the 18th century, the chief concern involved having been the South Sea Company. In return for an annual subsidy and a monopoly of the British South Sea trade, this company assumed responsibility for a large part of the national debt. The venture collapsed with substantial losses.

span of control. In organization theory, the number of subordinates who receive direction or supervision from a common leader or superior. The subordinates may in turn be leaders of sub-groups with their respective spans of control.

spearhead money. See explanation under OCCUPATION MONEY.

special assessment. As applied to public finance, a charge made by a government against a landowner for a public improvement adjacent to his property which, while generally beneficial to the community, is especially beneficial to the landowner assessed. See also ASSESSMENT.

special-assessment bond. See explanation under BOND.

special depositary. A bank, not necessarily a member of the Federal Reserve System, authorized, under specified conditions, to retain as deposits for the United States Treasury funds received from the sale of United States government securities. See also DEPOSITARY.

special indorsement. An indorsement that specifies to whose order a check, note, or similar paper is payable or to whom the paper is assigned, and which requires the additional indorsement of the indorsee before payment can be made or the paper can be assigned to another. The term is used in contradistinction to BLANK INDORSEMENT. See also INDORSEMENT.

specialist. As applied to stockbrokers, a broker who buys and sells certain securities on his own account.

specialization of labor. The condition which exists when certain craftsmen confine their work to the production of a specific commodity. Thus, certain craftsmen may make shoes, others may make hats, etc. The term is often used interchangeably with DIVISION OF LABOR.

specialized agency. As applied to the UNITED NATIONS, an international organization, operating within a particular social and economic field, either newly created by the ECONOMIC AND SOCIAL COUNCIL or already established and co-operating with the council for the accomplishment of the general objectives of that body.

specialized capital good. A capital good which can be used for only one purpose or for a very limited number of purposes. The term is used in contradistinction to FREE CAPITAL GOOD. See also CAPITAL GOOD.

specialized management trust. An investment trust whose purchases of securities are confined to those issued by firms in one specific field of industry. See also INVESTMENT TRUST.

special-privilege monopoly. A monopoly resulting from legislative enactments or special favors granted by private companies. Thus, a tariff sufficiently high to prohibit the importation of a commodity might conceivably give a domestic producer complete control of the domestic supply of the commodity in question. The practice, once common among railroads, of granting rebates to certain shippers often enabled those so favored to drive competitors out of business. Historically, special-privilege monopolies were often established by special grant of the sovereign. See also MONOPOLY, TRADE MONOPOLY.

special stock. See explanation under CAPITAL STOCK.

specie. Metallic money.

Specie Circular. An order by President Jackson in 1836 directing that payments for public lands be made in specie. See also SPECIE.

specific duty. A customs duty based on weight, quantity, or other physical characteristics of imported goods. The term is used in contradistinction to AD VALOREM DUTY. See also CUSTOMS DUTY.

speculation. The practice of buying at one time and selling at another time to take advantage of price changes that have occurred during the interval.

speed-up. Any means used to secure more work from employees per hour or day. This may be attempted by raising the minimum standards of work performance, or, if the operations are controlled wholly by machinery, by increasing the speed of the machines.

spending unit. A statistical term normally used to identify a family or other collective group that pools resources and income and spends as a single unit. The term may, however, also embrace individuals.

split-up. The issuance of two or more shares of stock for each share outstanding. This increase in the number of shares outstanding decreases the value per share but does not change the total liability of the issuing corporation for the outstanding capital stock.

spot delivery. Immediate delivery.

spread. The difference between the price bid and the price asked. See also BACK SPREAD, PRICE SPREAD.

stabilization. The prevention of fluctuations in some phase of economic life. Thus, price stabilization means an attempt to keep prices at a constant level. Business stabilization suggests any policy designed to maintain a steady volume of economic activity.

stable money. Money that maintains a reasonably constant value in terms of the commodities and services which it will purchase. See also MONEY.

stamped bond. See explanation under BOND.

stamp tax. A tax, payment of which is secured through the purchase by the taxpayers of stamps of various denominations issued by the taxing authorities, the latter requiring that such stamps be affixed to articles or documents before they may be lawfully sold, purchased, or used. See also TAX.

standard deviation. A statistical measure of the extent of absolute dispersion. variability, or scatter in a FREQUENCY DISTRIBUTION (*q.v.*), obtained by extracting the square root of the ARITHMETIC MEAN of the squares of the deviations from the arithmetic mean of the frequency distribution.

The standard deviation, although the most commonly used measure of dispersion, emphasizes extreme values because the deviations are squared.

This computation is known also as the *quadratic mean* and *root-mean-square average*, the generalized formula being:

$$M_q = \sqrt{\frac{\Sigma(X)^2}{N}}$$

when

M_q = quadratic mean,
X = the numbers to be averaged,
N = the total number of items to be averaged.

Example:

Class interval	Midpoint	Frequency	Deviation from mean (2.454)	Deviation from mean squared	Multiplied by frequency
−0.5 to 0.4	0	10	−2.454	6.022	60.220
0.5 to 1.4	1	30	−1.454	2.114	63.420
1.5 to 2.4	2	40	−0.454	0.206	8.240
2.5 to 3.4	3	50	0.546	0.298	14.900
3.5 to 4.4	4	25	1.546	2.390	59.750
4.5 to 5.4	5	8	2.546	6.482	51.856
		163			258.386

$$\text{Standard deviation} = \sqrt{\frac{258.386}{163}} = \sqrt{1.585} = 1.26.$$

standard error of estimate. See explanation under SCATTER CHART.

standard error of the mean. See explanation under SAMPLING.

standardization. As applied to marketing, the identification of a definite grade, quality, or size of a product by a known term or symbol. Certain standards are first determined, then the product thus standardized is inspected and graded according to those standards and is assigned the appropriate term or symbol.

standard money. Money consisting of a commodity of specified weight and purity, the value of which, as a commodity, equals its value as money. It should be noted, however, that in legal nomenclature the United States silver dollar is referred to as "standard money" although its value as metal is less than its face value. As defined elsewhere in this dictionary, the silver dollar is FIDUCIARY MONEY. There has been no standard money, as here defined, in circulation in the United States since 1933. Previous to that time standard money was in circulation in the form of gold coins. The government accepted gold bullion in unlimited quantities at the rate determined by law which was then $22.67 per ounce of fine gold. Gold could not be bought, therefore, for less than that amount; and as gold bullion could always be secured from the mint at that amount, it could not be sold for more. The face value of gold coins, therefore, always equaled their value as a commodity. Also called *primary money*. See also MONEY.

standard of living. The minimum of the necessities or luxuries of life to which a person or a group may be accustomed or to which they aspire.

Standard Oil case. One of two cases, *Standard Oil Company* v. *United States*, 221 U. S. 1 (1911) and *United States* v. *American Tobacco Company*, 221 U. S. 106 (1911), in which the Supreme Court of the United States announced the famous "rule of reason" in interpreting the provisions of the Sherman Antitrust Act. The court declared that the act did not intend that every combination in interstate commerce should be considered *ipso facto* invalid; on the contrary, reason should be used in identifying the combinations which the act intended to prohibit. Unless such an interpretation were used, said the court, the provisions of the act would be so comprehensive as to be unworkable. The actual combinations involved in the American Tobacco and Standard Oil cases were mergers of competing companies effected through stock purchase. These the court ordered dissolved. See also SHERMAN ANTITRUST ACT, RULE OF REASON.

stand-by controls. Government credit, commodity, or other economic controls that are legally authorized but are held in abeyance by administrative authorities pending conditions that may require the establishment of the controls. See also CONTROL.

state bank. An incorporated or nonincorporated banking institution chartered or carrying on business under the laws of one of the states of the United States. A state bank may be a COMMERCIAL BANK, a PRIVATE BANK, or a SAVINGS BANK. See also BANK.

state bond. See explanation under BOND.

state capitalism. A vague and somewhat ambiguous term usually indicating some degree of state ownership and control of CAPITAL. As thus used, it is often made synonymous with SOCIALISM or STATE SOCIALISM. See also CAPITALISM.

state medicine. Professional health care provided for the public and paid for from public funds. Also called *socialized medicine*.

state socialism. A term used somewhat loosely to suggest a moderate degree of socialism. It may comprehend the nationalization of key industries or government regulation of industry to curb monopolistic tendencies and to stabilize economic life. Sometimes it is used to describe social-welfare legislation or other paternalistic measures, and it may even be used to describe a policy of PROGRESSIVE TAXATION to reduce high incomes. See also SOCIALISM.

state tax immunity case. A case, *Graves* v. *New York* ex rel. *O'Keefe*, 306 U. S. 466 (1939), in which the Supreme Court of the United States reversed the old rule that salaries of federal employees were immune from state taxation and sustained the application of the New York state income-tax law to the salary of an employee of the Home Owners Loan Corporation, an instrumentality of the United States government.

state use system. The use of convict labor for the production of commodities not for public sale but exclusively for the use of the institutions of the state and its subdivisions. See also CONTRACT SYSTEM, CONVICT LEASE SYSTEM, PUBLIC WORKS AND WAYS SYSTEM.

static economics. See explanation under GENERAL EQUILIBRIUM.

statism. A term sometimes used to describe a trend toward governmental control of economic life. It is applied especially to a condition where the government, through public ECONOMIC PLANNING and the NATIONALIZATION of KEY INDUSTRIES, acquires a predominant influence in directing the economic life of a nation.

statute of limitations. A law which limits the time in which action can be taken to collect debts, enforce judgments, or prosecute criminals.

stay law. A legislative act prescribing a delay in the execution of legal remedies; for example, a mortgage moratorium or a postponement of the execution of judgments.

sterilized gold. In the United States, new acquisitions of gold placed in an inactive fund by the United States Treasury. The gold becomes active or *desterilized* when it is deposited in the FEDERAL RESERVE BANKS in the form of GOLD CERTIFICATES. For example, newly mined or imported gold is delivered to the assay office of the United States Treasury, which issues a check in payment. The check is deposited in a bank, redeposited in the district federal reserve bank, and from there forwarded to the treasury for payment. It may be paid to the federal reserve bank in gold certificates; but if the policy of the treasury is to sterilize gold the bank will be paid from a government deposit in some COMMERCIAL BANK. The gold is then said to be inactive, meaning that it is placed in the Treasury General Fund where it cannot become the basis for credit.

sterling area. An association of countries with inconvertible currencies which, under British leadership, developed currency and trade policies that were mutually favorable and essentially discriminatory as against the rest of the world. The various associated countries gave a preference to goods which could be purchased from one another and pooled their holdings of scarce currencies, such as American dollars, using the scarce currencies only for essential imports. The sterling area replaced the STERLING BLOC (*q.v.*) in 1939. The sterling area embraced Iran, Iceland, Egypt, Eire, and the whole of the British Empire including all the dominions except Canada. It formerly included the Scandinavian countries and Argentina, but these countries withdrew after the outbreak of World War II. Under the provisions of the Anglo-American Loan Agreement, signed July 15, 1946, the sterling area was to be liquidated by July 15, 1947. These provisions, however, were subsequently modified.

sterling bloc. A loose association of countries whose trade depended upon Great Britain, whose monetary policies were, in general, the same as those of Great Britain, and whose currencies were kept at parity with the pound sterling by means of a central monetary reserve deposited in London. The sterling bloc included all of the Scandinavian countries, the Latin-American countries of Uruguay and Bolivia, most of the countries of the British Empire, and, in a limited way, Argentina and Japan. The term began to be used when Britain abandoned the GOLD STANDARD in 1931. The sterling bloc ended with the establishment of the STERLING AREA (*q.v.*) in 1939. See also EXCHANGE CONTROL.

steward. As applied to labor relations, an employee, elected by his fellow employees within an establishment or department, to represent them in negotiations with the employer.

***Steward Machine Co.* v. *Davis*.** See SOCIAL-SECURITY CASES.

stipend. See SALARY.

stock certificate. See explanation under CAPITAL STOCK.

stock dividend. A dividend paid in shares of capital stock. A stock dividend does not change the financial condition of the corporation. The ASSETS remain the same and the LIABILITIES are changed only in that the undivided profits are decreased and capital stock is increased.

stock exchange. 1. A place where buyers and sellers meet to trade in securities. 2. An organization, usually unincorporated, which, among other things, provides a place where members trade in securities both on their own account and for the account of others. Also called *security exchange*.

stockholder. A person who holds a share or shares of the capital stock of a corporation.

stockpiling. See explanation under STRATEGIC MATERIALS.

stock rights. The privilege accorded stockholders to purchase shares of a new issue of the corporation's stock at a stipulated price, in quantities limited to some proportion of their existing holdings. Such rights are customarily evidenced by a document called a *stock warrant*. If the relation between the market price of the existing stock and the purchase price of the new issue is favorable, the stock rights may have a cash value. See also CUM RIGHTS, EX RIGHTS.

stock savings bank. A bank organized under state laws as a profit-making institution with the customary capital stock and stockholders and which caters particularly to individuals who wish to make time deposits for the purpose of saving. Stock savings banks in the United States are located in the Middle West and are relatively small institutions. Many now accept DEMAND DEPOSITS as well as TIME DEPOSITS, and make short-term loans; hence they are hardly distinguishable from COMMERCIAL BANKS. See also SAVINGS BANK.

stock warrant. See explanation under STOCK RIGHTS.

Stone* v. *Farmers' Loan and Trust Co. A case, 116 U. S. 307 (1886), in which the United States Supreme Court suggested that the rate for a public utility, fixed in a legislative enactment, might not necessarily be final, despite an apparently contrary doctrine developed in the Granger cases and *MUNN* v. *ILLINOIS* (*q.v.*), since the courts would necessarily be the tribunal of last resort in determining whether or not a rate, thus fixed, was reasonable. Four years later, in a Minnesota rate case, *Chicago, Milwaukee, and St. Paul Railroad Co.* v. *Minnesota*, 134 U. S. 418, the United States Supreme Court definitely established the finality of judicial review of legislative rates by declaring that the reasonableness of a rate was a judicial question, and any rate found by the court to be unreasonable would be set aside.

stop-loss order. An order to a stockbroker to sell at a stipulated price on a falling market, or to buy at a stipulated price on a rising market. Stop-loss orders are given in cases where a trader has been BUYING ON MARGIN or SELLING SHORT (*qq.v.*).

store credit. Credit extended by means of a charge account covering merchandise bought. Store credit was used extensively to finance the colonial planters along the North Atlantic seaboard during the 17th and 18th centuries. With the development of more formal methods of extending long- and intermediate-term credit, store credit has ceased to occupy its former position of importance, being confined today largely to use in emergencies and in extending short-term consumer credit in retail establishments.

straight bill of lading. A nonnegotiable bill of lading stating that the goods are consigned to a person specified. See also BILL OF LADING.

straight letter of credit. See explanation under LETTER OF CREDIT.

straight-life plan of life insurance. A plan according to which a life-insurance company agrees to pay a stipulated sum of money upon the death of an insured person in return for an annual premium of a fixed amount during that person's lifetime.

strategic materials. Raw materials or other commodities, essential to national defense, of which a particular nation's actual or potential supply falls below needs anticipated for a period of national emergency and which are therefore accumulated or stock-piled before an emergency develops. Under the Strategic and Critical Materials Stock-Piling Act of 1946, a special defense agency of the United States government is authorized to determine from time to time which commodities are strategic and which are *critical*, the only difference between these two categories being the magnitude of the supply which it is thought desirable to accumulate. This agency also recommends the quantities of such commodities which are to be accumulated in national stock piles.

stratified sample. A limited number of observations selected from an entire aggregate of phenomena by separating the entire aggregate into homogeneous groups and drawing samples from each group at random. For example, suppose that an estimate is desired of the price of grade-A eggs in New York City, and there is known to be a price differential between the chain stores and the independents. The proportion of chain stores to independents in the sample, then, might be made to conform to the proportion obtaining in the whole area. See also SAMPLING.

street certificate. A stock certificate evidencing ownership of a specified number of shares of the capital stock of a corporation and containing a BLANK INDORSEMENT by a registered owner whose signature is guaranteed by a broker. A street certificate may be sold and resold in the financial market without formal transfer on the books of the corporation.

stretch-out. An increase of work without a commensurate increase in wages.

strike. A planned and concerted work stoppage, on the part of employees in a plant or industry, in an effort to enforce certain demands having to do with their continued employment. Also called *walkout*. See also DIRECT STRIKE, GENERAL STRIKE, ILLEGAL

STRIKE, JURISDICTIONAL STRIKE, SIT-DOWN STRIKE, SLOWDOWN STRIKE, SYMPATHETIC STRIKE.

strikebreaker. One employed during a labor dispute to replace an employee on strike. The term refers particularly to a person employed only for the duration of the strike. See also SCAB.

***Sturges* v. *Crowninshield*.** A case, 4 Wheaton 122 (1819), in which the United States Supreme Court established the rule that, although the Constitution delegates powers over bankruptcy to Congress, the states of the United States may make their own bankruptcy laws, and that such laws are valid as long as they do not conflict with federal legislation.

subscription price. As applied to stock purchases, the fixed price at which new or additional shares issued by a corporation may be purchased. The subscription price may, and usually does, differ from the MARKET PRICE that is ultimately established for the stock in question.

subsidiary coin. In the United States a silver coin of a value less than $1. The term sometimes includes bronze and copper coins although such coins, being made of base metal, are usually called MINOR COINS. See also COIN.

subsidiary company. A business enterprise, the operations of which are subject to the control of another corporation. The control is usually established through the ownership of a sufficient quantity of capital stock.

subsidy. Financial assistance or its equivalent given for a service which, though uneconomic from a profit-making standpoint, is considered essential to the public welfare. Also a grant made by a central government to its political subdivisions for the support of certain public services.

subsistence. A sufficient quantity of the necessities of life to maintain a bare livelihood.

subsistence theory of wages. See IRON LAW OF WAGES.

substitution, law of. The principle that, when one commodity can be substituted for another, the price of the latter commodity, if it is to continue in use, cannot be much higher than that of the substitute.

subtreasury system. See INDEPENDENT TREASURY SYSTEM.

subvention. Support or assistance. Particularly a grant or subsidy from a government or a foundation.

Suffolk Bank system. A plan put into effect after the economic crisis of 1837 whereby the Suffolk and seven other banks in Boston, Mass., agreed to accept and pay only the notes of those out-of-town banks that maintained a redemption deposit account with the Suffolk and sister banks. The plan had the effect of maintaining at par value the entire bank note circulation of the state.

sumptuary laws. Laws which propose to prevent the consumption of goods believed to be injurious to the health of individuals or to the welfare of society.

sunk cost. An initial, nonrecurring item in production costs. In manufacturing metal stampings, for example, the cost of the die is a sunk cost. Once made, an indefinite number of units can be produced from it. See also COST.

Sunshine Anthracite Coal Co. v. Adkins. See BITUMINOUS COAL CASES.

sunspot theory of the business cycle. See ASTRONOMICAL THEORY OF THE BUSINESS CYCLE.

supermarket. A spacious retail store, usually located in one story on the street level, where goods are conspicuously displayed and so arranged that customers may select what is wanted without clerical service. Purchases are customarily collected in a small pushcart and conveyed to a check-out counter where the bill is computed. Sales are generally for cash, with an extra charge for delivery if such service is provided. Food products and household supplies are commonly sold in supermarkets, although many are now offering a wide variety of other consumer goods. Most supermarkets are units of large corporations operating over a wide area.

superseniority. A preferred rank given special groups in the interpretation of seniority privileges. The term is frequently applied to the seniority accorded to veterans.

supplementary costs. See FIXED COSTS.

supply. The quantity of an economic good available for sale in the market. In its most limited sense the term may mean the quantity of an economic good that will be offered at a given price at a particular time. Thus, if 200 units will be offered for sale at $5 and 100 units at $4, we may say that the supply is 200 at $5 and 100 at $4.

The term also has the broader meaning of the quantity of an economic good that will be offered at all possible prices at a particular time. This is called *schedule supply.*

Price	First-period Supply	Second-period Supply
$5	500	600
4	400	500
3	300	400
2	200	300
1	100	200

In the table on p. 321 the schedule supply of a good is indicated at various prices, at two different periods.

It will be noted that during the interval between the first and second periods, the schedule supply increased; that is, there was an increased offering of the good at all prices. These two schedule supplies are represented by lines *a–a′* and *b–b′* in the following diagram.

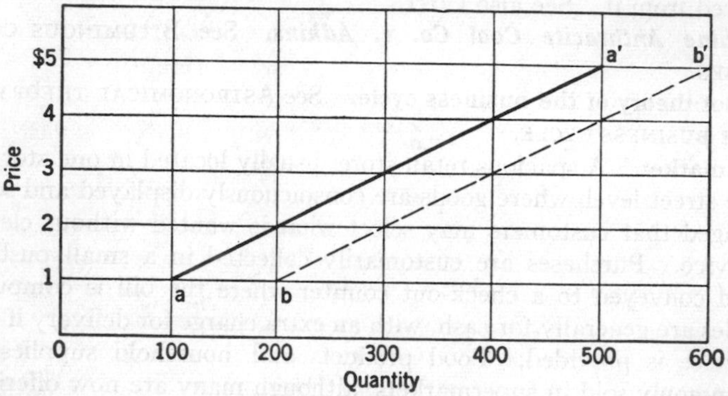

See also COMPOSITE SUPPLY, ELASTIC SUPPLY, INELASTIC SUPPLY.

supply and demand, law of. The assertion that price varies directly, but not necessarily proportionately, with demand, and inversely, but not necessarily proportionately, with supply. See also DEMAND, DEMAND AND SUPPLY CURVES, SUPPLY.

surety bond. A contract in which one party guarantees a second that he, the first party, will fulfill an obligation originally assumed by a third party, if the latter fails to fulfill it. See also BOND.

suretyship insurance. See FIDELITY INSURANCE.

surplus. That which remains after immediate needs have been fulfilled. In a business enterprise surplus is the sum of the ASSETS less the sum of the LIABILITIES. It is usually designated as *capital surplus.* Capital surplus may be an EARNED SURPLUS or a PAID-IN SURPLUS.

surplus labor and value theory. A theory, developed by Karl Marx and other socialist writers, which assumes that the value of a commodity is the amount of human labor necessary to produce it. From this premise it is argued that although the worker is entitled to all of the value thus produced, he receives only that portion necessary for his upkeep; the remainder passes to the capitalist as profit or surplus value. The theory assumes that the labor expended on the commodities necessary for the worker's upkeep is less than the labor expended on the commodities he creates. Also called *theory of surplus value.* See also LABOR, VALUE.

Surplus Property Act. An act of Congress, 1944, which provided for the disposal of United States property declared surplus at the end of World War II. Supervision of the actual disposition of surplus property in the United States and its territories and the transfer of such property between federal agencies was placed under the control of the War Assets Administration in 1946.

surplus value, theory of. See SURPLUS LABOR AND VALUE THEORY.

surtax. An additional tax on the same tax base after one tax has already been applied. For example, in calculating income taxes in the United States, a sum is first calculated on the tax base on the basis of PROPORTIONAL TAXATION, and then an added sum or surtax is calculated on the basis of PROGRESSIVE TAXATION. See also TAX.

survivorship annuity. An annuity paid to a beneficiary after the death of the person providing for such annuity. An annuity which continues in whole or in part to a surviving beneficiary after the death of the annuitant. See also ANNUITY.

survivors' insurance. See explanation under OLD-AGE AND SURVIVORS' INSURANCE.

suspense account. A bookkeeping account containing a balance which is of doubtful value and hence placed in suspense before finally being charged to the profit-and-loss account; also an account containing items which temporarily have not been allocated to a regular account. See also ACCOUNT.

sweating. Employing labor, usually on a piecework basis, at low wages and long hours, and perhaps under unhealthful conditions.

symmetallism. The use of an amalgam of precious metals in coins. The term has also been used to indicate a monetary system in which paper money is backed by gold and silver bullion and is redeemable in specified proportions of each.

sympathetic strike. A strike by workers who have no grievance against their own employer, but who stop work in order to aid other workers, presumably members of some allied union. Also called *secondary strike.* See also STRIKE.

syndicalism. An economic system that would place the ownership and control of the means of production in the hands of the workers. Each industry would be organized as an autonomous unit managed by the workers, and these autonomous units would be combined in a federation for the promulgation of measures in the interests of the public. Coercive government would hold no important place in a syndicalist regime and, theoretically, might disappear altogether. See also ECONOMIC SYSTEM.

syndicate. A group of individuals, business organizations, or banks associated together for the purpose of carrying out an undertaking requiring a large amount of capital. See also COMBINATION.

T

Tableau économique. A graphic representation of what was believed to be the flow of wealth in an economy, published in 1758 by François Quesnay (1694–1774), a French physician. The *Tableau économique* envisaged three classes in the economy: (1) a productive class consisting principally of agriculturalists; (2) a proprietary class made up of property owners and government officials; and (3) a sterile class consisting of merchants, manufacturers, and servants. All wealth was thought to be created by the productive class; some was retained for its maintenance, and the rest circulated in the economy, only to return to that class eventually. In his presentation Quesnay used the figure of 5 milliard (billion) francs as the value of wealth created by the productive class within a specified period of time. Of this, 2 milliard francs were retained for maintenance, 1 milliard francs were paid to the sterile class for manufactured goods required in agriculture, and 2 milliard were paid to the proprietary class for taxes and rents. Of the 2 milliard paid to the proprietary class, 1 milliard were spent for food and hence returned to the original source, and 1 milliard were paid to the sterile class for various purchases. This 1 milliard francs received by the sterile class together with the 1 milliard francs originally received from the productive class were both repaid to the productive class for food and raw materials. Thus, of the 3 milliard francs originally emanating from the productive class, all were eventually returned to that source.

Although an ingenious conception, and the first attempt at MACROECONOMICS in the field of DISTRIBUTION, the explanation has little relation to the operation of economic life as now interpreted.

tabular standard of value. A plan by which contractual obligations in terms of money may be altered according to the purchasing power of money at the time the payment is due. A certain number of specific commodities are selected, and the sum or average of the prices of these commodities is accepted as a standard. If, at the time the payment is due, this sum or average has advanced or declined, a proportionate additional or lesser amount of money is paid in settlement of the contractual obligation.

Taft-Hartley Act. See LABOR-MANAGEMENT RELATIONS (TAFT-HARTLEY) ACT.

Taft-Hartley Injunction Case. A case, *United Steelworkers of America v. United States*, 361 U. S. 39 (1959), in which the United States Supreme Court upheld the action of a federal district court in enjoining the nationwide steel strike of 1959. The strike had lasted 116 days and was the longest on record. The high court held that the injunction was an appropriate exercise of judicial power in overcoming a threat to the "national health," authority for its exercise having been conferred upon the courts by Congress in Sections 208–210 of the LABOR-MANAGEMENT RELATIONS (TAFT-HARTLEY) ACT. The injunction was issued following the expiration of the Act's so-called "cooling-off" period of 80 days and had the effect of compelling some one half million steelworkers to return to their jobs.

tangible property. A right or interest in things that have substance, as distinct from property rights in relatively immaterial concepts such as a patent, a claim against a debtor, or the good will of a business. The term may also refer to any property that can be accurately appraised. See also PROPERTY.

tare. A deduction from a gross weight for the weight of a container.

tariff. 1. A schedule of fixed rates or charges, usually those of a common carrier; for example, a passenger tariff published by a railroad. 2. A schedule or system of duties authorized by a government and imposed upon commodities exported or imported. For the more important kinds of tariff systems, see AUTONOMOUS TARIFF SYSTEM, CONVENTIONAL TARIFF SYSTEM, EDUCATIONAL TARIFF, FLEXIBLE TARIFF, MAXIMUM AND MINIMUM TARIFF SYSTEM, MULTIPLE TARIFF SYSTEM, PROTECTIVE TARIFF, SINGLE-SCHEDULE TARIFF, SLIDING-SCALE TARIFF, TARIFF FOR REVENUE ONLY. See also CUSTOMS DUTY.

Tariff Act of 1922. See FORDNEY-MCCUMBER TARIFF.

tariff for revenue only. A system of tariff duties which, theoretically, is not intended to protect home industry but only to produce revenue for the government. See also TARIFF.

Tariff Information Catalogue. An encyclopedia compiled by the United States Tariff Commission giving information concerning commodities subject to import duties. The document contains such information as the volume of commodities imported and exported, costs of production, and the extent of foreign competition.

Tariff of Abominations. The United States Tariff Act of 1828. It represented the most extreme protective legislation up to that date, was rather generally criticized, and led to the nullification movement in South Carolina.

tariff union. See CUSTOMS UNION.

tariff war. Competition between two or more countries, carried on by means of tariff discriminations, commercial concessions and demands, and the like.

task. As applied to wage systems, the amount of work that must be done within a given length of time in order to secure the minimum wage assigned to any particular job. The term is usually applied to cases where a bonus of some kind is paid for production beyond a certain prescribed minimum within a given length of time.

tax. A contribution exacted of persons, corporations, and other organizations by the government, according to law, for the government's general support and for the maintenance of public services. Besides its compulsory character another distinguishing characteristic of a tax is the fact that there is no exact correlation between the amount paid and the value of the public services from which the taxpayer benefits. For specific kinds of taxes see APPORTIONED TAX, CAPITAL-GAINS TAX, CAPITAL-STOCK TAX, CHAIN-STORE TAX, DIRECT TAX, ESTATE TAX, EXCESS-PROFITS TAX, EXCISE TAX, FRANCHISE TAX, GIFT TAX, GRADED TAX, HEAD TAX, HIDDEN TAX, INCOME TAX, INDIRECT TAX, INHERITANCE TAX, LAND-VALUE TAX, LUXURY TAX, NUISANCE TAX, OCCUPATIONAL TAX, PAY-ROLL TAX, SALES TAX, SEVERANCE TAX, SINGLE TAX, SOCIAL-SECURITY TAX, STAMP TAX, SURTAX, UNDISTRIBUTED-PROFITS TAX, USE TAX, WAR-PROFITS TAX. See also DUTY.

tax-anticipation bond. See explanation under BOND.

tax assessment. See explanation under ASSESSMENT.

tax avoidance. Exploitation by a taxpayer of legally permissible alternative tax rates or methods of assessing taxable property or income, or of reporting taxable property or income, in order to reduce tax liability. The term may be extended to include situations where a person refrains from engaging in some activity or enjoying some privilege in order to avoid the incidental taxation; for example, failure to import goods because of unwillingness to pay the duty. Sometimes referred to as *tax dodging*. See also TAX EVASION.

tax base. The unit of value or some privilege or object upon which a tax is actually levied and the tax return is calculated. It may be property owned by the taxpayer, annual net income, the value of the estate of a deceased person, a corporate franchise, an occupation, or the volume, number, quality, or other characteristic of certain specified articles. In the case of the poll tax, the tax base would be the individual taxed.

tax collector. A local government official charged with the responsibility of collecting certain taxes, particularly those levied on property.

tax commission. An administrative agency of one of the states of the United States whose members are either elected or appointed. It usually supervises local taxation, administers taxes not collected locally, and attends to the EQUALIZATION OF ASSESSMENTS throughout the state.

Tax Court of the United States. A special 16-member tribunal created by the Revenue Act of 1924 and given its present title in 1942. Its most important prerogative is that of deciding cases or controversies arising under most of the federal tax laws which involve alleged overpayment of taxes or tax deficiencies certified by the Commissioner of Internal Revenue. It may also review denials by the Commissioner of excess-profits-tax refund claims. A few of its decisions are final but most may, under certain circumstances, be reviewed by a federal appellate court and in some cases an appeal may be taken to the United States Supreme Court.

tax dodging. See TAX AVOIDANCE, TAX EVASION.

tax evasion. Illegal efforts to avoid payment of a tax; for example, failure to report taxable income or property. Sometimes referred to as *tax dodging.* See also TAX AVOIDANCE.

tax exemption. Legal freedom from the obligation to pay taxes, a privilege applicable to properties used by educational and eleemosynary organizations or to the income of certain nonprofit corporations.

tax farming. A practice, common in the ancient Greek cities and in the early period of the Roman Republic, of delegating to private individuals or institutions the right to collect public revenue in return for specified lump-sum payments to the public treasury. As a rule a profit or commission was derived by collecting from taxpayers more than was paid to the treasury.

tax limit. A constitutional or statutory limitation upon the kind of tax or the maximum rate of taxation which a tax authority, usually a political subdivision, may impose. Normally, this is coupled with provisions for securing additional funds to meet emergencies.

taxpayer. As applied to real estate, a temporary building the income from which will pay for the operating expenses and amortization charges and yield something in addition to apply on the carrying charges of the ground. See also AMORTIZATION.

tax rate. The proportion of the appraised monetary value of a tax base which a government actually collects as a tax. See also TAX BASE.

tax selling. **1.** The selling of securities, usually in order to realize losses for income-tax purposes. In the United States it is permissible, under income-tax regulations (1949), to offset capital gains with capital losses. If capital gains have been realized during the year, therefore, while other securities show a loss at the market price, sales are frequently made in order that the losses may also be realized and tax liability thereby reduced. **2.** The sale of real property for the nonpayment of assessed taxes.

tax sharing. The practice of having one political jurisdiction levy and collect a tax and share the proceeds with other political jurisdictions. In certain states of the United States a general property tax is sometimes levied and collected by the county or other local governmental body, part of the proceeds then being allocated to the central state government and other political subdivisions according to a formula previously established. Sometimes, as in the case of a sales or other excise tax, the central administration of the state may levy and collect the tax and then apportion a part of the proceeds to the state's subdivisions.

Taylorism. A term used to designate scientific management and work efficiency, so called because of the pioneer research in the field done by Frederick W. Taylor early in the 20th century.

technocracy. A body of doctrine prominent in the depression years of 1932 and 1933. The technocrats — economists, architects, and industrial engineers — claimed that industrial efficiency was being maintained at a high cost in premature obsolescence of machines. They argued that the savings resulting from laborsaving machinery never reached consumers but were absorbed by creditors and investors. This, they said, deprived the mass of people of purchasing power and created a surplus of goods. The goods were wanted and needed, but could not be bought at the prices asked.

technological unemployment. The unemployment that results when machines replace men. If the machines reduce production costs, competition reduces selling prices, and reduced selling prices increase demand, re-employment may occur in due course providing new skills to meet the new conditions can be acquired by the workers. To the extent that prices are not reduced, technological unemployment tends to be prolonged. See also UNEMPLOYMENT.

technology. Industrial science, particularly its application to the replacement of skilled labor by modern machinery.

teller. In banks of the United States, an employee who receives deposits, issues withdrawals, or collects amounts due on promissory notes and other commercial paper payable to the bank.

temporal distribution. See explanation under TIME-SERIES CHART.

temporary admission. A term applied to goods admitted to a country for eventual export. Under specified conditions no CUSTOMS DUTY is paid on such goods, and hence no DRAWBACK is claimed. Identical with *ADMISSION TEMPORAIRE.*

Temporary National Economic Committee. A committee authorized by congressional resolution in 1938 to conduct a comprehensive study of monopoly and the concentration of economic power in the United States. The committee consisted of three senators, three representatives, and appointees from the United States Departments of Justice, Treasury, Commerce, and Labor, from the FEDERAL TRADE COMMISSION, and from the SECURITIES AND EXCHANGE COMMISSION. Among the important monographs published by the committee might be mentioned *Competition and Monopoly in American Industry, The Structure of Industry*, and *Distribution of Ownership in the 200 Largest Nonfinancial Corporations.*

ten-forty bond. A popular term applied to certain United States bonds issued in 1864. The bonds were redeemable any time after 10 years, were payable at the end of 40 years, and yielded 5 per cent interest. See also BOND.

Tennessee Valley Authority. A public corporation chartered by Congress in 1933 to build dams, power structures, and flood-control works along the Tennessee River and tributary streams, and to produce hydroelectric power and fertilizer. Its activities have greatly aided in promoting rehabilitation throughout the Tennessee Valley, an area of some 40,000 square miles. The work of the authority is financed through the sale of bonds to the investing public, public appropriations, and the income from the sale of products and services.

terminal bond. See explanation under BOND.

terminal wage. See DISMISSAL WAGE.

term plan of life insurance. A plan by which a life-insurance company agrees to pay a stipulated sum of money upon the death of the insured if his death occurs within the term fixed by the insurance policy—usually 5 or 10 years. In return for the protection, the insured pays an annual premium of a fixed amount during the period for which the insurance is in force. See also LIFE INSURANCE.

terms of trade. The conditions under which a nation carries on foreign trade, with reference particularly to the question whether such conditions are favorable or unfavorable. Among the factors which determine the terms of a nation's trade are the nature of its economy with particular reference to the degree of its dependence on foreign trade; the presence or absence of certain advantages in production, particularly production for export; and the world price level. In an inflationary period, for example, a nation that imports most of its foodstuffs and raw materials for industry is likely to find that the value differential between imported raw commodities and finished goods is less than in a period when prices are declining on world markets. Hence, the terms of trade for such a nation are likely to be more favorable when the world price level is declining than when it is rising.

territorial bond. See explanation under BOND.

Texas and New Orleans R.R. Co.* v. *Brotherhood of Railway and Steamship Clerks. A case, 281 U. S. 548 (1930), in which the Supreme Court of the United States sustained an act of Congress, passed in 1926, protecting the rights of railway employees to organize and select collective-bargaining representatives without employer interference. The court virtually overruled earlier decisions like that in *COPPAGE* v. *KANSAS* and *ADAIR* v. *UNITED STATES* (*qq.v.*) by declaring the employees' rights of collective bargaining to be beyond question, and by further stating that such rights would become a "mockery" if employers were permitted to interfere with employees' freedom in choosing their bargaining representatives.

theory. A statement setting forth an apparent relationship among observed facts, which relationship has been repeatedly verified by independent investigators. See also explanation under INDUCTIVE METHOD.

thin market. See NARROW MARKET.

through bill of lading. A bill of lading used for shipments which are handled by more than one carrier before they reach their destination. It relieves the shipper of the necessity of accepting and reshipping the goods at connecting points. See also BILL OF LADING.

tied loan. A term sometimes used to indicate a foreign loan made on the condition that the borrower will purchase in the lending country such materials as are required to carry out the purpose of the loan. See also LOAN.

tie-in sale. A sale made with the stipulation that some article other than the one purchased must also be purchased. See also TYING CONTRACTS.

till money. A relatively small reserve of money kept in the vaults of banks for the purpose of paying out such cash as is demanded. See also MONEY.

time bill. See explanation under BILL.

time deposit. A bank deposit subject to withdrawal only after a certain number of days' notice. See also BANK DEPOSIT.

time draft. See explanation under DRAFT.

time loan. A loan made for a definite period of time. The term is used in contradistinction to CALL LOAN.

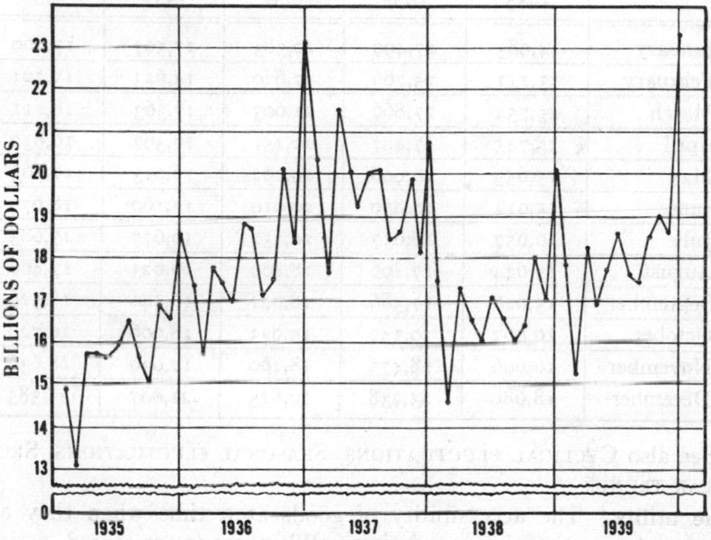

time reversal test. A method for determining the mathematical validity of an INDEX NUMBER (*q.v.*). The base period is changed from the period originally so designated to some subsequent period for which an index number has been calculated; then a new index number is computed for the former base period and multiplied by the original index number. If the product is unity, the original index number is a valid one mathematically. AGGREGATIVE INDEX NUMBERS and FISHER'S IDEAL INDEX meet this test. RELATIVE-VALUE INDEX NUMBERS meet this test only if computed by the GEOMETRIC MEAN. See also FACTOR REVERSAL TEST.

time-series chart. A graphic representation of statistical data in which the independent variable, plotted along the horizontal axis, is time, and the values of the dependent variable, plotted along the vertical axis, are shown at various intervals of time, these values being connected by straight lines to form a continuous curve extending over the entire period covered by the chart. Also called *temporal distribution.* The diagram on p. 331 shows a time-series chart of BANK DEBITS in the United States outside of New York City, by months, from 1935 to 1939, inclusive, as follows:

	Millions of dollars				
	1935	1936	1937	1938	1939
January	14,983	17,499	20,383	17,597	17,860
February	13,111	15,766	17,620	14,623	15,201
March	15,754	17,866	21,605	17,363	18,211
April	15,745	17,497	20,151	16,597	16,832
May	15,655	16,998	19,292	16,013	17,763
June	15,914	18,880	20,019	17,160	18,676
July	16,657	18,617	20,152	16,677	17,683
August	15,644	17,106	18,409	16,023	17,496
September	15,016	17,586	18,642	16,440	18,526
October	16,962	20,142	19,923	18,096	19,029
November	16,696	18,475	18,160	17,039	18,636
December	18,689	23,238	20,825	21,087	23,385

See also CYCLICAL FLUCTUATIONS, SEASONAL FLUCTUATIONS, SECULAR TREND.

time utility. The accessibility of goods at a time when they are wanted to satisfy human desires. When goods are stored, a time utility may be created. Ice harvested in the winter and distributed in summer is an example. See also UTILITY.

timework. A wage system by which an employee is paid a certain amount per hour or per day for a given job.

token coin. A coin, the face value of which is less than its value as metal. Thus defined, the term is used in contradistinction to standard-money coins. Sometimes the term is synonymous with MINOR COINS, and sometimes its meaning includes both SUBSIDIARY COINS and minor coins. See also COIN, STANDARD MONEY.

tolerance. A permitted variation of quality or size. For example, in manufacturing certain INTERCHANGEABLE PARTS a tolerance of

.003 in., plus or minus the standard measurement, may be permitted.

toll. A charge made for the use of something. The term is usually applied to a charge made for the use of something of a public nature such as a road or a bridge. It is occasionally used more in the sense of a price, such as in the case of a charge made by a miller for grinding grain belonging to another person.

tonnage. 1. As applied to ships, the cubical contents expressed usually in units of 100 cu. ft. Each such unit is called a registered ton, the word "ton" as thus used having no relation to the unit of weight. 2. Also a tax on ships, based on their capacity.

total utility. The sum of the utility of all units constituting a supply of goods, such supply being affected by the principle of diminishing utility. Thus, if the diminishing utility of a supply of five units of a good is represented by the figures 5, 4, 3, 2, 1, then the total utility of the supply is 15. The term is sometimes defined, however, as the marginal utility times the number of items constituting the supply. Considered thus, the total utility in the above example would be 5×1 (marginal utility) or 5. See also MARGINAL UTILITY.

tourist expenditures. Expenditures of tourists in a foreign country. Such expenditures are an invisible item of trade and have the same effect on the balance of payments of the tourists' home country as an import of merchandise from the country in which the expenditures are made.

Townsend plan. A proposal that the United States government grant a pension of $200 a month to every person 60 years of age and over. According to the sponsors of the plan, the money spent by the recipients of the pensions would stimulate a demand for goods and services and thus assure prosperity. The plan was proposed during the economic depression, beginning in 1929, and is named after the proposer, Dr. Francis E. Townsend.

trade acceptance. A time draft drawn by a seller on a buyer and accepted by the buyer, who thereby promises to pay at a specific time and place the amount of an invoice covering a current sale of goods. See also DRAFT.

trade agreement. A contract between a labor union and an employer or employers, setting forth the terms of employment for a stipulated length of time. Also known as a *labor agreement* or labor contract. The term also refers to trade treaties, particularly RECIPROCAL TRADE AGREEMENTS.

Trade Agreements Act. An act of Congress, 1934, which amended the Hawley-Smoot Tariff Act of 1930, thus permitting the President of the United States to negotiate trade agreements with foreign countries reducing American import duties as much as 50 per cent in return for appropriate concessions granted to American exports. The Trade Expansion Act of 1962 greatly extended the President's discretion, permitting him, in the case of certain manufactures, to waive tariffs altogether when America and negotiating countries accounted for at least 80 per cent of total product in world trade.

trade association. An organization of business establishments in one trade or field of work designed to further the common interests of that particular activity. According to the Department of Commerce of the United States, a trade association is concerned with statistics, cost accounting, research, public relations, trade relations, credit, insurance, employer-employee relations, and traffic and transportation, in so far as these relate to the area of interest of the particular association.

trade barrier. Any regulation which interferes with the free exchange of goods and services among different political jurisdictions. CUSTOMS DUTIES and IMPORT QUOTAS are common trade barriers, but international EXCHANGE CONTROL and sanitary and health regulations may be used for the same purpose.

trade bloc. Two or more nations which adopt a common policy regarding customs duties and other trade regulations applicable to other political jurisdictions.

trade deficit. See UNFAVORABLE BALANCE OF TRADE.

trade discount. A deduction from a basic or list price expressed as a percentage. By using a trade discount manufacturers and jobbers need not constantly reissue catalogues or price lists as market prices change. The published prices thus remain fixed, but the actual selling prices are advanced or reduced by adjusting the amount of trade discount.

trade dollar. A special United States silver coin minted from 1873 to 1885. It contained more silver than the standard silver dollar and was intended to facilitate trade with China and Japan.

trade-mark. A mark or symbol used to identify a specific seller or manufacturer. A trade-mark is usually stamped on, or attached to, a commodity and frequently appears in the advertising and on the letterheads of the individual or concern making or marketing the product. A trade-mark may be registered with the Patent Office in the United States.

trade monopoly. A special-privilege monopoly created by a public authority permitting a private trading company to monopolize commerce between the country granting the privilege and some other area, usually a colony. Such companies were especially active during the 17th and 18th centuries. Probably the most famous was the British East India Company which monopolized trade between England and India and enjoyed governmental powers in India. Similar companies existed in France, Holland, and elsewhere. See also MONOPOLY, SPECIAL-PRIVILEGE MONOPOLY.

trading stamp. A stamp given to customers by retail merchants, usually with each 10 cents' worth of goods purchased, which the customer may redeem for various articles when a sufficient quantity of stamps has accumulated. The trading stamp is thus a promotional device to attract and hold customers. The retail merchant customarily buys the stamps in bulk from a stamp company which advertises the premiums available and redeems the stamps from collectors. The use of trading stamps has increased steadily since their origin, in modern form, during the 1890's. In 1956, sales of stamps to retail merchants are said to have amounted to $600 million, with almost half of the families in the United States regularly collecting and redeeming them.

transactions tax. See explanation under SALES TAX.

transfer agent. A person who records changes in the ownership of a corporation's stock and who, therefore, records changes in ownership as the stock of the corporation is bought and sold. If a corporation does not maintain its own transfer office, it appoints an agent, frequently a bank or a trust company, for the purpose.

transfer payment. A term used by the United States Department of Commerce to indicate money disbursed by business or government in return for which no services are rendered. Allocations to cover bad debts and gifts to nonprofit, charitable, and educational institutions are examples of business transfer payments. Government transfer payments include such items as payments for relief and veterans' aid.

Trans-Missouri Freight Association case. An early antitrust case, *United States* v. *Trans-Missouri Freight Assn.*, 166 U. S. 290 (1897), in which the Supreme Court of the United States ruled that a contract between railroads to maintain rates violated the Sherman Antitrust Act. The court interpreted the Sherman Act rather broadly and implied that it proscribed any contract in restraint of interstate trade whether or not it might be construed as reasonable.

Transportation Act. 1. An act of Congress, 1920, known as the ESCH-CUMMINS ACT (*q.v.*). 2. An act of Congress, 1940. It authorized the Interstate Commerce Commission to assume jurisdiction over coastal and inland waterways in order to facilitate a more unified national system of water, rail, and motor transportation.

traveler's check. A check or draft payable at sight, issued principally by banks and express companies in various denominations and sold to travelers who sign the document once when purchasing it, and again, for purposes of identification, in the presence of the person who is asked to cash it. See also CHECK, DRAFT.

traveler's letter of credit. See explanation under LETTER OF CREDIT.

Treasurer of the United States (Office of). A part of the fiscal service branch of the United States Department of the Treasury which is responsible for the receipts and disbursements of public moneys, for the issue and redemption of United States paper money and coin, the payment of interest and principal on the national debt, and the safekeeping of securities deposited with the federal government as collateral.

treasury bill. A short-term obligation of the United States government, usually maturing in less than 1 year.

treasury note. A short-term obligation of the United States government, usually maturing in from 1 to 5 years. The term also applies to two kinds of United States paper money—GREENBACKS and treasury notes of 1890, or *Sherman notes*. The latter have been called for redemption.

treasury stock. See explanation under CAPITAL STOCK.

Trenton Potteries case. A case, *United States* v. *Trenton Potteries Co.*, 273 U. S. 392 (1927), in which the Supreme Court of the United States ruled that a specific agreement among producers in a trade association to fix and maintain prices for their commodities, however reasonable the prices may be, is a violation of the federal antitrust statutes and therefore void.

trial balance. The sum of all the debit balances in a general ledger compared with the sum of all the credit balances. When the two sums are equal, the ledger is said to be in balance; that is, for every amount debited there is a corresponding amount credited.

triangular trade. A situation in foreign trade in which equilibrium — that is, a balance of exports and imports — is maintained over any period of time by an exchange pattern involving three rather than only two countries. Where such a pattern exists, Country A may export to Country B which, in turn, may export to Country C. Country C then completes the three-way pattern, or triangle, by exporting goods to Country A, thereby offsetting, or balancing, the flow of goods from Country A to Country B. A classic example of such a situation is afforded by part of the trade of the American colonies in the 18th century. The colonies exported rum to the West Coast of Africa in exchange for slaves; these were transported to the West Indies in exchange for sugar; in turn, this commodity was taken back to the colonies to be manufactured into more rum for the African trade.

Tripartite Currency Agreement. A declaration issued by France, Great Britain, and the United States in 1936, and later by Switzerland, the Netherlands, and Belgium, in which co-operation in the stabilization of their several currencies was pledged. The understanding became inoperative after the occupation of France and other countries by Germany.

***Truax* v. *Corrigan*.** A case, 257 U. S. 312 (1921), which involved a statute of the state of Arizona barring the use of injunctions in labor disputes. By a bare majority, the Supreme Court of the United States invalidated the Arizona statute on the ground, among others, that the denial of injunctive relief in labor disputes, access to such relief being continued in practically all other situations where principles of equity were applicable, constituted an arbitrary and unreasonable legislative classification and violated the equal protection clause of the 14th Amendment of the United States Constitution.

true interest. See PURE INTEREST.

Truman Plan. See POINT 4 PROGRAM.

trust. 1. Property held and administered by an individual or organization for the benefit of another individual or organization. The administrator of the trust is known as the *trustee*. See also COMMON TRUST, INVESTMENT TRUST, MASSACHUSETTS TRUST, TRUST COMPANY, TRUST FUND, VOTING TRUST. 2. A corollary of the above definition, applied to business organization, is a plan whereby the voting rights of the majority of the voting stock of two or more corporations are assigned to a designated number of trustees who then direct the affairs of the corporations to the mutual advantage of all the stockholders. 3. More recently, the term has been used to designate any large corporation or combination of corporations exercising a monopolistic or semimonopolistic control over the production or distribution of some commodity or service. See also COMBINATION.

trust company. A financial organization, usually performing the customary commercial banking functions of accepting deposits and making loans, and in addition having the authority to act as agent, trustee, or fiduciary in many capacities. It also acts as executor and administrator of estates, and as custodian of valuables deposited for safekeeping. Many COMMERCIAL BANKS have trust departments. See also BANK, TRUST.

trustee. See TRUST.

Trusteeship Council. A special organ of the United Nations intended to protect the peoples of dependent areas, particularly those administered as trusteeships or trust areas by members of the United Nations. Membership of the council includes those nations administering such trust areas, the five permanent members of the United Nations SECURITY COUNCIL, and others. Half of the membership must at all times consist of nations not administering trust areas. The council operates under the authority of the GENERAL ASSEMBLY OF THE UNITED NATIONS.

trustee stock. See explanation under CAPITAL STOCK.

trust fund. Funds administered by a trustee, frequently a bank. The investment policies pursued by the trustee may be specified by the maker of the trust fund. Where they are not so specified, the investment policies pursued by the trustee are governed by law. See also TRUST.

trust receipt. A document acknowledging responsibility for property enumerated therein and held in trust for some designated party. A trust receipt is sometimes executed when a DRAFT attached to an ORDER BILL OF LADING cannot be met by the buyer. The bank through which the draft has been drawn may then issue a trust receipt which is signed by the buyer. The bank retains title to the property; the buyer sells the property and remits the proceeds to the bank.

turnover tax. See explanation under SALES TAX.

two-dollar broker. A stockbroker who transacts business only with other brokers. The term originated from the commission once charged, which was $2 for every 100 shares of stock bought or sold. The commissions now depend upon the price of the stock. Two-dollar brokers absorb overflow business from other brokers during busy periods.

two-name paper. One of various types of short-term, negotiable instruments in which two persons guarantee payment.

tying contracts. Clauses in contracts to sell goods or lease property according to which the buyer or lessee is forbidden to use the goods of competing sellers or lessors in connection with the goods or property bought or leased. Various statutes, including the CLAYTON ACT, prohibit tying clauses in contracts. See also TIE-IN SALE.

***Tyson* v. *Banton*.** A case, 273 U. S. 418 (1927), in which the Supreme Court of the United States invalidated a New York State statute attempting to regulate the resale price of theater tickets. The court based its adverse decision on the ground that selling tickets for theatrical exhibitions was not "business affected with a public interest" and hence not subject to regulation under the state's police power.

U

unconfirmed letter of credit. See explanation under LETTER OF CREDIT.

underdeveloped area. A term popularly used to indicate a region which, compared with Western standards, suffers from low levels of living. Ineffective use of natural resources and lack of industrialization are often associated with the concept of underdevelopment, although an area may be "underdeveloped" in other respects.

underemployment equilibrium. A condition in which the sum of the investment items and consumer expenditures in the GROSS NATIONAL PRODUCT balance with a NATIONAL INCOME insufficient in volume to absorb the entire working force of the nation. Some authorities hold that this is the trend in a highly industrialized economy. The reasons cited are: (1) decline in the PROPENSITY TO CONSUME; (2) decline in the MARGINAL EFFICIENCY OF CAPITAL; and (3) strengthening of LIQUIDITY PREFERENCE because of low interest rates, which, in turn, result in low PROPENSITY TO INVEST and national income insufficient to absorb the entire working force. See also KEYNESIAN ECONOMICS, KEYNES' LAW OF CONSUMPTION.

underlying bond. See explanation under BOND.

Underwood Tariff. The United States Tariff Act of 1913. It enlarged the FREE LIST, increasing only a few items to correct previous errors. Certain COMPENSATORY DUTIES were abolished, and in many cases SPECIFIC DUTIES were replaced by AD VALOREM DUTIES. In general this tariff attempted to reduce duties, such a policy being advocated as a means of bringing foreign competition to bear upon domestic monopolies.

underwriting. As applied to investment banking, the purchase for resale of a large block of a new security issue by one or more investment bankers, and the written agreements pertaining to such a transaction.

undistributed-profits tax. A progressive tax on corporation profits not distributed as dividends, levied by the United States government in 1936. See also PROGRESSIVE TAXATION, TAX.

unearned income. 1. Income received as rent, interest, dividend payments, or in any form other than gain or compensation resulting directly from the recipient's personal efforts. 2. As applied to accounting, payments received that have not been earned. Such items as rent and interest are frequently received in advance of the time when they are earned. The sums thus received are treated as liabilities until such time as they are actually earned.

The items are then credited to an income account. Sometimes called *deferred income.* See also INCOME.

unearned increment. Generally, appreciation in the value of property, not anticipated by the owner and not in any way due to his personal efforts, intelligence, or skill. More particularly, the value added to land because of increased population, the growth of cities, and the building of railroads, highways, and other such improvements; hence, value added to land apart from any effort or expense applied on the land in question by the owners thereof.

uneconomic. A term applicable to any action or process which does not add to the total sum of useful goods and services; or which produces goods or services less effectively or at a greater cost than is warranted by existing technical knowledge.

unemployment. The condition of being unable to find gainful employment when able and willing to work. In any developed economic system there is always a certain amount of unemployment caused by changing jobs, vacations between jobs, and similar circumstances. In the United States, 3.9 million were unemployed, or not at work if employed, in November, 1963. The total civilian labor force at that time numbered 73.3 million persons. See also CYCLICAL UNEMPLOYMENT, DISGUISED UNEMPLOYMENT, FRICTIONAL UNEMPLOYMENT, SEASONAL UNEMPLOYMENT, TECHNOLOGICAL UNEMPLOYMENT.

unemployment insurance. A system of insurance designed to afford protection against financial loss due to inability to find gainful employment. In the United States, nation-wide compulsory unemployment insurance for most categories of employed workers is authorized in the SOCIAL SECURITY ACT of 1935. There is a federal tax on payrolls which may be offset, within limits, by contributions to an approved state unemployment fund. This provision has practically forced the states to adopt unemployment-insurance plans, and all states now have such plans. The proportion of the payroll tax which goes to the federal government is used to aid the states in administering their respective unemployment-insurance systems. See also INSURANCE.

unfair trade practice. Any business practice intended to deceive or to secure an advantage by means that are morally reprehensible. Examples: false and misleading ADVERTISING, inaccurate labeling, price cutting to ruin a competitor, and creation of a MONOPOLY.

unfavorable balance of trade. A condition said to obtain in the international trade of a given country when the money value of its merchandise imports exceeds the money value of its merchandise exports for a particular period of time. The term originated in the theory of MERCANTILISM (*q.v.*) and should not today be considered synonymous with "undesirable balance of trade." Also called *passive trade balance* and *trade deficit*. See also BALANCE OF TRADE.

unified bond. See explanation under BOND.

unilateral agreement. An agreement the terms of which impose a specific obligation, or obligations, on one party in return for a promise by the other.

unilinear tariff. See SINGLE-SCHEDULE TARIFF.

union certification. Certification by an appropriate government agency, in the United States by the National Labor Relations Board, to the effect that a particular labor union has fulfilled the legal requirements to qualify as the bargaining agent for the employees of an establishment and is to be recognized as such.

union label. A label or stamp placed on commodities to indicate that they have been made in a union shop or that the labor expended upon them has been that of workers belonging to a labor union. See also LABOR UNION, UNION SHOP.

union security clause. Any provision in a labor or wage contract that protects a labor union against loss of members. See also LABOR UNION, TRADE AGREEMENT.

union shop. A plant or enterprise in which all the workers must belong to the union; nonunion workers may be employed, however, on condition that they join the union. See also CLOSED SHOP, MODIFIED UNION SHOP.

unissued stock. See explanation under CAPITAL STOCK.

unit banking. A banking system in which banks are separate corporate or unincorporated entities not legally affiliated with one another. See also BANKING SYSTEM.

unit cost. The total cost of a single article or unit of service. It includes the VARIABLE COST, plus a proportionate share of the FIXED COST. See also COST.

United Federal Workers of America. A second labor organization for United States government employees established in 1937. Once affiliated with the CONGRESS OF INDUSTRIAL ORGANIZATIONS.

United Mine Workers v. Coronado Coal Co. See CORONADO CASE.

United Nations. An association of 113 (1964) nations organized to maintain international peace and security and to encourage such economic and social conditions throughout the world as promise to further this objective. A conference at Washington, D. C. (Dumbarton Oaks), laid the foundations of the United Nations and led to the calling of the United Nations Conference on International Organization at San Francisco in 1945, at which place and time the charter of the United Nations was drafted and signed by 50 participating nations. See also Economic and Social Council, General Assembly of the United Nations, International Court of Justice, Security Council.

United Nations Educational, Scientific and Cultural Organization. A special agency of the United Nations organized in 1945, and consisting (1964) of 113 member states. It promotes collaboration among nations by advancing knowledge, particularly through instruments of mass communication; by establishing numerous educational standards and opportunities; and by maintaining, increasing, and diffusing mankind's cultural heritage. See also United Nations.

United Nations Monetary and Financial Conference. See explanation under International Bank for Reconstruction and Development and International Monetary Fund.

United Nations Relief and Rehabilitation Administration. An international agency of 51 member governments, established in 1943. Its primary purpose was to provide relief for European countries, lacking foreign-exchange resources, which had been liberated by the victor countries in World War II. Later it carried on relief and rehabilitation operations on a global basis. The terminal date of the activities of the administration was originally March 31, 1946. In August, 1946, at a meeting of the administration's governing council in Geneva, all health and social-welfare functions were transferred to other agencies. Operations having to do with displaced persons, however, were continued for a brief period. See also United Nations.

United States Atomic Energy Commission. A five-man commission of the United States government charged by law with the development of policies which will promote public and private research in nuclear fission, the dissemination and exchange of scientific information on such research, governmental ownership and exploitation of fissionable materials in the interests of national security, and the application of atomic energy to industrial pursuits after proper international safeguards have been provided.

United States Chamber of Commerce. A federation of local boards of trade, chambers of commerce, and similar organizations including some trade associations. It represents the commercial interests of the United States as a whole, its chief functions being to give voice to the views of its member bodies in matters relating to public commercial policies and to furnish information having to do with industrial and commercial interests. See also Board of trade, Trade association.

United States Court of Customs and Patent Appeals. A specialized federal appellate court having to do with the settlement of controversies arising from customs and patent matters. It was established in 1910 under a clause in the Payne-Aldrich Tariff Act of 1909. In 1929 its jurisdiction was extended by Congress to include appeals from decisions of the United States Patent Office in matters relating to patents and trade-marks.

United States Customs Court. A court having to do with the settlement of controversies arising under the customs laws. It was created by act of Congress in 1890 under the name of the Board of United States General Appraisers. The name was changed to its present form in 1926.

United States Employment Service. Part of the Labor Department's Bureau of Employment Security which supervises a system of nationwide, free, public employment offices, adminstered by the states and paid for with federal funds when minimum federal standards are maintained.

United States Fish and Wildlife Service. A unit of the Department of the Interior, created in 1940, to conserve and promote the efficient use of wildlife resources, including wild birds, fish, and other fauna.

United States Mutual Security Agency. Administers United States foreign aid. Successor (1962) is Agency for International Development.

United States note. See GREENBACK, TREASURY NOTE.

United States Office of Education. A branch of the Department of Health, Education and Welfare. Among its functions are the preparation and dissemination of statistical and other information relating to education in the various states and territories, and the administration of federal funds appropriated to aid education.

United States Public Health Service. A branch of the Department of Health, Education and Welfare. Among its functions are the carrying on of research studies relating to physical and mental diseases, the control of the spread in the United States of diseases originating abroad, the dissemination of health information, and the collection and publication of vital statistics.

United States Steel case. A case, *United States* v. *United States Steel Corp.*, 251 U. S. 417 (1920), in which the Supreme Court of the United States refused to order the dissolution of the United States Steel Corporation which counsel for the government had indicated controlled more than one-half of the business of the industry and which counsel had sought to partition on the ground that it violated the antitrust statutes. The court held that the antitrust statutes did "not make mere size an offense," and pointed out in support of its decision that competition existed in the industry and that price-fixing agreements had been terminated.

United States Tariff Commission. An independent administrative agency of the United States government, consisting of six members appointed by the President and Senate to study the effects of the tariff and related legislation on the economic life of the nation and to conduct research on matters relating to international commercial policy. The commission's investigations cover such matters as foreign export bounties, competition of foreign products with those produced at home, and preferential provisions in trade treaties. It also advises the President on the negotiation of RECIPROCAL TRADE AGREEMENTS with foreign countries and on the administration of the FLEXIBLE TARIFF.

United States* v. *Addyston Pipe and Steel Co. See ADDYSTON PIPE AND STEEL CASE.

United States* v. *American Linseed Oil Co. See LINSEED OIL INDUSTRY CASE.

United States* v. *American Tobacco Co. See STANDARD OIL CASE.

***United States* v. *Butler*.** See HOOSAC MILLS CASE.

United States* v. *Darby Lumber Co. A case, 312 U. S. 100 (1941), in which the Supreme Court of the United States upheld the constitutionality of the minimum-wage and maximum-hour provisions and, by implication, other provisions (including the proscription of child labor) contained in the FAIR LABOR STANDARDS ACT of 1938. In coming to this decision, the court developed the doctrine that the power of Congress over interstate commerce includes authority to prevent the transportation of proscribed goods — in this instance goods made under substandard working conditions. This authority, moreover, is not vitiated even if it results in congressional regulation of manufacture. By implication, therefore, an implication expressly confirmed in the court's opinion, this case overrules the CHILD-LABOR CASE (*q.v.*) of *Hammer* v. *Dagenhart*. It also opens the way for national regulation of almost every phase of production and changes materially the historic distinction between the powers of Congress and those of the states.

United States* v. *E. C. Knight Co. See KNIGHT CASE.

United States* v. *International Harvester Co. See INTERNATIONAL HARVESTER CASE.

United States* v. *South-Eastern Underwriters Assn. See INSURANCE CASE.

United States* v. *Trans-Missouri Freight Assn. See TRANS-MISSOURI FREIGHT ASSOCIATION CASE.

United States* v. *Trenton Potteries Co. See TRENTON POTTERIES CASE.

United States* v. *United Shoe Machinery Corp. See SHOE MACHINERY CASE.

United States* v. *United States Steel Corp. See UNITED STATES STEEL CASE.

United States Warehouse Act. An act of Congress, 1916, which sought to provide improved storage facilities for agricultural products and more economical credit to farmers on loans secured by warehouse receipts.

Universal Postal Union. An organization with headquarters in Bern, Switzerland, created in 1863 and having 124 member nations (1964). Under the terms of various conventions developed by congresses of the union, member states have agreed to the reciprocal free exchange of mailable matter, and, for reasonable compensation, each member has agreed to forward external mail to its destination in its own territory by the most expeditious means.

unlisted stock. See explanation under CAPITAL STOCK.

unparted bullion. Bullion from which the baser metals have not been extracted. See also BULLION.

unproductive consumption. A term sometimes applied to the condition which obtains when consumers receive an income for services which do not produce goods for the market; for example, the services of household servants. Some early economists have argued that unproductive consumption of this nature is the way out of depression because it will create more spending and still not add to the accumulation of goods. See also CONSUMPTION.

usance. A period of time, established by law or custom, for the payment of certain bills of exchange. See also BILL OF EXCHANGE.

use-and-occupancy insurance. Protection through insurance against the loss of net profits or specific charges such as taxes, royalties, or salaries when a fire or other catastrophe makes it impossible to carry on a business for a certain length of time. Also called *business interruption insurance.* See also INSURANCE.

user cost. A Keynesian term which identifies DEPRECIATION in UNIT COST on the basis of the amount that the discounted expected future earnings of the capital equipment has been reduced because of producing that unit. Instead of being calculated on the basis of a percentage which absorbs the cost of the capital equipment over a span of years, presumably its period of usefulness, depreciation is thus made dependent upon future costs and selling prices as reflected in the estimated future earnings of the capital equipment. See also

COST, MARGINAL EFFICIENCY OF CAPITAL.

use tax. A tax levied on the use of particular articles. During World War II the government of the United States imposed a use tax on automobiles and boats. A use tax is frequently resorted to in order to reach persons who attempt to escape a local sales tax by purchasing in localities where the sales tax is not applicable. See also TAX.

usury. Interest in excess of a maximum established by laws applicable to various types of loan transactions. In popular speech the term is frequently applied to any rate of interest considered to be unfair and unjust.

utility. The ability to satisfy a human want or desire. There is no unit of measure for utility. It is a subjective appraisal depending upon the individual concerned and the object considered. See also FORM UTILITY, MARGINAL UTILITY, PLACE UTILITY, POSSESSION UTILITY, SERVICE UTILITY, TIME UTILITY.

utility theory of value. The theory that explains value according to the degree to which the thing valued contributes to man's most urgent necessities. The obvious objection that some commodities like diamonds, which contribute nothing to the actual physical needs of existence, may stand high in value, and other commodities like water, which do contribute to basic physical needs, may stand low in the scale of values, led to the modification of the utility theory of value and the development of the FINAL UTILITY THEORY OF VALUE (*q.v.*). See also VALUE.

utopia. An imaginative account of an ideal society. Examples: Francis Bacon's *New Atlantis*, Edward Bellamy's *Looking Backward*, Tommaso Campanella's *City of the Sun*, Laurence Gronlund's *Cooperative Commonwealth*, Sir Thomas More's *Utopia*, William Morris' *News from Nowhere*, Plato's *Republic*.

utopian socialism. A name applied to the ideas of a number of social reformers of the latter part of the 18th and early part of the 19th centuries who believed that the ills of society could all be resolved by some preconceived plan of voluntary association. Among the prominent utopian socialists were Robert Owen, a wealthy manufacturer of England; Charles Fourier, the son of a wealthy French merchant; and Louis Blanc, a French historian. Their ideas as to the specific organization of an ideal society differed, but all were essentially communistic. Numerous colonies, both in Europe and in the United States, were established by the utopian socialists. Robert Owen established such a colony in New Harmony, Ind., in 1825; and in Massachusetts, the Brook Farm experiment was begun in 1841. See also SOCIALISM.

V

valorization. The establishment of an arbitrary price or value for a commodity, usually through government action such as, for example, price fixing or making public loans to agricultural producers on commodities the value of which may be established by government order above or below prevailing market prices.

valuation. The process of appraising the worth of property according to some recognized criteria, a process necessarily preliminary to the fixing of fair and reasonable rates for a public utility by a public-service commission. Criteria which may be used are CAPITALIZED-VALUE STANDARD, EARNING-CAPACITY STANDARD, ORIGINAL-COST STANDARD, PRUDENT-INVESTMENT-COST STANDARD, REPLACEMENT-COST STANDARD, REPRODUCTION-COST STANDARD. See also FAIR RETURN.

value. The quantity of one thing that will be given in exchange for another thing. Thus, if 2 bu. of corn will exchange for 1 bu. of wheat, the value of corn in terms of wheat is ½, whereas the value of wheat in terms of corn is 2. The value of goods and services is usually expressed in terms of the standard medium of exchange; that is, the amount of money for which they can be exchanged at any given time. For some of the more important theories of value see COST-OF-PRODUCTION THEORY OF VALUE, FINAL UTILITY THEORY OF VALUE, LABOR THEORY OF VALUE, NEOCLASSICAL THEORY OF VALUE, SURPLUS LABOR AND VALUE THEORY, UTILITY THEORY OF VALUE. See also BOOK VALUE, CAPITALIZED VALUE, DENOMINATIONAL VALUE, GOING VALUE, INTRINSIC VALUE, PAR VALUE, SCARCITY VALUE.

value added. For a given enterprise, the market price of goods completed, less the cost of materials purchased from others. Value added may be gross or net. Gross value added includes payments for taxes, interest, rent, profits, reserves for depreciation, and compensation to management and other employees, including social security. Net value added excludes depreciation. The GROSS NATIONAL PRODUCT is the total gross value added by all the productive enterprises in the economy.

variable cost. A cost which increases or decreases as the total volume of production increases or decreases. The costs of raw material and labor are examples. Also called *direct*, *prime*, *running*, and *operating cost*. See also COST.

variable proportions, law of. See PROPORTIONALITY, LAW OF.

***Veazie Bank* v. *Fenno*.** A case, 8 Wallace 533 (1869), in which the

Supreme Court of the United States upheld a federal tax of 10 per cent on the amount of all state bank notes circulating as money on the ground, among others, that such a tax was an exercise of Congress' constitutional power to provide a sound and uniform currency for the entire country, and that the exercise of such a right included the power to restrain the circulation of notes not issued under congressional authority. The practical effect of the tax, thus sustained, was to drive all state bank notes out of circulation and to ensure that the circulation privilege for bank notes would, at the time the decision was rendered, belong to the then recently created national banks.

velocity of circulation. The rapidity with which MONEY, money substitutes, or both combined, change hands during a given period of time. The velocity of circulation of money alone has been estimated at from 20 to 25 times a year. Inasmuch as payments by check account for approximately 90 per cent of the goods and services purchased in the United States, velocity of circulation is often calculated on the basis of BANK DEPOSITS alone. Income velocity, or payments for final goods and services exclusively, is usually measured by dividing the NET NATIONAL PRODUCT for a given year by the MONEY IN CIRCULATION plus the DEMAND DEPOSITS standing to the credit of bank customers during that year. Exchange or transactions velocity, which includes not only transactions involving final goods and services but also all intermediate transactions, is measured by dividing BANK DEBITS during a specific period of time by demand deposits existing during that same period.

venture capital. Capital subject to a considerable risk; hence, also called *risk capital*. The term is used in contradistinction to SECURITY CAPITAL. Capital invested in a new business, where the chances of success are uncertain, is an example. Venture capital is usually represented by common stock in the case of incorporated organizations. See also CAPITAL.

vertical expansion. Expansion of a business establishment by gaining control of the operations involved in the production and sale of a commodity all the way from obtaining the original raw materials to the fabrication and final marketing of the commodity.

vertical labor union. See INDUSTRIAL UNION.

vested interests. Established claims to real or personal property. The term is sometimes used to identify the moneyed, or property-owning, classes in society.

Veterans Administration. An independent establishment of the United States Government, organized under the President, to which is confided the execution of all laws enacted for the benefit of war veterans. Such benefits include special compensation and allowances, pensions, vocational rehabilitation, education, insurance, loans, and hospitalization and medical care.

Veterans' Reemployment Rights, Bureau of. A unit of the Department of Labor of the United States established under act of Congress, March 31, 1947, and supplementary legislation. It assists former members of the armed services in securing their re-employment rights in civilian pursuits as set forth in the Selective Training and Service Act of 1940 and amendments.

vice-consul. See explanation under CONSUL.

visible items of trade. Exports and imports of merchandise and specie. The term is used in contradistinction to INVISIBLE ITEMS OF TRADE. Both the visible and invisible items are considered in the BALANCE OF PAYMENTS.

vital statistics. Statistics having to do with births, deaths, marriages, health, disease, and related matters.

Vocational Education Act. See explanation under SMITH-HUGHES ACT.

voluntary bankruptcy. See explanation under BANKRUPTCY.

voluntary checkoff. See explanation under CHECKOFF.

voting trust. See explanation under TRUST 2.

voting-trust certificate. A document issued to stockholders of a corporation when they assign the voting rights of their stock to a trustee or trustees. The voting-trust certificates are evidence of an interest in the corporation identical with the interest evidenced by the stock certificates, except for the voting rights. Unlike voting rights transferred by means of a PROXY, a voting-trust certificate indicates that such rights have been assigned for a relatively extended period of time.

voucher. A document that establishes the accuracy of the entries in books of account or other alleged facts. The term often refers specifically to a receipt for a sum of money.

W

wage. A payment for labor. See also DISMISSAL WAGE, INCENTIVE WAGE SYSTEM; MINIMUM WAGE, MONEY WAGE, REAL WAGE.

Wage and Hour and Public Contracts Divisions. Major units of the Department of Labor of the United States. Under one administrator they enforce the provisions of the FAIR LABOR STANDARDS ACT and the WALSH-HEALEY PUBLIC CONTRACTS ACT.

Wage and Hour Law. See FAIR LABOR STANDARDS ACT.

wage and salary control. Any effort to fix the level of wages or salaries by law or administrative decree. See also CONTROL, DEFENSE PRODUCTION ACT.

wage dividend. A bonus paid to employees of a corporation, in addition to their annual wages, which bears a definite relation to dividends paid on the capital stock of the corporation.

wage-fund theory. A doctrine developed by John Stuart Mill, to the effect that wages depend upon the relationship that exists at any particular time between the number of workers and the quantity of capital employed for the payment of wages; the only way wages can be increased, therefore, is to reduce the number of workers or to increase the amount of capital used for the payment of wages.

wage leadership. The influence exerted over the wage level of an entire industry or labor market by a wage settlement arrived at in one large industrial establishment or group of establishments.

wage-price spiral. A continuous succession of wage advances followed by higher prices, and, because of the higher prices by further advances in wages. See also ROUND-OF-WAGE INCREASES.

Wagner-Connery Act. See NATIONAL LABOR RELATIONS ACT.

Walker Tariff. The United States Tariff Act of 1846. It embodied the principle of TARIFF FOR REVENUE ONLY. Maximum duties were placed on luxuries.

walkout. See STRIKE.

Walsh-Healey Public Contracts Act. An act of Congress, 1936, which, with subsequent amendments, requires the inclusion, in government supply contracts involving sums in excess of $10,000, of stipulations calling for the payment of prevailing minimum wages as determined by the Secretary of Labor, overtime pay at the rate of time and one half, a basic 8-hour day or a 40-hour week, safety and health standards, and restrictions on child and convict labor.

want. A need or desire not necessarily accompanied by the power to satisfy it.

war economy. The condition obtaining in economic life when, through governmental CONTROLS, allocations of scarce materials, rationing, and the imposition of similar restrictions, production for civilian use is curbed, and the production of war materials is greatly expanded.

war-profits tax. A tax designed to recapture excessive private profits due to abnormal war demands, especially excess profits due to the demand for goods by the government in wartime. See also TAX.

warrant. As applied to the purchase of stock, a right granted a stockholder to buy additional shares at a specified price within a certain length of time.

wash sale. A fictitious sale in which the seller himself becomes the buyer of what he sells. The term is usually applied to stocks, the object being, as a rule, to induce others to buy and thus stimulate demand.

wasting asset. An asset which cannot be replaced, and the life of which cannot be prolonged by repairs. A coal mine is an example of a wasting asset. See also ASSET.

watered stock. See explanation under CAPITAL STOCK.

waybill. A receipt showing a list of the goods accepted for shipment, issued to a shipper by a common land carrier.

wealth. Material objects that are external to man, inherently useful, appropriable, and relatively scarce. Most economists exclude from the meaning of the term "wealth" all property rights such as stocks, bonds, and mortgages, these being regarded as evidences of ownership of wealth, but not wealth itself. Others argue that such property rights must be included in the concept because the manner or degree in which ownership of wealth is divided may affect the usefulness of that wealth and that the division, therefore, cannot be considered apart from the thing divided. Likewise there is a difference of opinion regarding the inclusion of money within the meaning of wealth. Money as such — that is, exclusive of its possible usefulness as a commodity — is not generally regarded as wealth in the technical sense of that term. Some authorities, however, argue that, aside from any intrinsic usefulness which certain forms of money may have, money is a particular kind of wealth because it is external to man, appropriable, relatively scarce, and useful indirectly as a medium of exchange. Wealth as defined above is often referred to as *economic wealth.*

The term "wealth" as used in general business practice includes money, evidences of ownership, and, in general, anything that has money value.

In popular speech "wealth" is sometimes given a still broader meaning by the inclusion of attributes of man such as health and skills and, in fact, even man himself if he is not owned as a slave. Likewise in popular speech the term may include inappropriable items such as climate or a beautiful landscape. Such items are sometimes designated as SOCIAL WEALTH but it should be noted that the term "social wealth" is given other meanings as well. See also NATIONAL WEALTH.

Webb-Pomerene Act. An act of Congress, 1918, which authorizes American exporters to organize approved associations for the carrying on of export trade, such associations being exempted from the operation of the antitrust laws.

weighted average. An average in which the numbers to be averaged are augmented by certain values called *weights*. Following are examples of a weighted ARITHMETIC MEAN, GEOMETRIC MEAN, and HARMONIC MEAN.

Weights (w)	Numbers to Be Averaged (m)
1	10
2	8
3	5

$$\text{Weighted arithmetic mean} = \frac{\Sigma wm}{\Sigma w} = \frac{41}{6} = 6.833.$$

$$\text{Weighted geometric mean} = \sqrt[\Sigma w]{m_1^{w_1} \times m_2^{w_2} \times m_3^{w_3}} = \sqrt[6]{80{,}000} = 6.564.$$

$$\text{Weighted harmonic mean} = \frac{\Sigma w}{\dfrac{w_1}{m_1} + \dfrac{w_2}{m_2} + \dfrac{w_3}{m_3}} = \frac{6}{0.95} = 6.316.$$

In economic computation, weighted averages are frequently used in the construction of INDEX NUMBERS. In computing central tendency in a FREQUENCY DISTRIBUTION, the frequencies are weights. See also MEAN.

welfare economics. Consideration of the extent to which an economic system attains predetermined goals assumed to maximize human welfare, and the evaluation of public policies designed to effect economic changes directed to those ends. The term is associated with the work of Arthur Cecil Pigou, a British economist, who conceives costs of production as including certain social costs such as the impairment of the health of employees or air pollution due to fumes from a factory chimney, and who recognizes social gains that may result from production quite apart from private profit. The phrase is also applied to current economic policies of government which seek to improve social conditions.

welfare state. A term used to characterize a government sponsoring social welfare programs such as public housing, farm subsidies, health insurance, and the like. The term is used in a somewhat derogatory sense.

***West Coast Hotel Co.* v. *Parrish*.** See MINIMUM-WAGE CASES.

Western Hemisphere Trade Corporation. A domestic trade or business corporation conducting all of its business in North, Central, or South America, the West Indies, or Newfoundland, at least 95 per cent of whose gross income is derived from sources outside of the United States. Certain tax advantages are granted Western Hemisphere trade corporations, the object being to foster trade with, and to encourage the economic development of, countries within the regions named. See also CORPORATION.

Wheeler-Lea Act. An act of Congress, 1938, which amends the Federal Trade Commission Act in several important respects. As thus amended, that act prohibits not only "unfair methods of competition" but also "unfair or deceptive acts or practices in commerce," provides civil penalties in suits instituted by the United States Department of Justice for any violation of a final order of the Federal Trade Commission, and empowers the commission to enjoin dissemination of false advertising of foods, drugs, and other products, pending a final order of the commission regarding such dissemination or the institution of appropriate suits through the Justice Department.

wildcat banking era. The period following the dissolution of the second Bank of the United States in 1836. Because state banking laws of the time lacked conservative standards and varied greatly from state to state, banks inspired little confidence in prospective depositors, and the nation's money and credit structure was most unstable.

wildcat strike. See ILLEGAL STRIKE.

Willcox* v. *Consolidated Gas Co. A case, 212 U. S. 19 (1909), in which the United States Supreme Court, in attempting to provide a definition for "fair return" to a utility, declared that there was no particular rate of return which was to be deemed "fair" for invested capital. Degree of risk, location, prevailing rates on investment, and other factors must all be considered in determining the fairness of a rate for any particular enterprise.

Wilson-Gorman Tariff. The United States Tariff Act of 1894. It changed the tariff rates but slightly. Such changes as were made were in the direction of lower duties.

***Wilson* v. *New*.** A case, 243 U. S. 332 (1917), in which the United States Supreme Court upheld the provisions of the ADAMSON ACT (*q.v.*) establishing a maximum 8-hr. day and an appropriate wage structure for interstate railway employees. The court ruled that failure of employers and employees to secure a collective wage-and-hour agreement on railways justified such legislation even if it involved the fixing of wages. The court also suggested that Congress could compel adjustments by arbitration of labor disputes on interstate railways.

windfall profit. A profit in excess of that which can be considered normal. See also PROFIT.

Wisconsin rate case. A case, *Railroad Commission of Wisconsin* v. *Chicago, Burlington and Quincy R.R. Co.*, 257 U. S. 563 (1922), in which the Supreme Court of the United States extended the doctrine of the Shreveport case that the federal government, operating through appropriate administrative authority, may remove discrimination between interstate and intrastate railway rates by ordering the latter to be raised to a level with interstate rates. The power was held to belong to the federal government because it is necessary to any effective policy of national control of interstate commerce. See also SHREVEPORT CASE.

withholding tax. See explanation under CURRENT TAX PAYMENT ACT.

***Wolff Packing Co.* v. *Industrial Court of Kansas*.** A case, 262 U. S. 522 (1923), in which the Supreme Court of the United States invalidated provisions of a Kansas statute setting up an industrial-relations court and empowering it to hear and determine labor controversies in certain businesses declared to be "affected with a public interest." The court held that some of the businesses subjected to this statutory regulation, notably those having to do with food, fuel, and clothing, did not come within the judicially accepted category of businesses "affected with a public interest"; hence, the statute's requirement that labor controversies in which such businesses might be involved must in certain instances be submitted to compulsory adjudication constituted an unreasonable interference with the contractual freedom of employer and employee and violated the due process clause of the 14th Amendment. Subsequent cases, notably the MILK-CONTROL CASE, have greatly modified at least the judicial premises upon which the decision turned in this case.

Women's Bureau. A major unit of the United States Department of Labor, established in 1918. The bureau is concerned with the welfare of wage-earning women. It formulates standards for improving their working conditions and suggests ways for advancing their employment opportunities and increasing their efficiency. Continuous research is carried on by the bureau to provide the necessary data for carrying out its program.

working capital. The amount of the current assets less the amount of the current liabilities. That part of the current assets equal to the current liabilities must be used to meet short-term debts. What remains of current assets is free for other uses in the business, and hence is working capital. See also CAPITAL, CURRENT ASSETS, CURRENT LIABILITIES.

workmen's compensation laws. Laws enacted by various states of the United States which set forth the liability of employers in cases of industrial accidents or diseases contracted as a direct result of certain conditions of employment. Such laws are increasingly replacing or supplementing the common-law rules of liability. Most states commit the administration of their laws to special boards or commissions. Also called *employers' liability laws*.

work relief. Employment provided by the government or by private social agencies primarily to ameliorate distress and to stimulate recovery from a depression stage in the business cycle by increasing purchasing power. See also BUSINESS CYCLE, PURCHASING POWER.

work-sharing. As applied to labor relations, an attempt to prevent dismissal of some employees by placing all employees on a part-time basis.

World Federation of Trade Unions. An international organization established for the purpose of furthering trade-union interests throughout the world. The federation came into being in Paris in 1945. Sixty countries were represented and by the end of the year the federation claimed a membership of 71 million. The only large national trade-union organization that remained outside the federation was the AMERICAN FEDERATION OF LABOR. During 1949 dissension appeared within the federation and many national groups withdrew because the federation was communist-dominated. Under the leadership of American, British, and other western trade-union organizations, those seceding national groups and the American Federation of Labor created a new world labor organization, the INTERNATIONAL CONFEDERATION OF FREE TRADE UNIONS (*q.v.*) in 1949.

World Health Organization. Since April 7, 1948, a SPECIALIZED AGENCY of the ECONOMIC AND SOCIAL COUNCIL of the UNITED NATIONS devoted to the improvement of health conditions throughout the world. Its permanent headquarters are in Geneva, Switzerland, and it has 117 members (1964).

Y

yardstick. A term first applied to the electric light and power rates established by the TENNESSEE VALLEY AUTHORITY in 1933. A low schedule of rates was established by the authority at that time in order to find out whether a low rate would increase demand and income, and how profits would be affected. It was anticipated that such data might influence the rates of privately owned establishments. See also TENNESSEE VALLEY AUTHORITY.

yellow-dog contract. An agreement entered into by an applicant for employment stating that he will not become a member of a labor union if employed. Yellow-dog contracts are generally illegal in the United States.

yellow seal dollar. See explanation under OCCUPATION CURRENCY.

yield to maturity. See NET YIELD.

Young plan. A plan for the payment of reparations owed by Germany under the Treaty of Versailles and put into effect in 1929. The Young plan superseded the DAWES PLAN. It reduced the total amount of reparations to be paid, specified a definite schedule of sums to be paid during a stipulated length of time, and did away with most of the supervisory controls on German economy then in existence. The plan was named for Owen D. Young, chairman of the committee that devised the plan.

***Youngstown Sheet & Tube Co.* v. *Sawyer*.** A case, 343 U. S. 579 (1952), in which the Supreme Court of the United States passed upon the so-called emergency powers of the President. The case arose out of an executive order by President Truman for governmental seizure and operation of the nation's steel mills because of a threatened strike. Although the Court left open the question of executive discretion in the absence of pertinent Congressional legislation, and although it suggested that there might be occasions when the President could rely upon inherent constitutional authority to counter threats to the nation's safety, the majority of the Court, in this instance, took the position that the President had failed to follow the procedure for settling labor disputes which Congress had provided in the LABOR-MANAGEMENT RELATIONS (TAFT-HARTLEY) ACT (*q.v.*), and that, hence, he was invading the legislative province of Congress.

Z

***Zollverein*.** The German word for a CUSTOMS UNION. Such unions were formed in 1833 between Prussia and various independent German states wherein it was agreed to impose no tariff duties among themselves, and to adopt uniform duties applicable to the rest of the world.

zoning. The practice of planning a municipality or wider area in such a way that, as population increases, maximum convenience, utility, and beauty are assured the residents. To that end districts are zoned or earmarked for manufacturing enterprises, retail trade, and various classes of residences. See also *Euclid* v. *Ambler Realty Co.*

zoning case. See *Euclid* v. *Ambler Realty Co.*

APPENDIX

A.

Specimen financial statements analyzed in terms defined in this dictionary. Terms defined are indicated by CAPITAL LETTERS.

National Income and Product Account

Consolidated Balance Sheet of Federal Reserve Banks

Consolidated Balance Sheet of Member and Nonmember Banks

Balance Sheet, International Monetary Fund

B.

National Monetary Units

NATIONAL INCOME AND

1	**National income**	**239.0**
	Compensation of employees	**153.3**
2	*Wages and salaries*	*145.8*
	Private	123.6
	Military	5.1
	Government civilian	17.2
3	Supplements to wages and salaries	7.5
	Proprietors' and rental income	**44.0**
4	Business and professional	22.3
5	Farm	13.7
6	Rental income of persons	8.0
	Corporate profits and inventory valuation adjustment	**36.2**
7	*Corporate profits before tax*	*41.4*
8	Corporate profits tax liability	18.6
	Corporate profits after tax	22.8
9	Inventory valuation adjustment	−5.1
10	**Net interest**	**5.4**

1. NATIONAL INCOME[2] measures the total FACTOR COST of all final GOODS and services produced in the nation's economy during a specific period of time, except those emanating from illegal activities and the services of housewives. Government INTEREST is also excluded. The economy covered is that of the continental United States.

2. BONUS, COMMISSION, GRATUITY, payment IN KIND, SALARY, WAGE. Includes employee contributions to OLD-AGE AND SURVIVORS' INSURANCE and other SOCIAL INSURANCE funds.

3. Employer contributions to OLD-AGE AND SURVIVORS' INSURANCE, and other SOCIAL INSURANCE funds, private PENSION and other welfare FUNDS. DISABILITY BENEFITS, FEES paid to DIRECTORS, juries, witnesses, and justices of the peace, pay for military RESERVES for part-time service, and compensation paid to inmates of prisons.

4. NET INCOME, both monetary and payments IN KIND of enterprises that are not CORPORATIONS, such as INDIVIDUAL PROPRIETORSHIPS, and PARTNERSHIPS. Includes noncorporate INVENTORY VALUATION ADJUSTMENTS. Includes also net income of PRODUCERS' CO-OPERATIVES. Capital gains and losses are not included, nor are DEPLETION ALLOWANCES.

5. Computed by deducting total PRODUCTION expense from the sum of: (1) cash RECEIPTS from the sale of farm products, (2) receipts from government sources, (3) VALUE of farm products consumed at home, (4) rental value of farm residences, (5) value of any change in the physical volume of farm INVENTORIES of livestock and crops.

6. Net monetary RENT from individually tenant-occupied REAL PROPERTY (except that of REAL ESTATE operators) net IMPUTED RENT to owner occupants of nonfarm residences, net ROYALTIES realized by individuals from PATENTS, COPYRIGHTS, and rights to NATURAL RESOURCES.

7. PROFIT before federal and state INCOME TAXES. Intercorporate DIVIDENDS are eliminated from the PROFITS of domestic CORPORATIONS. Net RECEIPTS of dividends and branch profits from abroad are added.

8. Federal and state TAXES levied on corporate earnings. Tax refunds are deducted from the tax LIABILITY in the year the tax liability was incurred.

9. INVENTORY VALUATION ADJUSTMENT.

10. Monetary INTEREST received from private business and from abroad. Monetary VALUE of services IN KIND rendered by certain financial institutions calculated by subtracting from the total amount of interest and DIVIDENDS received by such institutions, the amount of interest and dividends actually disbursed by them to the owners of the FUNDS entrusted to the institutions in question. Interest accruing to but withheld from LIFE INSURANCE policyholders and depositors in mutual BANKS. Government interest payments to business arbitrarily deducted from the sum of the above items to compensate for their inclusion in corporate PROFITS and in the INCOME of unincorporated institutions.

---

[1]As published periodically in the *Federal Reserve Bulletin,* Board of Governors of the Federal Reserve System, Washington, D.C.—Billions of dollars.

[2]Terms appearing in CAPITAL LETTERS are defined in this dictionary.

PRODUCT ACCOUNT, 1950[1]

11	**Gross national product**	**282.6**
12	**Personal consumption expenditures**	**193.6**
	Durable goods	29.2
	Nondurable goods	102.3
	Services	62.1
13	**Gross private domestic investment**	**48.9**
	New construction	*22.1*
	Residential, nonfarm	12.6
	Other	9.5
	Producers' durable equipment	22.5
	Change in business inventories	4.3
	Nonfarm only	3.6
14	**Net foreign investment**	**−2.3**
15	**Government purchases of goods and services**	**42.5**
	Federal	*22.8*
	National security	19.1
	Other	3.9
	Less: Government sales	.2
	State and local	19.7

11. The GROSS NATIONAL PRODUCT measures the purchases at MARKET VALUE of all final GOODS and services by various segments of the economy.

12. MARKET PRICE of GOODS and services purchased by individuals and nonprofit organizations. Includes the VALUE of goods and services IN KIND such as food and lodging furnished to employees, foods and fuel produced and consumed on farms just as though such items had been purchased. Rental value of owner-occupied houses.

13. Purchases of newly produced CAPITAL GOODS by private business and nonprofit organizations and the change in the VALUE of their INVENTORIES owing to increase or decrease in volume. All private new dwellings whether acquired by owner occupants or rented. Construction expense of crude petroleum and natural-gas drilling.

14. The difference between: (1) the VALUE of domestic output exported; (2) materials produced abroad by United States-owned resources; (3) cash gifts and contributions received from abroad, and: (1) IMPORTS from foreign producers, (2) material produced in the United States by foreign-owned resources; (3) cash gifts and contributions to foreigners. Computed by ascertaining the difference between foreign CURRENCIES bought with dollars and dollars bought with foreign currencies covering GOODS and services.

15. Purchases of GOODS and services by federal, state, and local government bodies such as compensation to employees, contributions to SOCIAL INSURANCE, purchases from business, purchases from abroad, and international contributions. Includes government-enterprise INVESTMENTS as these cannot be distinguished because of lack of statistical data. The volume of sales of government SURPLUS of CONSUMER GOODS, both foreign and domestic, is deducted from the above-named items.

	Gross national product	**282.6**
16	**Less: Capital consumption allowances**	**21.2**
17	**Indirect business tax and related liabilities**	**23.8**
18	**Business transfer payments**	**.8**
19	**Statistical discrepancy**	**−1.8**
20	**Plus: Subsidies less current surplus of government enterprises**	**.3**
	Equals: National income	**239.0**

16. CAPITAL CONSUMPTION allowance.

17. TAXES levied upon business exclusive of INCOME and other general taxes.

18. Business TRANSFER PAYMENTS.

19. Any difference in the independent estimates of the NATIONAL INCOME and the GROSS NATIONAL PRODUCT after consideration of reconciling items.

20. SUBSIDIES less SURPLUS of government enterprises.

CONSOLIDATED BALANCE SHEET OF

	Assets	
1	Gold certificates	19,878,903
2	Redemption fund for F. R. notes	628,764
3	Total gold certificate reserves	20,507,667
4	Other cash	298,842
5	Discounts and advances:	
	For member banks	528,754
	For nonmember banks, etc.	....
6	Industrial loans	5,188
7	U. S. Government securities:	
	Bills	654,820
	Certificates:	
	Special	....
	Other	....
	Notes	15,051,113
	Bonds	6,803,479
	Total U. S. Government securities	22,509,412
	Total loans and securities	23,043,354
8	Due from foreign banks	38
9	F. R. notes of other Banks	114,847
10	Uncollected cash items	2,959,221
	Bank premises	41,047
	Other assets	208,952
	Total assets	47,173,968

1. GOLD CERTIFICATE.[2] Issued to the FEDERAL RESERVE BANKS by the United States Treasury in return for CREDIT to a deposit ACCOUNT. See No. 13 below. The usual financial procedure for newly mined or imported gold is as follows: (1) gold delivered to the United States MINT by private owner who receives a treasury CHECK drawn on a federal reserve bank; (2) check deposited in MEMBER BANK and credited to deposit account of the private owner; (3) check sent to the federal reserve bank where it is credited to the deposit account of the member bank and charged to the deposit account of the United States Treasury; and (4) United States Treasury replenishes its deposit account by issuing gold certificates to the federal reserve bank. See also STERILIZED GOLD.

2. The law requires that each of the FEDERAL RESERVE BANKS deposit with the United States Treasury, in a redemption FUND, an amount of GOLD CERTIFICATES equal to 5 per cent of that portion of FEDERAL RESERVE NOTES issued to it and not secured by gold certificates pledged with the FEDERAL RESERVE AGENT. See No. 11 below.

3. The law requires a RESERVE in GOLD CERTIFICATES of at least 25 per cent of the FEDERAL RESERVE NOTES issued and the total deposits held. The percentage in this statement is:

$$\frac{20{,}507{,}667}{23{,}331{,}677 + 20{,}381{,}257} \text{ or } 46.9$$

or 21.9 per cent in excess of the minimum requirements.

4. COIN and PAPER MONEY other than GOLD CERTIFICATES and FEDERAL RESERVE NOTES.

5. BANK LOANS secured by COLLATERAL or arising through REDISCOUNT operations. See item No. 16 Consolidated Balance Sheet of Member and Nonmember Banks. The REDISCOUNT RATE is one means by which the FEDERAL RESERVE SYSTEM influences the amount of BANK RESERVES and hence the amount of BANK CREDIT available.

6. LOANS made directly to business concerns. The right to make such loans was granted to the FEDERAL RESERVE BANKS in 1933. Discontinued in 1959.

7. TREASURY BILL, TREASURY NOTE, CERTIFICATE OF INDEBTEDNESS, BOND (United States of America). The amount of government obligations that can be acquired by the FEDERAL RESERVE BANKS directly from the United States Treasury is limited by law. Government obligations are acquired for the most part, therefore, through OPEN-MARKET OPERATIONS. This is a second method by which the FEDERAL RESERVE SYSTEM influences BANK RESERVES and hence the amount of BANK CREDIT available.

---

[1]As published in the *Federal Reserve Bulletin*, Board of Governors of the Federal Reserve System, Washington, D.C.—Thousands of dollars.

[2]Terms appearing in CAPITAL LETTERS are defined in this dictionary.

FEDERAL RESERVE BANKS, MAY, 1951[1]

8. Deposit balances in foreign CENTRAL BANKS for account of the Federal Reserve Bank of New York. Other FEDERAL RESERVE BANKS participate through the New York bank.

9. FEDERAL RESERVE NOTES issued by one FEDERAL RESERVE BANK and received by another are returned to the BANK of issue for payment, or are sent to the United States Treasury for redemption.

10. CHECKS, DRAFTS, etc., deposited in the FEDERAL RESERVE BANKS, but not collected up to the time the statement was prepared. See also No. 15 below.

	Liabilities	
11	Federal Reserve notes	23,331,677
	Deposits:	
12	Member bank—reserve accounts	18,535,791
13	U. S. Treasurer—general account	665,888
14	Foreign	874,339
	Other	305,239
	Total deposits	20,381,257
15	Deferred availability cash items	2,521,370
16	Other liabilities and accrued dividends	15,973
	Total liabilities	46,250,277
	Capital Accounts	
17	Capital paid in	228,984
18	Surplus (Section 7)	510,022
19	Surplus (Section 13b)	27,543
	Other capital accounts	157,142
	Total liabilities and capital accounts	47,173,968

11. FEDERAL RESERVE NOTES in circulation. These are secured by GOLD CERTIFICATES, United States BONDS, and ELIGIBLE COMMERCIAL PAPER pledged with the FEDERAL RESERVE AGENT.

12. Each MEMBER BANK is required to hold its LEGAL RESERVES on deposit with the FEDERAL RESERVE BANK of the district where the member bank is located. See BANK RESERVES. See also item No. 7 Consolidated Balance Sheet of Member and Nonmember Banks. The amount of RESERVES is determined by the Board of Governors of the FEDERAL RESERVE SYSTEM within limits set by the Congress. This is a third method by which the Federal Reserve System influences the amount of BANK CREDIT available.

13. FEDERAL RESERVE BANKS act as FISCAL agents of the United States Treasury. As such, they hold deposits on ACCOUNT of the treasury, honor treasury CHECKS, pay INTEREST on United States SECURITIES, and redeem maturing United States securities when due or when provided by law.

14. Just as the Federal Reserve Bank of New York keeps deposits in foreign CENTRAL BANKS, so foreign central banks keep deposits with the Federal Reserve Bank of New York. Other FEDERAL RESERVE BANKS participate through the New York BANK.

15. Deposited CHECKS, DRAFTS, etc., in the process of collection, CREDIT for which is being deferred pending collection or expiration of the period estimated necessary for collection. See FEDERAL RESERVE BANK FLOAT.

16. DIVIDENDS paid by a FEDERAL RESERVE BANK are limited by law to 6 per cent of its paid-in CAPITAL.

17. The CAPITAL STOCK of FEDERAL RESERVE BANKS is owned by the MEMBER BANKS, each member bank being required to subscribe 6 per cent of its own paid-in CAPITAL and SURPLUS, one half of which has been paid and one half of which remains on call. See item No. 5, Balance Sheet of Member and Nonmember Banks.

18. Accumulated earnings from LOANS and INVESTMENTS. Should at any time the FEDERAL RESERVE BANKS be dissolved, the law requires that the SURPLUS be paid to the United States government.

19. FUNDS supplied by the United States government for the purpose of making commercial LOANS directly to business organizations. Earnings and losses resulting from the use of such funds are included.

CONSOLIDATED BALANCE SHEET OF MEMBER

	Item	1949 (Dec 31)
	Number of banks	**14,705**
1	**Assets, total**	**180,043**
	Loans, total	**49,828**
	Loans on real estate	18,350
2	Commercial and industrial loans (including open-market paper)	17,195
3	Other loans, including overdrafts	15,070
4	Less valuation reserves	787
5	**Securities, total**	**91,436**
	U. S. Government obligations, direct and guaranteed	78,754
	Obligations of States and political subdivisions	6,657
	Other bonds, notes, and debentures	5,505
	Corporate stocks, including stocks of Federal Reserve banks	520
6	**Currency and coin**	**2,185**
7	**Balances with other banks, including reserve balances and cash items in process of collection**	**34,491**
	Bank premises owned, furniture and fixtures	**1,173**
8	**Real estate owned other than bank premises**	**32**
	Investments and other assets indirectly representing bank premises or other real estate	**86**
9	**Customers' liability on acceptances outstanding**	**191**
10	**Interest, commissions, rent, and other income earned or accrued but not collected**	
11	**Other assets**	**621**

1. ASSETS.[2]

2. COMMERCIAL PAPER.

3. OVERDRAFTS.

4. RESERVES set aside to cover losses or shrinkage in VALUES.

5. INVESTMENT PORTFOLIO. CAPITAL STOCK of the FEDERAL RESERVE BANK is a legal requirement for MEMBER BANKS. See item No. 17 of the Consolidated Balance Sheet of Federal Reserve Banks. BOND, PROMISSORY NOTE.

6. CURRENCY. COIN. Cash on hand to meet the over-the-counter DEMAND of customers and possible CLEARINGHOUSE balances against the BANK.

7. DEPOSITS in other BANKS. RESERVE balances are legal BANK RESERVES deposited in the FEDERAL RESERVE BANKS. See item No. 12, Consolidated Balance Sheet of the Federal Reserve Banks.

8. REAL ESTATE.

9. BANK ACCEPTANCE. Offset by item No. 17 below. The difference is the sum advanced by customers of the BANK in payment for ACCEPTANCES not presented for payment at the time the statement was prepared.

10. INTEREST. COMMISSION.

11. ACCOUNTS RECEIVABLE. ACCRUED INTEREST.

---

[1]As published in the *Statistical Abstract of the United States*—Millions of dollars.

[2]Terms appearing in CAPITAL LETTERS are defined in this dictionary.

AND NONMEMBER BANKS, DECEMBER, 1949[1]

12	**Liabilities, total**	**166, 878**
	Deposits, total	165, 244
13	Deposits of individuals, partnerships, and corporations:	
	Demand	83, 454
	Time	54, 416
14	U. S. Government and postal savings deposits	3, 325
	Deposits of States and political subdivisions	8, 957
	Deposits of banks	12, 721
15	Other deposits (certified and cashiers' checks, etc.)	2, 371
16	Bills payable, rediscounts, and other liabilities for borrowed money	27
17	Acceptances executed by or for account of reporting banks and outstanding	222
18	Interest, discount, rent, and other income collected but not earned	
19	Interest, taxes, and other expenses accrued and unpaid	1, 385
20	Other liabilities	
	Capital accounts, total	**13, 165**
21	Capital notes and debentures	48
	Preferred stock	69
22	Common stock	3, 431
23	Surplus	6, 365
24	Undivided profits	2, 626
25	Reserves and retirement account for preferred stock and capital notes and debentures	606

12. LIABILITIES.

13. DEMAND DEPOSIT. TIME DEPOSIT.

14. POSTAL SAVINGS.

15. CERTIFIED CHECK. CASHIER'S CHECK.

16. BILLS PAYABLE. REDISCOUNT. See item No. 5 Consolidated Statement of Federal Reserve Banks.

17. See item No. 9 above. ACCEPTANCES outstanding do not represent extension of CREDIT by the BANK. The bank guarantees payment in return for a FEE and thus assumes LIABILITY, but the customers normally provide FUNDS to meet the obligations when due.

18. INTEREST. DISCOUNT (2). RENT. UNEARNED INCOME (2).

19. ACCRUED INTEREST. TAX.

20. ACCOUNTS PAYABLE, items in transit and other small ACCOUNTS.

21. DEBENTURES. PROMISSORY NOTE.

22. CAPITAL STOCK.

23. SURPLUS. Earnings invested in the BANK as additional CAPITAL.

24. Earnings available for DIVIDENDS, or for additions to SURPLUS.

25. RESERVES. Earnings set aside to be used eventually to retire amounts specified in items Nos. 21 and 22 above.

INTERNATIONAL MONETARY

		Jan 31 1951
1	**Gold (at 35 U. S. dollars per fine ounce)**	1,530.6
2	**Balances with Depositories**	766.4
3	**Members' Non-negotiable Non-interest-bearing Securities Payable at Face Value on Demand**	*4,963.9*
	Currency Adjustments Receivable	—
4	**Total Currency**	5,730.3
5	**Members' Subscriptions Receivable**	883.0
6	**Other Assets**	.8
7	**TOTAL ASSETS**	8,144.7

1, 2. The fund's holdings of gold and member CURRENCIES[2] are deposited with the CENTRAL BANK or some other designated DEPOSITARY in each member country.

3. Any member is permitted to substitute the described SECURITIES for the fund's holdings of its CURRENCY to the extent that the amount of currency held by the fund exceeds what the fund considers a normal working balance. As these securities are considered equivalent to currency they are included in that category.

4. No. 2 plus No. 3. Eligible members may purchase the CURRENCY of other members with their own currencies or with gold, subject to limitations. Such purchases are intended to assist members temporarily short of certain currencies. In general, a member is permitted to purchase other currencies only to the extent that the fund's holdings of that member's currency does not increase more than 25 per cent of its total quota (see No. 8 below) within any 12-month period, and does not at any time cause the fund's holdings of its currency to exceed an amount equal to twice its total quota.

EXAMPLE:

Quota 100 { 75 per cent currency; 25 per cent gold }

Year	Currency held	Currency added	Total
1	75	25	100
2	100	25	125
3	125	25	150
4	150	25	175
5	175	25	200 (Limit)

A member is obligated to repurchase its currency from the fund when conditions permit. Repurchases are made in gold or, within limits, in convertible currencies.

5. Balances due from members whose PAR EXCHANGE RATES have been established and balances not due from members whose par exchange rates have not been established.

6. IMPREST FUND, and other cash balances, accrued charges against members, advances for travel expenses, unexpired INSURANCE, etc.

7. ASSETS.

[1]As published in *International Financial Statistics,* International Monetary Fund.

[2]Terms appearing in CAPITAL LETTERS are defined in this dictionary.

SHEET[1]

FUND, JANUARY 31, 1951

	Capital:	
8	**Members' Authorized Subscriptions......**	***8,151.5***
9	**Less Excess of Expenditures Over Income from Inception to Date............**	***7.1***
10	**Net Capital.......................**	**8,144.4**
11	**Reserves and Liabilities................**	**.3**
	TOTAL CAPITAL AND LIABILITIES	**8,144.7**

8. Each member is required to subscribe to the fund a certain assigned quota which determines that member's voting privileges and the extent to which that member may make use of the fund's resources. (See No. 4 above.) The quota consists of gold and CURRENCY. The original members of the fund were required to subscribe in gold either 25 per cent of their quotas or 10 per cent of their net official holdings of gold and United States dollars as of Sept. 12, 1946, whichever was less. Minimum gold subscriptions for new members are determined by the fund.

9. DEFICIT to date.

10. No. 8 less No. 9. CAPITAL.

11. ACCOUNTS PAYABLE, UNEARNED INCOME (2), etc. RESERVE.

12. LIABILITIES.

NATIONAL MONETARY UNITS

Courtesy of Manufacturers Hanover Trust Co.

International Division, New York

Country	*Currency*	*Consisting of*
Aden	Shilling	100 Cents
Afghanistan	Afghani	100 Puls
Albania	Lek	100 Qintar
Algeria	New Franc	100 Centimes
Andorra	Peseta	100 Centimos
Angola	Escudo	100 Centavos
Antigua	Dollar	100 Cents
Argentina	Peso	100 Centavos
Australia	Pound	20 Shillings = 240 Pence
Austria	Schilling	100 Groschen
Azores	Escudo	100 Cents
Bahamas	Pound	20 Shillings = 240 Pence
Bahrain Islands	Indian Rupee	100 Naye Paise
Balearic Islands	Peseta	100 Centimos
Barbados	Dollar	100 Cents
Basutoland	Rand	100 Cents
Bechuanaland	Rand	100 Cents
Belgium	Franc	100 Centimes
Bermuda	Pound	20 Shillings = 240 Pence
Bolivia	Peso	100 Centavos
Brazil	Cruzeiro	100 Centavos
British Honduras	Dollar	100 Cents
Brunei	Dollar	100 Cents
Bulgaria	Lev	100 Stotinki
Burma	Kyat	100 Pyas
Cambodia	Riel	100 Sen
Cameroons	Franc	100 Centimes
Canada	Dollar	100 Cents
Canary Islands	Peseta	100 Centimos
Cape Verde Islands	Escudo	100 Centavos
Central African Republic	Franc	100 Centimes
Ceylon	Rupee	100 Cents
Chad	Franc	100 Centimes
Chile	Escudo	100 Centesimos
China	NT Dollar	100 Cents
Colombia	Peso	100 Centavos
Congo (Leopoldville)	Franc	100 Centimes
Congo (Brazzaville)	Franc	100 Centimes
Costa Rica	Colon	100 Centimos
Cuba	Peso	100 Centavos
Cyprus	Pound	1000 Mils
Czechoslovakia	Crown	100 Hellers
Dahomey	Franc	100 Centimes

Country	*Currency*	*Consisting of*
Denmark	Krone	100 Ore
Dominica	Dollar	100 Cents
Dominican Republic	Peso	100 Centavos
Dubai	Rupee	100 Naya Paise
Ecuador	Sucre	100 Centavos
Egypt	Pound	100 Piasters = 1000 Mill.
El Salvador	Colon	100 Centavos
Ethiopia	Dollar	100 Cents
Fiji Is.	Pound	20 Shillings = 240 Pence
Finland	Markka	100 Pennis
France	Franc	100 Centimes
French Somaliland	Franc	100 Centimes
Gabon	Franc	100 Centimes
Gambia	Pound	20 Shillings = 240 Pence
Germany (Western)	Deutsche Mark	100 Pfennig
Ghana	Pound	20 Shillings = 240 Pence
Gibraltar	Pound	20 Shillings = 240 Pence
Grand Cayman Is.	Pound	20 Shillings = 240 Pence
Greece	Drachma	100 Lepta
Grenada	Dollar	100 Cents
Guadeloupe	New Franc	100 Centimes
Guam	U. S. Dollar	100 Cents
Guatemala	Quetzal	100 Centavos
Guiana, British	Dollar	100 Cents
Guiana, French	New Franc	100 Centimes
Guinea	Franc	100 Centimes
Haiti	Gourde	100 Centimes
Honduras (Republic)	Lempira	100 Centavos
Hong Kong	Dollar	100 Cents
Hungary	Forint	100 Fillers
Iceland	Krona	100 Aurar
India	Rupee	100 Naye Paise
Indonesia	Rupiah	100 Sen
Iran	Rial	100 Dinars
Iraq	Dinar	1000 Fils
Ireland (Republic)	Pound	20 Shillings = 240 Pence
Israel	Pound	100 Agorot
Italy	Lira	100 Centesimi
Ivory Coast	Franc	100 Centimes
Jamaica	Pound	20 Shillings = 240 Pence
Japan	Yen	100 Sen
Jordan	Dinar	1000 Fils
Kenya	Shilling	100 Cents
Korea (South)	Won	100 Chon
Kuwait	Dinar	1000 Fils
Laos	Kip	100 At
Lebanon	Pound	100 Piasters
Liberia	U. S. Dollar	100 Cents
Libya	Pound	100 Piasters = 1000 Mill.
Liechtenstein	Franc	100 Centimes
Luxembourg	Franc	100 Centimes
Macao	Pataca	100 Avos

Country	*Currency*	*Consisting of*
Madeira	Escudo	100 Centavos
Malagasy (Madagascar)	Franc	100 Centimes
Malaysia	Dollar	100 Cents
Mali	Franc	100 Centimes
Malta	Pound	20 Shillings=240 Pence
Marshall Islands	U. S. Dollar	100 Cents
Martinique	New Franc	100 Centimes
Mauritania	Franc	100 Centimes
Mauritius	Rupee	100 Cents
Mexico	Peso	100 Centavos
Monaco	New Franc	100 Centimes
Montserrat	Dollar	100 Cents
Morocco	Dirham	100 Moroccan Francs
Mozambique	Escudo	100 Centavos
Nepal	Rupee	100 Pice
Netherlands	Guilder	100 Cents
Netherlands Antilles	Guilder	100 Cents
Nevis	Dollar	100 Cents
New Caledonia	Franc	100 Centimes
New Guinea	Pound	20 Shillings=240 Pence
New Hebrides Islands	Franc	100 Centimes
New Zealand	Pound	20 Shillings=240 Pence
Nicaragua	Cordoba	100 Centavos
Niger	Franc	100 Centimes
Nigeria	Pound	20 Shillings=240 Pence
Norway	Krone	100 Ore
Oceania (French)	Franc	100 Centimes
Pakistan	Rupee	100 Paisa
Panama	Balboa	100 Centesimos
Papua	Pound	20 Shillings=240 Pence
Paraguay	Guarani	100 Centimos
Peru	Sol	100 Centavos
Philippines	Peso	100 Centavos
Poland	Zloty	100 Grosze
Portugal	Escudo	100 Centavos
Portuguese Guinea	Escudo	100 Centavos
Puerto Rico	U. S. Dollar	100 Cents
Qatar	Rupee	100 Naye Paise
Reunion Is.	Franc	100 Centimes
Rhodesia-Nyasaland	Pound	20 Shillings=240 Pence
Romania	Leu	100 Bani
Ryukyu Islands	U. S. Dollar	100 Cents
St. Kitts	Dollar	100 Cents
St. Lucia	Dollar	100 Cents
St. Vincent	Dollar	100 Cents
Samoa (British)	New Zea. Pound	20 Shillings=240 Pence
Saudi Arabia	Riyal	20 Gurshes=100 Halalah
Senegal	Franc	100 Centimes
Seychelles	Rupee	100 Cents
Sierra Leone	Pound	20 Shillings=240 Pence

Country	*Currency*	*Consisting of*
Solomon Islands	Pound	20 Shillings = 240 Pence
Somalia	Somalo	100 Centesimi
South Africa (Republic)	Rand	100 Cents
South West Africa	Rand	100 Cents
Spain	Peseta	100 Centimos
Sudan	Pound	100 Piasters = 1000 Mill.
Surinam	Guilder	100 Cents
Swaziland	Rand	100 Cents
Sweden	Krona	100 Ore
Switzerland	Franc	100 Centimes
Syria	Pound	100 Piasters
Tahiti	Franc	100 Centimes
Tanganyika	Shilling	100 Cents
Thailand	Baht	100 Satang
Timor	Escudo	100 Centavos
Tobago	Dollar	100 Cents
Togo	Franc	100 Centimes
Tonga Islands	Pound	20 Shillings = 240 Pence
Trinidad	Dollar	100 Cents
Tunisia	Dinar	1000 Mill.
Turkey	Pound	100 Piasters
Uganda	Shilling	100 Cents
U. S. S. R.	Rouble	100 Kopecks
United Kingdom	Pound	20 Shillings = 240 Pence
Upper Volta	Franc	100 Centimes
Uruguay	Peso	100 Centesimos
Vatican City	Lira	100 Centesimi
Venezuela	Bolivar	100 Centimos
Viet-Nam	Piaster	100 Cents
Virgin Is. (U. S.)	U. S. Dollar	100 Cents
Yugoslavia	Dinar	100 Paras
Zanzibar	Shilling	100 Cents